FROM THE SACRED TO THE DIVINE

ANALECTA HUSSERLIANA

THE YEARBOOK OF PHENOMENOLOGICAL RESEARCH

VOLUME XLIII

Editor-in-Chief:

ANNA-TERESA TYMIENIECKA

The World Institute for Advanced Phenomenological Research and Learning
Belmont, Massachusetts

FROM THE SACRED
TO THE DIVINE

A New Phenomenological Approach

Edited by

ANNA-TERESA TYMIENIECKA

The World Phenomenology Institute

Published under the auspices of
The World Institute for Advanced Phenomenological Research and Learning
A-T. Tymieniecka, President

KLUWER ACADEMIC PUBLISHERS

DORDRECHT / BOSTON / LONDON

Library of Congress Cataloging-in-Publication Data

From the sacred to the divine : a new phenomenological approach /
  edited by Anna-Teresa Tymieniecka.
      p.   cm. -- (Analecta Husserliana ; v. 43)
  English and French.
  "Published under the auspices of the World Institute for Advanced
Phenomenological Research and Learning."
  Includes bibliographical references and index.
  ISBN 0-7923-2690-3
  1. Religion--Philosophy. 2. Holy, The. 3. Phenomenology.
I. Tymieniecka, Anna-Teresa. II. World Institute for Advanced
Phenomenological Research and Learning. III. Series.
B3279.H94A129 vol. 43
[BL51]
142'.7 s--dc20
[200]   93-49634

ISBN 0-7923-2690-3

Published by Kluwer Academic Publishers,
P.O. Box 17, 3300 AA Dordrecht, The Netherlands.

Kluwer Academic Publishers incorporates the publishing programmes
of D. Reidel, Martinus Nijhoff, Dr W. Junk and MTP Press.

Sold and distributed in the U.S.A. and Canada
by Kluwer Academic Publishers,
101 Philip Drive, Norwell, MA 02061, U.S.A.

In all other countries, sold and distributed
by Kluwer Academic Publishers Group,
P.O. Box 322, 3300 AH Dordrecht, The Netherlands.

Printed on acid-free paper.

Printed in the Netherlands.

ACKNOWLEDGEMENTS

The studies presented in this collection stem partly from two programs held by The World Phenomenology Institute in consecutive years at the annual meetings of the American Philosophical Association, Eastern Division, in Atlanta, Georgia, December 1989, and Boston, Massachusetts, December 1990; partly they stem from our other conventions or by invitation. We are grateful to our authors for their continuing participation in our work.

We acknowledge the permission to publish in translation the study by A-T. Tymieniecka, which appeared first in Italian in *Teologia Razionale, Filosofia della Religione, Linguaggio su Dio* (Herder/Lateran University Publishers, 1992).

Thanks are due to Miss Isabelle Houthakker and Mr Robert Wise for their expert editing of the papers, and to Mr Wise for proofreading the volume and preparing the Index.

A-T.T.

TABLE OF CONTENTS

vii

THE SACRED AS THE GROUND OF RELIGION: THE ITINERARY OF THE HUMAN SOUL IN HER YEARNING AND SEARCH FOR THE ULTIMATE

The contemporary revival of interest in the Sacred as a category of philosophical reflection upon religious experience seems to have been left to itself while the philosophy of the Divine is suspended over the cliff aloof from it.

It needed the phenomenology of life as the ground-field of all investigation pertaining to the human being, the human world of life, the human place and role in society and the cosmos, etc., to offer a plane upon which even the deepest stirrings of the human soul, as well as the highest and most audacious swings of the human spirit and imagination, would find the subterranean threads running through the entire conundrum of life's and the soul's fabric-in-process, ever advancing, creating ever new complexities, links, ties, etc., and would reveal the delineation of their mutual intertwinings.

Upon the field of the phenomenology of life, we discover, indeed, that far from being self-enclosed in separate realms, the experience of the Sacred and the conception – philosophical-intellectual – of the Divine are not, and could not be separated from each other. On the contrary, ascertaining the fulcrum of the genesis of the Sacred within the human soul situated at the very heart of the vital, psychic, creative, moral and intellectual forces, we discover that when the soul launches itself upon its quest for the *Ultimate*, it is the Divine which awaits it, lurking through the maze of life-experience at the end of its *itinerary*.

To take even the first step in this direction requires, however, an entire fermentation of the resources of life; for it to mature inwardly well enough to launch itself upon the quest a unique type of fortitude and determination is needed. To conduct the search after the Ultimate sense of existence does not mean following one beaten track; on the contrary it involves searching step-by-step new byways, seeking new territories, scrutinising old evidence for new hints, old tracks for new hitherto hidden destinations.

It takes a novel charting of the entire territory of life's experiences, feelings, emotions, desires, thoughts, attachments, volitions, aims, etc., with a new compass not given, not clear but just lurking in the dark. And yet once launched, the soul advances in her quest, marking an itinerary of unclear but *absolutely certain evidences* through which the soul orients herself moving further and further in her own transformations.

Hence, the present collection attempts to explore some of the perspective in which the itinerary of the Sacred toward the Divine takes its steps, forges its mark.

We do not attempt more than to lay the groundwork for the chain of evidence to be revealed.

A-T.T.

A group of participants in our session on the phenomenology of the Divine at the American Philosophical Association, Eastern Division Meeting, in Atlanta/Georgia, 1989 (at the back: Jude Dougherty, Thomas Ryba; in front: Steve Laycock, Edith Wyschogrod, Marlies Kronegger . . . among others).

INAUGURAL STUDY

ANNA-TERESA TYMIENIECKA

FROM THE SACRED TO THE DIVINE

MAIN THESIS

Phenomenological investigation consists of analyses, and in the detailed analyses that characterize it, we find outlines which offer a basis for ideas, recognitions and concepts, and ultimately we are able to provide answers to philosophical questions. It is a matter of adequately recognizing and appreciating them.

In this study we are above all trying to find and highlight the point in which the *significant intuition of the divine arises within* the field of the life-experience of the human soul. As can already be found in my previous writings,[1] the precise analyses of the soul's functional circuits sustain the inter-linked concepts and ideas in which our object of investigation is organized. Here, I attempt a further step, articulating some features of my analytical work. My intent is, on the one hand, to show how the human soul, in its development, is organized in cognitive-constitutive, valuative and volitive functionings, and, on the other hand, how, by setting off the search for 'ultimate meaning', it makes the genesis of the sacred possible.

Anticipating what will later be developed, one observes that the genesis of the *inward* sacred, pointed to in my treatise *The Three Movements of the Soul*,[2] leads to the point in which an entirely exceptional intuition detaches itself from the spiritual-empirical environment, that we are accustomed to call 'subjective' or 'personal', and which moves into further sacred-spiritual developments, gradually crystallizing itself in a meaningful 'trans-natural' complex. This complex provisionally uses the primary means of constitutive consciousness, however, by widening its own instruments, finally detaching itself from the intentional system.

'Inside' the soul, the intuition of the sacred 'dilates', expanding the soul 'outside' itself. Although 'inside' the man, this intuition of the sacred is, at the same time, independent of the control of the ego, of the influence of the flux of its experiences, as well as independent of all given entities accessible to man and all that forms the horizon of

3

A-T. Tymieniecka (ed.), Analecta Husserliana XLIII, 3–18.
© 1994 *Kluwer Academic Publishers. Printed in the Netherlands.*

his existential universe. In other words, the *sense* of this sacred meaning that crystallizes itself goes beyond all the possible references of the system of life, of the world and of the cosmos, beyond the very soul from which it arises, and beyond all 'rationality' of the intentional system. As a matter of fact, the thread proceeding from the 'inward sacred' of the soul leads to the Divine that man desires for its 'transcending' all.

In the new context that stands out as a result of these analyses, the problem of the divine, of God, of religion appears to be rooted in a first fundamental problem: "What are the conditions of revelation, of mystical experience, of religion?"

SECTION ONE

I. *In explaining how our further investigation poses itself in the orbit of phenomenological research*, I must first point out that its aim is to illuminate the very narrow passage from the empirical, aesthetic and spiritual experiential circuits in which the human soul advances forward in its genesis, to the tonality of the inward sacred and to the awareness – revelation? – of the Divine. For this reason, these analyses aim at the clarification of the human soul's acts and lived experiences, in which is found the crucial point at which these circuits allow the rise of meaning, which overcomes all and is, at the same time, as most intimately 'close' to the soul. Since it is an 'extraordinary' meaning which, however, emerges through *all* the functions of the human soul in the system of its vital forces, our investigation is situated in the *phenomenology of life at the heart of the new phenomenological critique of reason*.

The main questions in our reflection are: "Where and for which reasons and in which ways, does preoccupation with the divine emerge for man?" Moreover: "In what are his faith, his religious conviction and, in the end, religion itself, founded?". In short: "How is it possible that man, a captive of contingency, can, according to what he believes, go beyond it and 'speak' with the Divine, primarily conceived of as being beyond contingency and transcending all?" It appears that my approach through the inward sacred intersects other ways to clarify these problems and it will be opportune to make at least some reference to them. This allows us to fully situate my particular investigation in its own context. Proceeding backwards, I start from this last point.

In the perspective opening itself here, the philosophical preoccupation with questions concerning religion essentially focuses on explaining how the formation of this meaning, that is, the *ciphering* of the divine message, its 'revelation', comes from 'transcendence' and is possible for man, a finite being, thus, the question of "how God can speak to man."

II. From the beginning, phenomenology has always been preoccupied with the origins of meaning in all fields of human existence. Precisely because of this fundamental preoccupation, Husserl saw phenomenology primarily as:

(a) constitutive, that is, engaged with the analysis of the nature of meaning (*eidos*), with the constitution of cognitive processes (transcendental phenomenology) and with their 'position', thematization and predication; (b) seeking the origin and development of meaning in the genetic process of human consciousness – in the so-called transcendental genesis or transcendental constitution of the life-world; and (c) presupposing that the roots of meaning are at the pre-predicative, pre-constitutive level. All these approaches maintain the cognitive act of consciousness as a starting point and orientation, presupposing that it plays – thus attributing to it the character of playing – a main role in the intentional system sustaining transcendental consciousness.

The classical approaches here listed have allowed different perspectives on the problem of the Divine to open. However, each of them in turn excludes the interconnections among various human functionings and offers a truncated and partial perspective, either by maintaining the presupposition of intentionality, or by severing the link with it in the pre-constitutive region.

In contrast with these approaches, I have conducted a new phenomenological investigation which replaces the cognitive-constitutive act – a Cartesian inheritance that has polluted all modern and contemporary philosophy – as the starting point of philosophical research with the *creative act of man*. As a matter of fact, the creative act situates philosophical research in the fullness of human functioning, which is no longer limited by the intentional system, but is immersed in the complexity of man as a human being, and singles out the threads of that functioning by differentiating them and showing their orchestration. The creative approach discovers, in fact, the *human condition* in its interconnections with vital and cosmic forces, on the one hand, and with specific virtualities which allow the *human condition* to realize itself in the form of the human soul, on the other – a field in which the problems of human immanence and its transcendence meet.

III. In this field of the human soul, spreading on one side toward nature and cosmos, and on the other side toward the transcendental universe that man with his virtualities and his own faculties develops – his life-world and his spirit – we encounter three manners of investigation, different ways through which we can approach the question of the Divine. In the phenomenology of life, as a matter of fact, all modes of the soul are encountered and clearly shown.

Moreover, in the context of the phenomenology of life I have enlightened a stage, a particular territory in the development of the human soul on which – as will be shown at the end of these analyses – the questions that concern the Divine appear in their true two-fold human-Divine aspect, that is, in their human immanence-Divine transcendence. I call this stage of the development of the soul, the stage of the 'sacred'.

(a) At the first level is found a vital functioning circuit in the crystallization of the human condition, that closest to vital-cosmic roots. The human condition, as a primordial phase in the self-individualization of the living being that crystallizes its humanity, sets up this nascent human being in the vital network that he *shares with all living beings* at all levels of constructive progress of self-individuation.

One would hope that at this primeval vital-cosmic level this network of interconnections would establish the human psyche, the soul, in its very dense existential fabric, which would guarantee an indubitable certainty of being. But, on the contrary, through these interconnections the soul is shaken by existential anguish, which pushes it to investigate these same interconnections in relation to the mysteries of existence. A meaning arises from this work of the soul on its vital-cosmic relations of existence which the soul interiorizes. From its natural status the soul takes on a modality according to which it is linked with the unknown, mysterious, incomprehensible, marvelous. Moving from concreteness into direct commerce with all natural facts, modulated functioning circuits are present in the soul and lead it to the 'infinite' cosmos, full of the forces and mysterious powers which appear mixed in human life and need to be exorcised, flattered, tamed, befriended, and so forth. The modalities the soul acquires in these procedures raise it over the profanity of the concrete toward the conditions of that cosmos. In this process, its new moldings constitute a sphere beyond the concrete vital 'profane', that is, the sphere of the 'sacred.' (This first sphere of the sacred vital-cosmic is that of the so-called primitive societies studied by Lévi-Strauss, by Eliade *et al.* In phenomenology, A. Ales Bello is working on this.)

(b) At the second level of the development – that in which human consciousness draws constitutive fullness from the socio-cultural world and the full development of the spirit – the soul turns through intentional relations toward other consciousnesses and creates the universe of inter-subjectivity. In other words, the constitutive acts of all human beings, not only intersect in the construction of the universal life-world, common to all, but also develop in the relation founded between the acts of one and those of others. Therefore, Husserl could speak of the community of human consciousnesses, a community that, encompassing the human being, goes beyond everything that is concrete and transcends the singular boundaries of each individual. This system of human spirits, always in development and progressing with the stages of humanity – the spirituality shared by consciousnesses, in the sense of Husserl – can be identified with another level of existence that man considers as transcending the vital, the worldly concrete, the everydayness, in short the 'profane'.

At the level of the interconnections flowing from inter-subjective relations, the human soul enriches itself through the circuits of spiritual experiences which, referring to the highest spiritual levels, lead to the last point – ultimate consciousness – as the culminating point of spiritual development. In this way it is possible to see how the soul receives a spiritual molding of the sacred rooted in the network of the interconnections of human consciousness: the sacred shared with other consciousnesses.

From the philosophical point of view, however, there remain questions regarding the relation between these sacred spiritualities individuated at the two indicated levels and the properly religious experience. Is it truly this cosmic or communitarian transcendence of consciousness which appears in the authentically religious experience of the Divine? That there exist exemplary experiences of the religious act is a fact testified to by religions. Can we elucidate their nature, their origin, their significance against the background of these two sacred developments of the soul? We must answer negatively. Then, in which way does the authentic background or religiosity manifest itself? Since we cannot answer this question on the basis of the two indicated levels of the sacred, we approach a third way in which sacrality assumes a form. In fact, our thesis is that sacrality, the sacred, *the sacred molding of the human soul constitute the ground, the soil, on which all questions concerning the relation between man and the divine are played out.*

The creative analysis of the phenomenology of life that we mentioned at the beginning of our discourse – analysis which radically changes the starting point of research, coming to the Archimedean point of the extension of the functioning of the human being (that is, to all the circuits of its functioning, which link it to the cosmos, to nature, to other living beings and to other human beings) and comprehending the two other indicated modes – opens a regal path for reaching the central point of all approaches to the transcendent. Thus, it offers an elucidation of the meaning of the sacred itself.

(c) The third path is based on the psychic-vital-cosmic clarification of the primitive sacred and also on its transcendent-intentional clarification. But it distantiates itself from both by making a radical leap. Here on this third path a crucial point is nailed down – the critique of human reason is to put to use as a thread leading back, with the analysis of the creative act of man, to the sources of the encounter between the virtualities of the human condition with those of the vital human soul; its instruments correspond with those of the soul which crystallizes these virtualities in specifically human functions.

With these instruments the creative investigation discovers and illuminates the emergence and *genesis of the meaning of the sacred* in the flux of human existence. We intend here the genesis of the 'inward sacred', as I call it to distinguish it from the two functional levels previously mentioned. In this genesis, which we discover by means of the analysis, there is present, hidden to intentional observation, a deep work of the soul. In its authentic progress of molding, it simultaneously elaborates an authentic surge toward the crystallization of the religious act and progresses in the crystallization of the authentic meaning of the sacred. In fact, I want to underline my conviction, which will be briefly substantiated in this essay, according to which only in the elaboration of the inward sacred thus conceived is the emergence of the religious act, of the mystical experience, or the acceptance of 'revelation' of the Divine by man – the exemplary instances of the experience of the Divine – possible; this possibility is founded on the ground of the soul.

The two modes previously mentioned necessarily intersect with this last one which activates the exemplary acts of so-called religious experience, that is, of those experiences which sustain in an essential way all the religiosity of man. It is the creative analysis of the soul that gives access to the unfolding of the origin of the conditions which make

the main moments of the religious experience possible and their clarification: How revelation of the divine could be acknowledged as such
and accepted by man, or how God radically transcending all that is human
and the life-world in which man is apparently closed by his limited and
finite intentional circle, allows man to 'listen' and get in touch with Him.
In short, in the philosophy and psychology of religion it is a matter
of explaining the basis of religious faith, that is, of how man within
his boundaries could receive and recognize a Divine message coming
from elsewhere, or how God could speak to man. Our answer to these
questions will be given in the investigation of the genesis of the inward
sacred.

SECTION TWO
ANALYSIS OF THE GENESIS AND EMERGENCE
OF THE INWARD SACRED

*The Phenomenology of Life Shows the Strategic Position of the Soul
Among the Vital-Cosmic Forces and the Sphere of Human Creation*

The Cartesian starting point for the investigation of the cognitive act
has produced, as we know, various separations among the orbits of the
human universe submitted to philosophical reflection. Phenomenology
has sought, with Husserl, Merleau-Ponty, Sartre, to overcome the illegitimate separations between flesh, body, soul, spirit. However, moving
from an invalid starting point, it has not been able to discover the
authentic interconnections between the various areas of human functioning. In fact, phenomenological anthropology moved within an anthropomorphic field, whereas the creative phenomenology of life opens all
the doors so arbitrarily closed thus far, through which the soul communicates with all the circuits of being and becoming, psychic, vital,
organic and inorganic, cosmic circuits, as well as with those circuits
generated through the crystallization of the virtualities of the human
condition, circuits intellectual, social, cultural, spiritual, religious.

As I have shown in my treatise *Logos and Life*, the human soul
works on and with all virtualities as a lens of life, offering the ground
for their encounter and opening the space where it can intervene in
those virtualities and transform them in particular ways. Therefore, the
soul reveals itself as a strategic phase in the becoming and progress of
human existence at all levels.

The soul, thus revealed, by extending itself over all the functioning circuits of *man's-self-interpretation-in-existence*, but also by being open to the investigation of all the forces and their moldings – forces that lead and carry this development – reveals the subterranean threads which link the fragments of the genesis of the spiritual act deriving from these threads. By virtue of opening this extended field of the soul we can observe and evaluate the moments of this development in their meanings. The latter are not only instantaneous and evanescent, but also evasive, truncated, incomplete and evocative. A very delicate operation is necessary in order to recognize them, collect them and submit them to an evaluative reflection, on the basis of which we realize that what happens in our own inwardness has a germinal meaning completely different from that which we normally, expect, namely that all refers to ourselves and is reduced to our faculties. We become aware that it is not us, but the Divine.

With this quick glance at the new ground of phenomenological analysis we directly enter the field we intend to investigate.

In his treatise on the human passions, Descartes wonders if among all the natural – empirical – passions of the soul, the soul may possess a passion – or some passions – properly its own. The result of Descartes' reflection is that the soul generates from itself the passion of generosity. I entirely agree with this; or rather, going further, I would say that generosity seems to found all the passions of the moral life of man. (Compare my treatise: *The Passions of the Soul and the Ontopoiesis of Culture.*[3]) However, I suggest that not generosity the primary passion, but rather the passion of *understanding* which moves all reasoning functioning of the human being is primordial. It is starting from this passion, which constitutes the transcendental limit, that the transcendental activity of man organizes itself in all its effort and thus allows the constructive progress of life.

Following the threads of this primordial passion we will see the soul developing its own movements, the passions. In fact, it is by means of subterranean questioning, upsetting all the levels of the soul's circuits, and developing all the subliminal passions, allowing the soul to emerge from the preoccupations that till now dominate its empirical existence, the soul releases from its own sources drives, forces, inspirations that do not belong to empirical preoccupations, nor to other concerns referring to life, to the world, to society, to the concrete, nor even to the abstract, to the imaginative, to the intellectual. These drives seem to organize themselves in three successive pulses.

In my treatise on the genesis of the sacred, I distinguish, in fact, *three movements of the soul* (See *Logos and Life*, Vol. 2). Going over their course we can follow the genesis of the meaning of the divine in the development of the sacred from *the sacred molding of the soul itself*.

It is at the culminating point of this molding that sacred meaning appears in all its fullness in front of the *Witness* of all its existence, which corresponds to the pattern of the divine sought by man.

Now I will proceed to a brief presentation of the central points of the analysis of the genesis of the sacred that I extensively discussed in *The Three Movements of the Soul*. At the end of this essay I will try to go beyond those analyses to the thematic of the central problem, that is, to the culminating point of the genesis of the inward sacred: to the passage from the sacred to the Divine, from inner immanence to inwardness extending itself to transcendence.

a. *The Route of the First Movement of the Soul*

In the commerce of a living being with its vital environment there is always the matter of 'understanding'. To enter the most developed circuits of our reasoning functions is for man a vital necessity in order to single out the interconnections with things, events, reasonings, etc. Then, the causes, the reasons, the principles of events and of human actions, of thought and of feelings and so forth, are to be distinguished. However, at some point, while we are immersed in preoccupations concerning the world, life and ourselves, driven by ambitions, by inspirations, by desires, etc., a certain kind of inner disillusion arises in us and the following question imposes itself: "Why are we thrown in this course of life, why do we follow this path, why do we desire to behave in this way and not in another way . . . , why do we want to agitate ourselves in such matters; finally, why life as such?" Driven by this anxiety of understanding or rather because of the lack of meaning in everyday life and longing for understanding, moved by the inner forces of the soul, thus freed, we throw ourselves into reflecting upon all our proceedings, doubting them, denying all the partial justifications that can be offered in the search for sufficient, ultimate, complete reason. This investigation, that I have called 'radical investigation', makes all the reasons and justifications we have so far accepted vain. All the ways of establishing 'validity' of conduct, principles and their foundations, ultimately, all beliefs have lost their preestablished validity in this investigation. Suspended, these validities ask for another basis of legitimacy. Our inner universe, shaken in its foundations, has collapsed; without the possibility of saving some thing, this universe must be reconstructed on the bedrock of new convictions, with new modalities of application and legitimacy. (Thèrése of Lisieux seems to have gone through this shipwreck when she asked herself these questions also at the time of her Carmelite vocation.)

Starting from this radical investigation of the meaning of every thing, in which the soul submits all to doubt – without neglecting anything, analyzing all in all perspectives, from all points of view, throwing away all that has already been collected and accepted – it seeks inside itself new points for orientation over this unknown sea, in the effort of releasing from within some orientation toward a path which will lead to the reacquisition of an existential horizon.

And, as a matter of fact, gradually eliminating all that is already given, passionately searching out a new point of orientation, the soul acquires a new molding, it unwinds from its own center a new *sui generis*, trans-empirical, trans-natural propulsion. Transformed by this new molding, thus strengthened, the soul throws its entire self into a new movement.

b. *The Soul in Its Route Toward the Exaltation of the Ideal*

In this new molding, stripping itself of its natural values, the soul first throws itself into the 'idealizing' crystallizations of the moral, esthetic, social and religious modalities. In these subliminal modalities of experiences – rising from natural concreteness submitted to the interests and to the vital preoccupations of subliminal modalities – the soul extends its universe with more satisfying meanings that give place – give space – to the creative development of man. Seduced by the great ideals, people, in many cases, stop at this point in their development.

The artist, the architect, the political man, the humanitarian project their existence in the exaltation of the human spirit, which renewing itself with ever new goals and plans, keeps the human being above the trivialities of the concrete.

However . . . , and here we reach the third movement of our research.

c. *Toward the Trans-Natural Destiny of the Soul – the Inward Sacred*

Taking up again the thread of my thought, I discover that the ideal, the spiritual values are not enough to soothe the anxiety of the soul which does not find the absolute achievement of its ideals; 'perfect' beauty, love, justice, goodness are never reached; all the efforts of man to realize them only arrive to a certain point and then all the threads that link him to the world, to social business, etc., dissolve themselves and, as Saint Augustine said "time steals everything."

Submitted to this inner investigation of the meaning of things and wondering about the final meaning of human affairs – all of which, even the most noble and virtuous, dissolve in the flux of life – and seeing all the enthusiasms that have brought them forth falter, the soul becomes aware that its ideals do not satisfy its desire to understand the meaning of all and that this desire to justify life cannot be satisfied unless the 'absolute meaning' of 'all this' is found, meaning that will not disappear with the wind: the 'ultimate' and 'final' meaning of human affairs, of existence, of life, of the human being himself. Again, the investigation of ideals bring us to affirm their dissolution and that the valuation they involve dissolves itself in futility. The soul then finds itself thrown on its own in a stormy sea, without compass and swamped in total darkness: the light of reason, of the empirical life or of that devoted to higher values, has definitely disappeared.

In the two previous movements, however, the soul developed its own forces by, at the same time it faltered, crystallizing its subliminal virtualities; in the dark where it finds itself dispersed, its own search for orientation has now much improved, thinner and more precise 'instruments' by which to acknowledge its situation; it is able to recognize and evaluate its own drives, its own demands and the forces over which it must work from 'inside' (because the 'outside' has disappeared). The 'outside' has disappeared in the most radical way we can suspect. There, when we strip ourselves of our modalities of valuation of all attributes, dependencies and interconnections which our essential immersion involves – all that sustains the course of our *self-interpretation-in-existence*, of this same existence – in the life-world and in the human universe (that is the social, communitarian and spiritual world), we escape the fabric of interrelations with other men, of which man is the weaver. Man, weaving his own existence, does so in relation with others.

It is on their response to his own vital surges, to his own consciousness, on their acceptance, on their approval that the development of his
emotions, feelings, desires, ambitions, actions depends. By this I do
not want to say that man in himself is dependent on the community or
on others, but that man develops his own course of *auto-individuation
in existence* precisely inside this communitarian and social web through
his surges 'outside himself' in order to involve the participation of others
in his own goals. It is in such communication, in the communication
of feelings, appreciations, aspirations, convictions and tendencies that the
individual man finds his reaffirmation and his strengthening.

The soul, on emerging from that network, finds itself in empty space
on all sides. In the anguish that then floods his soul, the human being
does not find anyone able to understand him, because emerging from that
network of common vital-social convictions, from the convictions
imposed by the vital preoccupations of the moment, the questions to
which the soul seeks to respond, the questioning oscillations which it
would like to resolve, are outside the common existential context, have
become so uniquely personal that no one could penetrate its intentions,
just as much as no one is able to penetrate the unique bottom of the
soul from which they are born and agitate. Alone, the human being would
feel entirely abandoned, lost, condemned if . . .

Here we are at the central point of our investigation. In fact, a new
interrogative threat begins to which the soul now submits itself in its
inner conflicts. Now it is a matter of finding by *itself* all the answers.
How to do so? In truth, man turns, as always, incessantly to others in
order to explain his conduct, his preoccupations, his doubts and also
makes efforts to place his trust in others. In the thorny moments of this
tormenting and very intimate research he enters into anxious and feverish
communication with others. Unfortunately, even if he does not feel
rejected, the reactions, the answers of others appear to be elusive, vain,
and do not touch the knot, the point in which the interrogator feels the
meaning of existence, of being, of the most intimate destiny that he is
searching for. However, this very intimate and obscure intuition brings
him forward in recognizing his *inward destiny*, a destiny that he forges
step by step, modulating in ways radically different from the previous
ones (natural or high-subliminal), his tendencies, his attitudes, his
feelings, etc. In my treatise I sought to show the progress of the thread
of the trans-natural destiny of the soul, through innumerable myste-

rious moments (because they are not clear before the light of constitutive reason), inexplicable in their apparently sudden apparitions; it is a most delicate thread with innumerable ruptures, but discretely continuous. And every 'step' of this progress is signaled because of a moment, because of a new molding taking place in the abyss, in the lively circuits of the soul – a molding that concerns the meaning of all. In contrast with the natural, moral or high sense of the subliminal ideals and with every sense that has direct reference to life and its preoccupations, even with those more spiritual and higher, this sense does not assume the forms of transcendental constitution, does not proceed in its development through the intentionalities that link transcendental functioning to the life-world. If, in a traditional way, we call that sense that is constitutive of life, 'profane', we will have to assume that the other is that which we traditionally call 'sacred'.

Its fragments do not come into presence in the sense of the cognitive 'noema' and the acts in which this field of consciousness appears are not the 'positional' or presencing acts of constitutive consciousness. The truth, then, that these fragments bring is not that of the logic of intellectual functioning.

The soul in its course, however, becoming aware of these differences, does not comprehend them in their modality, in their proper nature. It notices this difference and becomes anxious. And at that point it always asks itself if it is on the 'right path', if it is not 'wrong', if it has remained 'normal', etc. It does not have an adequate measure of this strangeness which it has encountered.

Up to the point. . . . But here we must return to a question developed at the beginning of this section: the question of the perpetual effort of the person to find understanding of his torment in others. It is at this point that, after having sought to show the single, radically new level on which the life of the soul now proceeds in its course in order to follow a single destiny uniquely its own outside all vital connections, a trans-natural destiny, we must attest to the central factor of this course: the appeal of the *Witness* and the intuition of it that crystallizes itself along the trans-natural route.

SECTION THREE
THE INWARD SACRED OF THE SOUL FROM WHICH
THE *SUI GENERIS* INTUITION OF THE DIVINE ARISES

A. *The Witness that Leads to the Crystallization of Religious Acts*

Long and very delicate analytical fragments on the progress of the trans-
natural destiny are needed to show that during its entire path the soul
with yearning turns itself toward an ultimate point. If it realizes that
its events are entangled in the network of feelings, of inner tendencies
that urge on endlessly, and it tries to find some order among them, in
order to distinguish between the right and the wrong step, the soul is
the only one to know all that takes place in itself, and also that it is unable
to see all the elements from all points of view. Precisely when it tries
to become aware of itself and submits itself to a sincere and complete
examination of the failures and successes of all its life, does it find
itself 'innocent' in its tangled situation and in its weakness and, as if it
could neither make itself understood nor clear itself of blame, it invokes
a 'Witness', who "if he could know and see the entire tangled situation
in which it finds itself, it would understand."

'Understood', the soul would feel very humble, simply in all the
weakness of its mistakes, of its unawareness of many things, of its unjus-
tifiable hesitations on behalf of its spirit, of its lack of right understanding;
it would feel stripped of all, even of its good intentions, and it is in
that moment of extreme simplicity and of humbleness in recognizing
its own impotence that the soul turns in all its being toward this witness,
who 'if he would know all, would understand' and 'would forgive' and
'would accept it' in his intimacy.

In truth, this turning toward a possible, virtual, witness does not fall
into emptiness. On the contrary, it leads to a most intimate intuition,
an intuition that crystallizes itself in an 'inward reality' with an experience by which all the anxiety, torment, and efforts made to find some
answers, are accepted. We now submit: that is, we turn from the inward
dialogue with ourselves with all its evasive ramifications to the Witness.
How wonderful! We understand that we are not alone! The Witness is
a radiant presence, penetrating our existence in all its parts to the flesh
of the soul. Finally, there is the conviction that the destiny of our existence is discovered as the *new life of this soul*. It is a trans-natural life,
inside and outside us, contingent and absolute.

It is the extraordinary presence of the Witness in the soul which gives the culminating point to our trans-natural destiny. Moreover, *it is the modality of this presence which allows us to discover its true meaning.*

B. *The Modalities of the Presence of the Witness that Indicate the Trans-Natural Meaning: the 'Divine'*

As a matter of fact, the Witness that emerges in an intuition journeying through all the fluctuations of the life of the soul, affirms himself 'in his presence' absolutely distinct from the soul, as radically other. Radically other because he cannot identify himself with any living being, with anything known and with nothing that could be known, because he introduces himself as other, radically other, not only in relation to all that is present, but also to all that which is possible; in this way he introduces himself at the peak of being and of becoming, and knowing all, penetrating all, he is somehow aware of all. Thus present in the soul, the Witness is able to understand the human attitude in its totality as such and particularly that of the soul which invokes him.

In the first place, his presence detaches itself as distinct and autonomous compared to our efforts to invoke this presence, wanting to hold back and modify its ways. However, it appears inside the soul. It penetrates it from 'outside' and attracts it in all its movements toward a most intimate union. Moreover, attracting it toward himself, the Witness makes the soul extend itself in all its movements to the extreme of its capacities, of its yearnings and its own efforts. In the second place, he prolongs this extension toward himself, who is *outside the soul itself*, because the Witness appears ciphered, according to one of its statements, *as outside the soul.*

Does not the Witness that completely penetrates us, that participates in all our movements, that inspires all our being through his own presence, this Witness that the soul ciphers with an absolutely different meaning from its own self, as *absolutely other*, represent what we call by means of a concept the 'Divine'? We can summarize with Saint Augustine: "God within us and us outside ourselves."

Only now in the apparition of the Witness in the soul, in his entire presence which affirms himself in his trans-natural meaning, do we discover that our personal destiny, so much sought after was trans-natural, that the modality elaborated in our soul, was the modality of the sacred.

C. *The Genesis of the Soul As a Condition of Religious Experiences*

After this quick view of the genesis of the inward sacred that identifies itself with the development of special forces and of the appropriate
virtualities of the human soul, development that allows it to launch
itself on the trans-natural course, and after having recognized that in
that – as in its peak – the trans-natural presence of the Witness is manifested, we must go back to our initial proposal in order to appreciate
how the genesis of the inward sacred – or perhaps, to put it better, the
genesis of the soul in the sacred – corresponds to the thesis that we
have proposed.

How can God speak to man?

How can God, Who in the way we search Him postulates His radical
transcendence compared to man and to all the contingency of the life-
world and of the cosmos, come into contact with a contingent being?

These questions are specified in the context of our analysis in the
following way: if this exemplary communication and this exemplary
contact should realize itself through the 'revelation of a message', then
– assuming the radical transcendence and the limitation of man in his
contingent situation – exceptional conditions for this fulfilling would
be necessary. It seems that our investigation points out that the primary
condition of the revelation of a Divine message to man is the *genesis
of the inward sacred in the soul*. Not only must the soul let emerge an
impulse and a force from its own virtualities in order to follow its own
aspiration toward the nativity of the trans-natural destiny, but in the
course of the development of its own forces and sacred modalities, the
soul must prepare the means to become 'careful', to 'listen' and recognize the message of the Witness – the divine messenger. Finally, after
having overcome its boundaries, 'outside itself' toward the Divine, the
soul must still have prepared the *sacred meanings to cipher this message*.

The ciphering of the sacred message, that gives foundations to the
beliefs and to religion, belongs to another stage of research.

The World Phenomenology Institute

NOTES

[1] Anna-Teresa Tymieniecka, *Logos and Life*, Book 1, *Creative Experience and the Critique of Reason*, Part II (Dordrecht: Kluwer Academic Publishers, 1988).
[2] Anna-Teresa Tymieniecka, *Logos and Life*, Book 2, *The Three Movements of the Soul* (Dordrecht: Kluwer Academic Publishers, 1988).
[3] Anna-Teresa Tymieniecka, *Logos and Life*, Book 3 (Dordrecht: Kluwer Academic Publishers, 1990).

PART ONE

THE SACRED
AS A STATION TO TAKE OFF FROM . . .

From left to right: Krystyna Gorniak Kocikowska, Steve Laycock, Robert Sweeney, A-T. Tymieniecka, Thomas Ryba among others at the 'Phenomenology of the Sacred' session of the World Phenomenology Institute during the American Philosophical Associaton Annual Meeting of the Eastern Division in New York, 1990.

THOMAS RYBA

THE IDEA OF THE SACRED IN TWENTIETH-CENTURY THOUGHT: FOUR VIEWS (OTTO, SCHELER, NYGREN, TYMIENIECKA)

INTRODUCTION

Most of the contemporary notions of the Sacred developed by positive philosophers of religion have their origins in the Enlightenment and the Romantic movement. Especially foundational for this development was the Kantian philosophy, with its concern about the sublime and the possibility of a purely rational religion – concerns which were to set the ground rules for philosophical discourse about the idea of the Sacred for centuries to come. Parts of Kant's larger philosophical project – the notions of the *a priori* and the categorical constitution of reality, in particular – have left indelible marks on subsequent philosophical definitions of the Sacred. Indeed, if one wishes to understand why broadly phenomenological philosophies of religion have dealt with the Sacred in the way they have, then one must begin with the philosophy of Kant.

Although I recognize Kant as one of the fonts of subsequent formulations of the idea of the Sacred, it is not my purpose, in this paper, to rehearse the Kantian contributions to the philosophy of religion *in toto*, because it was not Kant's specific intent to create a philosophy of religion. Rather, my purpose here is to review the ways in which four subsequent thinkers formulated their notions of the Sacred, recognizing – as I do – that behind their discussions the point of the Kantian foil prodded them on; also I wish to rehearse the ways in which these four twentieth-century thinkers came to terms with the idea of the Sacred in response to the ground rules established in the Kantian epistemology. In short, I wish to rehearse the ways in which Rudolf Otto, Max Scheler, Anders Nygren and Anna-Teresa Tymieniecka formulated their notions of the Sacred against the background of Kantian epistemology. My intention to do this is simplified by the historical fact that, of the works of these four twentieth-century thinkers, Rudolf Otto's *The Idea of the Holy* was written earliest; it provided the point of departure for Scheler

A-T. Tymieniecka (ed.), Analecta Husserliana XLIII, 21–42.
© 1994 *Kluwer Academic Publishers. Printed in the Netherlands.*

and Nygren, whose writings about the *a priori* and categorical nature of the Sacred were responses to and critiques of it.

Rudolf Otto's *The Idea of the Holy* is one of the pivotal works of religious phenomenology in the twentieth century because in it Otto construed the phenomenological and formal characteristics of the Sacred with an intellectual audacity sufficient to make this work the reference point for all subsequent thinkers concerned with a similar goal. Although Otto's *Idea of the Holy* is his most remembered book, similar themes echo through his earlier works. The program delineated in *The Philosophy of Religion Based on Kant and Fries* also has considerable relevance for a contextualization of the philosophical development of the idea of the Sacred in the twentieth century. This is because in *The Philosophy of Religion* Otto makes explicit both his dependence on and reaction to the philosophy of Kant, two relations he usually shares with subsequent thinkers who extend or critique the formulation presented in his work *The Idea of the Holy*. Thus, both *The Idea of the Holy* and *The Philosophy of Religion* provide the impetus for many later theories of the Sacred, and the work of later twentieth-century thinkers, for the most part, can be described as having developed in subtle dialectic with both Otto and Kant. Here, I specifically have in mind the works of Max Scheler and Anders Nygren. In the case of Anna-Teresa Tymieniecka, her inclusion is not a matter of apparent positive or negative dependence upon Otto, even though her thinking evolved in a milieu in which Otto was an important influence. Tymieniecka's thought is included because it represents an original contemporary attempt to formulate a notion of the Sacred which readdresses – in an invigorated way – some of the Kantian assumptions underlying the formulations of the three preceding thinkers. Although it will be impossible to review all of the points of Otto's theory of the Sacred in the short space allotted, a discussion of its relevant features follows.

I. RUDOLF OTTO AND THE IDEA OF THE HOLY

Scheler, Wainwright, Dawson and others have recognized that Otto's philosophy falls into two major divisions, whose parts are not easily reconciled (Scheler: 286; Dawson: 284; Wainwright: 13–15). The first of these is Otto's attempt to describe the Sacred on the basis of its historical and experiential manifestations in various world religions, the descriptions of the Judaeo-Christian and Hindu conceptions being the

most well-developed of his treatments. The end of this first portion of
The Idea of the Holy is clearly signalled when Otto shifts from a discussion of the elements of religious experience to a section which
includes a discussion of the analogies of experience and to the two
chapters on the Sacred as an *a priori* category. The precise nature of
this transition has been hotly debated. Some, like Scheler, argue that
the first (or phenomenological) section stands on its own merits as a
purely descriptive section about the Sacred; others, like Dawson, argue
that the first section is tainted by the neo-Kantian philosophy which
obviously characterizes the latter portions of the work. Whatever the
integrity and precise relation between these sections, the presuppositions and argument contained therein may be summarized in more or less
the following terms.

Otto's chief concern would seem to be to preserve the Kantian epistemology as expressed in the three critiques, but only insofar as this
epistemology does not vitiate religious experience of the Sacred, a form
of experience which Otto construes as neither a matter of Kantian pure
reason, nor of Kantian practical reason, nor as the Kantian notion of
aesthetic judgment. This apparent concern accounts for the priority which
Otto assigns to the phenomenological evidences over and against
his theoretical explanations of them; that is to say, he thinks that phenomenological description ought to drive theoretical formulations and
not the other way around. (Otto, unself-consciously, never raises the
possibility that his own phenomenological descriptions may be tainted
with imported theoretical assumptions.)

In the phenomenological portion of his work, Otto describes the Sacred
as possessing prominent features (or "elements" as he calls them) which
are simultaneously rational and irrational. As experienced, the Sacred
is fearful, majestic and energetic. These elements are woven together
in a mix of rational and irrational components in the percipient's experience of the Sacred's tremendous quality (*tremendum*). On the other
hand, the Sacred's mysterious quality (*mysterium*) is intimately bound
up with the experience of it being "wholly other." Otto gives the interpretation of the phrase "*mysterium tremendum*" a peculiarly Kantian twist
by referring to the word "*tremendum*" as the "synthetic qualifying
attribute" under which the Sacred is understood, thus suggesting that
under the description of mystery (or wholly other), cognitive content is
particularly thin (Otto [1]: 25). The fearful, majestic and energetic dimension of the Sacred, on the other hand, has reference only to the rational

and irrational responses of the experiencing subject, and not to the properties of any external object. Here, Otto obviously interprets the tremendous aspect of the Sacred on an analogy with the Kantian understanding of sublime experience – about which more will be said later. Finally, the Sacred is also interpreted under its formal synthetic aspect as being fascinating, this last element serving as the contrasting attitudinal pole to the daunting aspect of the Sacred's tremendousness. In its fascinating aspect, the Sacred is described as "a potent charm, and the creature, who trembles before it, utterly cowed and cast down, has always at the same time the impulse to turn on it, nay even to make it somehow his own" (Otto [1]: 31). I leave it to the reader to look up all the details of content with which Otto fleshes out the phenomenological portions of his description, for my own interest lies in quite another direction – that of his description of the Sacred as categorical and *a priori*. However, before describing the unique features of Otto's notion of the Sacred *a priori*, a rehearsal of the Kantian notion of *aprioricity* is necessary, since it is the Kantian notion which is ancestor to Otto's own conception.

A. *The Notions of the* 'A Priori' *and* 'Category' *in Kantian Philosophy**

The criteria Kant provides for distinguishing *a priori* judgments from what he terms "empirical judgments" are fourfold: (1) they are thought of as necessary, (2) they cannot be "derived from any proposition except one which also have the validity of a necessary judgment" (that is to say, "they are not grounded in higher and more universal modes of knowledge"), (3) they allow no possibility of being interpreted otherwise and (4) they are ideal (they are not properties of the objects to which they refer) (Kant [2]: B3–B5, B188). In terms of modern epistemology, we may describe these criteria as the criteria of: (1) necessity, (2) nonderivability or foundationality (3) incorrigibility and (4) ideality. The same criteria presumably apply to all features of the Kantian system (that is, ideas, categories, knowledge) which are tagged as *a priori*.

Kant opts to demonstrate these criteria in a way which has reference to the "subjective sources of the possibility of an object in general" and is not in any fashion dependent upon an epistemological algorithm which would be contingent and empirical (Kant [2]: A149). He recognizes that the only valid proof of the existence of *a priori* judgments is a demonstration of the impossibility (for any subject) of knowledge which is not constituted by *a priori* concepts of pure understanding. He "proves" this by arguing that positive (synthetic) non trivial (non-analytic) knowledge must have a medium in which the synthesis occurs, and this medium consists of the inner sense, imagination or apperception of their *a priori* forms, time and space (Kant [2]: B194–B195, A155–A156). As he puts it: "Space and time contain a manifold of pure *a priori* intuition, but at the same time are the conditions for the pure receptivity of our mind – conditions under which alone it can receive representations of objects, and which therefore must also always affect the concept of these objects" (Kant [2]: B102, A73). No knowledge would exist were it not for such synthesis and the universal and *a priori* forms which make it possible (Kant [2]: B195, A156).

The universal principles to which Kant refers can be schematized according to four kinds of judgment, that is, according to: (1) quantity (universal, particular, singular judgments), (2) quality (affirmative, negative, infinite judgments), (3) relation (categorical, hypothetical, disjunctive judgments) and (4) modality (problematic, assertoric, apodeictic judgments). From these it is possible to derive the famous Kantian table of the categories. For Kant, categories classify the functions of understanding "completely and yield an exhaustive inventory of its powers" (Kant [2]: B107, A79). They also represent the *pure concepts of understanding* which apply *a priori* to the objects of intuition. Here, Kant describes epistemological constitution as a sequential movement from the given manifold of pure intuitions, through the synthesis of the manifold by the imagination, to the unification of the pure synthesis by the understanding through the categories. The categories function as the forms under which the manifold of intuition can be brought to understanding. They are developed from certain kinds of judgment, but their number and their location in pure understanding are inscrutable; their presence cannot be demonstrated inductively.

Kant's characterization of the *a priori* remains homogeneous throughout the three critiques, but its relevance to the constitution of experience varies with each one. The way in which the *a priori* is constitutive of aesthetic experience – an important theme of the *Critique of Judgment* – is directly germane to Otto's understanding of the Sacred, because it is the Kantian understanding of the constitution of aesthetic experience which establishes Otto's notion of the Sacred as an *a priori* category. Unlike judgments of pure reason (where considerations of satisfaction and interest are absent) or judgments of practical reason (where considerations of satisfaction and interest are both present), aesthetic judgments represent a sort of *via media*: they are judgments in which interest is absent but satisfaction is present. What this means is that the kind of *a priori* associated with aesthetic experience is not constitutive of an aesthetic object in the way that categories are, and that it does not consist of a necessary relation of pleasure or satisfaction which accompanies the experience of the object (as in moral objects); it is a passive satisfaction, a satisfaction which is "contemplative" in that it is the "consciousness of [58] the mere formal purposiveness in the play of the subject's cognitive powers . . . in respect to cognition in general, without . . . being limited to any definite cognition, and consequently contains a mere form of the subjective purposiveness of a representation in an aesthetical judgment" (Kant [1]: 57–58). Thus, pleasure or satisfaction is a necessary concomitant of aesthetic experience, but that satisfaction has no relation to the constituted object *per se*, nor can it be subsumed under one of the categories of understanding. It is the product of the experiencing subject alone. Pleasure results from a purposiveness attributed to the object, but not found in it. The beautiful, therefore, is completely exhausted in the effect an object has upon the percipient. The sublime has reference to the subject in the same fashion as the beautiful, though the cause of the disturbing effect of the sublime is in the experience of its boundlessness and in the fact that it produces indirect pleasure coupled with pain.

The *a priori* nature of aesthetic experience does not function constitutively to produce the object. Rather, it represents an *a priori* category which is not fundamentally rational in the same fashion as the categories or the judgments of pure reason. Aesthetic judgments are "singular judgments" which "do not combine their predicates of satisfaction with a concept, but [combine them] with a given, empirical representation" (Kant [1]: 37, 131). They can be referred to neither the categories nor the laws of pure reason. It is the universal validity of pleasure "perceived as mentally bound up with the mere judgment upon an object, which is represented *a priori*" in an aesthetic judgment taken "as a universal rule . . . and valid for everyone" (Kant [1]: 37, 131–132).

B. *The Notions of the 'A Priori' and 'Category' in the Thought of Otto*

In calling the Sacred an *a priori* category, Otto does not simplistically identify it with the Kantian categories of pure reason or understanding, nor does he allow its subsumption under Kantian practical reason or aesthetic experience. Otto accepts the notion that the category of the Sacred can be formed on an analogy with aesthetic objects, *especially* insofar as these aesthetic objects fall neither under the schematization of the categories of pure reason nor under moral laws.

Three distinguishable features of the Sacred contribute to its significance for the believer. First, the Sacred must in some sense find a form of mediation in the awareness of the religious believer. It will not do to reduce the experience of the Sacred to an aesthetic experience in the Kantian sense, because the judgment that emerges from the encounter with a sublime or beautiful object has reference only to the experiencing subject and is not about any extra-mental property which the object really possesses. In his unhappy reference to the Sacred as "wholly other," Otto is not suggesting that there is no point of experiential mediation between the Sacred and the percipient. Rather, he is in fact arguing that the Sacred is experienced precisely as something which is not to be confused with the subject. Thus, it is not a plausible object in the aesthetic or moral sense, but its otherness expresses instead an alterity which testifies to its reality (Otto [2]: 17). The wholly other is known for what it is precisely because it is so different from what we are, and were it not so different we would confuse it with our own estimation of a sublime or beautiful object. In fact, the Sacred can only be known via a "double negation." By this, Otto means that the percipient, in attempting to form a judgment about the Sacred object, first negates the features of the numinous object's rational and subjective constitution; then the conceptual void which remains is negated in the direction of something which is beyond the objective and subjective contributions to the constitution of experience.

Second – and this is consistent with what was just said – the Sacred transcends rational categories of thought. The alterity of the wholly other is such that it is not susceptible to objective constitution on the basis of the ideas of pure reason, nor is it reducible to an aesthetic judgment. But in arguing the point, Otto is not denying that any schematization of the Sacred according to the concepts of pure reason is impossible.

Yet any such schematization has no relation to the Sacred as a thing-in-itself. Particularly to the Sacred's character of *mysteriosum* do rational schematizations apply, and here they do so as the "*absoluteness* [of] all rational attributes applied to the Deity" (Otto [[1]: 140–141).

Third, Otto postulates a certain type of feeling as the intuitive guarantor of the relation between Sacred object and experiencing subject. To describe this feeling, Otto employs the German word 'Ahndung', a word rendered by "presentiment," "foreboding," "apprehension" or, to use Otto's preferred word for its associated faculty, "divination" (Otto [1]: Ch. XVIII). In calling *Ahndung* a "feeling," Otto intends something quite beyond the pale we usually associate with this phrase. "Feeling," in this context, is that which establishes between subject and object a relation which is causal, extra-cognitive, and yet a form of knowledge. Before Otto, Fries maintained that religious feeling and religious conviction were inseparably connected, so that if one tries to prove the truth of one's conviction one must have recourse to the kind of knowledge which undergirds it. This influences Otto to postulate feeling as a form of suprarational knowledge, a third variety of reason between pure and practical reason. He elevates what was aesthetic judgment for Kant to a new status by assigning to feeling a function which is not merely reducible to subjectivity. But the peculiarity of this "apprehension" of the Sacred is that it cannot be demonstrated along Kantian lines to be an *a priori* judgment. Otto makes it clear that he *does not* hold the Kantian view that a transcendental deduction of the categories is possible. Instead, when he attempts to justify the validity of the feeling of the Sacred, he bases his justification upon a supposed special faculty, inherent in religious *virtuosi*, which is activated by peculiar external circumstances. His justification of the validity of the feeling of the Sacred, therefore, amounts to little more than the assertion than there are certain specially endowed individuals who, under special circumstances, experience the Sacred with an intuitive intensity which makes the experience indubitable for them (Otto [2]: 18–19, 95–98).

II. THE SACRED IN THE THOUGHT OF MAX SCHELER

In his essay, "The Problems of Religion" contained in his book *On the Eternal in Man* (Leipzig: 1921), Max Scheler describes a phenomenology of religion which has the work of Otto and Schleiermacher as its points of departure. Like Otto, Scheler is interested in identifying the *a priori* aspect of the Sacred, but he does so in a fashion which is even further removed from the Kantian philosophy than the Friesian neo-Kantianism of Otto. In order to understand what Scheler is up to, it is necessary to recognize (1) that he is engaged in criticism as much as in constructive philosophy, and (2) that he makes an important distinction between "reconstructive" (or descriptive) phenomenology, on the one hand, and essential phenomenology, on the other.

Scheler's criticism of Otto is not entirely unqualified. He does admire the descriptive phenomenological portions of *The Idea of the Holy*, commenting that they show a "remarkable depth and subtlety" coming as they do from the pen of a "most estimable writer on the philosophy of religion" (Scheler: 169). His argument with Otto is not about the phenomenological experience of the Sacred, but about Otto's philosophical interpretation of that experience, with its heavy Kantian overtones. His judgment of this portion of Otto's work is clear. As he puts it: "It is . . . where Otto exerts himself to demonstrate that the holy is, in Kant's sense, an *a priori* category, that he begins to burden his fine study with a theory we must consider false and discredited – not only in this connection but *wherever* it is adduced in explanation of extra- and super-sensory phenomena in the field of object-perception" (Scheler: 286).

Scheler does not accept the Kantian view that "anything [anyone] . . . fails to find in the content of 'sensation' is added to sense-data by mental synthesis," nor the (Kantian and) Schleiermachian view that the basic phenomena of religious experience, concretely isolated, are merely the irreducible material – and not the form – of religious speculation and constructive theology (Scheler: 286). Thus, Scheler's first criticism of Otto calls into question the neo-Kantian procedure of analyzing religious phenomena in a way which is analogous to aesthetic phenomena, an approach which transforms the Sacred into "a subjective rational category 'coined' for certain sense data (and . . . not pre-existent as an attribute of the object)" (Scheler: 145). In this context, Scheler is particularly critical of Otto's "theoretic . . . 'deformation'" of the primary experiential elements which, Otto thought, described the numinous – the tremendous mystery and fascination of the Sacred, for example – and which Scheler sees as hopelessly dissociated from any extra-psychological object which they may seem to represent (Scheler: 286). But the problem with this approach is that it decides the case against the exis-

tence of asensual or supersensual objects by fiat, before the evidence
has been produced (291).

Following from this first difficulty is another. Both Otto and Schleiermacher "lay a disproportionate emphasis upon emotion in . . . [their]
definition[s] of the religious act" (Scheler: 287). Foreclosed is the
possibility – a possibility which Scheler upholds – that there are direct
religious acts which involve "percipient reason" (*ibid.*). By this last
phrase Scheler presumably means a kind of religious experience or
reason "which directly apprehends the essences of things" and thus cannot
be cut off from the extramental existence of its object (Scheler: 288).
This neglect of essential insight on Otto's part means that the intentionality of religious experience is a peculiar one; the associated
"value-aspect" of the Sacred being theoretically formed on analogy, again,
with that of the Kantian aesthetic object (*ibid.*). This means that,
according to Otto, the Sacred (like the Sublime or Beautiful) can only
be valued for the effect it has on the percipient, and that, though causally
related to an object in some sense, the value associated with that object
is never construed as one of its inherent properties. In place of this
view, Scheler opts for an understanding of religious emotion which makes
the intentionality of such emotions the very carrier of objective knowledge about the Sacred. Put another way, the Sacred "discloses itself to
us [through the focus of these emotions], and in the absence of these
emotional acts we could as little perceive it as a blind man colour"
(Scheler: 289). The emotions are enjoyed for themselves only at the
second moment of the religious experience.

Scheler does not think that once one has jettisoned the neo-Kantian
baggage in Otto's idea of the Sacred one can then move from Otto's
phenomenology of the Sacred directly to its correct conceptualization.
This is because Scheler makes an important distinction between the
two varieties of phenomenology which I alluded to previously.
Reconstructive (or descriptive) phenomenology – the brand practiced
by Otto in the earlier portions of *The Idea of the Holy* – must, by its
very nature, be relativistic and subjective. That this must be so derives
from the fact that reconstructive phenomenology can pursue the Sacred
only in terms of the "*given*" 'ideas,' because it is engaged primarily in
the process of reconstituting and reintuiting their original empirical
contents and "revitalizing [their] . . . original meaning and restoring
their perceptual validity for today" (OIEM, 18). As Scheler puts it:
"[R]econstructive phenomenology cannot be productive: . . . it can only

rediscover, therefore produce nothing new, for one cannot *re*discover what no one has ever observed" (*ibid.*). Also excluded by its very nature is involvement in most of the questions which have been perennially important to philosophy: questions of truth, adequacy, existence, formal validity, and so on. Reconstructive phenomenology is thus relativized to the context of the experience it investigates; it renders but does not explain, test or discover.

On the other hand, Scheler proposes *essential phenomenology* as the method which is truly philosophical and which supplements the deficiencies of a purely reconstructive phenomenology. This recommendation on Scheler's part is tantamount to an admission that a second *theoretical* moment is demanded in any approach to the Sacred. Scheler's feud with Otto is not, therefore, over whether there should be an explanation of what, whether or why the Sacred *is*, but is a matter of disagreement over which is the best method for providing these explanations. Description in every case calls for explanation; by itself, description cannot constitute an adequate science.

The essential phenomenology which is to replace Otto's categorical philosophy will not differ from it in its search for *a priori* structures. Scheler also thinks that the Sacred has something of the *a priori* about it. But he gives the notion of the *a priori* a different thematic slant, and looks for it in a different place than in neo-Kantian categories which are constitutive of consciousness (Scheler: 19). However, even Scheler is shy of maintaining that essential phenomenology will offer demonstrative "proofs" of the existence of the Sacred; proofs which move necessarily from essential knowledge of religious objects to their existence. Nevertheless, Scheler does argue that a method of essential *correlation* may be possible. He describes it as follows:

Although . . . [essential phenomenology] on no occasion allows one to assert the reality of a given object, . . . one yet knows *a priori* that the 'essential correlations' which it discovers, since they are true of this or that object, are also true of all possible contingent objects of the same 'nature' or essence, whence it follows that we can make true judgments about those objects. But reality itself can only be established, 'in accordance with' these essential co-relations, by some kind of *contingent* experience (. . . its subsequent thinking over, development, supplementation), and for supersensible objects this implies either metaphysics or God's positive self-communication. . . . (Scheler: 19)

Put concretely, Scheler's argument is that if there is a general, essential concept of the Sacred, then we should expect to find subsequent examples of the Sacred corresponding to it. However, subsequent

examples might prove the ultimate corrigibility of that essential conception because an essential analysis merely establishes the grounds
for the correlations of observed and anticipated characteristics. This is
a far cry from the categorical conception of the Sacred which Otto
attempted to provide. In fact, Scheler's conceptualization of essential phenomenology is an answer to Kantian philosophy of the categorical *a
priori*. Scheler does not wish to foreclose the possibility that a demonstration of the Sacred's *a priori* character can rely upon inductive
correlations or be disproven by them. Unlike Kant – who built incorrigibility and necessity into his definition of the *a priori*, thus ultimately
calling into question every variety of inductive demonstration of it –
Scheler does not construe the notion of the *a priori* as constitutive of
consciousness itself, but rather of objects in consciousness. This means
that a correctly formed judgment that is constitutive of an idea expresses
the *a priori* nature of the object to which that idea applies. The shift is
from the *a priori* nature of categories that are constitutive of consciousness to the *a priori* nature of objects that are constitutive of
consciousness.

Intent upon making clear the difference between his approach and
those of Otto and Schleiermacher, Scheler does not dwell upon the Sacred
in itself, but concentrates his discussion on the phenomenology of the
religious act (Scheler: 162).

III. THE SACRED IN THE THOUGHT OF ANDERS NYGREN

Also critical of the neo-Kantian groundwork laid by Rudolf Otto is
Anders Nygren, in one of his smaller works: "The Validity of Religious
Experience" (*Die Gültligkeit der religiösen Erfahrung* [Gütersloh: 1922]).
Unlike Scheler's works, this monograph of Nygren defines the other –
quite opposite – limit to the criticism of Otto's notion of the Sacred.
Nygren takes Otto to task not for the fundamental error of his depen-
dence upon Kant, but because Otto's derivative, Friesian neo-Kantianism
does not faithfully preserve Kant's fundamentally correct insights.

Nygren views Otto's criticism of the transcendental deduction as
equivalent to a rejection of a transcendental *a priori* in favor – as he
puts it – of the notion of an anthropological *a priori* consisting of a
productive or receptive religious faculty present in all humans (Nygren
[Watson]: 25). The error in Otto's conception of the Sacred as *a priori*
– as Nygren understands it – is its complete immanent psychologism,

which is susceptible to criticism on at least four grounds, according to Nygren.

First, Otto errs by not grasping the full depth of the Kantian criticism of metaphysics and ignores the Kantian approach to the establishment of the validity of metaphysics – an oversight which makes Otto's explanation of the Sacred little more than an unverifiable theory. In this, "Otto stands philosophically on pre-Kantian ground" (*ibid.*, 26). With respect to the significance of metaphysics, there has been no development from the thought of Kant to the thought of Otto, only a regression.

Second, by positing an inherent faculty which produces religious experiences, Otto involves himself in little more than a tautology (*ibid.*). This is tantamount to the assertion that the Sacred is what is experienced as Sacred. This approach provides no explanation at all, but merely pushes the problem further back. Why, for example, do we have such a faculty and how does it stand in relation to is supposed objects? The postulate of a faculty which secretes religious experience as the liver secretes bile has no explanatory value unless its function – at the very least – can be explained.

Third, the analogies which Otto draws between the religious individual and the prophet have only the dimmest resemblance to each other, at least according to Nygren's entrenched Christian sensibilities. For Nygren, "[a]nything suggestive of 'Invention, creation, composition and the spontaneous production of genius' is fundamentally alien to the prophet" (*ibid.*, 27). Nygren contests the spontaneity of Otto's (fundamentally) Romantic notion of religious experience because he himself accepts a notion of religious experience modelled on one of the notions of Christian revelation, according to which the percipient's passivity is emphasized with respect to the material content of the revelation, while his/her creativity is strictly limited with respect to the formal representation of that content. "The prophet is not an artist . . . of religion, freely creating and shaping religious values, but his creativity and his whole attitude is completely *sui generis*" (*ibid.*). The analogy between the aesthetic sense and the religious sense – an analogy freely traded upon by Otto and seemingly intimated by Kant – is to be rejected, according to Nygren. *Homo religiousus* is not primarily productive, but receptive.

Fourth, inasmuch as Otto construes the Sacred as an *a priori* category composed of rational and irrational elements, his losses far outweigh his gains, for though he attempts to rescue the Sacred from excessive rationalization, he paradoxically wishes to retain it as a "historico-philosophical criterion of value" (*ibid.*). But from Nygren's Kantian viewpoint, this undermines the Kantian underpinnings of the very notion of the *a priori*, while making it susceptible to psychologistic reductionism (*ibid.*). The Sacred's rational features become mere *rationalizations* and its irrational features are reduced to affective universals.

What, then, does Nygren offer as a positive reconstitution of the Kantian notion of the *a priori* of the Sacred? Nygren recommends nothing less than a return to a new transcendental deduction of the categories in order to demonstrate that the category of the Sacred can be necessarily derived. The task of the philosopher of religion is to "enquire how far a 'transcendental deduction of religion' is possible" (*ibid.*, 36). This means, according to Nygren, that the task incumbent upon the philosopher of religion is no less than that of demonstrating "an element in religious experience, of such a kind that, unless it is recognized, no experience is possible, . . . an element which must have validity if anything at all is to have validity" (*ibid.*, 47). What Nygren seeks is not a demonstration of each element of religion in its perfect richness but merely "the validity of the fundamental religious category or . . . value" (*ibid.*, 48). Here, the shift is away from the empirical descriptions of the numinous (like those provided by Otto) and back to the very demonstration which Otto denied had any sense: the rational establishment of an *a priori* religious category. In this demonstration, a much heavier burden is placed upon religious philosophy than any ever experienced by ethics or epistemology. According to Nygren, it is not sufficient to demonstrate that the category of the Sacred is based upon principles which insure the validity only of theoretical experience – as in the case of epistemology – nor is it sufficient to demonstrate that the category of the Sacred is based upon principles which insure the validity only of moral experience – as in the case of ethics – but rather, the category of the Sacred must be shown to be founded upon principles which are the basis of any experience! "That is to say, we must not merely show that no *religious* experience, but rather that no experience *of any kind* is possible without the fundamental religious category, or that there is any validity whatsoever except on a religious basis" (*ibid.*, 50). Such a demonstration will be free from the claims of specific cultural forms for limited durations, and the validity it possesses will transcend such limitations. Here, at the very heart of the notion of validity, Nygren claims that we

THE IDEA OF THE SACRED

find an intimation of this fundamentally religious category. For, if a transcendental validity is recognized, if a kind of validity which claims eternal applicability can actually be shown to be a limit-concept of knowledge, then the category of eternity must be constitutive of it. Thus, the transcendental notion of validity itself – in fact and by absolute necessity – depends upon the category of eternity.

The constitutive category of eternity is susceptible to an interpretation which makes all other judgments religious. Thus mathematical propositions, moral propositions, propositions of natural science and even of history, insofar as they are valid judgments of reason, might be construed as religious judgments. But Nygren denies this: such an extension of the notion of the Eternal would be to dilute it. Instead of opting for an interpretation of the Eternal as a category which subsumes the contents of all other judgments under it, Nygren distinguishes the Eternal's contribution to the possibility of experience according to its *validity* from its contribution according to its *content*. To found the validity of a judgment is as different from providing the content of a judgment as the pedestal which supports a statue is from the statue itself. Judgments of reason outside of the realm of religious philosophy "only presuppose the category of eternity for their validity, but they do not *contain* it" (*ibid.*, 55). "As regard its content, the category of eternity belongs to the realm of religion exactly as the theoretical categories belong to the realm of knowledge or the categorical imperative belongs to ethics" (*ibid.*, 56). It is "actually contained only in religious experience" (*ibid.*, 56).

In this way, the conflation between the Sacred and the Eternal is possible for Nygren, but it is a conflation which is never complete because the transcendental deduction of every aspect of all historical religions is, of course, impossible. The component of the Sacred which is *a priori* – the Eternal – is thus limited by Nygren to a number of general possibilities, even though as a Christian theologian he thinks they will be best and most concretely realized in Christianity. Without completely freeing himself of his Christian prejudices, he describes these general possibilities of the *a priori* category of the Sacred as follows:

[The] . . . 'eternal' must not be understood in the naive sense of an extension of time backwards and forwards, but the description of a form of existence which is raised above the temporal and finite. From a philosophical point of view, the eternal is described negatively, as that which is elevated above all temporal and spatial limitations, and positively, as that which is valid. From a religious point of view, the eternal is that which participates in the life of God, and therefore it must not simply be identified with the eschatological. The pious man is actually having a share in the life of God, not only in the sense that he is assured of it for a future existence, but that he is as a present possession. Just as there can be an element of validity in experience, although it is not grounded on experience, so there can also be something in the midst of this world, which is not "of this world" but of the nature of eternity. Religiosity reveals itself precisely in the theoretical and practical awareness that 'the reality given in sensible experience is not the whole of reality' (Stange), but that there is a world of eternity – which does not . . . stand in such an exclusive relation to our earthly world that we must [38] first leave this behind, before we can participate in the eternal. On the contrary, it is of the nature of piety to seek the traces of the eternal in all that is or happens; and the stronger it is, the less it excludes earthly things from the world of eternity, the more it makes every moment of life a religious moment, the more it views everything in existence *sub specie aeternitatis*. (*Ibid.*, 57–58)

IV. THE SACRED IN THE THOUGHT OF ANNA-TERESA TYMIENIECKA

It is difficult to disentangle Tymieniecka's notion of the Sacred from the extensive argument contained in *Logos and Life*, because this entire work can be read as having the definition of the Sacred as its primary theme. The first volume is preparatory to the second, where Tymieniecka's intention of discussing the Sacred is clearly central. Indeed, Volume One and 140 pages of Volume Two reach their climax in the third and final chapter of Volume Two: "The Secret Architecture of the Soul."

I have elsewhere written at length about Tymieniecka's contribution to the philosophy of religion in *Logos and Life*, and I am acutely aware of how difficult it is to write a brief summary of that material (Ryba [1]). Moreover, I have no intention of repeating what I have already written at length elsewhere. Nevertheless, the originality of Tymieniecka's approach to the Sacred makes its inclusion here important, especially inasmuch as it represents a fourth option which differs significantly from those of Otto, Scheler or Nygren. For these reasons, I would like to summarize in a few words the salient points of her view of the Sacred.

Like Nygren and Otto, Tymieniecka's theory of the Sacred stands against the horizon of Kantian epistemology. Like Otto, she is aware of the affinities between the sense of the Sacred and the aesthetic sense, and (again, like Otto) in explaining the nature of this affinity she accepts aspects of the Kantian theory of knowledge. Like Kant, Otto and Nygren, she recognizes that human experiences takes place within the *a priori* categories of space and time (among others), but she construes the constitution of these categories in a fashion which is more appreciative of the creative role of imagination. Specifically, she appreciates the Kantian view of creativity which postulates for imagination of mediatory role between passion and reason, and she employs this notion to contest the extremism of both the Husserlian and Sartrean notions.

On the one hand, she rejects the Husserlian notion of imagination because it turns creativity into a mere reflection of rational cognition; according to it creativity is nothing more than the unfolding of rational possibilities, an unfolding which is the result of the free play of eidetic variation constrained by the *a prioris* which are dictated by the conscious or preconscious constitution of the mental object (1: 374–375). On the other hand, she rejects the Sartrean notion of imagination which admits no features of structuration at all, but stresses the radical freedom of this faculty to the extent that it is construed as detachable from all forms of consciousness (1: 375). Here recognition of the fundamental sanity of the Kantian notion of imagination – as the compromise position between these extremes – does not preclude her criticizing its defects. Most markedly, she criticizes Kant's explanation of how the mediation of imagination occurs. She rejects the Kantian attempt to locate the mediatory role of imagination in cognition – and, more precisely, in perception – and postulates its location as a third place (and makes it a third thing) which is neither exclusively rational nor irrational; she calls this *tertium quid* the *Imaginatio Creatrix*. With great freedom, it creatively orchestrates both the materials of reason and materials of passion to produce new scientific and artistic ideas, constrained only by the materials upon which it works.

Likewise, in her appreciation of Kant's categorical schematization of reality, her retention of a few of its salient features is no more important than the modification she suggests. For example, she admits that human experience as "the individualization of life" takes place according to a *distantiation*. "That is, it installs a 'spatial' spread just as it installs the vitally significant experience of time: successiveness, simultaneity and futurity. *Life as individualization installs the space-time axis of its progress*" (1: 432). Even so, this categorical *a priori* is in no wise construed in the Kantian fashion. There is no question of apodeicity of a specific rational schematization here; space is not *a priori* Euclidian, nor do space and time have an *a priori* Dedekindian or Cantorian structure. Space and time – if they can be called categories – do not possess a determinate form. Though they are conditions for mundane human experience, they are also in a perpetual state of development as a result of the creativity which forges human experience. Their constitution is never final. They move toward constitution and rationality as the teleonomy of human striving approaches its asymptote.

Tymieniecka thus introduces into the discussion of the Sacred a view of human creativity and imagination which places them at the heart of all human experience. The Imaginatio Creatrix functions to orchestrate the rational and non-rational strivings of humanity in ever original ways, according to the various ends of human aspiration toward which these strivings stream. One of these ends is the experience of the Sacred, and associated with it is the teleonomic striving for transcendence.

Tymieniecka's notion of the Sacred can be discussed both with respect to (1) those occasions when she associates the Sacred with a transcendental object or the object of a specific intentional complex of strivings or (2) those occasions when she associates "sacredness" with the intentional complex (or complex of strivings) itself. In other words, the Sacred takes on two meanings for Tymieniecka: it is both *object* and the *process of striving* toward an object.

First and foremost, Tymieniecka's notion of the Sacred can be identified with that end toward which all human creativity is ordered. By this I mean that she thinks that when human creativity is examined in its fullness, two seemingly discontinuous moments are discovered which, nevertheless, possess a common "entelechial factor" (1: 22). The first of these is the *logos* of poetic achievement, "poetic achievement" here meaning the process of creation in its broadest sense. The second of these moments, the *antilogos* of spiritual achievement, seems to stand to the first moment as its negation or antithesis, since it seeks the ultimate dissolution of all human creations in its quest for absolute transcendence. In the realm of high culture, this entelechy drives the artist, the philosopher, the musician, the novelist to move beyond the words of the past; in the realm of the Spirit, all possible works of culture are abandoned in the movement toward a trans-natural destiny. Put another way, the drive to transcend, in Tymieniecka's philosophy, consists of an ontogenetic *a priori* which can be read as evidence for the existence of the Sacred.

In particular, the *antilogos* of spiritual achievement most clearly reveals the Sacred because spiritual achievement cuts to the ground of everything typically associated with cultural achievement in an attempt to reconstitute it anew. This process Tymieniecka describes in detail as the three sequential movements of the Soul.

The first of these, radical examination, occurs when an individual recognizes a deficit of meaning in the world of culture, a meaninglessness which leads to an existential crisis, or a "shaking of foundations" in Tillich's happy phrase. As a result, a desire emerges to search for a new meaning beyond the pale of cultural life, beyond anything productive that creativity has to offer.

This leads to a second moment, the moment of exalted existence where the individual momentarily believes in the attainability of a circumscribable absolute, a belief whose shattering frustration leads to a third moment in which the whole question of transcendence is reformulated in such a fashion that a correct insight into the nature of transcendence is secured. Here, the perennial utterances of the Mystics no longer fall on deaf ears, and the spiritual voyager realizes that the entelechial factor which essentially characterizes human striving is without an intentional or achievable object. Also realized is the futility of continuing the spiritual quest outside of the reciprocity of the human community, for the other provides a needed foil to, and the regulation of, our own complacently conceived paths to transcendence. Interaction with an other is, in fact, a form of transcendence.

Thus, for Tymieniecka the Sacred has a primary referent in the transcendental object of spiritual attainment. But the form of "inward Sacredness" also refers to the process of spiritual self-constitution which is equivalent to the quest for the transcendent. Because her major work on the philosophy of religion, *The Three Movements of the Soul*, is not pitched as a response to Otto and only indirectly to Kant, I have not had to rehearse at great length the difficulty she finds in either. Rather, my discussion of her work has emphasized her constructive contribution to a definition of the Sacred. This is not to say, however, that Tymieniecka's writing was accomplished in a vacuum. As much as any contemporary philosopher, she has inherited a way of conceptualizing the Sacred which is dependent upon the broader tradition represented only partially in my discussion of Otto, Scheler and Nygren. Despite her originality, there are significant continuities between her thought and the thought of these three.

Like Otto (and Kant before him), Tymieniecka sees that the key to understanding the awareness of the Sacred is understanding the aesthetic process. But Tymieniecka and Otto are at odds in their thinking

about what this relation is. Whereas Otto and Kant viewed the analogies between the sense of the Sacred and the sense of the sublime as
consisting of a passivity with respect to the object – a passivity in which
the unique experiences of the sublime, beautiful and Sacred are sub-
jectively but preconsciously constituted – Tymieniecka sees "inward
Sacredness" as a project to be accomplished consciously, a form of life
to be forged.

Like Scheler, Tymieniecka posits the Sacred as an *a priori* in a sense
which is not bound to epistemic categories but to an ontology, though
the ontology she associates with the Sacred is far more dynamic than
Scheler's relatively static essentialism. In seeing the Sacred revealed in
the teleonomic striving for transcendence, Tymieniecka does not posit an
external object or essence to be grasped, but a general course to be
pursued. Ideas can be interpreted as *a priori*, but they are *a priori teloi*.
They are not cut and dried, but draw creativity toward themselves; their
realization is forever in an incomplete process of fulfillment. Any Sacred
worthy of the name is not to be circumscribed within the categories of
human thought or action – even though its reality may be revealed in
the process of human transcendence. In this sense, Tymieniecka's Sacred
is both immanent and transcendent.

Finally, Tymieniecka (like Nygren) would admit that the single most
fitting epithet for the Sacred is the Eternal. There is much in Nygren's
characterization with which she would no doubt agree. But she and
Nygren part company when he interprets this description – in Kantian
fashion – as having reference to a principle which founds the possibility of all validity. Her interest in the Sacred is not connected with
the necessity of saving the Sacred by deriving it through a modified transcendental deduction of the categories. Rather, the title "the Eternal"
for Tymieniecka refers to the presence of the Sacred permeating unique
moments of human creativity. As she puts it:

Eternity only consists of unique present moment, moments which – after long periods
of germination – thrust their roots into blind and deaf matter and spread their branches
and proceed through the work of time. These moments (which have passed through the
filter of our personal experience) traverse our unique spiritual route and attach themselves to the first designs of Creation before all time. Moments live and we live through
them. Our destiny is established by them. Our destiny, ineffaceable, causes this life to
enter gloriously into all eternity. (Tymieniecka 2: 180)

CONCLUSIONS

We have reached an appropriate point to ask, What is the cash value of the whole preceding description, aside from providing some historical background for subsequent papers in this section?

It seems to me that the preceding description puts us into a position to understand the general contours of the problematic of the Sacred as it has been framed in the twentieth century. In this problematic, Kant is the Archimedean point in the movement of modern notions of the Sacred, since much of this problematic uses his epistemology as a fulcrum by which to move thoughts in one direction or another. Also, from the preceding sketch, we are in a position to see how conceptualizations of the Sacred follow from and very directly depend upon respective ideals of philosophic method. Nygren – the most radical Kantian of the four – cannot rest content until he has posited the Eternal as the foundational category of all categories. Otto – on the other hand – appreciates the Kantian epistemological structure, but tries to free the Sacred from identification with orthodox Kantian notions of pure reason, practical reason or aesthetic judgment. Scheler – the dyed-in-the-wool essentialist – finds the Sacred given in phenomenologically derived essences, and Tymieniecka sees the Sacred shining through the process of self-creation and its transcendental goal.

The Sacred (as *a priori*) is conceptualized and also driven by the philosophical presuppositions of each thinker. For the Kantians, it is either categorically constitutive of reality (Nygren) and thus prior to it, psychologically constitutive of religious experience (Otto) and thus prior to it, or – in the case of Scheler – its *a priori* nature is a function of its prior intelligibility as an essence possessing necessary characteristics conatural with the human intellect. Finally, in the case of Tymieniecka, the *a priori* nature of the Sacred is ontogenetic in that it is presupposed to be the driving force of all human creativity as well as its ultimate end. Nevertheless, all of the discussed thinkers agree at the most general level that the Sacred is, in some sense, an *a priori* of human experience. But how they construe it depends to a large extent upon how they believe human experience to be constituted or constructed. The notions of the Sacred thus subserve epistemology in each case.

All it takes is a bit of cynicism to broach the question of whether the Sacred – so often recreated in the image of likeness of some pet philosophical system – is not merely an invention stemming from the parts of that system and the yearnings and imaginations of its adherents; but such cynicism is also susceptible to a reversal. Perhaps the richness and ubiquity of the ideas of the Sacred in the twentieth-century philosophy of religion are a testimony to the inseparability of thought from the religious dimension of human experience. Perhaps the real *aprioricity* of the Sacred derives from the fact that all human experience takes place within the horizon of sanctity. But to say this is merely to inflate the more homely words of Paul of Tarsus, who described the Sacred as that in which "we live and move and have our being" (Acts 17: 28).

St. Thomas Aquinas Center
Purdue University

NOTE

* At certain points, Sections 'a' and 'b' of Part One closely follow my exposition of Kant and Otto, which first appeared in: Thomas Ryba, "The Philosophical Loadings of Rudolf Otto's Idea of the Sacred," *Method and Theory in the Study of Religion*, Vol. **3**, #1, 1991, 24–40.

BIBLIOGRAPHY

Dawson, Lorne, "Otto and Freud on the Uncanny and Beyond," *JAAR* **LVII**, #2 (1989): 282–311.

Kant, Immanuel. *The Critique of Judgment*. New York: Hafner Press, 1951 (= Kant [1]).

Kant, Immanuel. *The Critique of Pure Reason*. New York: St. Martin's Press, 1965 (= Kant [2]).

Nygren, Anders. "The Validity of Religious Experience" [Philip Watson's unpublished translation of *Die Gültigkeit der religiösen Erfahrung*. Gütersloh: 1922].

Otto, Rudolf. *The Idea of the Holy*. London: Oxford, 1976 (= Otto [1]).

Otto, Rudolf. *The Philosophy of Religion*. New York: Richard R. Smith, 1931 (= Otto [2]).

Ryba, Thomas. "Anna-Teresa Tymieniecka's Contribution to the Philosophical Psychology of Religion," *Phenomenological Inquiry* **XIV** (October, 1990): 30–52 (= Ryba [1]).

Ryba, Thomas, "The Philosophical Loadings of Rudolf Otto's Idea of the Sacred," *Method and Theory in the Study of Religion* **III**, #1 (1991): 24–40 (= Ryba [2]).

Scheler, Max. *On the Eternal in Man*. Hamden: Archon Press, 1972.

Tymieniecka, Anna-Teresa. *Logos and Life*. Book One: *Creative Experience and the Critique of Reason*. Dordrecht, Boston, London: Kluwer Academic Publishers, 1988.

Tymieniecka, Anna-Teresa. *Logos and Life*. Book Two: *The Three Movements of the Soul*. Dordrecht, Boston, London: Kluwer Academic Publishers, 1988.

Wainwright, William J. "Rudolf Otto," *Encyclopedia of Philosophy*. Vol. 6. New York: Macmillan, 1967: 13–15.

STEVEN W. LAYCOCK

TELIC DIVINITY AND ITS ATELIC GROUND

I

It may be claimed with unquestionable cogency that the Husserlian theology, embracing as it does a dipolar Deity, a God-in-process, a Divinity unintelligible apart from its endless teleological free-fall toward the ideal realization of the world's absolute presence, must stand in frontal contradiction against an ontological vision which in principle excludes the self-subsistence and sempeternity of any god, a vision in which dispersion, duality and dipolarity are ontologically relative and derivative, a vision which rejects in any ultimate acceptation both *telos* and teleology. Over the preceding several years, as certain aspects of Buddhist thought have become increasingly satisfying and sensible for me as solutions or resolutions of theological quandaries, the incompatibility of the two views has come to demand, with ever greater insistence, either reconciliation or resolution. Is it possible, then, that the Husserlian God depicted in the *Foundations for a Phenomenological Theology*[1] may be rooted in a non-polar, non-processive and atelic Ground, a Ground profoundly affiliated with the absolute "Emptiness" (*sunyata*) of Buddhist thought? I offer here an affirmative answer. And though my response will perhaps be exuberantly speculative, if I am able to show, not that Husserl himself actually adopted such a stance, but more modestly that Husserlian theology is at least logically tolerant of the Buddhist vision, then the transformation which my own thinking has undergone will be blessed with a certain degree of continuity and grace.

I have come increasingly to feel that Husserl is best venerated by the attempt to tread the phenomenological path which his life-work opened up for us, and to imbibe in some measure his uncompromising intellectual rectitude, even though the conclusions at which we arrive may diverge from an orthodox alignment with the positions which he took. For Husserl, the "perpetual beginner," no position enjoys the privilege of finality. Yet, throughout his variegated attempts and starts was woven a consistent though seldom apparent theological thread, which, when it rose resplendently to the surface of the fabric, was given

43

A-T. Tymieniecka (ed.), Analecta Husserliana XLIII, 43–54.
© 1994 *Kluwer Academic Publishers. Printed in the Netherlands.*

voice in such categorical proclamations as his rejoinder to Roman Ingarden. To his student's inquiry concerning the fundamental problem of philosophy, Husserl's response was unhesitating: "The problem of God, *of course*."[2] Clearly, Husserl's manifold "beginnings" were dedicated to the "end" of theological vision.

II

The Husserlian God, a God in flux, is, in Husserl's arresting phrase, the "self-realization process of the Godhead."[3] Perhaps the most natural gloss would assign to the word "Godhead" (the German: "*Gottheit*") the sense of "Divinity." On this reading, it is Deity which is "realized" and which "realizes" itself in "self-realization". But a second reading is both possible and, I believe, preferable. A venerable strain of Rhineland mysticism grounds the personal God with all its deific attributes in the "Godhead," the prepersonal *Gottheit*, which differs from God in its very *absence* of determination. And though Husserl was not of a discernibly "mystic" cast of mind, his employment of "*Gottheit*" may still resonate with the appropriate overtones. And on this reading, the one I prefer, it would not be God, but "Godliness," the "God-Being," the Ground, perhaps *Abgrund*, of the divine life, which "realizes" itself through God.

It would of course be extravagant to suspend an assessment of Husserl's intent upon so slender a thread. But there are considerations which would suggest the cogency of this two-tiered vision of the Ground and of the deific exfoliation which draws its nourishment from it. First, the Husserlian God is dipolar. God is neither subject nor object, but, in formal terms, the binary operation which in effect transforms the one into the other. This movement of explication is simply inconceivable in the absence of a prior distinction of divine Subject from divine Object. And the field of this distinction, the continuous ground subtending the wall of partition, is, in my select sense, the *Gottheit*. God is therefore inconceivable apart from Godhead. But second, suppose that the ready interpretation were indeed correct. A process of "self-realization" makes tacit and ineliminable allusion to a non-realized state. Yet if God is "realization" itself, an essentially *binary* function, this process is always and necessarily *in medias res*. Being ineluctably monadic, the "zero-state" could at best serve as the Alpha-pole of deific procession. But that is unintelligibly to relegate the full field to half of itself, Ground to divine

subjectivity. *Aporia* thus greets the purportedly "natural" reading of
"*Gottheit*," and transforms the apparently less natural interpretation into
the more natural one.

Let me illustrate my notion of the Ground, not by appealing to
Husserl's own reflections, but with Sartre's mythological musings
regarding the "upsurge" of the for-itself. "Everything happens," Sartre
claims, "as if, in order to free the affirmation *of* self from the heart of
being, there is necessary a decompression of being" (*BN*, 27–8). Here
"being" does not refer to the ontological domain of the in-itself, for
the in-itself is unintelligible except as being-*for* that which is *for*-itself;
and prior to "decompression," there *is* no for-itself, for the for-itself is
precisely the very "decompression" of being. In primordial "being," there
is no "affirmation *of* self," no internal distantiation which would permit
an aerial reflection *upon* self, and thus, since "self" is constituted solely
in reflection, no *self* at all. In Sartre's words,

The in-self cannot found *itself* without introducing the *self* of a reflective, nihilating
reference into the absolute identity of its being and consequently degenerating into
for-itself. (*Being and Nothingness*, 133)

Yet, in Vaihingerian cadence, it is "*as if*" prior to the for-itself, prior
to the very possibility of purposive agency, primordial being acted
"in order to" effect a distantiated self-affirmation, "in order to" found
itself, the for-itself being the "means" to this "end." The conditions of
primordial being are strictly inconsistent with the demand for an intelligible description of the very possibility of purposiveness. And we might
for this reason be tempted to reject the Sartrean position outright as
simply and straightforwardly incoherent. Yet the mythological "*als ob*"
curiously relaxes what otherwise would seem to be an insupportable
logical tension. The doctrine of non-purposive being and the myth of
its purposiveness roll on separate tracks: the one ontological and the other,
as I have called it, "mythological." Or if it be granted that the discourse
of phenomenology is, as I believe, inevitably imbedded in the matrix
of the "as if," and is thus in this specific sense "mythological," it becomes
apparent that the *ontological* claims that being is non-purposive is in
no danger of colliding with the *phenomenological* description that it is
exactly *as if* being were to act "in order to" realize the end of self-
reflection and self-founding.

A second and poignantly similar illustration, taken from the tradition of Buddhism, is in order. "In the beginning, which is really no beginning," Suzuki writes:

the will wants to know itself, and consciousness is awakened, and with the awakening of consciousness the will is split in two. The one will, whole and complete in itself, is now at once actor and observer. Conflict is inevitable; for the actor now wants to be free from the limitations under which he has been obliged to put himself in his desire for consciousness. He has in one sense been enabled to see, but at the same time there is something which he, as observer, cannot see.[4]

What sense could possibly be assigned to the supposition of a pre-conscious "willing" or "wanting"? Understanding "consciousness" as intentional, and "will" as one of its specific modalities, how could there be, in the beginningless "beginning," a non-intentional exemplification of intentionality? All of this is reduced to patent nonsense unless, once again, we bear in mind that ontology and phenomenology have the ghostly capacity of penetrating one another without touching. For those who, like myself, cannot accept the evident dispersion, the exteriority, the dividedness of things as ontologically primary, and those who more specifically cannot accept this evidence as confirming an *ontological* verity at all, it is fitting that a story be told, a "myth," a description in the mode of the "*als ob*" which *cannot* conflict with one's ontological insight, but which remains, if not "true" then "true-to" one's experience.

Is it accordingly possible to regard the Husserlian theology as a hypothetical "story," a "myth"? Our "myth" would not, of course, be a theoretical "account," a story designed to *explain*. This would make of Husserl's vision an empirical generalization an account inevitably under-determined by its data, and this result is patently at variance with Husserl's intent. Nor should "myth," in our sense, be regarded as mere fantasy. For it must, with all the rigor of phenomenological method, quite patently and irresistibly appear exactly *as if* our myth were no "myth" at all, but unproblematically *true*. As I have suggested, it must be "true-to" experience as it is lived. No "myth" is to be considered valid and appropriate which does not partake of this curious irony. A good "myth," in our sense, *appears true*. But we shall not, for all that, remove it from the matrix of the "*als ob*."

Phenomenology neither contravenes nor falsifies ontology. Yet we must resist an unnuanced assimilation of the two. For in phenomenology, ontology is "infinitely deferred," as it were. The deific Ground is disclosed in every presentational act. But this disclosure is primordially

and ineluctably "empty." It *cannot* be "filled," for, as we shall see, presentational omniscience is phenomenologically incoherent. And though
this "impossibility" represents the "infinite deferral" of absolute presence,
it stands simultaneously as the very "possibility" of the endless enrich-
ment of relative presence.

If we, like Sartre and like Suzuki, were to compose a "myth" of self-
realization, what would be the "self" thus realized? What would its
"realization" be? And what relationship would be born by this "realization" to its Ground? The "realization," we know, is God. And the
"self" of *Gottheit*, a "self" deferred, dislocated, decentered, a "self"
which cannot be present within the Ground "itself," is the divine *telos*:
the absolute presence of the world as the ultimate terminus of all intentional activity. This "self" is constituted within the grounded, not the
Ground. Yet it is only thus, by grounding that which though distinct
nonetheless constitutes "itself," that the Ground may possess a "self"
at all. Or rather, the Ground "itself" exists only by giving "itself" to God.
It is self-*renouncing*, not self-*possessive*. Indeed, the Ground *is* the very
"giving" of "itself." It *is*, in the Buddhist idiom, the "emptying" of self
manifest in absolute world-presence. Absolute presence is the Ground's
gift of "self" to the Divine, and to us as well inasmuch as "[e]very human
is . . . a ray of the unfolding of the divine being."[5] Nothing, no "self,"
no presence, no self-presence, remains of the Ground. It is, mythologi-
cally, "as if" the Ground, upon gazing ingenuously outward, were to
see nothing at all; "as if" its emanating illumination were to fall upon
nothing at all. And it is "as if" Deity were to arise in response to the
primordial desideratum that there be vision, manifestation, presence, self-
presence. Again, it is "as if" God were a mirror of the Ground, reflecting
within it the presence which is the Ground's bestowal of self. And it is
"as if" a certain reflex, or reflux, of "reflected" presence were thus
remitted upon the Ground. Yet it is also "as if" the Ground, incapable
of "taking" or "possessing," were therefore incapable of taking into itself
and possessing this very reflux of self-presence as if "self"; "as if" the
Ground were incapable of absorption, opacity, and could only transmit
this illumination without impedance; "as if," therefore, the only adequate
image of the Ground were that of luminous transparency.

The deific Alpha and Omega, Subject and Object, the "domain" and
"range" of the universal operation of "self-realization," are not to be
regarded as analogous to the fixed termini of a powerful electric arc.
The Divine is perhaps more adequately, though not unproblematically,

imaged as the vast fiery proflux of solar plasma heaved from the sun's blazing surface and, at the end of its arc, merging once again with the surging inferno which gave it birth. Or, in an image somewhat less dramatic, God is seen as that movement of realization whereby the world-body, as lived from within, the world as *Leib*, seeks to know itself as objective, as *Körper*. God is the transformation of lived-world into world-object, of World-Horizon into World-Pole.

The atelic Ground of God, the "sun" in our first image and the existence which subtends lived and objectivated body in our second, is not, however, *both* the deific Alpha *and* the divine Omega, or Beginning *and* End. It is not both world-*Leib* and world-*Körper*, but is rather the plane whereon this very distinction is drawn, and thus neither. The "Neither" occasions, gives opportunity to, the "Both." But the "Both," the subject/object dipolarity of God, is intrinsic to God, not to the deific Ground. The Ground cannot intelligibly be said to "seek" its own realization, for "seeking" presupposes the very dichotomy of Beginning and End, *nisus* and *finis*, which in principle cannot inform the "Neither." We need, rather, a "myth." We must be prepared to say in the phenomenological mode of the "*als ob*" that everything happens *as if*, in order to realize itself, there must be drawn a distinction between striving and striven-for. Indeed, we have said as much, though in an analytic vein. Husserl's teleological God, the "self-realization process of the Godhead," is simply inconceivable in the absence of this distinction. And since the "Both" is, in its turn, inconceivable without the "Neither," it is certainly "as if" the Neither, though ontologically incapable of purpose, has nonetheless purposefully given rise to the Both.

III

Let me conclude with a brief meditation on the "End" of things. What would it be like if the divine *telos* were perfectly realized? At the "end," when the plasmic arc will have completed its exuberant surge, it will merge indistinguishably with its solar matrix, "beginning" and "end" being themselves indiscernible. At the "end," when the subject-body will have thoroughly objectified itself, no distinction will remain between subject and object, as no such distinction was present in the primordial subject-object. And though this "end" is, as Husserl cogently argues, unobtainable by perceptual attainment and hyletic illustration, its structure is nonetheless available to a certain intuition. The moment of ideal teleological fulfillment is exactly the moment of immersion in the Ground. Circuitously, we can thus read the physiognomy of the Ground of perceptual experience in the structuration of the "ideal" of this experience. And we shall see, as promised, that the deific Ground is remarkably consonant with the Buddhist conception of "emptiness" (*śūnyatā*).

Perception enacts the *écart*, the parturition, of figural object from horizoning ground.[6] Figure appears *upon* ground, and as arising *from* its ground; inseparable, yet distinct. And if the ground is in turn thematized and objectified, it must arise from, and be manifest against, some more primitive ground, thus establishing a "genealogical" succession of intentional matrices. The "World-Horizon" of Husserl's phenomenology is the primordial Matrix, the Context of all possible contexts, the Ground of all perceptual grounds. It is the ultimate and final Horizon within which whatever figural object may manifest itself finds its manifestation. But as such, as prethematic horizon, the world stands at the farthest remove from the conscious intensity which marks the focus of the field. The World-Horizon is, if you will, the deific Body as prethematically lived. Its unity and ultimacy are lost to the ingenuous and naive prereflective consciousness, absorbed, as it is, in the objects and affairs of the "natural attitude," and are revealed only to a reflective consciousness capable of apprehending the word not merely as pre-objectual context, but as the universally invariant locus of manifestation. In transcendental reflection, the world is thus seen as the invariant "maypole" to which are tethered all the colored streamers of our intentional life. The "objects" of our world, no longer taken as termini of intentional activity, no longer simply "thrown in the way" (*ob-jectus*) of intentional illumination, lose their objectuality, their opacity, becoming thus "translucent" media of world-disclosure. Remarkably resonant is Suzuki's poignant description of the *Dharmadhātu*, the world as revealed through the exercise of "wisdom" (*prajñā*):

everything [is] transparent and luminous, for luminosity is the only possible earthly representation that conveys the idea of universal interpretation . . . no shadows are visible anywhere. The clouds themselves are luminous bodies. . . .[7]

The Husserlian God is World-Consciousness: the teleological process whereby the peripheral and merely apperceived "World-Horizon" is progressively transformed into the fulfilled disclosure of the world itself as the ultimate sanctuary, the locus of rest for all of the possible motions of intentionality. So long as the transcendental gaze is fixed upon the divine *telos*, the World-Pole, all the objects within the world glow with the luminosity of the world. All is "transparent and luminous."

Objects thus come to function as distinct "modes of givenness" whereby the World-Pole is manifest. But as such, as translucent "objects," world-disclosures appear "through" one another, thus coming to light as reciprocally integral and intrinsic. The World-Pole is always incompletely constituted. It *is* only *as* it is given, though it is given in rich variation. The world cannot be disclosed apart from its varying modes of manifestation. Every mode of presentation is the distinct perspectival disclosure of other modes of manifestation, the world being thus informed by the *Ineinander* integrity of its modes of givenness. However, since the world is, like any transcendent intentional locus, an ideal invariant constituted across the potentially endless variation of its appearances, since it is "the never completed but always more closely approached synthesis of all perspectives,"[8] *no* world-profile can disclose *all possible* world-profiles. We do, however, advance in our enjoyment of the world's endlessly variable modes of manifestation, thus progressively enriching the manifold of world-profiles accessible through any given world-profilee. At the ideal and never fully actualizable limit of this process lies the "absolute presence" of the world, the plenary display of the world as it would be simultaneously given to a putatively omniscient mind in all its possible modes of disclosure.

With his "Mirrored Cell,"[9] the Greek-born experimental artist Lucas Samaras (b. 1936) provides an irresistible trope for the World-Pole. The "Cell" is a construction of mirrors – walls, ceiling, floor, and objects within the cell all comprised of mirrors – each reflecting all the others within it. To stand within it is to loose one's bearings, to be de-centered, or rather, to find one's center infinitely distributed about one. It is to *experience*, not merely to conceive, the fallaciousness of simple location. Reflections within reflections offer to the eye the expectable *mise-en-abîme*, the "abyss," the *Abgrund*, of infinite iteration. One's externalized body is reflected and infinitely replicated from every angle.

The "flaw" of the Cell, if indeed it is one, is that, so long as I stand within it the opacity of my body blocks the inter-reflection of opposite mirrors. Yet this "flaw" provides an even more serviceable metaphor for our purposes. In Husserl's vision, we shall never succeed in removing the opacity at the center. Omniscience is phenomenologically incoherent; absolute presence is perpetually out of reach. For in the omniscient envisionment, the transcendent object would be "immanentized" without remainder. And inasmuch as an omniscient mind, simply by definition would see things *as they are*, omniscience would *per impossible* abrogate and abolish the phenomenologically ineliminable distinction between immanence and transcendence.[10] Teleological advance in the direction of absolute presence does, of course, amount to the "de-opacitization" of the occluding opacity. Yet only the fully realized *telos* finds this opacity utterly dissolved. Only in the ideal, the unrealizable, is perfect inter-penetration attained.

The congruent Buddhist conception of *prātitya-samutpāda*, the conditioned arising-together of all things, or as I would prefer, their man-ifestation-in-horizon, is founded in a simple and lucid insight: nothing is, nothing can be, the origin of itself, since nothing pre-exists itself. Nothing, then, is self-existent. Each thing owes its very existence, its very "self," to that which lies beyond itself. As Nāgārjuna, the Buddhist philosopher of "emptiness," writes, "Whatever comes into existence presupposing something else is without self-existence (*svabhavatā*)."[11] Its manifest existence, its "self," is thus "distributed," factored out, among those horizoning conditions which sustain it.

Like Samaras, the ancient Hua-yen master Fa-tsang is said to have erected a "Mirrored Cell" for the edification of the Empress Wu, placing in the center of his chamber a golden statue of the Buddha, and com-menting that

This is a demonstration of Totality in the dharmadhatu. In each and every mirror within this room you will find the reflections of all the other mirrors with the Buddha's image in them. . . . The principle of interpenetration and (mutual) containment is clearly shown by this demonstration. Right here we seen an example of one in all and all in one – the mystery of realm embracing realm ad infinitum is thus revealed.[12]

As helpful as Fa-tsang's demonstration might be, it holds at its heart an image of the Buddha, a central occlusion which prevents unin-hibited inter-reflection. This seems to be once again a "flaw," since, in Fa-tsang's vision:

The progression is infinite, like the jewels of Celestial Lord Indra's Net: a realm-embracing-realm ad infinitum is thus established, and is called the realm of Indra's Net.[13]

In reality, all things are present in one another like the jewels of Indra's Net. Yet also, *in reality*, though the statue might be removed, the lesson of the chamber received its experiential certification only through the insertion within it of one's own opaque body. In the Realm of Truth, the *Dharmadhātu*, Suzuki comments, "what we have . . . is an infinite mutual fusion or penetration of all things, each with its own individuality yet with something universal in it."[14] Yet in the *Lokadhātu*, the region of naive and "natural" consciousness where "simple location" and unequivocal centering hold sway, this truth cannot be modeled. And having no model, no perceptual illustration, the perfect interpenetration of the *Dharmadhātu* would seem to be beyond our conception.

Emptiness and absolute presence are "beyond conception" in a deeper sense as well. In absolute presence, the fully constituted World-Pole would be seen as the "identical X-meant," constituted across a manifold of disclosures which embraces not merely all *actual*, but fully all *possible*, manifestations. Yet the entire domain of manifestational possibility cannot be simultaneously actualized without massive incoherence. The world *can* be manifest in my presence here before you. And the world *can* be manifest in my present absence. The world *cannot*, however, be manifest in my simultaneous presence and absence. Emptiness, likewise, is regarded as the universal fund of possibility, the intrinsic incoherence which can only be perceptually manifest in the impermanence, process, flux of *saṃsāra*, since its simultaneous instantiation is impossible.

Were Husserl correct in his unwavering insistence that the strata of meaning, sense, ideality, universality, are ineluctably founded in perceptual presence, we could have no intuition of the structure of absolute presence. However, though the Husserlian refutation of omniscience may well place limits upon perceptual illustration, upon the enjoyment of presence, it does not thereby confine intelligibility. Otherwise, the provision of endless progress toward the ideal would render the ideal itself eidetically mysterious. In restricting the exercise of *Wesensschau* to the domain of perceptually founded idealities we must, *pace* Husserl, posit a mode of "unrestricted" intuition, a mode of intuition not relativized to a given fund of perceptual presence. The Buddhist *prajñā*, which lucidly certifies both the impossibility of self-existence and its entailment, universal interpenetration, is unmistakably a form of such "absolute" intuition. Interpenetration is not a truth of perceptual *presence*, nor of its relative *absence*, the absence *of* presence. *Prajñā* sees "through" presence, in its immanent or transcendent modalities, and discloses the "transparent and luminous" Ground (*śūnyatā*) which offers its "self" in presence, thus retaining not the least trace of opacity. The reciprocal

and endlessly repeated reflective insertion of one mode of manifestation within another constitutes an "abyss." *Grund*, in its deepest sense,
is *Abgrund*; and in the deepest sense, to be "grounded" is not to rest
secure upon some ostensible *fundamentum inconcussum*, but rather to
"fall" endlessly and without harm through infinite space. The World-Pole
is not a rock upon which the myriad "objects" of the world are established, but the space, the interval, the vacuous matrix of interpenetration,
in which they "float." Yet every mirror in the chamber is simply *there,
as it is, such* as it is, there in its "suchness" (*tathatā*). And at the same
time, every mirror "empties" itself into all the other mirrors, being thus
"empty" (*śūnya*) of self.

University of Toledo
Toledo, Ohio

NOTES

[1] Steven W. Laycock, *Foundations for a Phenomenological Theology* (Lewiston: Edwin
Mellen Press, 1988). See also "God as Ideal: The All-of-Monads and the All-
Consciousness," in Daniel Guerrière, ed., *Phenomenology of the Truth Proper to Religion*
(Albany: SUNY Press, 1990); "Toward an Overview of Phenomenological Theology"
(introducing essay) and "The Intersubjective Dimension of Husserl's Theology," in *Essays
in Phenomenological Theology* (Albany: SUNY Press, 1986), co-edited with Prof. James
G. Hart.
[2] Quoted in Louis Dupré, "Husserl's Thought on God and Faith," in *Philosophy and
Phenomenological Research* **29** (1968).
[3] "Selbstrealisierungsprozess der Gottheit," Edmund Husserl, ms. A V 22, p. 47, quoted
in Stephan Strasser, "History, Teleology, and God," in A-T. Tymieniecka, ed., *Analecta
Husserliana*, Vol. **IX**, p. 278.
[4] D. T. Suzuki, *Essays in Zen Buddhism*, First Series (London: Rider and Co., 1970),
p. 131.
[5] Edmund Husserl, *Drei Vorlesungen über Fichtes Menschheitsideal*, ms. F I,
p. 49, quoted in Strasser, "History, Teleology, and God in the Philosophy of Husserl,"
op. cit., pp. 325–6.
[6] This is true, it must be said, of "ordinary" or "unenlightened" perception. For "[i]n
the shunyata experience, the attention is on the field rather than on its contents." Herbert
V. Guenther and Chogyam Trungpa, *The Dawn of Tantra* (Boulder: Shambhala, 1965),
p. 27.
[7] D. T. Suzuki, *Essays in Zen Buddhism*, Third Series, ed. by Christmas Humphreys (New
York: Samuel Weiser, Inc., 1976), pp. 77–8.
[8] James M. Edie, *Speaking and Meaning: The Phenomenology of Language* (Bloomington: Indiana University Press, 1976), p. 8.
[9] Dated 1969/88.

[10]   Husserl insists that even God is debarred from the perception of objects *"without any mediation through 'appearances'*," and regards as a "fundamental error" the notion of God as "the Subject of absolutely perfect knowledge, and therefore also of every possible adequate perception, [who] naturally possesses what to us finite beings is denied, the perception of things in themselves." Such a deposition is, in Husserl's view, "nonsensical," or indeed "countersensical" (*Wiedersinn*). "It implies that there is no *essential difference* between transcendent and immanent, that in the postulated divine intuition a spatial thing is a real (*reeles*) constituent, and indeed an experience itself, a constituent of the stream of the divine consciousness and the divine experience." (Edmund Husserl, *Ideas: General Introduction to Pure Phenomenology*, W. R. Gibson, trans. [New York: Macmillan, 1931], p. 123.) See my essay, "Actual and Potential Omniscience," in *The International Journal of Philosophy of Religion* **26** (1989).

[11]   Nagarjuna, "Fundamentals of the Middle Way: *Mūlamādhyamakakarika*," trans. Fredrick J. Streng, in *Emptiness: A Study in Religious Meaning* (New York: Abingdon Press, 1967), 7: 16, p. 191.

[12]   Fa-tsang, "On the Golden Lion," Garma C. C. Chang, trans., in *The Buddhist Teaching of Totality* (University Park: Pennsylvania State University Press, 1977), p. 23.

[13]   Fa-tsang, "On the Golden Lion," Chang, trans., in *The Buddhist Teaching of Totality*, p. 229.

[14]   D. T. Suzuki, *Essays in Zen Buddhism*, Third Series, pp. 77–8. Compare Plotinus's scintillating vision: "all is transparent, nothing dark, nothing resistant; every being is lucid to every other, in breadth and depth; light runs through light. And each of them contains all within itself, and at the same time sees all in every other, so that everywhere there is all, and all is all and each is all, and infinite the glory." (Plotinus, *The Enneads*, trans. Stephen MacKenna [London: Farber and Farber, 1969], V viii 4, p. 425.)

J. N. MOHANTY

RELIGION AND THE SACRED

I begin with the remark that "is sacred," like "is beautiful," but unlike "is red" is not a determining, but rather a modifying predicate (in Brentano's sense of that distinction). The way I am now using the distinction between determining and modifying predicates has to be understood in the following manner.

For one thing, determining predicates and modifying predicates are not simply different predicates, but are *qua predicates* different. They are *radically* different predicates. Now, modifying predicates themselves are of various kinds; of these I choose two for my present purpose. These are aesthetic predicates such as "is beautiful" and "is sublime," and religious predicates such as "is sacred," or Rudolf Otto's "mysterium tremendum." I want first to press the point that these predicates express the *how* of a certain mode of working. To say that a thing is beautiful or that it is sublime is to say that it is working upon the speaker in an appropriate manner. Let me call it, using an inelegant locution, 'beautiful-working,' 'sublime-working.' A beautiful thing, i.e., a thing described as beautiful is one which works on the describer as beautiful, it produces on him an impression-of-beauty. This is what 'beautiful working' consists in. Note that the impression of beauty is not a beautiful impression, it is rather an impression of beauty (or of-elegance, or of-sublimity). When one is speaking of a clear or a fleeting impression, one describes the impression. But an impression of beauty is such that beauty is its immanent, constituent object (not as red resides on the surface of a piece of red paper). The same, I contend, is true of "is sacred." If I describe a thing as sacred, the thing is working on me in a certain manner, this working consists in producing in me an impression-of-sacredness.

Let me again go back to aesthetic effects. As Josef König pointed out—and my present ideas go back to him[1]—when Goethe says that

55

A-T. Tymieniecka (ed.), Analecta Husserliana XLIII, 55–59.
© 1994 Kluwer Academic Publishers. Printed in the Netherlands.

art works maintain one in the face of the destructive power of the world, this maintaining is very different from the sense in which an air raid or tornado shelter protects you from a bombing or the fury of a tornado. This 'working-as maintaining,' which is not a *real* protecting is an aesthetic effect. Looking at the Strasbourg cathedral, Goethe said that it raised him to the heavens. This 'working as lifting one up to the heavens' is an aesthetic effect. This does not mean that the cathedral produced in Goethe an effect which raised him up to the heavens.

Contrast with this the feeling good which some news may produce in me. The news is a thing. The feeling good is a thing (a mental state). This is a case of non-aesthetic effect. The pleasant news *eo ipso* pleases someone, in this case, me. A sublime landscape works-as-sublime, not *for* any one. Its being sublime and its working-as-sublime are one and the same.

A non-aesthetic impression may be investigated by either physiology or psychology. An aesthetic effect is not a possible subject matter for investigation by a special science.

Describing a non-aesthetic impression ("It pleases me," or "That is red") is "describing" in a radically different sense than that in which describing an aesthetic impression is so. This difference may be expressed thus:

One who describes a thing may describe it correctly or incorrectly, describe well or poorly. One who describes poorly also describes. But a bad poet is not a poet. The aesthetic impression is its own description, it is itself poetic. The description of an art work is like description of a thing. But an aesthetic impression is not. It speaks, as it were, for itself, bears its own testimony. "X is beautiful" describes the impression-of-beauty. Aesthetic sensing and aesthetic describing are inseparable moments of one experience of beauty. This is what "is beautiful" means, and it should not be construed to mean that X only appears to be beautiful. We are not permitted to make that distinction between being-beautiful and appearing-to-be-beautiful. The aesthetic judgment is objective.

If you want other examples, here are some: an impression-of-spatial-depth is what originally presents spatial depth. But if something appears as a man, it may or may not be one; similarly, an impression-of-vitality is what originally presents vitality. The same is true of impression-of-sublimity. The important question is, by what mechanism can such an impression be produced from without? My contention is, it cannot be. But this last assertion only gives rise to problems of great difficulty, which I cannot attempt to answer on this occasion.

The sentence "A is blond" is true if and only if A is in fact blond. Here truth is, in some sense, correspondence. The poetic speech "That is beautiful" is true by the very occasioning of the utterance, and its truth is the ground of the fact that the fact is as the sentence says it is. The meaning of 'truth' in the two cases is radically different.

I will pursue this strange contrast one step further, and maintain that we have here two senses of 'being': in the one case, being is simple *Vorhandenheit* (as Heidegger understands it), in the other case, it means *acting* in a certain manner, being efficacious, being in the verbal, intensive sense. In the latter sense, to be is to be efficacious, to produce an effect. Such an entity, working in such and such a manner, is, qua so acting, a being that is essentially so— beautiful or sublime or sacred, as the case may be. No 'Sein' holds good of all such cases as a generic property, but each one has its own being. In an important sense, this *distributive*, particularised sense of 'being' as being-efficacious-in a-certain-manner, is the only sense of 'being' which does not allow itself to be analysed as 'being the value of a variable' (Quine) or 'being a thetic predicate which is the correlate of an act of believing' (Husserl). Shall we then say, as opposed to the suspicion that being-beautiful or being-sublime is merely subjective being, rather the very opposite, that only in such efficacy does one encounter being as such ?

Everything that I have said, following Josef König's most remarkable thoughts, I want to say about the modifying predicate "is sacred." To say, on originary evidence, that something is sacred, is to be acted upon by that thing in a certain manner, and this working *is* being-sacred. It is in and through the feeling of sacredness (impression-of-sacredness) that a sacred being is precisely as it is. A sacred being (like a sublime or a beautiful being) is not first a *vorhandenes* entity, which then has a property called sacredness (sublimity or beauty)—just as a red thing is first a *vorhandenes* thing which, over and above that, has the property of being red. It is sacred, its very being consists in acting-as-sacred, it is an activity. With this, I have sought to capture both of the two claims about the sacred—that the sacred must be an original being, and that it is a power, not a thing (*Ding*).

After having presented in barest outlines what I would regard as the nature of the originary concept of the sacred, I would now, again very briefly, indicate how I think the relation of this concept to religious needs is to be best construed.

Here, a paper by Dr. Pratt of New Zealand, which I heard being presented at the Australasian Society of Phenomenology meetings this past Fall in Melbourne, showed me the way, just when I was groping for it. Pratt distinguished between what he called pre-religion and religion. If I understood him aright, the contrast is between an original religiosity exhibited, e.g., in the founder prophets and apostles or the experiences underlying the basic texts, and its objectification and institutionalization in texts, dogmas and churches. The importance of this distinction is much lessened if we simply relegate pre-religion to the chronological beginning of every religion. It becomes a more interesting distinction if one recognises that the pre-religious and the religious co-exist as but two strata of religious life, with the latter founded upon and yet covering up the former, and with the former making the latter possible as its originary source and continuing support. Taking the distinction in this sense, the closest that one need look for illumination of it within phenomenology is to Merleau-Ponty's distinction between the pre-objective and the objective. The objective world (correlatively, objective thought) is founded upon pre-objective perception. The task of phenomenology is to grasp the objective world as it emerges out of the pre-objective background of operative intentionalities.

My contention is, that although within the established religions with their objective texts, dogmas, rituals, institutions, laws, communities there is the distinction between the sacred and the profane, the originary source of meaning of the predicate "sacred" lies in the pre-objective impression/feeling-of-sacredness, through which the *event* of working-as-sacred emerges into the world.

Temple University

NOTE

1. For the relevant works of Josef König, reference may be made to his *Sein und Denken* (Halle: Max Niemeyer, 1937) and *Vorträge und Aufsätze*, ed. G. Patzig, Munich: Alber Verlag, 1978.

EDITH WYSCHOGROD

LAYCOCK, A PHENOMENOLOGICAL WHITEHEADIAN?

The astonishing question of what is it like to be God and to see the world as God sees it is the subject of Steven Laycock's *Foundations for a Phenomenological Theology*. The extraordinary audacity of this project is mitigated somewhat by a more moderate epistemological claim: "God sees through and only through our eyes."(p. 1) Thus, on his view, the divine envisagement of the world is comprehensible because it is structurally homologous with our own.

But God's accessibility to human cognition carries a price tag: a restriction or hemming of the divine nature. Thus, the epistemological moderation of Laycock's project is offset by its audacity at the metaphysical level. For on the plane of God as object, God is understood as "the intersubjective community of finite minds,"(p. 197) or, in proto-Kantian language as "the ideal presumptive synthesis of all subjective vantage points, the telos of unimpeded intersubjective interpenetration."(p. 1) Although I am in sympathy with Laycock's project of scaling down the received view of divine omniscience—Laycock's work is, in fact, a brilliant rethinking of this issue—I shall consider four difficulties that I believe necessitate further reflection.

I shall argue first that Laycock seems to strive for a Whiteheadian/Husserlian amalgam, a synthesis which is partially achieved because of genuine parallels between a phenomenologically articulated description of consciousness and Whitehead's view of God's primordial nature. Yet what Laycock *actually* borrows from Whitehead is the dynamism of a process God so that, in effect, the specular character of phenomenology's God is altered. Because the specular and the dynamic are incompatible in important respects, his goal of fusing the two is achieved less by an appeal to conceptual overlaps than by an appeal to their differences. A Whiteheadian/Husserlian God, I shall argue opens up fundamental incongruities in the divine nature.

A-T. Tymieniecka (ed.), Analecta Husserliana XLIII, 61–69.
© 1994 Kluwer Academic Publishers. Printed in the Netherlands.

Second, I shall insist that the dimension of mystery is absent from Laycock's god. This is bound up with his treatment of non-being as chaos which can—even if it need not—succumb to categorial ordering.

Third, I contend that the problem of evil is omitted from Laycock's book, perhaps, one hopes, to become the subject of some future work. Yet even in the absence of explicit analysis, some implications for his understanding of evil can be teased from his theology. If I am right, these gleanings about evil highlight some difficulties in his conception of the divine nature.

Finally, I shall consider how, on his view, individuals are to be construed as everlasting and whether such perdurance is worthwhile.

Process and a Phenomenological Theology

Consider my first contention that "Laycock's method is the method of Husserl, but his metaphysics is the metaphysics of Whitehead" (to echo *Genesis* 27). Although he does not develop the parallels between phenomenological method and Whiteheadian metaphysics in any extended fashion, I do not merely infer that Laycock connects the two. He explicitly states that Husserl's belief that the "divine entelechy's empty intending of the world-pole" is another way of describing Whitehead's "primordial nature" and that a phenomenological account of God as the "active [synthesis] of finite historical advance" is congruent with Whitehead's understanding of God's "consequent nature."(p. 76) In short, Laycock argues for a Whiteheadian dipolar God whose deific nature can be expressed in Husserlian language.

Phenomenologically speaking, God is like the individual subject, not constituted but a constituting empty intentionality. At another level there is the divine self-objectification, the world-pole as "'the never completed but always more closely approached synthesis of all perspectives,'" (James Edie, cited on p. 204), a world-pole realized in an infinite series of finite actualizations as a "gallery of pictures" temporally displayed. Laycock is not arguing for a universe formed out of nothing or from a primal dust by a creator or for an eternal stuff hurtling forth new forms. He claims instead (astonishingly) that the hyletic primordium or matter is "the concrete flux of intersubjective life," what Husserl called "transcendental subjectivity," and that this matter receives its form from a logos which orders the hyle of divine subjectivity.(p. 155)

Although Laycock does not enter into Whiteheadian niceties, Laycock's divine intending act can be redescribed in Whitehead's terms as "unlimited conceptual realization of the absolute wealth of potentiality." Awaiting fulfillment by a noematic content, Husserl's empty intention, in Whiteheadian language, is "'deficiently actual,'...an unconditioned actuality at the base of things."(Whitehead, p. 523) Similarly, what is, for Husserl, God as the fulfilled divine intention or realized world-pole can be thought of as Whitehead's consequent nature of God, "the realization of the actual world...the weaving of God's physical feelings upon his primordial concepts. [It is] derived from the temporal world, [which] then acquires integration with the primordial side.   It is determinate, incomplete, consequent,...fully actual and conscious."(Whitehead, p. 524)

What is attractive in phenomenology is its sophisticated account of perception as multi-perspectival, the idea of meaning bestowal, the apprehension of objects as unities, and the multiple strategies of bracketing that provide access to the workings of consciousness. The method yields a phenomenologically comprehensible God whose nature comprises multiple centers of consciousness, whose sphere of operations is an infinite space, an omni-temporal (but not atemporal) divine subject, who looks through (by way of) *us* and is " the bottom of the well of our subjectivity."(p. 228) Through process thought, even when it is not foregrounded in his work, Laycock expects to bring out the dynamism of deific intelligence.

It may be useful to resort to a trope, to an opthalmological metaphor, to assess the consistency of Laycock's phenomenological focus and his use of process thought. When I have my eyes examined, my opthalmologist employes a two-pronged strategy. First, he looks for signs of disease or malfunction of the eyes by examining them as anatomical objects. Second, he tries to learn what my visual deficits are by seeing things through my eyes. Thus, he asks me to read letters and numbers from a chart and, in a second test, requests that I press a button when I see flickering pinpoints of light inside a spherical apparatus that resembles a brightened sky chart, lights which are either foregrounded or at the periphery of this artificial horizon. He is relieved when I can convey what I see and frustrated if I fail to do so because my visual field must become transparent to him so that he can see it as I do. In the tests by which he tries to see things through my eyes, his knowledge is parasitic upon my experience and that of all his other patients, all of whom are related to one another through an internal system of relations which come together in his specular subjectivity. In sum, he sees with all of their eyes as anatomical objects from outside (again, not all at once) in a totalizing view. By contrast, it is possible for each patient to see the eyes of all the others but not his or her own. I introduce this figure because it suggests the strengths of Laycock's position—his magnificent account of the divine engagement—as well as its limitations when he hitches a Husserlian God to the process.

To make this point, it may be useful to sketch Laycock's account of God as specular intelligence. He begins with the pre-reflective experience of God as radiance, in the double sense of radii that emanate from a divine center and of illumination. In accordance with his commitment to strict phenomenological method, he proceeds to reveal God in the self-evidence of phenomenologically reduced experience, not as factually known but as an eidetically reduced content, then. Because this is *all* that can be known of God's existence, Laycock does not have to offer proofs of God's existence but needs only to disclose God's nature as eidetically apprehended. It is taken for granted that God is mind and exhibits the properties of all minds, "intentionality, teleological directedness and intersubjectivity." (p. 24)

I noted earlier that, for Laycock, divine consciousness like its human counterpart is intentional. But divine consciousness is also perceptual, the object of its perception being the world-pole, the center of "all possible intentional reference" and "the ultimate locus of value."(p. 29) Laycock inquires into how objects are perceived and shows that they are grasped through the multiple profiles they present. An object cannot be numerically distinct from its profiles, but the object is not merely their sum. This is because an object is also an ideality, its identity, the one thing that it is, through its many manifestations.(p. 41)

This ideality not only shows itself in the organization of objects in space but also in the construing of experience as temporal. Intentionality guarantees the temporal continuity of experience in that the "mutual externality of the now-points" of multiple intentional acts "is resolved in the continuity of the time continuum." This analysis is deepened in Laycock's depiction of God as subject. To be a subject one must already have fallen into time. In technical Husserlian language, "passive time-synthesis establishes the way in which an agent becomes a sub/ject."(p. 146) This synthesis is universal, "a single activity at the base of the multitude of finite minds."(p. 147)

Laycock goes on to analyze the modalities of appearance: *transparent appearance*, the apprehension of meaning without taking cognizance of its constitutive conditions (recall my opthalmologist's seeing my seeing of the letters, numbers, and flashes of light) and *opaque appearance*, seeing the constitutive conditions of experience (recall my opthalmologist's examination of the anatomical eye). Of course, the analogy is imperfect in that the constitutive conditions for the opthalmologist are the physical eye, a naivete that would never pass muster with Husserl. To see opaquely is to grasp the way that appearance is generated, to be "on to" its *tromp l'oeil* character even though appearances do not give away the secret of their constitutive conditions in immediate apprehension. A God's eye view can never be only transparent: the world appearances together with their circumambient conditions are given as an ensemble to the divine ocularity.(p. 92)

Laycock also wants to allow for an increment in the divine cognition. Thus, he avoids positing all manner of self-coincidence of the divine mind. For example, he criticizes the Hegelian Absolute's sublation of individual egos by making them deducible from the Absolute Idea so that, in the end, the Absolute is coincident with itself. He also rejects Leibniz's view-from-nowhere description of God's mind as losing the richness of individual perspectives generated by the situatedness of individual subjects.

Especially important for Laycock is the fact that empty intentionality can never fully coincide with its object because the object's aspects are infinite. "Absolute presence remains relatively approximable" but never attainable.(p. 130) This means that we distance ourselves from "a zero point which establishes a direction or vector" and proceed toward absolute presence which is always receding from us. We are, to be sure, further from our starting point but not nearer our goal. Yet this is no reason for discouragement in that we can enjoy the "endless possible incremental realization" of the ideal construed as "the possibility of limitless advance...not a static affair-complex but a *pathway*."(pp. 130-131) With the analysis of God's non-identity with himself, it seems clear that Laycock means to introduce a dynamism into deific consciousness consonant with Whitehead's depiction of the self-transcending character of actual entities, of "the universe [as] a creative advance into novelty [whose] alternative is a static morphological universe."(Whitehead, p. 340)

Laycock's consummatory final chapter—a remarkable articulation of the entailments of the divine nature construed as a collective ocular intelligence—is best summed up in his own words:

> God...is 'entelechial' (intentional) *activity*, an activity whose actualizing telos is the world pole. God is at least the empty intending of the world-pole. But God is much more. Empty world-reference is an ineluctable feature of the 'necessary nature' of God. But to carry through the Whiteheadean/ Harteshornian vision of dipolarity, God is also contingently natured. We have rejected the very possibility of omniscience, but we have by no means rejected the possibility of endlessly progressive 'appropriation' of the divine *de jure* 'self.'(p. 169)

Laycock goes on to say that the "structures of divine envisagement" are to be taken as "the 'field' of consciousness mediating divine intentional access to the world-pole" and that "the intersubjective totality of finite minds is precisely identical with [a] divine envisagement,...composed entirely of finite minds."(p. 169)

Despite its richness, Laycock's opthalmological account cannot convey the dynamic character of a process God. To be sure, a phenomenologically construed divine intentionality and Whitehead's view of God's primordial nature overlap—in part because of the Platonic elements in each, for example, Whitehead's eternal objects, which he equated with Platonic forms (Whitehead, p. 70), and Husserl's doctrine of essences. But even if there is an opthalmological *element* in Whitehead, there is certainly no opthalmological *core.* For Husserl, finite minds are "pictures of the world" into which motion is introduced by the image of streaming. Thus, a phenomenological God is "the non-streaming Stream of all finite streaming, that within which is represented the flowing of each finite mind."(p. 216) Advance is constituted by the movement of the in-streaming towards the divine focus. On Laycock's reading, not only are we observers of God's nature but God becomes the Ur-phenomenologist, the pre-eminent ocular subject, a spectator God.

This is not the God of Whitehead's philosophy of organism whose dynamic character is largely dependent upon God's non-ocular features: first, upon the traits of an organism itself; second, upon the primacy of feeling; and finally upon a radically interpreted becoming. Briefly, the character of an organism hinges on its basic unit of significance, the cell-complex. Cells are alive: moving, grasping, gobbling appropriators, "prehending" what they need from the basic elements of the universe. Cell-complexes cannot be construed opthalmologically.

Bound up with the cell theory, is the idea of feeling. For Whitehead, feeling is not a possible modification of the way consciousness "intends" but a feature of all actual entities through which growth and satisfaction come about. For Whitehead process also involves the creation of radical novelty. Think of his often cited comment: "There is a becoming of continuity but no continuity of becoming...extensiveness becomes, but becoming is not itself extensive" (Whitehead, p.53), which reflects his rejection of the idea of serial advance based on a metaphysics of substance. These remarks are intended not to endorse Whitehead's God but to indicate an incompatibility between a process God and phenomenology.

The Divine Depth, Evil, and Immortality

I turn now to some difficulties in Laycock's account that are unrelated to the inherent strains in his attempt to relate phenomenology and process thought. Let us consider first Laycock's treatment of nothingness within the divine nature. Because phenomenology's task is to bring what is before consciousness into plenary presence, there can, strictly speaking, be no divine void, no ultimate mystery, but only a prior formlessness awaiting shape. Thus, Laycock writes: "But what then of 'chaos,' of 'creativity,' of the 'meontic'? If elemental hyle could exist utterly devoid of form, we could not so much as conceive of it, let alone know of its existence. And the supposition of such an inconceivable I know not what would be phenomenologically lethal."(p. 156) Yet a host of religious figures from Eckhart and Boehme to Mahayana Buddhist metaphysicians have attested the experience of mystery and identified it with a void and nothingness.

What is more, a phenomenological treatment of the divine depth is so bound up with form that little attention is paid to the problem of language, a problem which exercised the medieval mystics and which paved the way for postmodern speculation about the language of negation. Here a hint from Derrida may be useful. He writes:

> This which is called X is neither this nor that.... Despite appearances, then, this X is neither a concept nor even a name; it lends itself to a series of names, calls for another syntax, and exceeds even the order and the structure of predicative discourse; it is not and does not say what is. It is written completely otherwise.(Jacques Derrida, unpublished translation of an address on negative theology delivered at Hebrew University, Jerusalem, 1988)

Connected to the problem of non-being and deity, is the question of evil. Because it does not appear in the index of the present book, I do hope Laycock is thinking about a future work on God and moral matters. If, as in the present work, God is construed as total consciousness, as "the synoptic envisagement of the visual fields of all finite minds," these alternatives present themselves: *either* God will remain the perpetual onlooker, indifferent to evil (as, for example, the bird who watches while another bird eats the sweet fruit as described in the Mandukya Upanisad), *or* God is construed as active but still coextensive with finite minds and is implicated in the bloody crimes of history.

Finally, there is the question of immortality, which is connected for Laycock with the idea of what he calls the *Gotteswelt*, "the ideal of maximal empathic interpenetration of communal existence *partes inter partes*" to be approached asymptotically through "the endless actualization of all possible minds."(p. 76) If minds would fall into oblivion after death, no progress would be made in approximating the *Gotteswelt*. But Laycock's view of progress presumes that a good God would not allow an ultimate slippage into nothingness, an assumption which is tenable if one does not make the divine nature coextensive with finite minds. But if God is not other than the synoptic envisagement of finite subjects, then God's forestalling of final annihilation cannot be taken for granted. What is more, because Laycock's immortality is placed on an impersonal footing, the most that can be hoped for is the retention of a self that is a kind of conatus towards the *Gotteswelt*. On this view we can anticipate an immortality without personality, one in which the value of the human individual is lost.

My questions to Laycock are intended less as critique than as an acknowledgment of the profound questions which the book provokes. It is an extraordinary work of metaphysical imagination written with great flair, perhaps the most powerful speculative theology by a younger philosopher of religion that I have read in years.

Queens College
City University of New York

Whitehead, Alfred North. *Process and Reality: An Essay in Cosmology*. New York: Harper and Row, 1960.

ANGELA ALES BELLO

THE CRITIQUE OF REASON, CREATIVITY, AND MYSTICAL EXPERIENCE

The aim of Anna Teresa Tymieniecka's recent researches, published in two volumes: *Logos and Life*, Book 1: *Creative Experience
and the Critique of Reason. Introduction to the Phenomenology of Life
and the Human Condition* and Book 2: *The Three Movements of the
Soul* (Dordrecht: Kluwer Academic Publishers, 1988), is that of
proposing a global interpretation of reality by means of an analysis
defined as phenomenological. The phenomenological intuition,
indeed, forms part and parcel of the methodological approach taken:
the Author runs over the very movement of life and thus traces back
without making any prior assumptions; her analysis, therefore,
tends towards things themselves and is full of confidence in the
possibility of describing them just as they present themselves in
their vital manifestation. Life, potent but mysterious, becomes clear
to anyone who patiently dedicates himself to examining its process
and development. Here, therefore, we have a description that
believes in the results attained and does not consider them as merely
provisional viewpoints.

This motive constitutes the strongest and most valid link between the research of Tymieniecka and the phenomenology of
Edmund Husserl, though she deviates from his phenomenology both
in the concrete performance of her analysis and in the results
obtained: contrary to what one might suppose, indeed, the field of
inquiry—life—is not suggested to the Author by the theme of the life-
world but rather by her focus on the moment of creativity. This
moment, even though it underlies all artistic creation and has been
thoroughly examined in numerous other works of the Author, cannot
be reduced to this expression of creation alone but characterizes the
whole of the life process, assuming various forms. In this general
perspective a central position is assumed by the question of the
contraposition of life and thought, of creativity and intellectual

A-T. Tymieniecka (ed.), Analecta Husserliana XLIII, 71–74.
© 1994 *Kluwer Academic Publishers. Printed in the Netherlands.*

order, a contraposition that has often been sustained, especially in our own day.

The primary function Tymieniecka attributes to life enables her to understand the significance of reason itself. Indeed, the intention of the first volume is to proceed to a 'critique of reason' that would reveal the intrinsic intellectualism of the transcendental viewpoints of Kant and Husserl and thus throw them into a state of crisis. Here, indeed, we have the polemical term of the Author's inquiry. *Logos* and life indicate the confines within which the Author's search unfolds: it moves from the *logos* as the horizon of all philosophizing, paying attention—above all—to the Kantian and Husserlian perspective, and it grasps the profundity of life in its development towards the *logos*, which must not, however, be understood as a purely intellectual activity but rather as a substantially spiritual one.

It is precisely on account of its analytical character that the description calls for a patient effort; but the reader's constancy is rewarded by a gradual widening of the horizon, for the trend of the search is such that, moving from the creative act as the phenomenological access to the human condition, there unfolds the image of man as creator in his advance toward a threefold *telos*: from an intitial spontaneity there unfold his various activities, specifically, aesthetic activity, ethical activity, and cognitive activity.

Teleological interpretation presupposes a core virtuality, what is here called an "entelechy," using the classical notion used from Aristotle to Leibniz. Virtuality, spontaneity, and creativity: these are the constitutive elements of life, which moves forward from a kind of indifferentiation, arrives at an ever more complex articulation, bursts into human activity and human production, and eventually achieves self-awareness.

What renders the research of Tymieniecka both new and original is the role that she attributes to creativity as a neutral condition that can assume many connotations. Creativity and aesthetics are profoundly connected, but it is impossible to reduce creativity to the aesthetic dimension; *eros* and *logos* are contraposed but have a common origin in creativity. Reason may make claims to justifying everything, but it is of limited significance in the great ocean of life;

there is an apparent anti-intellectualism here if the intellect is considered to be absolute, but in actual fact what we have here is a redimensioning of intellectualism through the discovery of the sense of intelligibility from which rationalism eventually emerges. The discernment of such senses is the basis of a 'critique of reason' in which the fundamental schemes on which a great part of modern and contemporary philosophy has been constructed are turned upside down: reason no longer enjoys primacy, even though the importance of the self-reflective moment is fully recognized.

This patient work of excavation is used for examining and analyzing the 'human condition.' Here we have a reconsideration—right from the beginning—of the philosophical questions, a reconsideration that presents to us, as it were in a great fresco, the subtle interwoven plots which are reality.

In this radical analysis there could not be absent the search for the ultimate significance of all things, and the Author undertakes this search by proceeding from man's self-interpretation-in-the-sacred. Here we have the argument of the second volume, which can be understood only when seen in relation to the first.

These books underscore the need for going beyond the constructivity peculiar to the intellect; they develop the creative orchestration of specifically human existence. The Author clarifies this by proposing the simile of a triptych. In the first panel the poetical *logos* that presides over man's creative work is probed; in the central panel the creatively orchestrated intellect that establishes the lines of a plurirational system and therefore of structures, laws, and principles is investigated; the third panel (which is Book 2) is a vision of the spiritual *antilogos* that strains to discover the ultimate truths.

It is at this point that the Author comes to grips with the problem of the soul, describing its three movements, which are: (a) the radical examination of oneself, (b) the discovery of one's own finitude and the search for possibilities of overcoming it, and (c) the discovery of the life of the spirit. We thus have the beginnings of a very subtle description of the "movement" of the soul in what is commonly described as its ascent to God, culminating in mystical union. This process is indeed studied by the Author in a wholly novel manner, but the analysis is a very complex one and in this brief note one cannot go beyond indicating some of its results.

The vibration of the soul leads to a state that can be defined as ecstasy, but, whereas ecstasy is limited to a moment, authentic vibration of the soul is rather a continuous endeavor to become oriented towards a *telos*. Here we have the beginnings of the straining towards the absolute.

All this leads the Author to posit an "internal sacrality," the presence of which is illustrated in such figures as Ignatius Loyola, Theresa of Avila, and Thérèse of Lisieux. Tymieniecka wonders whether we are here concerned with an 'invention' or with a 'discovery,' i.e., whether or not there is a personal contribution in this movement. She eventually answers this question by concluding that the work and the personal effort do not follow a preordained road, that there is a spontaneous development "...in our collaboration—in the strong sense—in the work of universal Creation."(p. 147) An "elevated tonality" of the soul is thus attained: "Transported by a being elevated to a superior affectivity, we uncover new resources of enthusiasm, generosity, hope, and love—this 'ordo amoris' that Pascal speaks of. Similarly, the *joie de vivre* by which these affective effusions are illuminated shows us multiple prospects ignored until now."(p. 151)

In this process of elevation, in which "our dazzled souls see infinite splendors by meeting in one personal Principle and are lost in a divination of this Unique Being"(*ibid.*), forgetting oneself does not mean abolition of the personality, because the impulses pass through the filter of the personality.

Two final observations may be made here. First, in contrast to the challenging or even devaluation of human intellect and rationality in our day, these two volumes present us with a full-fledged 'critique of reason' in which reason itself is found to stretch further than the human orbit alone, to extend to the furthest horizons of life itself. By this measure of reason, irrationalism is avoided. Secondly, the analysis of the relationship between *logos* and *antilogos* leads the Author to inquire into the dimension of interior sacrality in such way as to propose a "new mysticism" or, better, a new interpretation of the mystic experience and, more generally, a new philosophical point of view on the phenomenon of religion.

Centro Italiano delle Ricerche Fenomenologiche

JADWIGA S. SMITH

THE COMMUNICATION OF THE SACRED
IN TYMIENIECKA'S *THE THREE*
MOVEMENTS OF THE SOUL

Points have we all of us within our souls
Where all stand single; this I feel, and make
Breathings for incommunicable powers;
But is not each memory to himself ?
—Wordsworth
Prelude Book III, 189-191

Great is this power of memory, exceeding
great, Oh my God, a vast and unlimited inner
chamber. Who has plumbed its depths? Yet,
this is power of my mind and it belongs to my
nature; I myself do not grasp all that I am. Is
then the mind too narrow to hide itself, so
that the questions arise; where is this thing
which belongs to it and it cannot grasp?
Would it be outside it and not in it? How then
does it not grasp it?
—Augustine
Confessions Book X, 15

The above epigraphs are fitting for an article on the inward
sacred as presented in *The Three Movements of the Soul,* the second
book of Anna-Teresa Tymieniecka's *Logos and Life.* The incommunicable part of the human being's most inward experience challenges our abilities to express ourselves by some common means of
language or signs. In other words, we are tempted to place it in some
larger system, in a structure which would objectify it and, as a
result, separate it from human life. Thus, the individual human life
poses a task of seeing it either as a rare and singular specimen of
particular consciousness or as a case belonging to some encompassing structure or system.

Tymieniecka wants to avoid the latter, to escape cognitive

A-T. Tymieniecka (ed.), Analecta Husserliana XLIII, 75–81.

constructivism or ontic structuration of objectivity, by means of striking at "the heart of givenness-in-becoming" (p. 5). Thus, the cognitive function of man cannot be separated from the very enactment of human life. In other words, the problem of the givenness of the real world, the ever challenging issue in phenomenology, has a solution, according to Tymieniecka, in stressing the conditions of life itself.

Whether we consider Husserl's transcendental phenomenology or Ingarden's eidetic version, we can see both as products of abstract reduction and out of touch, even if only temporarily, with the concrete relationships of a being within a flow of the life-world. For example, a fundamental difficulty in Ingarden's concept of the real individual is that though this individual is endowed with motion, action, and interaction, he still is perceived as remaining in a stationary stage. In other words, access to the essential, the core, the "true" identity of man becomes a paradoxical search for the unattainable, as the attempt to place it in some comprehensible structure necessarily tampers with the meaning of this search.

What Ingarden's eidetic analysis does not provide is the principle of the individual's intimate development. Tymieniecka's solution is *the entelechial factor,* the living individual, carrying out the progress of the being's particular identification. Thus her equation of being human with being creative gives prominence to the creative act—the act of the human being who has to cope with and who ultimately protests against the interpretation of human destiny in the particular constituted world given to him in time. The "specifically human" is to be found now in the study of a conscious process rather than in an ideal structural ontology. The role of consciousness is continuous transformation, continuous multiple exchange with external reality. The emphasis in *The Three Movements of the Soul* on constant process-in-the-making, quest, spiritual journey is striking, but the reader begins to get the impression that, despite this stress on ever-transforming consciousness, Tymieniecka's recognition of the role of the empirical does not preclude any system building which would ultimately lead to yet another perverted concept of human beings.

Instead, Tymieniecka initiates the study of a reverse process—

the "transmutation of sense" turning from the empirical, aesthetic, and moral quest to the "transnatural quest" for the ultimate destiny of the human being, all this process being a fundamental task of the human soul. The soul's "deepest life involvements" lead eventually to "the installation of a circuit of special significance, that of the 'inward sacred' " (p. 19).

At a certain point, because of a sense of culmination in creative accomplishment, the soul is ready to leap for the ultimate, innermost destiny of the human being. The three movements of the soul (radical examination—in response to the current of man's life; exalted existence—in response to the discovery of the finiteness of life; and transcending—in response to the opening up of the spiritual life) blaze a path to a spiritual readiness of the soul which culminates in the establishment of the inward sacred:

> The inward sacred springs from life's tightest entanglements and yet it unfolds itself over against them; its search expresses our crucial concern with the meaningfulness of life, and yet it turns out that it defies that; it promises to attain, in its progress, the peak of the exercise of reason, and yet it leads us to its complete devaluation, to its dissolution in the direction of the *anti-logos*. (p.19)

At this point the issue of communication emerges as being central to the discussion of the inward sacred. Hence it is my intention here to pursue that issue, beginning with the initial problem of the incommunicable suggested by the two epigraphs.

How one can even begin to talk of the inward sacred? This seems to be a contradiction of terms. Still at the same time, it is only through various forms of communication that we can work on our readiness to accept the escalating challenges made as the soul ascends to higher levels of spirituality.

Tymieniecka's first volume of *Logos and Life*, subtitled *Creative Experience and the Critique of Reason*, established the crucial role of creative acts in the life of the human being. Thus, the existential need for creation presupposes the existence of the recipient, even if this recipient happens to be the creator himself or herself. It follows then that the creator translates his or her interaction with an understanding of an empirical reality into an object. This object

succumbs to some principles of translation which are dictated by
the need to communicate within a certain context of empirical
reality. Tymieniecka acknowledges the need for an exterior point of
reference, the need for communication. One cannot fully give life a
meaning on the basis of personal aspirations and virtualities, and
so communication and the individual's relations with other people
are back on the agenda. Also, since the soul cannot communicate
directly with God and can only yearn for "passing beyond,"

> other human beings are the soul's only and last hope.... We can know
> nothing of this being (the One), and he can never be an end that
> corresponds to our natural powers. This Unknowable One is, however,
> our star in the attempt to surpass finiteness. This attempt is born and
> is maintained in communication with the other. (p. 86)

This passage, because it appears just before the section on the third
movement of the soul, that opening out toward the transcendent,
underscores the paradoxical role of communication pointed out at
the beginning of this article. Tymieniecka herself observes that: "It
is paradoxical that we are granted at the very first the solitude and
retrenchment of the soul. But this world of soul is actually pursued
in and through communication...towards transcendence" (p.105).

   She continues this paradoxical exploration of the relationship
of an individual human being with other fellow human beings in the
search for certitude. First, she explores the ill-fated search for
permanent human values, but the outcome does not lead her to
Nietzscheian pessimism. Rather, she discovers that when the soul
reaches the abyss of being closed in upon itself, "stripped of
contingent forms," it discovers, unlike Nietzsche, that it cannot
come out of the abyss by itself. It can do so only in communication
with other people because: "Authentic human values could not arise
in an isolated consciousness.... There is no world without values, and
values are born from communication with other people" (p. 120).

   The other person or persons are, then, in need of clarification
of our convictions and, by the same token, we ourselves question
these convictions. In such a radical interrogation and
"destructuring" in which the rules of "worldly" communication
are abandoned, all the rules of finitude are also gone. In other words,

in this communication without any reservations, the soul has its chance to taste transcendence. However short-lived this taste is, it still gives the soul an inkling into the sacred.

At the same time, the possibility of the human being's grasping an "extra-worldly" message while entangled in his finite, empirical reality encounters such difficulties that one more time a seemingly paradoxical observation emerges in that only through communication within these finite, empirical boundaries can one not only break barriers but also advance spiritually. A sense of communal effort among people "oriented in the same direction" gives rise to the idea of progress (p. 140).

On the individual level, one cannot grasp this "dynamic progression" in any discursive form, but one can, nevertheless, perceive a common "backbone" in one's consciousness. The presence of the "spiritual motif" is recognized by Tymieniecka as "the most powerful tool of the interior mechanism of our existence" (p. 158).

One of the stages in the dynamic progression just mentioned is an awareness of the confrontation with the "Unique Witness." This awareness is a product of the dynamic that triggers communication. Tymieniecka goes so far as to call communication "a dynamic which carries the dialectic of our existence" or "the very root of our spiritual genesis" (p. 163). Thus, the closer the reader is to Tymieniecka's culminating explication of inward sacred, the more he or she becomes involved in the issue of communication.

In our critical analysis of our progress in discovering "the ultimate course," we our engaged in our interior confrontation with ourselves, and, as a result, we are being involved in communication with ourselves as if we stood apart and tried to convince some other person about the goodness of our actions or their failure. We yearn for the approval of this "Witness." And it is in the presence of this Witness, at the end of our life, that we grasp the truth of the totality of our being and the discovery of "our destiny in our soul as the *life* of this very soul, arising from the obscurity of empirical actions and from our dependent psyche" (p. 166). This truth, ignored earlier, out of fear of the unknown, now allows transcendence to diffuse "our being while reabsorbing it into

Infinity" (p. 166).

Thus, through various stages of communication with the witness, distinct from the soul, the soul finds, at last, approval—the condition allowing infinitude, peace, and thus "communion with the Divine" (p. 168). Moreover, the moment the witness of our soul is discovered, we are aware of the true meaning of the fundamental dichotomy:

> The development of our being is a part of nature, which takes place in the organized cosmos according to objective laws. The creation of supernatural destiny, however, is brought about at the most personal and untranslatable depth—in objective terms—of our subjectivity, by its own choices. (p. 168)

The discovery of the Witness, connected with the time of agony, means being granted the privilege of seeing the path of life just trodden and of understand it at last, or using Tymieniecka's words: "Agony is a time of full lucidity before empirical disintegration begins, a time for pause...somewhat outside the ongoing movement" (p. 169). The role of our consciousness in making the world becomes clear, and as a result, "we see the present moment stretching to infinity outside of every event which has become a temporality" (pp. 169-70).

Finally, it becomes clear that "the *Unique Witness* is present before the beginning and presides at the beginning of time" (p. 174). The witness guards the soul in its search by preparing some "landmarks" and "illuminations" according to the soul's gradual advancement. In other words, Tymieniecka warns against some easy illuminations or instantaneous conversions. The readiness of the soul is a primary condition. The three movements of the soul prepare the way for the inward sacred and finally for the Unique Witness.

The revelation of the sacred message at the time of agony and union with the Witness are related to the spiritual development of the soul. The buried content of this development is ignored in the same way as is its transnatural aspect. A final understanding of all of the resources of the soul means the accomplishment of its destiny and leaving "the frame of contingency" and its temporality; the soul is "inserted into the first sketch of original creation" (p. 179).

The question of communication appears one more time in the closing sections of *The Three Movements of the Soul* when Tymieniecka emphasizes the fundamental role of communication between the self and the other person by means of "inward creative reciprocity" (p. 181) which is "a functional-ontological state of the human person" (p. 182). However, Tymieniecka warns against a total identification of the pursuit of one's destiny with the creative process of the artist. We introduce the "other self " into our creative quest, investigating our own being in existence by comparing ourselves with this "other self " in a reciprocal way. Still, each self conducts its own quest in separation. The process of communication between the two of them, even though failing to produce a common ground describable in an objective, rational way, nevertheless allows the recognition of the common anxiety of human destiny. Yet, this communication can break down at any moment, and then the soul, freed from empirical ties:

> finds herself lost "nowhere" and with "no one" to turn to. Cut off from the world, all her spontaneities flow into the urgent impetus of her quest. On the other side of the abyss that opens, the soul discovers the *Radical Other* abiding with her face to face. (p. 189)

Thus, according to Tymieniecka, the ultimate encounter with the inward sacred emerges from, on the one hand, the empirical, which is left behind, and, on the other hand, the transempirical which reaches its apex in the Absolute, Radical Other and which, thus, does not allow any further explanation.

Bridgewater State College

Tymieniecka, Anna-Teresa. *Logos and Life*, Book II: *The Three Movements of the Soul*. (Dordrecht, Boston, London: Kluwer Academic Press, 1990)

MARLIES E. KRONEGGER

A-T. TYMIENIECKA'S CHALLENGES:
FROM A SPIRITUAL WASTELAND
TO TRANSCENDENCE

I. Intuition and Reason

Tymieniecka's intuitions are cosmic and timeless in scope. If this makes her appear a visionary, it is because she is inspired by a substantive imagination which enables her to see beyond the wall of rationalism and chauvinistic attitudes, a fallacy of perception dramatically exposed in Plato's Allegory of the Cave. Her perceptions of meaning come like shooting stars in flashes of insight, and the inner light that radiates in her comes to life in her poetic language.

With Tymieniecka, vision is the spontaneous response of the poetic imagination to the challenges which life puts to man. If we follow Tymieniecka's path, neither a discipline or a program, freedom is self-motivation and spontaneity. In her *The Three Movements of the Soul*,[1] she shows us how to transcend the conditions of our life-world, achieving the full potential of human personality in the creative orchestration of all the faculties and in relation to *everything-there-is-alive*.

In a flashing moment of intuition, something opens. We see from within the integrity of life based on *re-ligio* in its original meaning of "to link back, to join, to make a connection, to weave, and to let stream again from infinite depths the living waters of the inexhaustible source." The control over nature that Western man considers a rational triumph over nature yields in Tymieniecka to sympathy with nature and expressive joy over striking a chord in harmony with nature: she proposes to act in such a way that our actions and most recent thoughts not only do not impede the harmony of which they are an element but actually cause, create, and radiate it. Whereas the rational mind breaks the world into elements, here reality is experienced as a harmonious totality. The achievement of this view is to create in man peace, trust, and sensitivity, is to listen to his intuition, a mode of instantaneous, total, coercive understanding full of the conviction of truth.

A-T. Tymieniecka (ed.), Analecta Husserliana XLIII, 83–87.
© 1994 *Kluwer Academic Publishers. Printed in the Netherlands.*

II. The Polyphonic Symphony of Human Life and of Everything-There-Is-Alive

Life is seen as an ever-expanding creative coherence that sur-passes itself at every instant. Tymieniecka elucidates the human condition within the context of *everything-there-is-alive*, seen as an orchestration of all the voices of sense within the "gigantic game of human creation."(xxvii)

Her efforts are illuminated by superior ideals; her creative elan passes beyond personal and individual frameworks; she calls upon all our faculties, all spiritual impulses, to combine to become bene-factors of mankind in an exalted existence, reflecting the universal harmony of creation.

Tymieniecka demonstrates that the creative act of man is the royal road of access to the Human Condition. Having replaced the predominantly intellectual "I can" of Husserl—the primogenital source of all cognition, volition, and action—with the creative act/ thrill/tremor, she has given the Husserlian aspiration to radicalism its ultimate form. With Tymieniecka, the realism of man's creative virtualities marks the point of departure of a new awareness. With this sacred awareness, the world is transfigured by a quality of the spirit projected onto external objects: inward sacredness, as used here, refers to the heightened quality of sense perceptions, and also to both religion and transcendental intimations. Above all, inward sacredness is characterized by an intense feeling of joy and libera-tion which is not given by any other experience as it brings "a meaningful heart to the hazardous work of cosmic creation."(150) Her cosmic apprehension of existence is an extreme development of inward sacredness. This takes us to her view that the most vital function of phenomenology is to foster the unfolding of the individual's integrity in accord with himself (the microcosm), his culture (the mesocosm), and the universe (the macrocosm), and with the ultimate mystery both beyond and within himself and in all things, in life and death, in inward sacredness and transcendence.

III. Inward Sacredness and Transcendence

Tymieniecka's investigations into the *inward sacred* in the human condition are to be likened to a stream of pristine spontaneity. They follow *the three movements of the soul* in an arc which begins in the twilight of nowhere, of the anti-logos, arrives at its zenith in the luminosity of the creative process, and sets in twilight as all human works lose luminosity and light, descending back into the nowhere of the anti-logos. The spiritual act, the zenith of man's creative orchestration, establishes itself polyphonically, using the fundamental registers that are the powers of the soul—"passions, emotions, sensibility, intellectuality, volition, attaining a complex harmonization in both moral life and creation."(178) Tymieniecka holds that the sacred is a "springboard towards transcendence."(179) Consciousness passes through progressive stages of intensification and unification culminating in the ecstatic identification of self and the world. Original creation is closely associated with the qualities of youth when she advocates freshness and spontaneity (120), the creative life-giving richness of human existence, and the ability to awaken the dormant life of a natural force not based on reason in order to give moral birth and spiritual development to life powers above reason. We attain a higher level of existence. Renewing the act of caring, she restores to existence the quality of risk, at once shattering and reintegrating the already known in the sacrificial creative fire of life in depth and in process here and now, for "true man is an authentic person who unfolds, who progresses in the bursting forth of ecstatic actions."(155) Tymieniecka defines her sacred mission: "With extreme intensity of will, we desire to elevate the other person toward the 'summits,' but we want him to rise in a free act. We take charge of the itinerary of others; we make it our own affair, the ultimate meaning of our accomplishment."(160-161)

Tymieniecka raises questions for which the only answer is one's own whole being, the expression of creative synergies which are unavailing against the sensuality, ignorance, and blind violence in man. Creative consciousness, a unique condition for life, recreates a lost harmony with nature. Tymieniecka defends the spiritual act in the longing for both creativity and spontaneity which communicates both truth and faith with apodictic certitude. The spiritual act participates in and identifies with the struggles and processes of life against finitude. Tymieniecka does not speak of nature that wipes out our spiritual creation in death, but of nature, the subliminal soil,

a synergetic center of forces, containing life's germinal virtualities in
the subterranean stream, the inward sacredness of the human
being.

Inward sacredness means to escape from the narrow confines of
personal existence in time to higher world of timelessness: the
density of the ecstatic experience is the result of the "creative,
glorious power in us to work with the first spontaneities flowing into
the soul which are as much cosmic, vegetal as uniquely the soul's
own."(179)

The power of the sacred, then, is no longer the power only to unite
animate and inanimate nature in a rhythmic symphony of enchantment and ecstasy, but rather the capacity to grasp the change-filled,
death-bound beauty of life at the crossroads where being and
transience meet. Tymieniecka transforms the fear of pain and death
into something joyful, vital, and heroic as she realizes: "Nothing,
except death, could shatter our work. This energy is what raises our
enterprise to the highest ideal: we give to our existence heroic
significance."(163) She compels the elemental forces of love and
death to confront each other. Her investigation spans life and death,
reason and emotionality, control over nature and sympathetic fusion
with nature. Underlying all of these antinomies is the intimation of
a fundamental unity between life and death as the inseparable poles
of a single reality. The magic of Tymieniecka's elan makes visible
and communicable a hidden harmony and reveals the unity in which
life and death appear as ultimate parts of the same continuum. This
justifies the reason why Christ had to die: "Christ had to die, having
in His passion lived and assumed all human finiteness and having
embraced every man, past, present, and future,—in the creator's
maternity. Delivered from the servitude of contingency, He infused
His entire affective, moral, supernatural being into humanity.
Indeed, 'God died from having loved man.' Of all the gifts of love, only
death can satisfy man."(161-162)

IV. Time and Eternity

How can the present moment be linked to Eternity? Tymieniecka
affirms: "Eternity only consists of unique present moments....
Moments live, and we live through them. Our destiny is established

by them. Our destiny, ineffaceable, causes this life to enter gloriously into *all* eternity."(179-180) The past, the present, and the
future merge into a single evolving totality, and in the intervals of
time disappear altogether (time with its implication of succession
and separation). Time has disappeared, and an Eternity of bliss
reigns.

The inner challenges with which Tymieniecka confronts us
make us realize our true nature and let us see into our being. In sum,
the coming to be and passing away of the world involves for her an
intuitive, playful knowledge. The spiritual act proper embodies an
anti-rational, anti-Promethean strain. The soul, our inward sacred
river, lays the groundwork for the life of the spirit. Tymieniecka
seems to open every inner door to our infinite nature.

Michigan State University

NOTE
1. Tymieniecka, Anna-Teresa. *Logos and Life*, Book Two: *The Three Movements of
the Soul*. Dordrecht, Boston, London: Kluwer Academic Publ., 1988.

PART TWO

THE METAPHOR OF THE SACRED
AND "ORIGINS"

GÉRARD BUCHER

THE METAPHOR OF THE SACRED,
OR THE ALLEGORY OF ORIGIN

> The poetic act consists in suddenly seeing that an idea
> divides itself in a number of motives of equal value,
> and in grouping them. . . .
>
> L'acte poétique consiste à voir soudain qu'une idée se
> fractionne en un nombre de motifs égaux par valeur
> et à les grouper. . . .
>
> S. Mallarmé

The difficulty of theorizing metaphor – with regard to the paradoxes
that such theorizing confronts – undoubtedly lies in the focal role and
extreme complexity of the object under scrutiny. Paul Ricoeur postulates that metaphor is the symptom of a mysterious generativity, a generic
vivacity in language. But his enterprise is hindered by his inscription
of metaphor in the framework of traditional metaphysics (*La métaphore
vive*, Seuil, 1975). For his part, Jacques Derrida suggests that metaphor
encompasses metaphysics, that it is a motive which actually confers on
metaphysics its configuration and tenor. But he offers no insight which
would allow us to circumscribe metaphor's extra-metaphysical positivity ("La métaphore blanche" in *Marges*, Minuit, 1972, pp. 247–324).
In fact, neither of these theoreticians explored the mythical antecedents
of metaphor, and it is no doubt for that reason that they engaged in a
polemic which, in the final analysis, only prolongs the antagonism
between idealism and criticism which has characterized our tradition since
its origins ("Le retrait de la métaphore" in *Psyché*, Gallilée, 1987, pp.
68–93). So the question is: will we be able to transcend our metaphysical tradition by bringing the genetic paradoxes of metaphor to the
foreground?

In the perspective which I call logoanalytic or thanatogenetic (*La
vision et l'énigme*, éditions du Cerf, 1989, and *Le testament poétique*,
forthcoming), metaphor is equated with the symptom ever reverber-
ating in language of the poetic origin of language itself. In consequence,
only an investigation of the *genealogy of metaphor* or of the myste-

91

A-T. Tymieniecka (ed.), Analecta Husserliana XLIII, 91–99.

rious origin of language echoed *in* history or *as* history could make patent the Phenomenon of the *poesis* of language which has already been exploited and concealed by onto-theology (in both the constructs of faith and reason).

The touchstone of the hypothesis is to achieve a renewed correlation between meaning and the sacred. At the first stage, all sacred practices in primitive cultures (funeral and sacrificial rites, rites of possession, of purification, etc.) are conceived of as a nascent symbolic process anchored in the ritualization of death. At the core of every rite the symbolic matrix is assimilated to a silent individual as well as collective metaphorization of death. It is the turmoil of the mind and heart, the confrontation with tainted chaos in the ritualized ordeal of mourning, which may have been the condition needed for the genesis of meaning and the sacred.

As a matter of fact, what allowed man to objectify or re-present the individual *and* collective ingestion of death or of the lived experience of chaos was the odyssey of the dead, its transition from the diabolically tainted to a tutelary hereafter. By delivering the Ancestor from the hell of dissolution, the community in effect produced its own delivery into humanity. Thus did the human animal's leap out of death perpetuate the belief in a mythical hereafter, thus did man become the eye of death *in* or *on* life. The unfolding of the symbolic was complete from the beginning; it set up a reflexive semiogenetic structure which originally was neither the prerogative of the subject nor that of the community.

In the thanatogenetic perspective, the vision of the Ancestor's or mediator's odyssey – the cycle of metamorphosis from man to the dead and the god – is considered to be the condition for man's introduction to the realm of meaning, the condition for the original deployment of logos itself; hence the vital significance attached by our forefathers to sacred practices and the necessity for a permanent recurrence of tests of loss and recreation. Anchored in religious practices, the poetics of language (or of metaphor) appears to be the source of human genius itself.

The hypothesis thus summarized leads to an epistemological distinction between two modes of the symbolic: First, a fundamental tacit logos deriving from man's religious practices is centered on the extraction of a pure substratum from the impure (originally the extraction of the relics of the dead in a purification process for the decaying corpse, that which "has no name in any language"), then, derived from the previous, there is the linguistic sphere of the spoken word, a sphere which actually encompasses the threefold co-emergence of language, the conscious speaking subject and the world of empiricity in general (what Husserl called *Lebenswelt* or life-world).

The homology of the two logoi centers on the notion of trace. In other words, it hinges on a primordial semiotic function. I borrow here from the models developed by Jacques Derrida, particularly in *Of Grammatology*; however, I give them a new dimension, since I relate them to the domain of ritual and myth. The ritualization of death is indeed interpreted as a tacit operation of inscription (by mortification and purification) and of collective reading of a trace (of the relics of the dead or of any other purely idolatrous manifestation). Consequently, any linguistic performance (and thus any metaphor) partakes of a pure trace or sign which, in the linguistic field, is inseparable from the production of phonemes or of the spoken word.

The verification of the thanatogenetic hypothesis would require a two-phase inquiry. The hypothetical unity of meaning and of the sacred implies a general recasting of our *episteme*: based on religious anthropology, the philosophical (Kantian) reflection on the conditions of possibility of experience would come to fruition not as theory, but as an epiphany of the poetry of metaphor, at the very chiasmus of being and thought. In this context, recognition of the reflective power of the word or of metaphor as a principle of our survival should supplant any "first causes" – God, the subject, matter (understood for example in its modern version as the physiologically grounded psychic capacities of the brain, etc.).

However, what is required first and foremost is an inquiry into the historical erasure of the difference between the two logoi. How could (or how can) the ritualization of death be explicitly transposed as metaphor? Conversely, how is historical destiny itself dependent upon an implicit reflection, through words, of our idolatrous origins? Finally, how can a reversal be achieved that would bring about the overcoming of the primeval ambivalence of violence *and* oblation characteristic of primitive rituals? The very notion of the *sacer* is indeed marked by a double postulation of veneration and repulsion. As a matter of fact, such an overcoming of our innate idolatrous violence is the task that has weighed upon us from the beginning. The answer to these questions pertains of course to Judeo-Christianity, i.e., to Hebrew thought in both its Judaic and Christian versions. It can come to fruition only as a poetic revelation of the death of God (an inquiry into the intimate connection between the experiences of death and of the divine).

If we wish to unravel this history, it is appropriate to recognize from the outset that the transgression of idolatry, as Epiphany of the word or as sacred metaphorization, must have necessarily taken on a reflexive form. In fact, the schema of ritualization of death had to loop back upon itself in order to achieve the self-reflective purification of its own archaic givens. Concretely, the leap from idolatrous primitivity to religions of the word is concomitant to the assimilation of the religious primitive with the impure or with death. It was by dint of this assimilation that a total shift of the primeval tacit or ritualized symbolism (the secret-sacred logos) towards the word (the profferred logos) could be achieved.

The linguistic metaphorization of primitive idolatry coincides with Moses's Revelation: the vision of a good and just God who anticipated man in the enunciation of his Word. The Exodus, the departure of the Jewish people from the kingdom of slavery, in other words their deliverance from the Egyptian realm of death, was the condition for such a vision. Here the Epiphany of *saying* (as voice and text) changed the order of the pure and the impure. It was henceforth only the propensity to defy God (as exemplified in the story of the Fall) or to affirm oneself to the detriment of the other (as in the Cain and Abel episode) which counted as sin or as impure behavior threatening the very humanity of man.

It was by means of an integral metaphoric transposition of the fundamental tenets of primitive religion that the Jewish people succeeded in escaping death. An entirely coherent reformulation of the unity of meaning and of the sacred allowed the ancient Hebrews to derive a radical force of renewal from their withdrawal from the surrounding pagan world. Of all events, the only one which might have entirely modified the destiny of man stemmed from his innermost symbolic conditioning. Only reflexive souls-searching can open unforeseen perspectives at the edge of the abyss. The Jewish people appear thus as an Orphic people whose escape from death required an unprecedented reformulation both of moral conscience and of the idea of God.

Throughout the fifteen centuries which followed the Sinai revelation, Judaic thought remained incessantly focussed on the full realization of its distinct humanity. Awareness of having been chosen had to be constantly reexamined at an ever greater depth, and then revitalized. The temporal ordeals of the Jewish people (particularly the Babylonian captivity and the confrontations with Greek and Roman hegemony) provided occasions for astounding spiritual growth. The advent of Christianity must be placed in this context of the constant Judaic quest for messianic fulfillment.

In its turn, the sudden appearance of the Christian faith may be seen as a thorough reinterpretation of both pagan and Judaic religious givens. A powerful interpretive apparatus was set into motion, inducing a radical schism. It accomplished both the disqualification of traditional Judaism (which was relegated to the rank of surrounding paganism) and its global metaphorization as pure vision of God made Word.

The distinct originality of the Christian transposition, as "nachträglich" or as an after-effect of Judaism, was the passage from a collective to an individual problematic. It brought about concurrently a pure epiphany of the sign-text (an epiphany of the poetic word) perceived in its permanent generativity. Christianity may indeed be seen as an almost explicit reformulation of the ritualization of death. At the very center of the symbolic blossoming which induced the faith in Jesus Christ, we do indeed recognize the archaic figures of man, the dead, and God. The unity of these three figures centers on the character of a unique and universal Mediator, the explicit incarnation of the new Adam in whom the destiny of both man and God are fulfilled.

By making manifest the schema of ritualization of death which subtends Judaism, the Christian myth presents itself as an absolute myth. Its inchoativity is intrinsic; it proposes a meaning which is perpetually in a nascent state. In fact, the procedure of its original invention was unremittingly renewed for all Christian readers by dint of a necessary exposure to the ordeal of the death and resurrection of meaning itself. Thus, the extraordinary semiogenetic power captured by the Gospels could be verified by the fact that a fiction was able to project itself on history as "real presence". It is because it delivered the secret of history from *alpha* to *omega* that the coming of the word of Jesus Christ was able to impose itself on the Ancient World. These themes must now be amplified by an explanation of their contents, as they resulted from the invention of the Gospel story itself.

From the point of view of thanatogenetic analysis, the Pentecost is the event which coincides with the Gospel's original invention. In an atmosphere of desolation and ruin (that of the dereliction of the Jewish

people who were crushed under the yoke of Roman occupation), the story
of the Holy Spirit descending on the Apostles is a patent manifestation
of the overwhelming, eschatological comprehension which permitted a
systematic revision of traditional Judaic givens. The Pentecost is the
allegory *par excellence* of a renewed comprehension of the symbol, the
radical *metanoia* which fomented the encounter with the altogether
Other.

Divided between the recognition of a presupposed miscomprehen-
sion or oblivion and the foreseeing of the imminent return of the Absent
(present in a glorious after-life), we will assert that the story of the coming
of the Spirit corresponds with the Event of the prime crystallization of
the Christian myth which is illustrated by the Proclamation of the first
Kerygma (in the Epistles of Paul and the Acts of the Apostles). Just as
the redeeming mission of Israel was to be ignored by the Nations (such
is the underlying theme of Isaiah's famous "Songs of the Servant of
Yahweh"), so Christ had not been recognized by his own people; he
had been put to death and had come back to life on the third day (besides
the frequent theme of death and resurrection in various palingenetic pagan
myths, the theme of resurrection had become, as we know, a very
common topic of speculation in post-Babylonian Judaism).

We must now understand how the two cardinal sequences of the story
of the Passion – death and resurrection – result from a sublime
metaphorization of the primitive pagan ritualization of death.

The crucifixion scene is indeed an explicit metaphorization of the
God-man's agony. The mirror relation of identification of the Christian
reader to the primordial dead is no longer concentrated on the corpse
(as in the archaic scheme), but rather on the poignant scandal of personal
death, and by extension on the dissolution of meaning itself, which is
expressed specifically by Christ's final cry of dereliction: "Eli, Eli, lama
sabachthani".

Consequently, the meaning of impurity ends up being entirely transposed, and it acquires a strictly moral value. The imperative facing the
Christian/reader is, in effect, to lose his propensity for all violent soli-
darity. Relentlessly exposed to the evocation of his abyssal mortality,
the believer, in taking Christ's place, must in effect assume the pain of
the *other*'s agony. This dissociation from the immemorial expulsion of
the dead/impure (the collective murder of others through sacrifice) thus
leads to a conversion of the mind and heart. By assimilating the whole
semiogenetic test to the abyss of dying, by profoundly reorganizing the

ethical and aesthetic drama of man still scattered in Judaism, the vision of Christ on the cross accomplished an integral metaphorization, which exposed and made explicit the tacit primitive ritualization of death.

As a result, the Christian vision of the crucifixion is in itself for every believer (or every reader/Christian for whom the full sense of the Passion is revealed) tantamount to a *metanoia*, a blossoming of an entirely regenerated subjective identity. The assumption of abysmal death and the ethical consequences which followed from it thus established the sublime reality of Christ on the cross. By seeing themselves in him, people could recognize and renew the very meaning of their humanity. It is therefore understandable that this incomparable scene, in which the integrity of the symbol was summarized in a transcendent mode, could make a mark on history as a distinguished event or as true myth, devoid of mystification and deception.

Complementing the crucifixion scene, the resurrection sequence brought to completion the metaphorization of death as epiphany of the sign/text and its complementary operation of reading. Here again, in an explicit but displaced fashion, absence, emptiness and oblivion commanded the emergence of a sublimated meaning. We find the perfect allegory of the word (or linguistic text and sign) in the figure of the empty tomb which offers, as it were, a reflexion *en abîme* of the entire Gospel text. Here the collected power of the symbol, which reverses all pagan ritualizations, emblematically volatilizes death.

First of all, the Holy Women's visit to the tomb on Easter morning can be assimilated to the deciphering of a trace, the vision, in spirit, of an already deferred glorious presence. Both indexed and eclipsed, the event of the resurrection must in fact be deduced from the reading of a cipher (or of a zero, the point of origin of any affirmation of being) which summons up memory (the women, who had forgotten the foretelling of the resurrection, had gone to the tomb to anoint the corpse of Christ) and opens up a horizon of glorious expectancy, or Parousia. Indeed the Second Coming is an event both already realized and imminent, delayed indefinitely since it coincides with the end of time itself (even if said event is also prefigured, for the sake of narrative coherence, by Christ's apparitions after his death). The sequence of the resurrection thus primarily coincides with the source point of the Christian message. The overwhelming surge of comprehension by means of an inaugural reading is legitimated by the conversion of these "readers of horizons" (S. Mallarmé), the first readers/Christians (the women and then the Apostles).

The resurrection of memory here occasions the total recreation of self: delivered from death, the subject accedes to a superior consciousness, a new sense of identity based on the hypostatizing of nothingness, a hollow in the order of presence. This apotheosis of self is one with the unification of the symbol: it is the deployment of the metaphor of the sacred in its entirety.

But this opening of the tomb is all the more fabulous in that it is also an obvious allegory of the subversion of the archaic. Indeed, the genesis of the Christian message demonstrates the emptiness of the primitive sepulchre. Idolatrous beliefs, metaphorically transposed, are now invalidated. There is no body in the tomb. Henceforth the blemish is strictly moral. It is the desire to murder which all harbor secretly in their hearts, while the emergence of a pure instance ends up being assimilated to the most subtle possible substratum: the Gospel text as text, and the testimony (or voice) of the first believers.

Finally, the opening of the tomb also emblematizes the overcoming of Judaic closure. By concentrating a previously dispersed thematic on the epiphany of the text and the voice – an epiphany which springs from a confrontation with death – Christianity presents itself as the eschatological version of a universalized Judaism. The Christian message is in effect Catholic: it is intelligible to all men because it contains the secret of the birth of man himself. (In formulating this hypothesis, I do not at all affirm the superiority of one religion over another; I only measure degrees of complexity and integration relative to the shared base matrix of the ritualization of death.)

At the conclusion of this rapid genealogical deduction, the irruption of the Christian myth presents itself as a self-reflective story in which the essence of the symbol or the divine drama of man himself are crystalized. The transposition of the primeval givens was the condition for the emergence of an absolute myth, detached from idolatrous references. Just as in the workings of dreams, each narrative motive derives from an underlying process of displacement and condensation. Here everything is subject to an imperative which, being oriented by the search for a perfect coherence of the symbol, is at once eminently abstract and figurative (allegorical). Thanks to a metamorphosis of the meaning of the impure, what became concurrently possible was an unprecedented ethical conversion, a plenary apotheosis of liberty and personal responsibility against a permanent backdrop of absence.

At the conclusion of a cycle of history, the task of analysis may thus be to make explicit the unknown work of interpretation which gave birth to all mythical and religious expressions of the human epic, especially of Judaism and Christianity. For it is only when the primitive idea of God has itself been taken to the sepulchre that poetry, whose matrix coincides with the *poesis* of metaphor, can reach full emancipation. Retrospectively, the Christian text may then appear as the paradigm of every poetic text in which the metaphorical exhibition of the secret of our origins is prefigured.

The complete Epiphany of metaphor which furthers the still hidden unfolding of Judeo-Christianity will thus aim to extend the splendour of the word to cover nothingness. It will confer an ultimate meaning upon the idea of a creation *ex nihilo* (we know that Mallarmé spoke of his great project in terms of a "Spiritual Conception of Nothingness"). From this point of view again, the demonstration of the unity of meaning and of the sacred through the ever mysterious unfolding of metaphor does not lead to scepticism at all; it makes the marvel of the human (divine) genius of the word more remarkable. It reconciles atheism and faith, and reinscribes our confrontation with the night (our innate Orphic mystery) at the very heart of the human drama.

State University of New York at Buffalo

Translated with the help of Maureen Jameson.

DOMENICO A. CONCI AND ANGELA ALES BELLO

PHENOMENOLOGY AS THE SEMIOTICS OF ARCHAIC OR "DIFFERENT" LIFE EXPERIENCES – TOWARD AN ANALYSIS OF THE SACRED

A significant segment of the human sciences have in our century done valuable work in deepening our knowledge of expressions and ways of life different from those that characterize Western civilization and have sought to define autonomous research methods that guarantee the validity of their inquiries. Though the attempt is undoubtedly worth all of the effort put into it, these sciences are encountering obstacles and difficulties that derive from the very structure of Western culture, characterized as it is by tension between philosophy and the sciences, between the philosophic *logos* and the scientific *logos*. The human sciences therefore experience difficulty in finding their proper orientation within this opposition.

In this situation one is led to wonder whether the problematics we have just outlined do not drive us towards a work of inquiry and excavation that will make possible a global reexamination of the significance of the Western *logos* itself. Critical reviews of the history of Western culture have already been attempted in spates, by Nietzsche and Heidegger, notably, but practically all of these attempts have been made in a philosophical perspective, so that, all said and done, they have tended to remain within the bounds of Western culture itself. The problem could be tackled in a more valid manner by situating oneself on the terrain of a confrontation of cultures making it possible then to trace the characteristic structures of modes of expression of logics that differ from the logic of Western thought. In such a perspective, indeed, Western thought could be illumined—from "outside" as it were—and better understood.

Posed in this manner, the problem therefore requires us to

A-T. Tymieniecka (ed.), Analecta Husserliana XLIII, 101–123.
© 1994 *Kluwer Academic Publishers. Printed in the Netherlands.*

identify the level at which this type of inquiry should be carried out, and it is in this connection that—among all the instruments made available by our culture—we find a truly pertinent suggestion in the phenomenological analyses left us by Edmund Husserl. The inquiries of this philosopher, though they in many ways must be considered to be well integrated examples of the Western mentality and perspective (since he assigns a fundamental role to philosophical rationality, feeling himself to be heir to the great upheaval brought about by Greek speculation, within which, indeed, one has to seek the profound connotations of our civilization), offer us some starting points or hints of considerable interest for the purposes of the analysis of other cultures.

Already in the early thirties he had set himself the problem of the relationship between the *Western logos* and the world's other cultural expressions, stimulated to this end by the studies in the field of cultural anthropology carried out by Lévy-Bruhl, with whom he was in epistolary contact.[1] Though he shared the conviction of the French anthropologist that the 'primitives' "... have a logic of their own, a view of the world of their own," because "... such as is man, such also is his world, his science, his art, his God, etc.,"[2] the inquiry—at least as regards the significance of this logic, this view of the world—never went beyond a generic recognition that it formed a part of a tradition, a view of the world, of the mythico-religious type; rather, the most conspicuous result of the analysis was obtained in connection with the Western mentality: "We Europeans [tend to] construct a method of universal thought, on the basis of which we then remove from ourselves all the mythologico-religious apperceptions and elaborate a 'scientific consideration of the world, a sober and factual (*nüchtern sachlich*) way of inquiry' that abolishes all the national and generational idols and seeks and constructs a truth and an objective world."[3] This is the basis on which Western philosophic thought is delineated.

Nevertheless, Husserl's analyses contain some brief observations that are indicative of a special attention paid to the so-called primitive world, a case in point being the comments found in Ms. trans. E III 7, *Der Mensch im Schicksal. Religion und Wissenschaft* (20-25.1.1934): firstly, an apperception of the animist type that prevents any distinction between things and animals; secondly, a way of understanding causality, be it in a context of normality or in that of anomalies, that attributes it to spiritual agencies. In actual fact, however, these spiritual agencies have to be identified with a world of spirits or demons that have to be placated by means of prayers, offerings, gifts, and this both individually and collectively: it is in this way that one configures primitive religiousness and explains its omnipervasiveness.[4]

Taken by themselves, these observations are not extraordinary for anyone who has studied the "primitive" world: what is really striking is that a thinker like Husserl whose field of inquiry would seem to be far removed from these problematics and who had previously concerned himself with subtle questions of a logico-gnoseological nature, should at a certain point of his search feel the need for overstepping the confines of his culture—still considering it to be emblematic—in order to observe other world-views with respect and intellectual curiosity. But this is not the only aspect of interest to those desirous of undertaking an in-depth inquiry into the world of the so-called primitives. As we have already said above, the problem shifts to the cognitive instruments appropriate to such a research project, and it is here that Husserl's phenomenology can offer us some valid suggestions regarding a concrete method of inquiry.

These suggestions, moreover, are of primary importance, for they derive from some fundamental positions assumed by Husserl, positions that are characteristic of his perspective, including the need for a 'reduction,' one which leads to the highlighting of 'lived experiences,' and his insistence on a work of excavation, which he defines as 'archeological' and which consists of a Rückfrage, a regressive questioning that can lead one to explore regions that have long since become covered by cultural sedimentations.

All the same, one has to underscore—and this is the purpose of the present note—that it does not seem possible to crystallize phenomenological analysis as being *primordially* an *archeology of the lived experiences* of the signs of ancient and different cultures and to use nothing but this archeology in executing a phenomenology of the lived experiences of the signs of Western culture; or, at least, it does not seem possible using only the instruments of the static and genetic method offered us by orthodox (Husserlian) phenomenology.

Without calling into question the undoubted merits of classical phenomenology, and fully recognizing that the instruments it prepared were as refined and efficient as its analyses were rich and exemplary, it yet seems fated to do its work only on the "surface," for it barely scrapes the top of the ground in which the Western *logos* is embedded.

Husserl's phenomenology, working in the concrete soil of analysis, has ploughed and broken up the *humus* in which the tree of Western culture has sprouted and grown, and has carried out minute and perspicacious studies with the aim of reinvigorating its growth: but this has little or nothing to do with the "abyssal" surveys of a radical phenomenology that, as the archeology of basic lived experiences, penetrates into the "lower" strata of cultures that are distant in either time or space and does so without ideological or methodological ethnocentricity.

Certainly, a resolute attempt to turn Husserl's methods in a privileged analytical direction having a seemingly antiquarian or exotic flavor, as an end in itself, may at first sight seem excursive or even altogether gratuitous. But a more painstaking phenomenological evaluation of the results that can be obtained by means of an appropriate reform of Husserl's methodology brings out the fact, and very clearly so, that the last goal pursued by Husserl, namely, that of a 'real' understanding (*Verständnis*) of the lived experiences of the *logos*, cannot be attained without grasping and reanimating the lived experiences of 'different' *logoi*, especially those deposited in the signs of non-Western cultures or, in any case, cultures that have not been influenced by the Greek *logos*.

De re nostra agitur, therefore. The term 'nostra' here has to be understood as referring to both 'them' and 'us,' jointly assumed to be and understood univocally as 'animals' in possession of a highly complex and, above all, multivalent rational and cultural brain, the results of which are never readily predictable and cannot exhaust themselves in any one given cultural model that, no matter how pragmatically victorious that model may prove to be in relation to others, can be elevated to the level of metacultural significances and values

Radical phenomenology is therefore destined to face the tough trial of finding possible answers to both ancient and recent anthropological and epistemological enigmas: identifying the morphology of the Western *logos* and the other *logoi,* isolating the mechanisms of the genesis of these *logoi*—each in its concrete specificity—and the nature of the possible relations between them, reconsidering the lived sense of the evident, the true, and the objective, thematizing (using the new instruments of analysis) the sacral (magico-religious) dimensions, as well as the philosophic, artistic, and scientific dimensions (*the global nature of the signs of all cultures*), and, lastly, establishing by its own means a precise sense of identification that will involve both new and old methods and results in univocal theoretical and operational modalities.

Consequently, and especially in view of the tasks that have just been sketched in telegraphic fashion, this phenomenology cannot but reveal itself as a singular and universal form of semiotics, though always phenomenological semiotics, be it made clear, namely, *an analysis of the lived experiences that fill the signs of all the cultures.*[5] We are here concerned with cultural semiotics, because what is to be studied are the signs (understood very broadly) of man, but the nature of these semiotics is phenomenological, because what is studied are not the signs as they 'objectively' present themselves, but as they are phenomenologically reduced to the corresponding basic lived experiences that constitute their only possible genesis and signification. Here we come up against the technical note of Husserl's epoche, which undoubtedly constitutes one of the most complex and most criticized aspects of the classical phenomenological method.

Let it be said right away that the phenomenological tasks listed above go well beyond the possible reach of that method, so that some essential technical and sense connotations of the classical approach would have to be revised and appropriately reformulated. When we discussed the matter of phenomenological semiotics and said that this would have to be preceded by an epoche that would strike down and neutralize the residual *objective* valence of the manifestative starting level, thus making possible the subsequent definition of the reduced phenomenological terrain of the lived experiences and their 'essential lawfulness,' we used the term 'objective' in a very precise technical acceptance that is not the one usually to be found in Husserlian texts. And this, to be sure, is not by any means of marginal importance

The epoche, which Husserl reproposes in different forms and via different reductive paths (*Wege der Reduktion*) constitutes the focal moment of his research, the essential feature of his method. Indeed, he defines it as the *Urmethode der Phänomenologie* in Ms. trans. C 7 I:[6] "In the epoche I have consciousness of the world and the modified known world, and this even in the mode of abstention (*des Enthaltens*) from the life of the natural world and all its interests." In Ms. trans. B I 5 VII, again he writes as follows:

> What must one understand by universal epoche and what does one bring about by means of it? Our answer is: rather than exercising our activity continuously and specifically on the terrain of the passively given world at every moment of life, in particular and primarily by having active experience thereof, and rather than turning this experience with its credence of being—activated for this very purpose—into the basis of scientific judgements (...), we begin, quite consciously and quite universally, by depriving ourselves of this theoretical terrain.[7]

The terrain in question is the one on which there is constituted all objective theoretical and practical knowledge, i.e., the world of values and the positive sciences:

> Under the title 'pregiven world' and under the titles 'passive pre-experience' and 'active experience,' there is comprised the concrete intersubjective world and, just like doing and having human impulses, be they those of an individual or those of the community, so also all the objective operations, language, art, science, the state etc., belong to the dimension of experience of the world or to the horizon in which we have the world—as already given at any one particular moment—as the horizon of possible experience.[8]

What we have to do is to call into question the whole of tradition and, more particularly, the questions posed by this selfsame philosophical tradition, be they of a logical, structural, teleological, or esthetic type, or any other; this radicality does not leave "an empty void"[9] as long as there remains a potential of the conscious type, an ambit of consciousness. "A new interest has to be activated" as Husserl underscores in Ms. trans. C 7 I, "the interest in the universe of subjectivity, where the world has its sense of being for me and where, consequently, my selfsame human being attains its sense of being."[10]

In Husserl, therefore, the mundane (i.e., naturalistic) valence is made to coincide equivocally with the valence of the objective. However, this reading, quite apart from being far too reductive to grasp the sphere of the objective in all its breadth and in all the multiformity of its aspects, would seem to be phenomenologically unreliable and to remain untenable even if the mundane should be ambiguously dilated to the very limit, to the point of embracing also the sphere of the *eidetic* in the proper sense of the term,[11] including the altogether particular sense of the ontological region, 'consciousness,' which is the theme of a pure psychophenomenology that, in his eyes, is not yet an authentically transcendental phenomenology.

This particular underlying attitude inevitably determines both the nature and the function of the epoche, and all this ends up having repercussions—and, indeed, very substantial ones—on the general methodological approach of Husserl's phenomenology.

The Primacy of the Egological

Husserl's underlying and unexplored assumption is thus the privilege or the primacy or the egological, whose 'manifestative' valence hinges on the assumption and on the use—in an analytical sense—of the certainty of the Cartesian *cogito*, notwithstanding the fact that its original significance and use were, quite to the contrary, notoriously speculative and constructive.[12]

This is the most conspicuous result of the famous text of *Ideas Pertaining to a Pure Phenomenology*,[13] in which the polemical anti-Cartesian moment—the impossibility of a radical negation of the existence of the world—goes hand in hand with an acceptance of the subject as 'absolute,' given that notwithstanding this radical negation—subjectivity is and remains the pole and point of reference.

Just as the attention that Husserl pays to the genetic aspect of the questions leads him to examine the origin of the eidetic by means of the variation/invariance relationship, so also does it drive him to fractionate the absoluteness of the I in the intersubjective dimension, and this both in the static sense and in the genetic one. Two texts are highly indicative in this direction: an attempt at reduction to intersubjectivity already accomplished in 1914 in *Grundprobleme der Phänomenologie*,[14] and a description of the genesis of the subject that sees it—the I—emerge from a stage defined as *vor-ontisch* and *vor-weltlich* and *vor-reflexiv;* it is constituted *stufenweise,* step by step, moving from a sphere of primordial immanence to the sphere of intersubjectivity,[15] eventually attaining the reflective, transcendental dimension.

Having in this way delineated a transcendental subjective and intersubjective domain, to be understood as the primary spring of every intentionality constitutive of the senses of the world, Husserl conceives and erects a transcendental phenomenology as the singular analysis of the pure lived experiences of an originary I (*Ur-ich*), the ultimate residue that cannot be suspended in the aftermath of a definitive epoche that would have liquidated, once and for all, the ontology of the mundane, which per se is wholly devoid of autonomous sense

This gigantic undertaking, which probably constitutes—together with the neo-positivist attempt—the last great design of founding and justifying European rationality, was not to have a positive and conclusive outcome, not even in the analyses that Husserl made in his later years and to which we have drawn attention by citing the texts mentioned above.

Now, for the purposes of the future of phenomenology as a method of analysis, we feel that, especially in the context here considered, little or no weight attaches to any critical reflection that explores and explains Husserl's failure in this respect with the use of tools drawn from outside phenomenological technique itself. On the other hand, considerable interest attaches to the use of this selfsame phenomenological reflection, together with 'intuitive confrontation,' in order to grasp the intrinsic reasons for Husserl's failure, if any such exist, from within—as it were—his own methods.[16]

It is however quite obvious that this solution implies, de facto and right from the beginning, a particular analytical approach that, moving in a specific direction, namely, that of the identification of 'delusions' (i.e., 'deviations' with respect to the intuitive schema), will eventually arrive—always provided that the attempt prove successful—at a re-reading and a re-formulation of the phenomenological method.

Since one notes—on completing the analytical check—that Husserl's rich and laborious recordings coincide only to a limited extent with the horizon of presence (as rigidly assumed) and, further, realizes that these deviations, far from being occasional, reveal themselves to be recurring and regular as one continues the confrontation, one will have to suppose, first of all, the existence of 'impurities' in Husserl's erstwhile vision, his starting point, quite apart from the methodological defects of the instruments fabricated and used for the proposed development of his phenomenological analyses.

In this sense, therefore, one cannot but conclude that Husserl, even though he had formulated the important *principle of all principles* of phenomenological methodology, according to which "every vision that originarily presents itself is a legitimate source of knowledge, that everything that gives itself originarily in the intuition (in flesh and blood as it were) is to be assumed as it gives itself, but also and only within the limits in which it gives itself," he did not subsequently follow it in a rigorous manner, thereby greatly reducing the magnitude of the task that he had set for himself.

When this principle is assumed in a proper and rigorous manner, without dilution or translation, the project is so overwhelming on the methodological level as to be of itself sufficient reason to convert phenomenological analysis into an archeology of lived experiences. Indeed, it could not be otherwise.

There can be no doubt that the exceptional importance of this 'principle' for every authentically phenomenological method, that is to say, for every analysis of which the appeal to intuition is not just speculative coquetry of the old-fashioned type, appears much reduced in Husserl's version,[18] which is generic and laconic in formulation, wholly devoid of adequate further theoretical investigation and without the functional and operative details that would be necessary for a correct understanding and proper application of the 'principle' itself.[19]

Nevertheless, even this 'principle,' which obliges one to remain in keeping with the intuition and everything that is given by it, is nothing other than the phenomenological recording—in a live broadcast as it were—of a corresponding authentic *Selbstgebung*, which calls for a complete and adequate *Erfüllung*. The supreme principle of phenomenological analysis cannot come into being or assume a heteronomous collocation outside this analysis, but—self-aligning itself as it were—cannot but offer itself as an integral phenomenological presence (both in 'content' and in form)[20] We are thus inevitably brought back to the point from which we started.

All said and done, therefore, Husserl does not 'see properly' right from the beginning, this in the sense that even his first analytical explorations record fields of presence in which even what is not phenomenological is assumed to be such. His great 'principle' is therefore disregarded as far as the level of application is concerned, and it seems that Husserl does not succeed in grasping it adequately, that is to say, complete with the lived *Erfüllung* that corresponds to it: Husserl enounces the principle, but does not seem to 'see it' in flesh and blood (*leibhaft*). In other words, he does not seem to see it as the *Selbstgebung* of specific lived experiences, the very experiences that have generated it as such and confer phenomenological sense upon it.

What then, is the meaning of this partial 'blindness' that we lament in Husserl's phenomenological analyses, and how can one explain it?

No matter how one may understand phenomenology, its origin and sense are certainly consigned, in a manner that is both definitive and indubitable, to the methodology developed by Husserl. No analytical phenomenology of any kind would have been possible without this methodology. Nevertheless, there can be no doubt (and we already had to note this in connection with the necessary phenomenological *Erfüllung*, the only thing that can confer genesis and significance to any enunciation of phenomenology and even to the selfsame *principle of all principles* of phenomenology) that the first movements of a phenomenological analysis and even the instrument of the epoche—which places in parentheses or suspends everything that is destined to be suspended inasmuch as it is extraphenomenological—are possible and comprehensible solely on the one condition that they take place and run their course by faithfully recording a field of offering grasped and assumed in a direct and therefore intuitive manner.[21]

Consequently, the first phenomenological gesture, that of suspension, putting into parentheses, is not a mere 'act of the will,' as Husserl insistently underscores by using the expression *"ich will,"*[22] nor does it come about blindly, but is rather a way of obeying and unbarring the course of the vectors of the further revelation of the horizon of presence along the specific directions induced and imposed by the allusiveness of the horizon itself.

As we have already said, there are good reasons (and by this we mean phenomenological reasons) for concluding that the horizon of presence that motivates and guides Husserl right from the moment of taking his first steps is authentically phenomenological only to a greatly reduced extent.[23]

In the last resort, Husserl seems to have assumed more than what he sees or, if you prefer, affirms to have seen even what— rigorously speaking—can never come to manifest itself as an authentic phenomenological presence. The first and immediate consequence of this 'visual deficiency' is provided by the distinction—which in Husserl is indeed only barely perspicuous—between the sphere of what 'can be suspended' and the sphere of what 'cannot be suspended,' the latter being also known as the 'phenomenological residue.' In this way there is only a partial and rather approximate individuation of the dimension of *objectivation,* which Husserl, in the absence of a true phenomenology of the Greek or Western *logos* underlying the objectivist makeup of the elementary lived experiences and their reduction to the passive condition, always confuses with the sphere of the 'mundane' or the 'natural.' Consequently, an epoche that affects only the mundane outcome of the objectivation, broad or narrow as it may be, can yield as a residue nothing but the other pole of the objectivation, namely, the pole of the ego.

Now, neither the pole of the world, understood as the universe of things, even though reduced to 'noemata,' nor the egological pole or pole of the egos, even though it be understood as pure intentionality, are, or can ever be authentic phenomenological presences, that is to say, true *Selbstgegebenheiten.*

The *ego-centered* lived experiences isolated by Husserl cannot, therefore, attain to the standing of authentic phenomenological experiences in which the very interplay of the noetico-egological intentionalities that constitute the world 'reduced' to noemata cannot succeed in manifesting itself fully in the field of presence (*complex lived experiences*).[24]

The egological makeup of noesis and the speculative primacy of the I would thus seem to have induced Husserl, faced with the two real components of elementary lived experience, *noesis and hyle,* to privilege the intentional component, noesis, that is, and to give undue preference to noetic and functional analyses at the expense of hyletic and non-intentional analyses, which Husserl wrongly considered to be of inferior rank; he thereby performed a grave amputation and deprived the phenomenological *corpus* of an important organ.[25] In our opinion, therefore, the future of phenomenology will depend to a large extent on the redeeming of the egological mortgage that Husserl took out on 'noesis'—a redemption that will automatically suppress the merely egological precipitate that is the 'noema'—and on the internal rebalancing of the relationships between *noesis* and *hyle* in the morphology of the *Erlebnis,* thereby making a resolute start with a hyletic phenomenology in the true sense of the term that will no longer have anything to do with *new transcendental esthetics.*

The analysis of the relationship between the noetic moment and the hyletic moment, moving from perception, which Husserl deemed to be the foundation and the starting point of the cognitive process, prompted him on several occasions in the course of his inquiries to reflect *ex novo* about the problem that Kant had tackled in his transcendental esthetics. In particular, Ms. trans. D 2 (dated 2 August 1933) is dedicated to this theme. Husserl makes a distinction between transcendental esthetics in the wider sense as a doctrine of perception (*Wahrnehmungslehre*) and esthetics in the narrower sense, namely, the esthetics of nature. In this way he faces up to the problems of movement, of kinesthesis, of action in relation to living bodies (*Leiber*) and physical things. Nature becomes a specific theme, because it is characterized by extracorporeity (*Aussenkörperlichkeit*) and a constancy of configuration at the level of the *Wahrnehmung*. This is a constant and recurring motive in Husserl's analysis and aims at identifying the origin of the man-nature distinction, which he traces back to the fact that it possesses a *Kern*, a knowable core with ever constant characteristics that connotate the objects of nature. The objects of culture, on the other hand, can be grasped by means of an apperception that varies according to the particular historical and social context.[26] Here we are undoubtedly concerned with an empiricist residue that acts in Husserl's position, bearing witness to a dualism that, in its turn, can be referred to a particular vision of the world: the Western view.

Toward a Hyletic Phenomenology

The new transcendental esthetics proposed by Husserl, notwithstanding the introduction of an apperceptive moment claimed to be capable of explaining cultural transformations, do not succeed in grasping the differences of the cultural perspectives precisely with respect to nature. We do not here wish to repropose in all its detail the obscure theme of nature and that of the function of the *hyle* within the *complex Erlebnis* as they were conceived by Husserl and then inherited by the phenomenological school, which experienced considerable difficulty in interpreting them.[27]

The *hyle*, understood as the material substrate (*stoffliche Unterlage*) of an *Erlebnis*, of which the noesis in Husserl's analysis becomes equivocably confused with the I, is also assumed to be an 'egologic possession' (*Ichzuhabenheit*) and yet to be *Ichfremde*, i.e., to be extraneous to the I which 'comes up against it' and which, by means of the animation conferred upon the *hyle*, transforms this hyle into something other than what—phenomenologically speaking —it really is, that is to say, into a plexus of *Abschattungen*, adumbrations, qualities, determinations of 'things' that have been noematically assumed. "Rückfragend kommen wir auf die hyletische Sphäre; als das letzte Nicht-Ichliche. Aber vorher naturlich Rückfrage von dem vollen Weltphänomen und seiner ontischen Auslegung auf den passiven Kern der Welt, auf die 'blosse' Natur."[28] In these few lines of Ms. C 3 VI we have a compendium of Husserl's position with respect to the hyletic sphere, understood as the non-I, and the link with nature, understood as the passive core of the world. In this way, and as a direct consequence of the egological makeup of the noesis and therefore also of the entire *Erlebnis,* Husserl's 'experiential' reading reduces the *hyle* "...into a hybrid being that is refused by consciousness and cannot form part of the world."[29]

Nevertheless, it is a far more serious matter—at least in our opinion—that in Husserl the *hyle* does not play any specifically phenomenological part either within the elementary *Erlebnis* or within the ambit of phenomenology in general. Indeed, if phenomenology—in conformity with Husserl's canon—is to be understood as an analysis based on *intuition* or even on the *evidence* of lived experiences assumed just as they give themselves and within the limits in which they so give themselves, both phenomenological appearance and apprehension of these experiences reveal themselves to be authentic enigmas for classical phenomenology, which takes to be (phenomenologically relevant) *elementary Erlebnisse* what are really *complex Erlebnisse.* How can an egological *Erlebnis* be subjected to a true analysis of any kind whatsoever? What sense is there in using such terms as 'manifestation' and 'appearance' in relation to *Erlebnisse* that are lived by an I?

Frege, though in a different analytical context, has pointed out somewhat summarily that a thing can be seen, a representation can be had, a thought can be conceived, that is to say, it can be thought. This evidently means that while things are 'seen' and not 'had,' *egological Erlebnisse* (as acts of an I that perceives, that remembers, that waits, that expects, that imagines, that phantasizes, that identifies, that distinguishes, that believes, that supposes, that values, that has dispositions (*Gefühle*), that has feelings (*Stimmungen*), that wants (*Willen,* etc.) are 'had' and not 'seen.'[30]

And yet phenomenological experience attests to us that the

elementary lived experiences appear, manifest themselves, constitute authentic *Selbstgegebenheiten*, presences 'in flesh and blood,' and phenomenological analysis, which claims to remain firmly anchored to the ground of intuition and even evidence, exists and has sense precisely as a faithful recording of these manifestations—in which it 'becomes annulled'—and not as an improper, metaphorical or translated expression thereof.

The dynamics of their appearance and the element that induces them to manifest themselves come to be totally occluded when the *Erlebnisse* are egologically set up, because this way of reading, which records the hyletic valence in an experiential manner, hides the general function they perform within the *Erlebnis*, i.e., the function of being the *sole and exclusive source of visualization of themselves* and of the entire *non-egological Erlebnis* (*elementary Erlebnis*). The *Erlebnis* can only manifest itself through the *hyle* that it contains as its own real component. There is no *Erlebnis* that, as such, could be devoid of *hyle*. It therefore follows that a future 'noetic' and 'functional' phenomenology, a phenomenology no longer transcribed in the terms of Husserl's egological reading, will bring to the fore a noesis of which the primary function is precisely that of being the plurimodal center of 'activity' and 'affectivity,' thereby connotating whatever manifests itself phenomenologically as lived experience as such, but without in any way implying the egological and personal valence of that experience.

Thus, if the hyle induces the manifestation of both itself and the noesis i.e., the entire *Erlebnis*, the noesis 'animates' and bestows 'intention' on both the hyle and itself and thus 'apprehends' the entire *Erlebnis* as such. The *phenomenological apprehension* of the lived experiences that manifest themselves thanks to the hyle has to be performed by the general function of the noesis of the lived experience, which, by means of self-reference, grasps both itself and therefore also the entire *Erlebnis* for identification purposes, so that the *Erlebnis* is always learnt as it gives itself and in the limits within which it so gives itself.

Only a reform capable of laying bare from below the structural concretions of the Greek *logos*, the elementary *Erlebnis* as lived experience that manifests itself in flesh and blood (*leibhaft*), anonymous and impersonal, will confer sense and value upon a truly hyletic phenomenology that is almost wholly absent in classical phenomenology.

If we now turn, at least provisionally, to neurophysiology with a view to identifying—before we practice the *epoché* of our own body (*Leib*)—the sources of the hyletic materials that constitute the real and non-intentional component of the *Erlebnis*, we come up against three types of receptors, i.e., tissues or organs specialized in specific responses to forms of energy: the esteroceptors, the enteroceptors, and the proprioceptors.

The esteroceptors are receptors stimulated by events in the so-called 'external environment' (eye, nose, tongue, ear, skin). The enteroceptors are situated in the viscera (internal organs) and are stimulated by variations of the internal state (kinesthetic data, general sensations of the health or illness of one's own body) (*Empfindnisse*).

Lastly, the proprioceptors are receptors stimulated by variations of the *corporeal locomotor system,* cases in point being the semi-circular canals (movements and positions of the head), the muscles (pulling), the tendons (tension and pulling), and the joints (pulling and pressure). These constitute the very complex and impressive sphere of the kinesthesis that gives us a sense of balance and a notion of the position and the movement of the body in space.

If we now objectively exclude the valence of our own body (*Leib*) and the neurophysiology associated with it, the phenomenological residue is constituted by the general plexus of the hyletic data as the 'material' of a lived experience of which the noesis—be it clear—is impersonal in the sense recalled above. The phenomenological examination of this plexus shows that there are quite a few surprises in store for us.

First of all, it is difficult to collocate the sediments of the kinesthesis within the general hyletic sphere without thereby creating problems. This sphere, in fact, appears to be characterized—at least for our present purposes—by the connotation of 'passivity' in a very precise phenomenological sense: *it is wholly devoid of any autonomous intentionality.*

In this sense, however, such a connotation is fully satisfied by the data deposited by the esteroceptors and the enteroceptors, which have to be included in the hyletic ambit in the true sense of the term. The data of kinesthesis, on the other hand, are not wholly passive sediments. Husserl—in Ms. trans. D 10 I, a little-known manuscript—had already refused, and not by any means without reason, to consider kinesthesis simply as a particular kind of the wider category *hyle:*

> Are the kinestheses really nothing but a particular species of the wider category *hyle*? And what about the specific I-ness of affectivity and activity? Myths of the beginnings: confused unity of a total hyle, not separate per se, confused affection of the totality; permanent turn (*Zuwendung*) in the direction of a wide-awake attitude, permanent mutation in the mutation of the delineation, the coincidence and the formation of unity and multiplicity, of showing up and disappearing; intervention of the separation: the groups of the *hyle*—in the strict sense—attract our interest, touch our sentiments in an extraordinary manner, in disappearing they excite desire, instinctive trends, having provoked instinctive action, they course in the kinesthesis together with the *hyle*, in its mutation, in a continuous appearing and disappearing. Hence in this process: as the same unities return (there present themselves) provisionally the same kinestheses, something ever new for a new *hyle* and for kinestheses that course with it, the intention turned to the corresponding hyletic unities takes the form of the intention turned to the kinestheses to achieve the contemporary entry of the *hyle*, particularly to bring to completion the hyletic changes that lead to the unities 'themselves.' In the hyletic changes of the unities we have the formation of optimal moments, towards which the kinesthetic intention (to be understood) as means therefore comes to a halt. The kinesthetic changes, inasmuch as they are immediately egological, must be guided, the others are mediated through them, as their consequence.[31]

But recognition of the dynamic value of the kinesthetic data equivocably drives Husserl to attribute these data to the sphere of egological activities in the proper sense of the term.

On the other hand, if—in following the thread of the proposed phenomenological reform—we take due account in our kinesthetic analysis of the general active and affective function of the impersonal noesis, which must necessarily be called into play if any dynamism is to be understood, there will come be revealed the wholly particular nature of the kinesthetic sphere, whose data are *dynamic* because they record the fundamental conditions of the motility of the body as *Leib* (living body). Inasmuch as they are data, they undoubtedly form part of the sphere of the *hyle* in the proper sense of the term, but inasmuch as they are dynamic valences, they reveal a specific and elementary noetic component of 'constitution' and not of 'animation' from outside—which is the general one that the noesis transmits to every *hyle*.

A further specific contribution of a reformed phenomenology is thus that of the discovery of kinestheses as hybrid presences that are noetic and hyletic at one and the same time and, consequently, their discovery as a functional link, a bridge between the two 'real' components of the *noesis* and *hyle,* the intentional and the 'material.' Here the *Erlebnis* reveals—in the kinesthetic *hyle* above all— a true core (*Kern* of the lived experience), a 'heart' that seems to preside over the continuous exchanges between *noesis* and *hyle* and vice versa, that thereby guarantees the organic consistency of the *Erlebnis* itself. But, if we now add to the singular dynamics of this core (which is constituted, as we have said, of the kinesthetic *hyle*) specific dynamics of *noesis* also, one will have to attribute to the *elementary Erlebnis*—and conclusively so—a prevalent connotation of action, of movement that classical phenomenology only barely glimpsed. As Husserl notes in Ms. trans. D 10 I,

> The system of the kinestheses is not previously constituted, but its constitution is realized together with the constitution of the hyletic objects at which this system is aimed from time to time and for which the kinesthetic situations as unity are—according to the possibilities— the 'means,' the 'premise' and also the 'conclusions.' Through the availability of the complexes of the kinestheses every time they form, or, rather, through any formation of the complexes and the transformation of the complexes (that have become constituted as immediate availabilities), there becomes possible the mediated availability of hyletic objects.[32]

As far as the rest-motion relationship is concerned, Husserl thus affirms that: "The individual kinesthetic system, together with the unitary field that belongs to it, originarily makes possible the constitution of appearance modes of the identical, and precisely in the form of 'rest,' which comes first and, as already said, is not a mode of motion and is constitutive of corporeity."[33]

> The constitution of movement (motion) becomes sufficiently compre-
> hensible on the basis of the previously experienced modes of kines-
> thetic succession—though one must also bear in mind what this 'being
> comprehensible' presupposes. ...Movement presupposes a transfor-
> mation in the transformability of the relationships of the kinestheses,
> of the 'absolute nearness,' of how it belongs to the first, originary
> rest. Every thing that appears at rest has its stable place in the field,
> to each thing belongs a change of kinesthetic place that belongs to it.[34]

All this makes it possible to analyze the formation of the space
that is linked with the proprioceptors, especially the organs of the
tactile sense. Nevertheless, Husserl never takes the decisive step,
namely, that of considering the elementary *Erlebnis* as an *Erlebnis*
of action. The substantial dynamic component discovered by the
phenomenology of the elementary *Erlebnis* makes it possible to
explain why the myths are eminently ritually re-activated (sacral) *events of action*.

Conclusion
The first methodological steps needed on the way to an analytical
phenomenology—to be understood as an archeology of elementary
lived experiences—can therefore be summarized as follows:

1) Scrupulous fidelity to the dictates of the *principle of all
principles* of Husserlian phenomenology. This fidelity requires one
never to abandon the terrain of intuition and evidence (though this
terrain has become wholly impracticable in Western culture), so
much so as to consider these valences in conformity with Husserl's
will—as comprehensible and possible *only on the basis of phenomenology* and *not before it.*

2) Radical reform of Husserl's noetic analysis, since the
egological transcribing of the noetic moment has rendered the
noesis itself phenomenologically invisible and has unbalanced its
relationship with the *hyle.*

3) Elaboration of a new hyletic analysis to take its place beside
noetic analysis in perfect doctrinal equilibrium.

4) A morphological and connective phenomenology of *elemen-*

tary lived experiences—which have laws that are not those imposed by the Greek/Western *logos*.

This decisive turning point impressed upon phenomenology by the necessary revision of Husserl's analysis, *which yet remains the indispensable starting point and point of reference of the operation,* involves—as we have seen—the reform of a number of key concepts and even of the traditional lexicon of phenomenology. Thus, it is quite evident that the phenomenological residue of a radical epoche is constituted by a true 'cultural continent'—the dominant expression of man's life on the planet and of longer duration than any other—where the elementary lived experiences reveal a morphology and a lawfulness of connection which go beyond those already visualized by classical analysis, which has confined itself to complex Western experiences.

If we have nevertheless continued to use the lexicon handed down to us by Husserl and his school, this is not only because we want to facilitate comprehension and stress an underlying continuity, but also because, as is well known, the significance of a phenomenological formulation is a function of the faithful noetic recording of *Anschauungen* and of nothing else. All the same, we have to confess that, as progress is made and the volume of analysis continues to grow, such terms as 'categorial,' 'precategorial,' 'predicative,' 'antepredicative,' 'objective,' 'natural,' 'mundane,' etc., run the risk of becoming approximate and even equivocal, especially for those who are making their first approaches to phenomenology.

Likewise, the radical suspension blotting out the entire Greek/Western *logos* and all its consequences rather than just a partial aspect, a particular consequence thereof (in the case of Husserl, the naturalistic and mundane attitude), is and remains an epoche borrowed from Husserl's analysis.

Moreover, there can be no doubt that the Greek *logos* and objectivation constitute a single whole, but the term 'objectivation'—which we have used very freely and whose sense ambit is not that of truth and evidence—inevitably evokes the other pole of the pair, namely, the subject, which in the new phenomenology is integrally involved in the suspension.

A phenomenology of the structure of the Greek *logos* has thus clearly brought out the bipolar nature of this *logos*, where the functional relationship between the invariant pole and the level of the (metamorphico-individual) variations constitutes a cultural modality for setting up the lived experiences, experiences that are so *complex* that nothing similar is known among the other cultures of our planet. Undoubtedly, therefore, we can continue to describe this *logos* as precategorial and to apply the term 'precategorial' also to the residue after its definitive suspension. At least, that is what we have done.

But it is quite evident that in our case the use of these terms bends them to the point of their signifying two different cultural continents: the categorial thus no longer has anything to do with 'judgment,' 'predication,' 'higher level objectivity,' and the like, just as the precategorial has nothing to do with 'experience,' 'the antepredicative,' 'doxa,' 'praxis,' 'the life-world.'

Nevertheless, this singular and "lazy" lexical (and perhaps more than just lexical) fidelity to Husserl has an altogether particular and profound significance for us. The new phenomenology has isolated—for the very first time—the structure of the Greek *logos*, the hidden spring of Western *objectivation*, and has sent it off the playing field, as it were, to uncover beneath the complex lived experiences of this *logos* the elementary lived experiences of different and ancient *logoi*, where rationality does not express itself in scientific theories, but in myths, in magic, in religions, and this to an extent that is so all-pervasive and dominant as to have become incomprehensible for us Westerners. Husserl's indefatigable analyses have glimpsed all this, though often as if they were recording the outlines of images out of focus or otherwise deformed, and have thus laid the methodological foundations for further phenomenological insights.

University of Siena/Arezzo
Lateran University

NOTES

1. Particularly noteworthy is Husserl's letter to Lévy-Bruhl dated 11 March 1935.
2. Ms. trans. A VII 9, *Horizont*, 1933, p. 25.
3. Ms. trans. A VII 31, *Struktur der Erfahrung—Episteme und Doxa—Bekanntheit und Fremde*, 9 April 1934, p. 5.
4. Ms. trans. E III 7, *Der Mensch im Schicksal, Religion und Wissenschaft*, 1934, pp. 1-2.
5. Cfr. D.A. Conci, "Introduzione ad una epistemologia non fondante," *Epistemologia* V (Genoa: 1982), p. 18.
6. Ms. trans. C 7 I, *Von der Epoche aus eine Reduktion auf das primordiale Sein des Ego als urtümliches Strömen*, June–July 1932, p. 29.
7. Ms. trans. B I 5 VII, *Sinn und Funktion der Epoche*, 1930, p. 7.
8. *Ibid.*, pp. 10-11.
9. *Ibid.*, p. 12.
10. Ms. trans. C 7 I, *op. cit.*, p. 29.
11. Ms. trans. A VII 13, *Vorgegebenheit—Wissenschaft*, 1921, 1928, 1930.
12. Cfr. D.A. Conci, *Prolegomeni ad una fenomenologia del profondo* (Rome: 1970), pp. 270 *et seq.*
13. E. Husserl, *Ideen zu einer reinen Phänomenologie und phänomenologischen Philosophie, Allgemeine Einführung in die reine Phänomenologie*, Vol. I, Husserliana III (The Hague: 1950), par. 50.
14. *Grundprobleme der Phänomenologie*, in *Zur Phänomenologie der Intersubjektivität*, Husserliana XIII (The Hague).
15. Ms. trans. A VII 12, *Apperzeption—Probleme der Weltanschauung*, pp. 29-30.
16. Cfr. D.A. Conci, *La conclusione della filosofia categoriale. Per una fenomenologia del metodo fenomenologico* (Rome: 1967).
17. E. Husserl, *Ideen zu einer reinen Phänomenologie...*, *op. cit.*, Vol. I (Italian translation) (Rome: 1960), pp. 50-51.
18. "...every vision originarily presenting itself is a legitimate source of knowledge (...), everything that is originarily given in the intuition (in flesh and blood, as it were) is to be assumed as it is given, but also only within the limits in which it so gives itself. It is clear that any theory can draw its truth only from its originary data. Therefore (...) every affirmation that limits itself to expressing these data, explicating them with terms that are significatively in keeping therewith, effectively constitutes an absolute beginning, a *principium* in the genuine sense of foundation." *Ibid.*, pp. 50-51.
19. Cfr. D.A. Conci, "Per una fenomenologia dell'originario," *Il Contributo* II, no. 2 (Rome: 1978), pp. 3-12.
20. *Ibid.*, p. 11.
21. See, for example, E. Husserl, *Phantasie, Bildbewußtsein, Erinnerung 1898-1925. Zur Phänomenologie der anschaulichen Vergegenwärtigung*, Husserliana (The Hague: 1980), p. 3.
22. Ms. trans. C 7 I, *op. cit.*, p. 29.
23. Cfr. D.A. Conci, *Prolegomeni...*, *op. cit.*, pp. 12 *et seq.*

24. Unlike the *elementary Erlebnis*, the complex *Erlebnis* is the one structured by the Greek/Western *logos*.
25. ...a discipline of lower rank "far below noetic and functional phenomenology" (*Ideen, op. cit.*, p. 125).
26. Ms. trans. A V 19, *Doxische Aktivität und praktische Aktivität*, May 1932.
27. As regards the general thematics of the *hyle* and the problems partly connected with it (precategorial perception of the thing, *Leib, Einfühlung*, etc.) that are to be found in little-known Husserlian texts, see *Philosophie der Arithmetik. Psychlogische und logische Untersuchungen* (Halle a.d.S.: 1891), p. 71 and elsewhere; *Logische Untersuchungen*, Vol. II, Part II (Halle a.d.S.: 1922), par. 58, p. 180; *Ding und Raum Vorlesungen*, 1907, Husserliana XVI (The Hague: 1973), pp. 42-60; *Ideen*, Vol. I, *op. cit.*, pp. 79-81, pp. 207-216, pp. 241-245; *Zur Phänomenologie der Intersubjektivität*, Husserliana XIII–XV (The Hague: 1973), Vol. I, pp. 55-61; Vol. II, pp. 378-391, Beilagen XLVIII LV, pp. 461-467; Vol. III, Beilagen XXXVI-XXXVIII; *Analysen zur passiven Synthesis*, Husserliana XI (The Hague: 1966), pp. 3-24, pp. 65-116; *Formale und transzendentale Logik. Versuch einer Kritik der logischen Vernunft* (Halle a.d.S.: 1929), pp. 185-188. As regards the reform of Husserl's *Erlebnis*, see also "Il tempo e l'originario. Un dibattito fenomenologico tra A. Ales Bello e D.A. Conci," *Il Contributo* no. 5-6, (Rome: 1978), pp. 5-13.
28. Ms. trans. C 3 VI, *Rückfrage zur Hyle. Hyletische Urströmung und Zeitung*, 17 October 1931.
29. J.P. Sartre, *L'essere e il nulla*, trans. G. Del Bo (Milan: 1958), pp. 24-25.
30. G. Frege, "Der Gedanke. Eine logische Untersuchung," *Beiträge zur Philosophie des deutschen Idealismus* 1 (1918-1919); now also in *Logische Untersuchungen* (Göttingen: 1966), p. 44, note 5.
31. Ms. trans. D 10 I, *Zur Konstitution der physischen Natur. Zuerst Leib-Aussendung; dann rückführend auf Hyle und Kinästhese*, May 1932, pp. 20-21.
32. *Ibid*, pp. 22-23.
33. Ms. trans. D 18, *Notizen zur Raumkonstitution*, 10 May 1934, p. 14.
34. *Ibid.*, pp. 18 *et seq.*

PART THREE

THE ALLEGORY OF THE SACRED

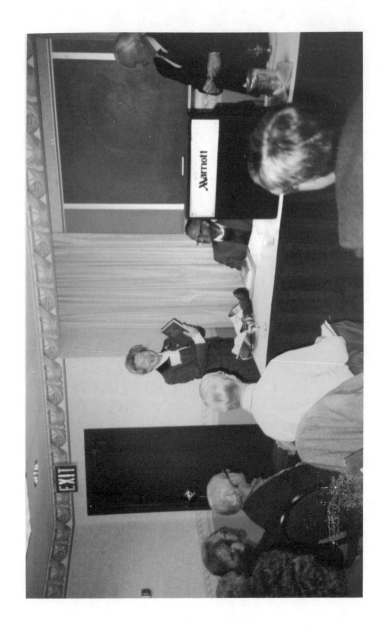

Anna-Teresa Tymieniecka showing the book dedicated to her which Marlies Kronegger presented her during the session on the Sacred at the 1990 American Philosophical Association annual convention. (J. N. Mohanty and George Williams look on.)

MARLIES E. KRONEGGER

ALLEGORICAL VOYAGES: LOUIS XIII
AND THE SACRED

Cet air, que je ne sçay quoy,
Qui fait vivre les images;
Et qui rend dignes d'un Roy,
Les moindres de ses ouvrages:
Cet air qui trompe les sens,
A des charmes si puissans,
Dans tout ce que fait cet homme,
Qu'on peut dire sans trop flatter,
Dire qu'Athenes & Rome,
Auroient voulu l'imiter.

"Toute l'oeuvre de Callot", Scudéry. *Le Cabinet* I, 1646, p. 159.

INTRODUCTION: PROFANE REALITY AND
SACRED ALLEGORY (1628–35)

Three major characteristics of Baroque aesthetics relate to allegory: metamorphosis, exuberance, and the inducement of vertiginous spaces. The disparity between the real and imaginary voyages of Louis XIII is small when the creative imagination of the author or the artist seeks to transcend the profane reality of which it is the touchstone. The word allegory derives from the Greek "alleon," meaning "other" or "different." Spiritual or allegorical truth transforms and regenerates the literal or historic sense of an event.

The allegories of poets, engravers, painters and composers, in particular those of Jacques Callot, Rubens and Louis XIII, often teach an atemporal lesson that is both cosmological and moral. As a sensuous reflection of the sacred, allegory is ambiguous according to the way one looks at the transfiguration of the hero or at the destruction of the enemy, at the ecstasy of the saint or even at the illumination, rapture or trance of the individual. Allegory reveals this paradoxical communion of being and non-being, of the absolute and the relative, of the eternal and the transient. Baroque allegory shows us how the immediate reality of the human transmutes itself in contact with supernatural reality.

127

A-T. Tymieniecka (ed.), Analecta Husserliana XLIII, 127–148.
© 1994 *Kluwer Academic Publishers. Printed in the Netherlands.*

The eruption of the sacred is the foundation of baroque allegory. It opens itself toward the transcendent and the transhistoric by a breakthrough of the sacred in artistic creations at the time of Louis XIII.

When the sacred manifests itself in an allegory based on religious history, myth, or a political event, a new dimension of absolute reality that transcends this world reveals itself.[1] The sacred manifests itself in a multitude of forms, in engravings, painting, music, and dance, and we will discuss those that make us discover a reality that does not belong to our natural, profane world.

We will note the extent to which the role of the artist, the musician and the poet is not only to elucidate the enigmas of history, but also to capture the invisible in the most manifest traces left by time. Thus, in the works of Piranese, it is not the memory of Caesar's achievements that evokes the grandeur of Rome, but a crumbling vault of a ruin, a reminder of Rome's glorious past. Such ruins designate that political and artistic body of Caesar which, unlike his physical remains, does not die. Similarly, Louis XIII, still in his minority, displayed publicly that the fullness of his sovereign majesty did not depend upon the perfection of the funeral rites in his honor. The king, sacred center of his court, nation and country, becomes the object of a cult which destroys the fundamental distinction between his person and his dignity.

Allegorical evocations of Louis XIII are expressed in a universal language, because they are adapted to the celebration of events that concern the people as much as the sovereign. Furthermore, a royal marriage, a peace treaty, an official "entrée" into a city, a tournament, or a victory unite in the same allegorical festivity and jubilation two or more nations. The ceremonial of Louis XIII, after all, is also a state ritual whose efficiency is assured by the multiplicity of allegories admired in fireworks as well as through painted, engraved, danced or sung allegories. No one sings alone. Even the stars and the angels in the sky sing in unison. And to praise the king is to praise God: Praise is the greatest motivator of artistic creation. It is the voice of the human condition. Praise as much as gratitude is the theme that comprises all allegories that glorify the king. These allegories signify the double nature of this king, who is corruptible because of his *humanitas*, but immortal because of his *dignitas*. We will see how allegory holds an important place: Through allusions, the engraver creates works of immediate relevance.

He is equally inspired by peace (universal harmony) or war (the miseries of war), by the victories over external enemies – against Protestants at Breda, Ré and La Rochelle, or by the splendors of inner strength in faith's resistance to evil (*The Temptation of Saint Anthony*).

I. TRIUMPHS OF LOUIS XIII; EXPANSION OF TERRITORY IN
IMAGINARY AND POLITICAL SPACES

1. *Rubens:* Marie de Médicis's Acceptance of the Regency
(March 1610)

When Rubens creates interferences between the imaginary and the real, he opens the door to infinite possibilities of putting into motion several temporal modes at once, in all directions (the present, the mythical past, the historical past, and the future), in several settings, and through several actions. (Copies of the works discussed follow the article.) The divine ascension of Louis XIII brings to light the sacred dimension of the prince. *Marie de Médicis's Acceptance of the Regency* presents us with a historical fact: Henry IV will soon leave, to make war in Germany against the aspirations of the Hapsburgs. In March of 1610, he turns the regency over to his spouse, Marie de Médicis, at the Luxembourg palace. The sovereign hands his wife the seal of power in the form of a globe strewn with fleur-de-lys, the symbol of celestial purity and French royalty. The globe in her hand represents the territory upon which her totalitarian authority will exert itself. The dauphin, who was eight years old at the time, and destined to reign, looks toward his mother who holds his hand. The aerial perspective opens up the horizon, suggesting that the king in his majority will also have total jurisdiction in his absolute power. The ram below the balcony in the middle of the portal ensures the renewal of the vital cycle of human life and of the seasons. The presence of the harnessed soldiers indicates their promise of loyalty in battle. On the right of the painting are two women, one of whom is Rubens's wife, his indispensable model, while the other represents Prudence, an allegorical figure, whose virtue is essential to the proper exercise of sovereignty.

2. *Mythological and Religious Elements of the Marvelous –*
Sea Voyages and the Search for Peace and a Spiritual Center

Rubens: The Majority of Louis XIII *(October 16, 1614)*

With a child's innocent soul, Louis XIII appears to escape the human
condition and contemplate the future on a stormy sea, in the ship of state-
craft which his mother, Marie de Médicis, had steered to safe ports
until she turned her power over to her son. This craft, in which sails
the allegorical figure of France, is guided by the four virtues, whose
emblems appear on the protective weaponry of various shields: the lion
represents divine forces; the altar, whose eyelet receives the spiritual light
of Religion, is encircled by the antagonistic symbol of a serpent; the
scales of Justice are balancing the visible and the invisible; the caduceus
(Mercury's winged rod entwined by two serpents) restores Peace and
Harmony to the universe. The constellation of Gemini with its stars
Castor and Pollux, the sons of Jupiter and Leda now transported to the
heavens, foreshadows the calm of the seas to be heralded in heaven
and on earth by the trumpet of a small angel hovering in the clouds.
All grace descends from the heavens.

Greek myth is visibly of primary and permanent importance to the
core of baroque culture. After his coronation on October 17, 1614 in
Reims, Louis XIII is sublimated not only in Rubens's paintings, but
also in a considerable number of allegorical prints and engravings. He
is shown in the guise of Hercules, son of Jupiter; Achilles, son of Thetis;
Phillip, son of Alexander the Great. The allegory thus appears to presage
the divine right which the king would enjoy throughout his life as one
who represented himself during his long career as Hercules, Jason, or
a saint. Through the unction of the coronation, the king acquires a
participatory status in the priesthood.

3. *The Victorious Battle: The New Coronation of the King and*
the Decisive Turning Point in French History; a Double Victory
over the English and the Huguenots

(a) The Battles of Breda, the Island of Ré, and La Rochelle *by Jacques*
  Callot (1630)

In the spring of 1627, Callot was for a short time in Flanders, where
he met Van Dyck and possibly Rubens. Then Louis XIII recalled Callot

from Nancy in 1629 and again in 1633. The first time, Richelieu asked him to glorify the victories at Breda, the island of Ré and La Rochelle; the second time, he was asked to glorify the victory at Nancy which Richelieu besieged from August 25 until September 25, 1633, when the city capitulated to Louis XIII. In *Entretiens sur les vies et sur les ouvrages des plus excellents peintres anciens et modernes*, Félibien confirms that Callot wished to cancel the assignment "because he was from Lorraine and believed he should do nothing against his country or his prince's honor."[2] Callot portrays the battlefields on land and on sea. The drawings "are each over 2 meters wide and 1.8 meters high"[3] and the ships intersect dramatically in curves and counter-curves. In sum, the war itself is a ceremonial which restores life and vigor to the kingdom threatened by the Huguenots and the English. Thus, once again, the defeat of the enemy and of heresy is sublimated to the king's advantage.

(b) Louis XIII as Jupiter *by G. Huret and J. Couvay (1630)*

The battle here, once again, is an allegory of another coronation of the king. Following the victories of Breda, Ré and La Rochelle, the defeat of the English and the destruction of the "canker" of heresy causes Louis XIII to believe in the reconstruction of a unified and interrelated world. This allegory does not express the world in which the king lives so much as the one which he is going to build. Louis XIII, astride his eagle with the smoke of La Rochelle's destruction at his feet, is seen as a planetary divinity, with the historical truth accepted and transformed into a universal affirmation of his religious triumph. He holds the symbol of lightning in his hand, and appears to incarnate the flash of lightning or of the celestial fire with tremendous power and formidable speed. He has been harmful to the heretics of La Rochelle, beneficial in reestablishing the Christian monarchy, and has for these merits been crowned by the heavenly father. His glory is heralded by the Seraphim beyond the gate of triumph where a painting portrays a battle scene of La Rochelle in microcosm. As the city burns, Neptune's shell arrives with his Tritons and salamander-tailed Nereids. Neptune looks upon Louis as Jupiter, confirming the joy caused by the eradication of heresy and the restoration of order.[4] Louis illuminates the people, like Jupiter, in imaginary space, a metaphor translated concretely by the nocturnal fireworks. Fireworks were used on many occasions, such as during one voyage made by Louis XIII to Lyons, where a lion was made to emerge from the Saône bearing fleur-de-lys and spitting flames. The air would suddenly fill with rockets, stars and a golden rain tumbling from the firmament and bursting into forms of serpents and girandoles. Louis XIII's ascension to higher cosmic levels confirms his sacred vocation.[5]

(c) Louis XIII as Equestrian Jupiter-Imperator, and Cardinal Richelieu
    by M. Lasne (1629)

Thanks to Louis-Jupiter, the monarchy is once again devoted to universal peace. It is the mythical distinction with regard to the historical event which elevates the king and the cardinal to the position of redeemers of humanity. The movement and the theme of this allegorical engraving is once again a sublimation of the king's sacred rights. The gaze is directed toward a search for a sublime victory. Riding a horse, the king appears like a thunderbolt. The horse, linked to fire and carrying life and death at once, is both destroyer and triumphant victor. Louis' legs touch the dead victims; the horse's raised forelegs are ready to crush yet more enemies, as yet invisible. The animal's pricked ears symbolize his obedience to the divine word and to Louis-Jupiter. He hurtles forward like an eagle, or an arrow released accidentally. The eagle, the king of birds and the messenger of celestial fire, accompanies Louis. His wings symbolize the soaring and liberation of the soul and spirit. He protects the king with his outstretched wing, which dissolves into clouds out of which the hand of the Jupiter-King will pull zigzagged thunderbolts. Lightning, the divine weapon of Louis-Jupiter, symbolizes the physical and moral storm launched upon the unbelievers. With the enemy vanquished, destroyed and dead, the battle crowns the king once more. Even war is a ceremonial which restores life and vigor to the kingdom threatened by the Protestants and the English. The battle leads to peace, ensured by Richelieu who is shown standing on the right. The cardinal, due to his intelligence and character, is going to conquer the king for good. The rock, the column encircled by palm leaves, a helmet and an eagle with arrows in its talons, and altar, the rope and bow all ensure peace. The rock's immobility and immutability could characterize the supreme and absolute Principle that inspires Richelieu, and calls to mind the Rock of Israel in the language of the psalms as well as the farewell canticle of Moses: He is the Rock, His work is perfect for on all roads He is the Law, Rectitude and Justice. The spiritual Rock from which the source of life flows is expressly identified with Christ by Saint Paul.[6] The curtain on the right symbolizes the passage from the former state to the new. The column and the rope are signs of the indissoluble alliance between heaven and earth. At its peak is the helmet which the hero has sacrificed and sanctified. The column is the axis of the sacred, the axis of Christian faith reestablished on earth. Seen from above, it is the center of the earth; from below, at the horizon, it is a slope to be climbed. The all-powerful king is sublimated by the promising gaze of the cardinal: peace will be restored; the monarchy will be unified, sanctified and consecrated by the battle.

II. THE OTHER SIDE OF THE COIN

1. *Voyages in the Beyond: The Miseries of the Human Condition*

(a) The Great Miseries of War: Hanging *(1633)*

As a symbol of life, the tree, in perpetual evolution and in ascension toward heaven, evokes all the symbolism of verticality in many prints and etchings by Callot and his contemporary, Perrier. The Tree of Life has lost its crown in *Hanging*,[7] a striking ritual presenting the putting to death of enemy soldiers, some of whom are hung from dry branches, while others, the lucky ones, are hung from branches with leaves. Here is the anagram of the tree of life: it is a tree of death in the form of a cross, the instrument of torture and redemption, that joins in one single category two extreme signifieds of this major signifier, the tree: death toward life, by the cross pointing toward the light, thus from the Passion to the blazing light. The victims, having confessed and been absolved, submit despite everything, knowing that the sacrifices required by God or the monarch must take place

(b) The Plague in Athens *by François Perrier (1630)*[8]

The triumph of death – *in illo tempore* – situates the unhappy event in the mythical past. The inscription, *Ignibus Hippocrates pestum Sedavit Athenis Peste Rochus Ticinum pectoris Igne levat*, summarizes the allegory of the plague, and in Latin, the sacred language, explains the theological sense of this engraving. Let us recall that Sophocles' tragedies

gave to the plague a universal signification of the tragic human condition of man menaced by the plague, combined with the allegory of fire,
of conflagration, of war. In this philosophical allegory, aesthetics and
metaphysics unite poetic creation intuitively. Refusing to dissociate art
from life, Perrier also founded the reconstruction of the human universe
on creative imagination, in the sense that Anna-Teresa Tymieniecka
uses the term, and on the orchestration of human existence and the
work of the poet, the artist and the philosopher. In July 1630, the plague
was prevalent in all of northern Italy, especially at Mantua, where it
claimed one million victims. Its ravages inspired François Perrier to
recreate the human condition of this period during which Louis XIII
had marched on to Piedmont after his victory over La Rochelle. The
allegory suggests a universal truth, deepened by the historical existence
of Roche, born in Montpellier (1300–1325), and Hippocrates, the Greek
physician (460–377 B.C.). The Saint is invoked as much as the physician in the apprenticeship of suffering and the discovery of divine love.
The one is known for his sermon that helps the victim to triumph over
physical Evil. The other gives peace of mind to the victim through
spiritual redemption. The curved line of this print expresses life, and
ascension to paradise and peace. It is no longer the tragic conception
of Christianity but its glorious and merciful aspect that reveals itself in
the ascension of the deceased through the flames and smoke of the plague
toward the light.

2. *The Diabolical Marvelous and the Sacred*:
The Temptation of Saint Anthony *(1635) by Jacques Callot*[9]

The historical Anthony (251–356) resisted a great number of temptations
in the Thebaid, a region in Egypt where the first Christian hermits
retreated into the desert. The marvelous infernal is found in the imagery
of poets, painters, engravers and dramatists. It inspired Dante, Milton,
Shakespeare, Tasso, Scudéry and Godeau, as well as Bosch, Brueghel
and Callot. Callot again creates the allegory of the "gran nemico
dell'umane genti," just as Tasse calls for the convocation of demons in
Gerusalemne. Callot knows how to express the immensity of space and
the *chiaroscuro* between the day that ends and the night that falls, and
of the night with all its mysteries. The temptation of Saint Anthony is
an apogee of the allegories of the cardinal sins that tempt him as the
sole victim of an army of monsters. The presence of monsters in the

engravings of Callot ("the Cardinal Sins," "the *petite passion*," Jesus being struck by a lance, or the ballet interludes engraved in France) recall the misery of the plague, war, hangings by invaders, thus all the forces of evil, multiplied to infinity, that appear like a great storm with a huge fireball and thunderclap. These monsters whirl about in all directions and constitute the center of the night, in contrast to the luminous center formed by the halo of the saint. Their open gullets spout forth flames and weapons; their fire is the fire of passions, of chastisement, of war; it burns, devours, and destroys by spitting out death. Callot has doubtlessly observed the whistling arrows, javelins and perhaps cannonballs hurled by the artillery in combat. The swift curves of the monsters occupy the fictitious depth of space. These fantastic creatures, half reptile (snakes, lizards, forked-tongued and scaly-tailed toads), half bird, with bat wings, possess all the characteristics of the unformed, chaotic, shadowy and abyssal. Are these the anguished expressions of the saint, or of the inhibition that prevents him from succumbing to their temptation and being thrown with them into subterranean caverns? Why is the saint placed at the border of this underground region of the cave? Will he be capable of resisting, and of killing the exterior monsters that are not yet part of his interior? His halo indicates his victory over the monsters within him and that he has killed within himself. His gesture, holding the raised cross in his right hand, symbolizes his gratitude toward the divine supremacy. This is the consecration of Saint Anthony on the verge of the unspeakable.

So art and religion also take the path that leads Saint Anthony beyond himself, toward a reality unknown yet foretold, that is revealed only if one sees it personally. Art and religion are founded upon the exaltation of human qualities, as Anna-Teresa Tymieniecka explains *Logos and Life*.

III. UNIVERSAL HARMONY; THE POLITICAL ASPECT OF THE MARVELOUS

1. *The Triumph of Louis XIII over Heresy: The Monarchy Unified by Christian and Universal Faith Suppresses Skepticism, Doubt, Hesitation, Revolt, Dissonance, the Mortal Canker of all True Art* [9]

"Ludovico decimo tertio iusto pio felice augusto invicto magno triomphatori italico britannico alemannico lotharingico Francie et Navarrae regi christianissimo. Aetatis suo anno 33 et sui regni 23" (J. Callot). The just, pious, felicitous, august, invincible and great king has triumphed over Italy, England, Germany, Lorraine, as the most Christian king of France and Navarre. Yet it is not this story that interests us, but rather the significance of a royal majesty who came into being for a great cause. Callot described the king in a combat setting with the intention of spiritualizing the combat. The triumphant horse is the privileged mount for the spiritual quest of the hero who was able to triumph over all the forces of evil. Louis XIII, the armor-clad hero, holds a lance in his hand, aiming to improve the world at his and his horse's feet. The trumpet of the Seraph bring together the sky and the earth in a common celebration of the glorious King Louis XIII. The myth of the glorious king, however, does not distance us from the story. Myth and history, allegory and reality, form a whole. Myth is also history, albeit symbolic. It also contains the memory of men in allegorical form. Louis XIII personifies history, his conquests have become myth. Allegory refers an ancient order to the present one and explains a sacred law: the sky serves as a mirror and offers a chance to penetrate the eternal.

There is a mysterious relation between the number of angels and the number of nations vanquished and reunited by Louis XIII. The smaller angels make up the army of God and the monarch, while the Seraph tear apart the sky, with the angels descending toward the king to reassert the fullness of his moral, political and religious victory. A seraph announces the king's eternal glory, dissipating all shadows.

The lightning and the arrow possess a quality of purification and illumination: they are the ignited prolongation of light. It is the image of fire that best reveals the means by which the celestial agents offer the halo to the triumphant king who is sanctified by glory. The royal crown, carried by the angel to the king, indicates the sacred and divine character of the king as the center of spiritual energy.

The trumpet of the Seraph, in bringing together the sky and earth in a common celebration of the king, symbolizes an important conjunction of elements and events: "per aeternitas," the note played by the Seraph indicates the surpassing of contradictions on the cosmic and spiritual planes. The king appears winged: he will attend to other battles without ever fighting. Bedecked in sunbeams from the celestial vault, he will allow light to triumph over darkness. The mind and eyes of the spectator are dazzled and filled with wonder by the unity of this allegory.

The king has accomplished the amazing feat of triumphing over his enemies, reestablishing universal harmony and ensuring eternal glory.

It is the revenge of Callot's creative imagination on the classic ideal of the Renaissance that tends to progressively impose itself. This allegory respects the laws of reality while opening a door to the invisible.

2. The Compositions of the King: From the Liturgy to the Bliss of the Royal Couple

According to the King and Queen's director of chamber music, Anthoine de Boesset, the musical phrase has the goal of training the listener, through the creation of a current strongly nourished by allegorical images. The expression of sound is used with two goals in mind: to call to the listener's spirit either a state of faith, or a state of joy. By participating in a state of bliss and happiness, the listener will thus believe he is immersed in the ritual of the Christian liturgy.

In the musical pastoral "Amaryllis," the king affirms his divine right by dancing. Amaryllis is the incarnation of beauty, sovereignty and virtue triumphing over the whole world, under the sun. The conjugal virtue, fidelity, is reflected in the royal couple. As a manifestation of divinity, Amaryllis is compared to the sun in the center of the heavens, the source of light and grace. Moreover, this version of the courtly aria is accompanied by a lyre, the instrument of Apollo and Orpheus. The seven strings of the lyre correspond to the seven planets: through their vibrations and cosmic revolutions, they are in tune with a very harmonious and spiritual state of mind. Thought and the contemplation of cosmic harmony are expressed by the harmony of the strings, the harmony of body and soul, and the harmony between the state and the starry heavens. This is Louis XIII's musical composition that best expresses the depths of the soul and the cosmos. For Louis XIII, to make the lyre vibrate was to make the cosmos vibrate.

In listening to the second version, written for harp, one has the impression that it describes a world of sleep and that it makes those who hear it irresistibly fall asleep and may even make them pass into the beyond. The harp unites heaven and earth and promises to cast its spell of happiness upon the people.

The organization of motifs is determined by the significance of the words of the text. We associate the motifs of sun, beauty, grace and faithfulness with light, hope, glory and everything that raises and transfigures the soul. This aesthetic tends to relieve the sentimental atmosphere that results from laudatory or sweet poetry. The soprano, the highest voice, predominates, and is accompanied by a lute. The counterpoint of the lowest voices, two tenors and one bass, moves in agile and supple vocal lines, and fully emphasizes the words grace, virtue, beauty and faithfulness, obeying a strict symmetry. The repeats are exchanged by uniting verses of equal length. Louis invites us to forget the unhappy human condition and proclaims the privileges that the divine ideal of Amaryllis grants to those who listen. Here again, the interplay between the imaginary and the real is put in motion several times in all directions, and the divine Amaryllis appears to be frozen in total sublimation. This musical pastoral, *Tu crois au beau soleil* ("Amaryllis") was commented on by Mersenne in *L'Harmonie universelle* (1635) and recommended as a model: "As for the Air in Four parts, it will serve as an example of those who are studying how to make good melodies and how to form parts which sing well in this matter, in which must be used a great multitude of details, which it is difficult to acquire without long exercise and a natural inclination."[10] Mersenne admires this courtly aria created by Louis XIII because it imposes its form and impetus on every musical passage: "This custom of wedding voice with instrument is very common in France, Italy and other countries. From this it can be inferred that it is good, and that the most subtle minds have perceived that the voice alone is not so mellow, rich and full for supplying to its recital the perfection desired, that one would encounter in a voice which would have all the parts together and which would have no need for breath or breaking off."[11] *Tu crois au beau soleil*, the "Diminutions" by La Barre for harp, constitute a tender, languorous and moving aria, which translates into a sort of sentimental transluscence. The flames of love dance, and emanations of the sun and of the world, grace, beauty and faithfulness, transcend them. Mersenne summarizes the ambitions of Louis XIII in the frontispiece of *L'Harmonie universelle*: Louis XIII-Goliath knew how to reaffirm national unity, and Louis XIII-David knew how to tame animals with the magic of his music.

Let us now turn to Louis XIII's favorite ballet, *The Ballet of the Merlaison*, presented at Chantilly on March 15, 1635 and again at Royaumont on March 17. According to Alexander Dumas, this ballet is comprised of sixteen entries. The king himself created the choreography and the costumes, composed the music, and danced twice, once in the role of the wife of the master Pierre de la Croix de Lorraine, and once as a farmer. The ballet is a distraction without dramatic unity. The thematic movements begin in wintertime and end in springtime, the end of the hunting season. The allegory of spring recites: "Here am I above the horizon, where I have come to make the world young again, I show the beautiful season that gives joy to [the] earth, and wave. . . . [winter] . . . seeing me, flees this place [where] I have come to establish the empire of love."[12] The great ballet with knights who invite us to an open dance brings this allegorical spectacle to a close and recalls the great Italian tournaments containing both surprise and enchantment, so well observed by Callot.

CONCLUSION

Allegory plays a fundamental role in art because it is a sort of transcendence that manifests itself in a sensitive form and is always ascending toward the invisible and the sacred. By refusing to dissociate art from life, love from knowledge, Louis XIII was able to found the reconstruction of the human universe on the creative imagination, on the orchestration of human existence, and on the work of the poet, the artist and the musician. The allegorical expression of his metaphysical and aesthetic philosophy intuitively and spontaneously unites the poetic and artistic creation of his time. The sacred is the source of all creativity; there is no salvation outside of the spirit of gratitude and faith.

Michigan State University

NOTES

[1] Mircia Eliade. *Le sacré et le profane*. Gallimard, 1965; *Briser le toit de la maison. La créativité et ses symboles*. Gallimard, 1986.
[2] Félibien. *Entretiens sur les vies et sur les oeuvres des plus excellents peintres*. Trévoux, 1723, vol. III.
[3] George Sadoul. *Jacques Callot miroir de son temps*. Gallimard, 1969.
[4] The painting by Rubens *Quos Ego Neptune Calming the Tempest* (1635) deals with the same event.
[5] Françoise Bardon. *Le portrait mythologique à la cour de France sous Henri IV et Louis XIII. Mythologie et Politique*. Paris: A. et J. Picard, 1974.
[6] Jean Chevalier and Alain Gheerbrant. *Dictionnaire des Symboles*. Paris: Robert Laffont/Jupiter, 1969.
[7] Professor Leonardy adds a lucid and relevant observation to this scene, based on *Justiz in alter Zeit. Mittelalterliches Kriminalmuseum*. Rothenburg ob der Tauber, 1989

(Band Vic der Schriftenreihe des Mittelalterlichen Kriminalmuseums Rothenburg ob der Tauber: "Es gab Vorschriften, die auf magische Weise Schutz bieten sollten. Der Strick mußte in bestimmter Weise hergestellt sein, der Galgen aus entrindetem Holz ('lichter Galgen') errichtet sein, damit keine Dämonen unter der Rinde verborgen sein könnten" (p. 280). "Der Galgen des Altertums war der Ast eines Baumes. Dazu benützte man nach Möglichkeit abgestorbene, laubfreie Bäume. Nach den religiösen Vorstellungen der damaligen Zeit ging von leblosen Baum lebenshemmende Kraft, also Kraft zum Töten aus" (p. 329).

[8]   Like Callot, Perrier went into exile in Rome, the eternal city, where he was the student of Lanfranco in 1629. In 1630 he visited Lyons, and then Paris, where he attached himself to Simon Vouet. In the context of the Eighteenth Century Exhibit in the Louvre, June 1991, see in particular P. de Champagne: *Louis XIII couronné par la victoire* (1630); Poussin, *L'inspiration du poète* (1630); F. Perrier, *Enée et ses compagnons combattant les harpies* (1630); Giovanni Lanfranco, *Le couronnement de la Vierge* (1630); Sébastien Stosskopff, *Statuette, livres, boîte de copeaux et coquillages* with the mise-en-abyme of Callot's prints – *Les statuette de bronze* with the mise-en-abyme of Callot's prints; *Guitariste Masqué et Gobbi* (1630).

[9]   C.-G. Dubois. *Le Baroque-profondeurs de l'apparence*. Larousse, 1973, pp. 99–110.

[10]   Marin Mersenne. *Harmonie Universelle* (1635), trans. Roger E. Chapman. The Hague: Martins Nijhoff, 1957, p. 120.

[11]   *Ibid.*, p. 121.

[12]   Bibliothèque du Conservatoire, Paris. Set to music by the Ancient Instrument ensemble, under Roger Cotte, for Nonesuch Records.

PAINTINGS DISCUSSED

1. Rubens. *Marie de Médicis's Acceptance of the Regency* (1610).
2. Rubens. *The Majority of Louis XIII* (October 20, 1614).
3. Jacques Callot. *The Battles of the Island of Ré.*
4. Jacques Callot. *The Battles of La Rochelle.*
5. G. Huret and J. Couvay. *Louis XIII as Jupiter* (1630).
6. Jacques Callot. *The Great Miseries of War: Hanging* (1633).
7. François Perrier. *The Plague in Athens* (1630).
8. Jacques Callot. *The Temptation of St. Anthony* (1635).

1. Rubens. *Marie de Médicis's Acceptance of the Regency* (1610).

142   MARLIES E. KRONEGGER

2. Rubens. *The Majority of Louis XIII* (October 20, 1614).

3. Jacques Callot. *The Battles of the Island of Ré*.

4. Jacques Callot. *The Battles of La Rochelle*.

5. G. Huret and J. Couvay. *Louis XIII as Jupiter* (1630).

6. Jacques Callot. *The Great Miseries of War: Hanging* (1633).

7. François Perrier. *The Plague in Athens* (1630).

8. Jacques Callot. *The Temptation of St. Anthony* (1635).

CATHERINE BÉDARD

L'AFFLEUREMENT ALLÉGORIQUE
DANS L'IMAGE DU COMBAT:
SUR LE *SAINT GEORGES* DE COSMÈ TURA*

Nous vous proposons une exploration du côté de l'image d'un duel qui
se serait affirmée, dans l'histoire, comme une manifestation exemplaire
d'une école de peinture dont on situe l'émergence vers la deuxième moitié
du *Quattrocentro*. Il s'agit de l'école de Ferrare et du *Saint Georges* de
Cosmè Tura (Fig. 1) que nous aborderons ici comme un portrait. Portrait
non pas d'un individu, ni même d'une société, mais portrait emblématique d'une école dont l'auteur serait le porte-parole privilégié.

   Ce duel que l'image présente, le combat de saint Georges contre le
dragon, s'est affirmé à Ferrare avec une obstination sans précédent. On
le trouve sur le portail principal de la façade du *Duomo* dès la fin
du Moyen Âge; on le retrouve à plusieurs endroits à l'intérieur de la
cathédrale et notamment dans un tombeau exécuté par Baroncelli à la
droite du choeur, oeuvre dont l'achèvement a été confié à Domenico
Paris. Il traverse la production locale des peintres et des sculpteurs, et
constitue l'un des sujets privilégiés de la miniature ferraraise qui se
développera tout au long du XVe siècle sous les règnes de Nicolo III,
de Leonello et de Borso d'Este, en relation étroite avec les recherches
des peintres et des penseurs invités à la Cour, tels Alberti, Pisanello,
Bellini, Donatello, Mantegna et Piero della Francesca. Le musée du
Duomo de Ferrare, où sont exposés vingt-deux antiphonaires produits par
l'atelier de la Cathédrale au XVe siècle, constitue à lui seul un abondant
corpus de l'image du saint. On a l'étrange impression, lorsqu'on entre
dans ce musée, d'entrer dans une collection thématique: fragments de
statues représentant le saint triomphant, tapisseries, antiphonaires ouverts
à la page où l'on reconnaît saint Georges, ou son homologue saint Michel,
traités selon des codes picturaux qui s'approchent davantage des effets
réalistes et naturalistes alors en vigueur chez des artistes comme
Mantegna que de la stylisation du gothique international.

   Cette présence de saint Georges à Ferrare s'explique en partie par le
culte qui lui sera voué dès le VIIe siècle, alors qu'il devient patron de
la ville. A ce corpus encore présent, il faut aussi ajouter toutes les oeuvres
produites pour la cour des Este, dont une grande partie est passée aux

149

A-T. Tymieniecka (ed.), Analecta Husserliana XLIII, 149–178.
© 1994 *Kluwer Academic Publishers. Printed in the Netherlands.*

Fig. 1. Cosmè Tura (avant 1430–1495), Saint Georges terrassant le dragon, Ferrare, Museo del Duomo. © Fratelli Alinari 1992, Firenze.

Fig. 2. Cosmè Tura, *Annonciation*, panneaux d'orgue, Ferrare, Museo del Duomo.© Fratelli Alinari 1992, Firenze.

Habsbourg à la mort du dernier duc de Modène. Ces oeuvres, maintenant en Autriche, ainsi que d'autres qui ont été produites à la suite
de celles-ci dans le style des gothiques germanique et autrichien, sans
compter les nombreuses copies du XIXe siècle, ont été exposées au
Castello Estense de Ferrare au printemps dernier.[1] Ceci n'a fait que
confirmer à quel point l'image de saint Georges, dans cette récurrence,
s'est figée peu à peu en un motif devenu emblématique de la ville, ou
plus précisément, de son histoire sous le règne de la famille Estense à
l'origine de son indépendance politique sous Boniface IX à la fin du XIVe
siècle, époque à laquelle Ferrare se libère de la souveraineté territoriale
de l'Église. Il est tout à fait intéressant que cette conquête politique
des Este et l'affirmation de leur pouvoir, qui s'inscrira de diverses façons
dans la ville (et notamment par la construction du château), croisent le
développement de l'image héroïque du chevalier combattant le monstre.
Ferrare se reconnaît dans cette image. Et la mémoire de cette image,
qui est aussi l'image d'un pouvoir, a trouvé dans le royaume d'Autriche
un lieu propice à sa conservation (symbolique et muséologique). C'est
par l'archiduc François-Ferdinand, qui portait aussi le nom des Este, et
qui a enrichi la collection de nouvelles pièces, que saint Georges devient
la figure emblématique d'une des dernières grandes monarchies
européennes.

L'intéressant problème que pose le corpus ferrarais, comme partie
d'un corpus plus vaste de la représentation de saint Georges dans
l'Italie des XVe et XVIe siècles, tient au fait qu'à travers cette récurrence et un processus de décontextualisation du combat du cavalier et
du monstre, il consacre une figure qui peu à peu devient "abstraite". Face
à cette répétition du même, que le regard finit par enregistrer comme
un motif absolu, s'est cristallisée l'idée d'une analogie essentielle avec
le combat du Vice et de la Vertu. On conçoit très facilement que les
conditions de possibilité de cette opération analogique consistent dans
la focalisation sur une figure de l'affrontement – au détriment de tout
contexte jugé secondaire – sur l'opposition de deux termes proposés
comme antithétiques, sous les traits de l'homme et de la bête, mais
plus précisément, de l'humain (ou du saint) et du monstrueux. Mais
encore doit-on ajouter que, pour que cette association s'établisse avec
évidence, cet affrontement doit déjà exposer dans sa structure le
déséquilibre des forces: ainsi le monstre est toujours présenté aux
pieds d'une oblique dominée par saint Georges, en pied ou à cheval,

comme sur le plateau le plus bas d'une balance, soit du côté des âmes livrées à Satan.

Si cette analogie s'établit dès lors comme un état de fait lorsque l'on considère la manifestation "abstraite" de ce duel qui nous est donnée presque systématiquement par la sculpture, les bas-reliefs, les médailles, et les objets d'art décoratif, alors les conditions de cette association en peinture entre le combat de saint Georges et le combat allégorique du Vice et de la Vertu méritent qu'on s'y attarde.

Il ne s'agit pas ici de postuler la signification allégorique de l'image. Ce serait non seulement limiter la portée de ce combat, les enjeux de cette figure, mais cela ne nous apporterait rien de nouveau quant aux stratégies critiques de l'image elle-même, en donnant plutôt à penser qu'elle est subordonnée au contenu discursif. Il s'agit au contraire d'y *observer les manifestations de faits picturaux pointant la dimension allégorique comme un problème de la représentation, troublant l'homogénéité de l'espace figuratif.*

Ce "fait pictural" par lequel l'allégorique se manifeste comme un lieu d'altérité dans le tableau est à entendre lui-même comme un duel. L'allégorique surgirait ici dans cet espace troublé suivant deux manières de situer la figure dans le lieu pictural: ces deux manières, à penser sur un mode dialectique, seraient l'emblématique et le narratif. Le *narratif*, soit cet ensemble de stratégies par lesquelles un récit, une *istoria* s'expose, dont une des règles tient à l'intégration des actants dans une logique ou une progression spatio-temporelle. L'*emblématique*, soit un détournement des figures dans une structure symbolique et qui consiste, à l'inverse des stratégies narratives, à privilégier le pouvoir d'abstraction de l'image. Il faut entendre ici par "abstraction" non seulement l'écart par rapport à la représentation du monde sensible, mais la part d'isolement, de séparation que ce concept implique. Ces deux modalités du rapport entre la figure et le lieu permettent du coup de faire émerger, à partir de ce cas précis, la complexité de la notion d'*istoria* telle qu'elle a été formulée par Alberti, notion qui identifie le sujet historié mais aussi, de façon plus générale et plus elliptique, l'histoire, le sujet, le tableau. On se rappellera que le mérite du peintre tient d'abord au choix d'une bonne *istoria* dont la composition est fournie d'emblée par le récit qui l'inspire.

[j]e conseille à chaque peintre qu'il se familiarise avec les poètes, les rhétoriciens et autres doctes lettrés; pour que ceux-ci lui donnent de nouvelles inventions et certes l'aident à

bien composer son *istoria*; ce sont ces inventions qui assureront sans conteste, à sa peinture, louange et réputation.[2]

Ainsi l'*istoria*, qui séduit par la seule *invenzione* même si Alberti ajoute que cette dernière, mise en peinture, plaira encore davantage, ne semble impliquer aucun changement, aucune modification, en termes de segmentation du récit ou de procédés narratifs, dans l'opération de transposition du textuel au pictural. Et pourtant, "travailler sur la composition c'est réfléchir sur l'*istoria*":

Je dis que la composition est une méthode de peindre selon laquelle les parties s'organisent dans l'oeuvre peinte. La plus grande oeuvre du peintre sera l'*istoria*: les corps font partie de l'*istoria*: les membres font partie des corps: les surfaces font partie des membres. [. . .] Tous les corps doivent en taille et en fonction s'accorder à ce qui se passe dans l'*istoria*.[3]

Voilà posé le rapport entre l'histoire, le sujet, le tableau, c'est-à-dire l'*istoria*, et l'ordonnance des éléments figuratifs, c'est-à-dire la *dispositio*. Retenons par ailleurs, à partir d'une enquête menée sur les normes imposées au peintre par les théoriciens, les académiciens ou les législateurs de l'Église, le définissant tour à tour comme illustrateur fidèle ou orateur, que:

Le peintre d'histoire est donc historien par l'organisation qu'il donne à l'événement, sa reconstruction; orateur, à travers les procédés qu'il emploie et qui produisent des effets de sens qui ne tiennent pas uniquement d'un récit prétendu neutre mais du discours [et qu'] "exposer un sujet" [c'est] le disposer de manière à mettre en vue ce qui semble, ce qui est (ou qu'on veut voir) considéré important".[4]

Les traitements narratif et emblématique tels qu'ils ont été présentés plus haut seraient à entendre ici comme les modalités conflictuelles produisant une perturbation de l'*istoria*.

Plus spécifiquement et à la suite d'une analyse des images du combat, nous dirions que le mode de représentation emblématique du duel se manifeste d'une part par un schéma de composition centripète, ou par une structure fermée où la tension des deux forces affrontées est maintenue dans l'espace qui les sépare (premier niveau d'abstraction, c'est-à-dire l'opération séparatrice, isolatrice); d'autre part, il se manifeste dans la compression bidimentionnelle de la figure, dans son aplatissement, qui tend à en faire davantage une forme découpée sur un fond qu'une configuration d'êtres dans l'espace. Telle opération privilégie, dans une convergence théorique tout à fait astucieuse, un traitement linéaire des figures affranchi de l'objectif strictement mimétique et qui s'affiche dans son pouvoir de schématisation, de stylisation, Le primat du *disegno*, à entendre dans sa double dimension, à la Renaissance, de dessin et d'idée, s'affiche ici, de façon singulière, comme passage privilégié à un autre niveau de discours, en l'occurence l'allégorique (second niveau d'abstraction, c'est-à-dire l'opération de mise à distance du réel).

Il faut entendre par "allégorique," dans ce cas précis que la peinture incarne et problématise, non pas la présentation de personnifications codifiées d'une idée abstraite ou le pouvoir de cohérence polysémique d'une définition illustrée, tel qu'on peut l'observer dans le registre inférieur des fresques de Giotto à Padoue, ou tel que l'a proposé Cesare Ripa sur le modèle de l'*impresa* dans son *Iconologia*,[5] mais la reconnaissance d'une structure qui appelle, par similitude, l'opposition du Vice et de la Vertu, ou du Bien et du Mal, soit la configuration paradigmatique de deux allégories antithétiques (c'est-à-dire qui se définissent l'une par rapport à l'autre). On se situe donc ici non pas seulement au niveau du double sens de l'allégorie[6] mais au niveau des *conditions d'apparition de ce double sens*. Cette mise en perspective du problème de l'allégorie, définie par Fontanier comme cette "proposition à double sens, par laquelle on présente une pensée sous l'image d'une autre pensée, propre à la rendre plus sensible et plus frappante que si elle était présentée directement et sans aucune espèce de voile",[7] nous permet de pointer, au-delà du sens caché-voilé ou du *concetto*, l'ingéniosité d'une démarche artistique confontée à l'expression symbolique.

Ce point de vue, celui de l'analyse des conditions d'apparition du double sens, nous semble d'autant plus intéressant et surtout pertinent, en regard des problèmes qu'exposent ces images, qu'il est celui même qui aura été envisagé à Ferrare dans le programme allégorique d'une fresque très peu connue de la *Casa del Sale*. Cette fresque, de l'école giottesque, montre parmi ses allégories personnifiées des Vices et des Vertus, deux médaillons quadrilobés contenant les figures affrontées, au caractère emblématique évident, de saint Georges et du dragon. Cette relation allégorique qui émerge d'un programme fonctionnant davantage par identification, par reconnaissance des attributs définissant les figures, il faut alors peut-être la lire comme le principe structural et sémantique de l'ensemble. Ces figures ne sont pas individuellement associables à un vice ou à une vertu en particulier, mais sont identifiables, de par leur affrontement, au combat du Vice et de la Vertu. Elles appartiennent à un niveau d'abstraction supérieur au reste des figures, qui illustrent le Vice ou la Vertu en des figures particulières. Situer le principe d'opposition dans la figure de saint Georges affrontant emblématiquement le dragon nous semble d'autant plus justifié que le contexte de production est Ferrare, qui trouve ici à s'inscrire par le biais de son image emblématique. Mais revenons à la peinture.

Il apparaît, dans les scènes historiées, que le combat de saint Georges soit ce lieu ambivalent – lieu de l'ambivalence par excellence – où se manifeste un aller-retour entre un désir d'abstraction et un désir de production de la réalité figurative. Désir d'abstraction qui, en peinture, signifie une résistance à la figurabilité, ou à l'insertion d'une figure dans l'espace, ou même, encore davantage, une résistance à la confrontation d'un archétype avec le réel mondain. Il y aurait manifestement, dans cette résistance à la fixation d'un signifié, ouverture à la signifiance; un désir de laisser en suspens l'opération de passage de l'invisible au visible, du sens (symbolique) au sensible, du texte ou de l'image mythique à l'image réelle, afin, paradoxalement, de maintenir à distance cette matière abstraite dans la matérialité de l'image. Nous croyons qu'en ce qui concerne le combat de saint Georges, l'intérêt n'est pas d'aller vers l'interprétation d'une configuration allégorique – de lever un voile – mais de *la proposer comme une altérité intrinsèque* en suggérant qu'il y a une crise dans le récit, que la narrativé picturale est troublée en son centre. Et que le symbolique affleure dans un motif cristallisé qui est le lieu où l'autre, un ordre autre, se manifeste. Cette altérité affectant la représentation devient alors le signe d'un conflit sous-jacent au conflit narratif.

Voilà donc, seulement esquissé bien sûr, l'un des aspects dialectiques les plus forts que propose ce tableau, mais que proposent aussi d'autres tableaux autour de lui. L'intérêt est que ce lieu duel ne soit qu'un des noeuds de cette toile dont l'oeuvre est tissée. Aussi nous approcherons-nous maintenant davantage du tableau de Cosmè Tura, en rappelant cette observation prudente que faisait Nicole Loraux, dans l'introduction des *Expériences de Tirésias . . .* , relativement aux dangers que court une pensée liée à une pratique hermétique des concepts oppositionnels ou des catégories antithétiques, observation qui a pour nous une portée théorique fondamentale si l'on pense aux interprétations traditionnelles qui viennent à l'assaut des représentations du combat de saint Georges contre de dragon: "A tenir ainsi la séparation pour acquise une fois pour toutes, on gagne quelque chose comme de l'évidence par mise à l'écart du trouble".[8]

Précurseur de l'art de la première Renaissance ferraraise, Cosmè Tura, lorsqu'il aura cessé d'être considéré comme ce maître à la tête d'un courant original mais néanmoins teinté d'un certain archaïsme, aura stimulé des descriptions passionnées, aux superlatifs anti-raphaélesques ou anti-léonardesques. Tourmenté, incisif, sec, compliqué mais doué d'une grande liberté créatrice, ce peintre au rythme diabolique et inquiet a une affinité pour le fantastique. Ses extravagances cruelles s'opposent à l'élégance douloureuse du jeune Bellini. C'était là un montage des réflexions de Roberto Longhi; télescopage un peu brutal, mais qui donne une idée de la nature d'un discours qui a fortement marqué l'histoire de l'art ferrarais.[9]

Le tableau de Cosmè Tura s'inscrit dans le contexte d'une école très longtemps marginalisée par la critique et l'histoire de l'art, puis qui a été "victime" de deux traditions discursives n'ayant réussi qu'en partie à en explorer les enjeux, en ne se frottant que trop superficiellement aux oeuvres, soit par le biais d'innombrables comparaisons stylistiques, soit par celui, à l'inverse, d'une surdétermination sémantique qui consiste plus ou moins en une idéologie de la transparence de l'image au savoir d'une époque. Cette première tradition est celle du *connaisseurship* tel que l'a pratiqué avec *maestria* Roberto Longhi, dont *L'atelier de Ferrare*, depuis sa première édition (maintes fois augmentée), fait désormais partie de ces "ouvrages incontournables" de l'histoire de l'art.

Écrit en 1934 en réponse à l'exposition de peinture ferraraise de la Renaissance tenue en 1933, ce texte consiste en une accumulation d'hypothèses d'attributions essentiellement présentées comme un correctif au catalogue de 1933. On y retrouve des arguments qui ne sont pas sans rappeler, bien qu'ils soient de nature plus littéraire que "scientifique," ceux invoqués aujourd'hui par les équipes de spécialistes chargés de défendre la destitution de telle ou telle oeuvre d'un maître. Même s'il faut reconnaître à Longhi certaines observations tout à fait intéressantes, que l'on regrette qu'il n'ait pas développées en les soumettant à l'analyse plus approfondie des oeuvres, il faut aussi reconnaître que la description comparative est essentiellement rhétorique et trouve souvent sa résolution dans la subjectivité des jugements de valeur apportés en dernière instance comme le décret du connaisseur, détenteur d'une crédibilité légitimée par l'étendue de son champ comparatif . . .

La seconde tradition est représentée par un ensemble très impressionnant de travaux qui consistent dans la reconnaissance plutôt que la

problématisation (ou l'approche des ambiguités) d'une culture humaniste locale, lisible dans une transparence implicite de l'oeuvre,
l'humanisme ferrarais étant considéré par ces historiens de l'art comme
cette quintessence dont a peinture devient un "produit dérivé".[10] Notre
position diffère: située sur les rives de cet humanisme dont les dimensions philosophique et sociale tiennent lieu de référence privilégiée, nous
aurions tendance à observer, au-delà des signes s'affichant comme les
éléments d'un langage codé, la dérive de l'oeuvre par rapport à ce centre
liquide, mouvant. Ces deux tendances que nous venons d'identifier très
rapidement représentent, quant à nous, deux façons de contourner l'objet,
son pouvoir discursif et sa spécificité, c'est-à-dire non pas son "individualité ineffable" mais *sa différence*. Aussi, en contrepoint à la réflexion
de Nicole Loraux que nous évoquions plus haut suite à notre première
analyse du duel, et pour pointer comment nous envisageons l'analyse
d'une oeuvre comme celle de Cosmè Tura (analyse affrontant deux
niveaux contextuels: le contexte d'exposition – soit le lieu et le dispositif
– et le contexte artistique élargi – soit l'inscription dans un corpus de
représentations en fonction duquel l'oeuvre se *positionne*), rappelons-
nous cette réflexion méthodologique que Barthes mettait à l'épreuve dans
son texte "La lutte avec l'ange":

> L'analyse textuelle cherche à "voir" le texte dans sa différence – ce qui ne veut pas dire
> dans son individualité ineffable, car cette différence est "tissée" dans des codes connus;
> pour elle, le texte est pris dans un réseau *ouvert*, qui est l'infini même du langage, lui-
> même structure sans clôture; l'analyse textuelle cherche à dire, non plus *d'où* vient le texte
> (critique historique), ni même *comment* il est fait (analyse structurale), mais comment il
> se défait, explose, se dissémine: selon quelles avenues codées il *s'en va*. [. . .] Le problème,
> du moins celui que je me pose, est en effet de parvenir à ne pas réduire le Texte à un
> signifié, quel qu'il soit (historique, économique, folklorique ou kérygmatique), mais à
> maintenir sa signifiance ouverte.[11]

Nous résistons cependant à cette séparation définitive opérée entre
l'analyse textuelle et l'analyse structurale. Nous croyons, pour la pertinence de l'entreprise, que l'analyse qui consiste à voir comment un
texte se défait, en l'occurence le texte pictural, est indissociable de
l'analyse qui se penche sur les relations paradigmatiques engendrées
par le texte.

Le tableau de Cosmè Tura est traversé d'une complexité dialectique;
il s'agit là d'une oeuvre qui est un faisceau de relations duelles qui ne
peuvent se manifester pleinement que dans l'appréhension et l'analyse
du fonctionnement global de l'objet peint, au-delà ou en-deça de sa

signification iconographique. Ainsi il ne suffit pas de reconnaître ici *un autre* saint Georges, dans un corpus très riche qui a connu d'ailleurs une grande fortune à la Renaissance et peut-être plus encore dans le maniérisme italien, qui en a produit d'étonnantes versions (ce qui fait ailleurs l'objet de notre recherche[12]), mais il faut voir comment ce sujet se singularise dans son rapport à un autre sujet, non moins canonique puisqu'il s'agit d'une *Annonciation* (Fig. 2): sujet autre qu'il réfléchit et qui le réfléchit à travers un dispositif qui les unit et les sépare à la fois, soit les portes de l'orgue du *Duomo* de Ferrare. Cette oeuvre fut exécutée en 1469, suite à la commande de l'évêque Lorenzo Roverella, pour orner le nouvel orgue de l'Église. Le peintre était donc confronté à l'exécution d'une oeuvre nécessairement fractionnée par les contraintes de sa fonction, qui consistait à dissimuler ou encadrer l'instrument de musique.

A orgue fermé apparaît le combat de saint Georges contre le dragon et la princesse en fuite, et à orgue ouvert, les panneaux rabattus montrent une *Annonciation*. D'une part donc, une représentation "stridente" (l'image d'un cri) visible dans le silence de l'Église, dans le lieu du recueillement, et le lieu par excellence de la rencontre spirituelle du fidèle avec Dieu; une représentation unifiée dans la clôture, dans la ferme-ture des portes qui est la mise au secret de l'instrument sonore ou de la Parole qui l'accompagne. D'autre part, une représentation scindée dont les deux parties sont séparées, éloignées l'une de l'autre par l'orgue découvert, offert à la vue pour s'offrir à l'oreille en interférence ou en communion avec le registre pictural qui l'encadre; et celui-ci ne se limite certes pas à un ornement mais refuse plutôt toute subordination en jouant, *en composant* (aux deux sens du terme) stratégiquement à la fois avec l'écart imposé par le dispositif, avec la relation différée à la représen-tation cachée – invisible mais présente – du combat de saint Georges et enfin avec le silence de l'image et de la rencontre sacrée comme un défi à la sonorité envahissante de l'orgue qui ne se taiera que pour céder à la puissance d'expression et à la volubilité de l'image du combat.

Il rapporto tematico tra il San Giorgio e l'Annunciazione puo essere visto sotto molteplici angolature critiche; ma in ogni caso il motivo fondamentale è quello della successiva inter-pretazione di due distinte manifestazioni della storia: la storia come azione e la storia come contemplazione. [. . .] L'azione certamente deve preparare la contemplazione [. . .]. All'aprirsi delle ante l'"azione" entra nell'oggetto stesso, la musica offre la chiave di inter-pretazione del mistero della eterna incarnazione del divino nel creato, l'intuizione viene sospinta verso elaborazioni più sottili dei dati della realtà fisica [. . .][13]

Pour saisir la singularité et la puissance d'ébranlement de cette oeuvre, une connaissance du répertoire des formules utilisées au *Quattrocento* pour représenter cet épisode de la vie de saint Georges s'impose. S'impose, dirions-nous, non pas comme une fatalité de la recherche qui se concentre sur un corpus précis dans une période donnée, mais s'impose dans la mesure où elle révèle la récurrence de certaines problématiques privilégiées par ce récit et surtout par l'opération qui consiste à passer d'un texte à sa représentation. Opération qui implique évidemment, et c'est bien là le problème majeur ou la plus belle amnésie de l'iconographie, des restes, des transformations, et des ajouts. Mais, comme notre objectif n'est pas d'ensevelir l'oeuvre ciblée sous l'accumulation – qui a sa part d'arbitraire d'ailleurs – des références possibles ou des éléments d'un champ artistique à partir duquel elle trouve à se positionner, nous ne ferons que souligner, empruntant ainsi un énorme raccourci, ce qui nous apparaît être en jeu de façon très forte dans les *Saint Georges* du XVe siècle italien, pour revenir ensuite à l'oeuvre de Cosmè Tura.

Le récit du combat de saint Georges est, en termes d'*istoria*, une invention tardive qui n'est pas signalée dans les premiers textes hagiographiques et qui apparaît notamment dans *La légende dorée* de Jacques de Voragine au XIIIe siècle. Ce n'est qu'au Xe siècle que serait apparu le motif du chevalier combattant le monstre, extrapolation de la légende originale issue des contaminations de mythes égyptiens (Horus, purificateur du Nil, combattant le crocodile) et grecs (Persée délivrant Andromède, Hercule délivrant Hésione) mais aussi de certaines croyances populaires véhiculant l'histoire de saints vainqueurs de serpents et de dragons, sans compter l'influence du combat des forces du Bien et du Mal illustrant la *Chute des Anges* et l'*Apocalypse*. Cette histoire est la suivante:

Georges vint dans une cité de Lybie qui était victime des menaces d'un dragon lacustre à qui l'on donnait en sacrifice tous les jours deux brebis, puis, les brebis venant à manquer, une brebis et un garçon ou une fille désignés par tirage au sort. Puis le sort tomba sur la fille du roi, que Georges aperçut par hasard en passant par là, au moment où celle-ci se dirigeait, escortée, vers l'étang. Georges lui demande ce qu'elle fait là, elle lui dit de se sauver et l'informe de l'événement à venir.

Or, après qu'elle l'eut instruit totalement, Georges lui dit: "Ma fille, ne crains point, car au nom de J.-C., je t'aiderai. [. . .] A l'instant Georges monta sur son cheval, et se fortifiant du signe de la croix, il attaque avec audace le dragon qui avançait sur lui: il brandit sa lance avec vigueur, se recommande à Dieu, frappe le monstre avec force et l'abat par terre.[14]

Ensuite, la princesse, ayant attaché sa ceinture au cou du monstre humilié, le traîne jusqu'à la ville. Georges fait à son tour du dragon un appât, en disant aux gens qu'il ne le tuera que s'ils se convertissent.

Dans la mesure où l'on considère *a priori* les oeuvres du corpus en ne tenant compte qu'avec méfiance ou du moins avec vigilance des influences généralement admises liant les artistes les uns aux autres, on peut avancer que deux tendances se dessinent. Celles-ci, traitant du rapport de l'action à la scène et au décor,[15] s'établissent indépendamment des pôles emblématique et narratif abordés plus haut. L'une, incluant le récit dans un dispositif discursif élargi ouvrant sur des réflexions multiples quant au cadre périphérique de l'action, réunirait les oeuvres de Paolo Uccello, de Jacopo Bellini, et de Vittore Carpaccio et conduirait aux représentations maniéristes brouillant le message théologique ou allégorique par divers procédés de détournement. L'autre, procédant par soustraction, par ellipse progressive des indications jugées secondaires, s'orienterait, notamment à partir des tableaux de Raphaël, vers une concentration presque exclusive de l'image sur l'affrontement de l'homme et de la bête qui nous mènerait aux combats baroquisants de Véronèse.

Ces deux tendances peuvent être nuancées, à leur tour, en fonction de la considération des actions archétypales qui déterminent l'être structural des personnages, au croisement de la situation syntagmatique, ponctuelle, et permettent d'analyser la complexité des rapports que les figures entretiennent dans ce récit et que la représentation figurée s'efforce d'exposer, ou dissimule. Désirer, communiquer, lutter: voilà les trois axes sémantiques, les "grandes articulations de la praxis",[16] selon lesquels s'ordonnent, par couples, les actants. Il s'avère que l'épreuve principale, qui constitue le syntagme de prédilection dans l'iconographie de la vie de saint Georges, occupe presque systématiquement le premier plan du tableau. Le duel prend diverses formes que l'on peut observer notamment à partir du tracé de l'axe monstre-cavalier. On peut avancer, en généralisant, que du milieu du XVe au milieu du XVIe siècle, deux tendances seront privilégiées par les artistes, soit: la translation axiale allant du vertical à l'horizontal (ex. Carpaccio) et/ou du plan à l'espace (ex. Uccello), cet axe étant presque toujours souligné par l'orientation de la lance; ou le maintien de la disposition traditionnelle (l'oblique en plan) narrativisée par divers procédés: torsion des corps qui signifie l'investissement d'un effort (ex. Cosmè Tura [Fig. 1], Véronèse, Rubens), compression des figures (ex. Sodoma), vide produit par l'absence de la lance qui accentue l'intensité du rapport d'opposition (ex. le Raphaël du Louvre, Vasari).

Dernier point: dans les tableaux montrant la lutte du saint Georges et celle de Persée, l'*istoria* inverse le rapport idéal entre nature et homme en donnant comme lieu à l'action le territoire du monstre. *C'est un territoire non balisé, irrationnel, sauvage, c'est-à-dire non maîtrisé par l'homme ou non codifié par la perspective selon le dispositif de représentation "objectif" de la Renaissance italienne.* C'est dans les représentations de *Saint Georges combattant le dragon*, foisonnant davantage au moment de l'engouement quattrocentesque pour les espaces architecturés, qu'apparaît le plus cette topologie duelle (Uccello, Carpaccio). Avec la ville reportée en périphérie, dans le décor, comme un simple objet figuratif ou le signe d'un espace *occupé* par l'homme, la construction linéaire n'a plus de prise et ne saurait organiser la représentation sans menacer l'intégrité symbolique du récit. Aussi, la perspective sera-t-elle limitée au décor ou évoquée sur la scène par la fonction vectorielle et structurante de la lance, ce trait tiré dans l'espace et dans le plan, une figure de résistance qui condense la valeur offensive de l'arme et de l'armature, au niveau du récit et de sa représentation. On y verra dans certains cas, comme dans celui de Paolo Uccello, une marque d'énonciation, alors que l'objet, offensif et déictique, indique par la spatialisation de son inscription linéaire le dispositif absent. La perspective est ainsi métaphoriquement narrativisée et l'épreuve est le discours de cette conquête.

Dans le tableau de Ferrare, la relative irrationalité de la représentation spatiale ou le désordre qui s'affiche dans la priorité accordée aux effets dramatiques des figures saisies dans l'instant de la terreur, dans cette volonté de produire une image qui aurait l'intensité de ce cri qu'elle raconte, qu'elle figure, cette irrationalité spatiale n'a de sens, nous semble-t-il, qu'en regard de l'organisation fortement rationalisée qui lui fait pendant. Et il ne suffit pas ici de relever un contraste qui se figerait dans un système bien stabilisé d'oppositions, mais d'en montrer les effets dynamiques.

Dans ce faisceau de relations duelles que nous signalions plus haut, il y en a une qui se manifeste dans le diptyque de *Saint Georges* (Fig. 1) et qui serait, au registre des modalités de la représentation de l'histoire, une confrontation entre la suggestion de mouvement ou la progression narrative – qui opérerait dans la partie gauche – et la production d'un effet emblématique opérant, lui, dans le panneau de droite. Cette séparation ne contredit pas ce que nous avancions au début en parlant de cette *altérité* qui travaille la figure circonscrite du duel. Au contraire, ce qui se produit ici c'est une *polarisation du narratif par rapport à ce centre altéré qu'est la figure du duel*. Aussi est-il plus juste de dire que le traitement narratif du panneau de gauche s'oppose au traitement ambivalent, c'est-à-dire narratif-emblématique, du panneau de droite. Cette polarisation ayant pour effet, dirons-nous, une explication du problème posé à droite, puisqu'elle en dissocie les termes. La progression narrative, à gauche, est due à la perception d'une conjonction ou d'une continuité très habilement ménagée entre l'axe scénique et l'axe contextuel, c'est-à-dire entre la pose de la princesse en fuite et sa position au pied de la montagne, et au terme d'une dénivellation très abrupte que sillonne un chemin tout en méandres.

Et les personnages au second plan de cet espace, rabattu sur le plan du panneau d'une manière volontairement primitive, contribuent à la production de cet effet de mouvement: ils sont les traces de ce déplacement et les signes des divers états du corps, de l'immobilité implorante à la course effrénée. Au milieu de cette déroute, et pour les besoins de la compréhension du récit, un homme s'arrête et désigne de son bras tendu la scène du combat. Un geste en négatif de celui de la princesse, qui instaure une relation de cause à effet. Encore plus haut, à l'origine de ce déplacement de plus en plus mouvementé le long d'un tracé serpentiforme, mais posé comme un horizon ontologique à la destinée des habitants qui fuient, apparaît une figure de la mort dans un corps à peine discernable, pendu au gibet à l'extérieur de la muraille, c'est-à-dire à l'extérieur du couloir menant à la cité. Ce que cette observation formelle révèle, de plus, c'est la nature ambiguë ou la fragilité du lien qui unit et sépare à la fois la princesse et la cité, au-delà du type d'association généralement privilégiée qui consiste à séparer, à dissocier de façon très tranchée, à couper le lien entre la cité et la princesse pour signifier le sacrifice de la vierge au monstre par l'exclusion de celle-ci du territoire protégé par le père. La princesse, exclue du rapport duel monstre-cavalier, occupe toujours, en termes narratifs, une position équivoque. Le point de vue d'une polarité action-réaction qui lui attribuerait une place privilégiée dans l'espace pictural s'avère bien discutable puisqu'*elle appartient à l'avant et à l'après*: elle est la cause apparente de l'épreuve (la cause profonde étant la colonisation chrétienne) et son résultat, ou la récompense du vainqueur (mais symboliquement, puisque son salut représente par anticipation celui du peuple). Aussi la retrouve-t-on, contrairement à la Vierge de l'*Annonciation*, à gauche comme à droite mais presque systématiquement à proximité de la ville, ou plus précisément, et dans la perspective d'une distance illusionniste (c'est-à-dire suggérée par l'espace représenté), entre la ville et la scène du combat. Par exemple, chez Crivelli, comme dans la plupart des cas d'ailleurs, le rapport de la princesse à la ville est suggéré par la convergence de deux types de proximité, picturale et spatiale, alors que dans le Raphaël de Washington seule la proximité spatiale est retenue et le lien narratif est ainsi distendu. Dans ce cas précis comme dans celui de Carpaccio, l'auréole couronnant la princesse justifierait, selon les critères d'ordonnance qu'expose et que préconise Bernard Lamblin dans *Peinture et Temps*,[17] sa position en fin de parcours, à l'extrémité du tableau en termes de lecture. L'auréole de la princesse condense la suite du récit en son cercle; elle est, à ce titre, une stratégie figurative fort habile. Figure parfaite, selon l'interprétation symbolique de la géométrie, et donc signe du divin, ell est ici le point final de la signification de l'épreuve. Que penser alors de la situation inverse où la dame apeurée est en fuite? Cosmè Tura ralentirait l'élan du regard en lui opposant le mouvement inverse de la princesse. Cette "collision perceptuelle" provoque un enregistrement de l'angoisse de la victime et accentue conséquemment le caractère dramatique du combat; mais elle dispose aussi le spectateur à interpréter l'issue du combat comme une solution, ou conditionne le fidèle à *espérer* la victoire du saint, c'est-à-dire de la Foi chrétienne. Du point de vue d'une temporalité de la lecture en fonction de la temporalité du récit, la présence de la princesse aux marges de la représentation de l'épreuve pose un intéressant problème. Car, alors que dans les *Annonciations* il pouvait sembler *logique* de voir la cause (l'Ange annonciateur) avant l'effet (la réaction de la Vierge), il est tout aussi logique de lire l'effet de la peur sur le visage ou dans l'attitude de la princesse avant qu'après la lutte du monstre et du cavalier, *puisque la figure du combat joint les antagonistes*: le monstre est la *cause* de cet effet et le héros, l'*agent* de son possible renversement. On peut donc seulement proposer qu'une solution soit plus chrétienne que l'autre! Le doute est un risque que l'Église ne peut courir . . .

Mais revenons, après ces réflexions concernant la relation princesse-cité, sur le couloir de cette étonnante montagne. Ce lien est très intéressant puisqu'il est lui-même passage, zone de transit, entre-deux, voie d'accès qui n'est pas sans rapport avec la fonction et l'aspect symbolique des portes qui en sont le support réel. Mais ce lien nous intéresse aussi parce qu'il est un filet, une ceinture, un tracé à la surface du tableau qui se poursuit ailleurs sous d'autres formes, ayant pour effet ainsi de resserer stratégiquement les liens distendus par le fractionnement de l'objet.

Dans le panneau de droite, qui concentre l'action dans une figure devenue emblématique (celle, figée et codée, du combat de l'homme contre la bête ou, plus justement, de l'image héroïque de sa domination comme nous l'avons déjà montré), la figure du lien, de la ceinture qui traverse le panneau de gauche, se resserrerait ici sur le corps lui-même médiateur du cheval. Le cheval est, du point de vue formel, ce moyen terme entre le divin et le bestial – et théologiquement ou substantiellement les deux à la fois, puisqu'il participe à la fois de ces deux natures: ce corps est devenu le centre nerveux de l'image et le support innervé du saint. Nous verrons d'ailleurs plus loin que ce corps ceintré, sur lequel le peintre attire l'attention, est aussi ce corps médiateur par lequel pourra advenir, à la surface et au croisement sémantique de cette image déjà emblématique, une autre image elle-même emblématique qui inscrira plus profondément le tableau au coeur même de l'humanisme ferrarais.

Les lacets que dessine sur le cheval ce rouge lumineux, lacets qui lui tiennent lieu de vêtement ornemental et de bride, on en retrouvera encore la figure dans l'*Annonciation*, sous la forme cette fois d'un mince filet qui retient l'écureuil à la colonne du fond comme un animal domestique. Cet élément du tableau nous permet encore de saisir jusqu'où un apparent détail peut nous mener lorsqu'on lui donne l'attention qu'il mérite: car si l'on observe bien, l'on verra qu'entre cette fragile attache et le coussin de pourpre qui en est le concentré matériel et pigmentaire, il y a un fil, certes le plus discret d'entre tous, qui ourle de haut en bas le vêtement de Marie pour se poursuivre dans la bordure du Livre Saint qu'elle tient ouvert sur ses genoux. Ce lacet, censé resserer, refermer le vêtement que le manteau bleu laisse entrevoir, se relâche progressivement pour laisser apparaître l'ouverture au niveau du ventre qui devient le signe, à la surface du corps virginal, à la fois de la réponse de Marie à l'annonce divine formulée par l'Ange, et du Mystère de l'Incarnation qui est conception sans effraction. Cette fente dans le vêtement est la figure de cette entrée interdite, figure du sexe de la Femme, déplacée sur l'enveloppe qu'est le vêtement. Mais cette fente est lisérée, montrée à la fois offerte et interdite, comme ouverte et fermée. Le fil établit figurativement ce lien mystique que l'Ange annonce entre le corps de la Vierge et la Parole divine. Il tisse dans la discursivité de l'image ce rapport intime et mystérieux entre l'humain et le divin, entre la substance divine et la chair de l'Homme.

A l'opposé de cette image, soit dans le panneau où émerge la montage – c'est-à-dire au dos du pendant *Ange annonciateur* de la Vierge – ce rapport entre l'Homme et Dieu resurgit dans on histoire plus archaïque encore, mais cette fois, à l'opposé, comme une catastrophe ou une rencontre interdite, dans une étonnante image de la Tour de Babel.[18] Il est tout à fait frappant que Cosmè Tura emprunte ici à la peinture et à la gravure un motif aussi fortement connoté qui produit une condensation des plus troublantes. Sa force tient sans aucun doute à l'association qu'elle engendre entre l'image de la terreur et l'évocation sonore d'un cri, que figure le diptyque de saint Georges, et l'histoire d'une catastrophe sociale, marquant une rupture fondamentale dans l'histoire de l'humanité qui passe par la confusion des langues. Il y aurait fort à dire sur l'association d'une Tour de Babel, symbole de la confusion, au territoire sauvage du monstre et à celui livré au désordre d'une construction irrationnelle de l'espace. Il y aurait fort à dire aussi sur le sens que prend cette évocation colossale, des points de vue théologique et théorique, émergeant ainsi au revers de l'*Annonciation*, quand l'interprétation exégétique propose que l'union perdue suite au châtiment de Dieu ne sera restaurée que dans le Christ sauveur (avec le miracle des langues à la Pentecôte), dont l'avènement est marqué en son origine par le miracle de l'Incarnation. Mais nous laissons en suspens cette idée qui nous semble mériter un développement éventuel.

Nous avons donc là, à travers les différents dérivés de ce tracé tout en méandres qui est à la fois, et tour à tour, parcours, lien, attache, une des modalités, subtile et puissante à la fois, par laquelle la peinture se montre réfléchissant cet intervalle difficile qu'elle a à gérer entre deux représentations distinctes, cette interférence symbolique et sémantique qu'elle propose et figure.

Ces réflexions sur le dispositif et le pouvoir condensatoire des figures posent la question fondamentale du virtuel dans l'oeuvre de Cosmè Tura.

Avant de poursuivre l'analyse des modalités de cette virtualisation du divin (virtualisation qui a pour effet de permettre non seulement l'expression d'un désir du corps divin mais d'un désir du corps humain lui-même virtualisé dans le corps peint) par le dispositif des portes, nous voudrions rappeler comment cette question du virtuel a été traitée par Louis Marin comme un des enjeux fondamentaux des *Annonciations*. Marin voit, dans les fables instauratrices du corps religieux chrétien, le récit toujours repris du don et du retrait du corps divin. Dans l'*Annonciation*, comme dans la *Visitation*, l'*Annonce à Zacharie*, la *Vision de Joseph*, la *Venue des femmes au tombeau*, qui sont toutes autant de fables d'une rencontre où s'énonce et s'annonce la venue *ici* ou la présence du vivant *ailleurs-déjà* de l'objet du désir, le corps divin a "sa position à l'horizon d'un *désir de présence*, partout et toujours, qui ne cessera de produire et d'altérer l'ordre des représentations qui s'y substitueront".[19] L'auteur s'attarde donc à l'une de ces représentations qu'est l'*Annonciation*, considérant cette rencontre fondatrice puisqu'elle met en contact les figures paradigmatiques de ce procès de virtualisation du corps divin, à savoir l'Ange et la Femme. L'ange est "*figure* de toutes les formes et de tous les procès de *transit*" et la femme "*figure* de l'ouverture d'un *espace* possible, pour les impossibles traces du désir".[20]

Entre l'Ange, messager du divin, de la Parole divine, et Marie, porteuse virtuelle du germe divin déposé en elle sans effraction de son corps virginal, de cette substance divine qui désormais l'habite, il y a cet intervalle sacré qui sera un défi pour la peinture. Défi puisqu'il est cet intervalle traversé par le divin, lui-même infigurable, invisible, incirconscriptible, dont la venue est figurée et annoncée par l'Ange situé à l'un des pôles de cette relation.[21] Concentrons-nous sur cet intervalle dans l'*Annonciation* de Cosmè Tura. Entre l'Ange et la Vierge, il y a, au-delà d'une bordure interne qui longe chaque panneau, l'orgue, le son de la musique sacrée qui surgit de l'espace du message divin qu'encadrent, annoncent et protègent (symboliquement) les portes peintes. Mais cet intervalle sonore est nié, dans une certaine mesure, par la construction spatiale qui lie étroitement dans la distance les deux panneaux. Aussi s'attendrait-on à trouver, sur les marges internes de ces panneaux physiquement séparés mais unis par la force de leur dispositif spatial, quelque élément tendant à *marquer* l'espace séparant les figures, *signifiant* d'une manière ou d'une autre cet entre-deux sacré que le divin franchit, tel un vase rempli de lys (ex. Filippo Lippi), une ouverture sur un jardin (ex. Lorenzo di Credi), une colonnade, ou le tracé perspectif d'un dallage fuyant vers le fond, vers un infini qui serait symboliquement produit par la construction rationnelle de l'espace (ex. Bartolommeo della Gatta). Ici, au contraire et malgré la force du dispositif spatial, l'intervalle est souligné lourdement; non pas simplement signifié ou tracé, délimité par le dispositif architectural, comme on le voit dans plusieurs *Annonciations* telles que celle de Piero della Francesca, mais comblé par celui-ci, si lourdement et si hermétiquement qu'il va même jusqu'à menacer cet espace de rencontre.

Deux colonnes accolées, qui pourraient même être deux pilastres (cet élément d'architecture à fonction décorative et non constructive) . . . Cette ambiguité est d'autant plus intéressante qu'elle est directement liée à la perception incertaine d'un objet situé sur le plan de la représentation, à cet endroit précis ou la jonction entre surface peinte et espace représenté s'affirme comme lieu contradictoire, lieu fragile où la production de l'illusion (qui est l'un des acquis, des défis de la peinture renaissante) est menacée, ou tenue en suspens, par l'exhibition de la planéité du support, du plan de la représentation, suspens qui est aussi démonstration audacieuse, périlleuse du savoir-faire du peintre.

Ces colonnes accolées dissimulent en grande partie l'espace sacré que les quatre colonnes extérieures déterminent, tout en délimitant deux à deux un autre lieu cette fois, un lieu signifié dans l'espace représenté comme lieu de représentation, soit les huit tableaux de figures peintes ornant les murs de cette étonnante architecture.

Il semble ici que Cosmè Tura opère encore une fois dans l'ambivalence, trouvant deux façons opposées de régler le problème de figurabilité de cet espace mystique, problème que est posé explicitement dans la conscience affirmée du rapport au spectateur. Ainsi, l'artiste propose d'une part un détournement du regard au profit d'une contemplation des figures murales, et d'autre part il lui interdit la vue de cet espace mitoyen en lui opposant une paroi ostentatoirement dissimulatrice. Montrer et cacher. Distraire et intriguer. Deux façons d'évoquer, de souligner, en face de cette relation mystérieuse entre l'Ange et Marie, la présence d'un tiers exclus. Ce tiers, qui est d'emblée postulé par tout secret, qui est cette référence abstraite par rapport à laquelle la communication du secret s'établit, c'est le spectateur qui est pleinement intégré, à ce titre, à la fois à la structure mystique de l'énonciation et à la structure théorique de la représentation.

Ce spectateur, deux fois postulé par la structure dans cette *Annonciation*, sera théoriquement *renversé* à la vue du revers de cette image, renversé tout comme la bête . . . Ici, aucune structure énonciative ou représentationnelle ne le présuppose.

Mais revenons encore un moment à l'*Annonciation* et à la double cloison centrale qui est au foyer de ce faisceau de relations duelles qui nous occupe. Dans le contexte de cette émergence d'un art humaniste dans la Ferrare de la seconde moitié du *Quattrocento*, dont Cosmè Tura est considéré comme le principal protagoniste, il est tout à fait significatif que, par rapport au centre artistique que constitue Florence et notamment pour ce qui concerne les transformations de l'organisation spatiale et l'utilisation de la perspective, cette oeuvre trouve le moyen d'assumer une telle marginalité tout en s'inscrivant habilement dans le droit fil de ces "conquêtes" nouvelles. Il faut savoir ici qu'à cette période des artistes comme Piero della Francesca et Mantegna, à la suite de Pisanello et de Rogier Van der Weiden (pour ne nommer qu'eux), ont été appelés à la cour de Ferrare par le duc Borso d'Este. Il faut savoir aussi qu'en 1438, Leonello rencontrait Alberti et l'invitait à la cour de Ferrare. Par la cohérence rationnelle de son élaboration architectonique, l'*Annonciation* est le fruit de ce contact avec les nouvelles théories de la représentation de l'espace; on ne peut que constater l'adhésion à ce principe albertien qu'est la correspondance, au niveau du plan du tableau, entre point de vue et point de fuite situés sur l'axe central (en l'occurence, à la jonction des panneaux qu'il faut assembler imaginairement – si l'on tient compte du dispositif original – mais que les documents actuels nous montrent ainsi, de toute façon, puisque les panneaux ont été démontés, puis artificiellement réunis en tableau). Mais alors que la *costruzzione legitima* a pour objectif d'unifier l'espace par la convergence des lignes en un point situé à l'infini dans l'espace représenté, il semble ici que ce procès d'unification soit paradoxalement tenu en suspens à son origine, soit en ce point précis où tout converge, le point de fuite. Ce point de fuite est situé un peu au-dessous du registre des gestes, et, en quelque sorte, *au bout* du regard de l'Ange (ce qui paraît tout à fait logique si l'on associe à cette origine, qui est aussi l'infini, Dieu), soit en plein centre de l'image et surtout, *entre* les deux colonnes centrales, dans cet intervalle d'où il faut entendre surgir la musique envahissante, invisible et incirconscriptible. Ainsi retrouvons-nous cet entre-deux par lequel l'oeuvre dans son ensemble s'organise, entre-deux dont nous avons analysé les implications fondamentales, comme lieu de l'origine et de l'infini, lieu d'où la représentation spatiale tire sa cohérence.

Voilà donc que se manifeste ici un superbe paradoxe. Ce centre organisateur, qui a aussi une valeur symbolique et historique puisqu'il est ce que l'humanisme toscan a livré de plus moderne (il constitue une rupture épistémologique), n'a pas sa place dans le tableau. Pointer, par le tracé convergent des lignes de fuite, cet entre-deux par lequel la représentation est unifiée, c'est du même coup pointer une fissure qui traverse l'image, une désunion fondamentale puisqu'elle atteint le centre narratif, structural, symbolique et théorique. Elle atteint ce point central qui, dans le *Saint Georges*, sera explicitement nié par un dédoublement excentré qui trouve désormais son lieu névralgique à l'axe central de chacun des panneaux.

Pour saisir la portée de ce paradoxe, son caractère subversif, il suffit de penser aux différentes stratégies utilisées par les peintres pour signifier ou marquer ce point en lui substituant, dans le plan de l'image, un objet figuratif, ou en l'inscrivant dans un lieu marqué symboliquement. Pensons aux *Épousailles de la Vierge* de Raphaël où le point de fuite est localisé dans l'ouverture traversant un temple circulaire qui le circonscrit; ou, à l'opposé, aux nombreuses *Annonciations* où le point de fuite est logé dans l'*hortus conclusus*, le jardin sacré de la Vierge, tout au fond du tableau. Et encore, à l'inverse, à celles où l'axe central est marqué par une colonne ou un pilastre. Toutes autant de stratégies qui font de l'origine-infini un lieu privilégié et problématique que l'on dérobe à la vue, *puisque régulateur, il est infigurable*.

Voilà sans doute pourquoi aura-t-il semblé tout à fait naturel et d'ailleurs beaucoup plus orthodoxe à Giovan Battista Cozza de procéder à une véritable "chirurgie esthétique", en 1735, qui consistait à fondre les deux colonnes centrales en une, après avoir amputé les deux bords internes du tableau. Cette scission trop affirmée par Cosmè Tura lui aura sans aucun doute semblé insupportable sinon disharmonieuse. Évidemment, cette opération avait pour effet de fausser l'architecture, et l'on a rendu plus tard au tableau sa double cloison originale.

Ainsi, dans ce dyptique, deux systèmes rivalisent: les rêts de la construction rationnelle et les méandres expressifs de la ligne qui résiste à la domination d'un processus unificateur. Dans ces deux systèmes de représentation qui se côtoient, une transformation se manifeste, qui est celle du Moyen Âge à la Renaissance, ou d'un primitivisme plus expressif à une volonté de saisir le monde rationnellement, de faire de la peinture une *cosa mentale*. Les rochers du paysage de l'*Annonciation* sont davantage architecturés; et les poses des figures peintes en grisaille sur les parois architecturales s'affichent comme un répertoire du savoir-faire du peintre en matière de maîtrise du savoir anatomique et d'observation du corps humain.

La puissance de cette oeuvre tiendrait donc à ce travail sur l'avers et le revers, ainsi qu'aux effets polysémiques de ces associations virtuelles qu'il faut penser sur le modèle de la médaille, qui tient ses deux faces à distance mais dans l'unité de l'objet. Cette puissance d'association virtuelle s'actualise dans le moment où se rabat le panneau, dans ce mouvement qui fait passer d'un côté à l'autre, mais aussi d'un lieu à un autre, et où l'*istoria* s'enrichit tout à coup de cette superposition de sens ou de cette confrontation signifiante (à la fois narrativement, figurativement et théoriquement). L'image de saint Georges s'ouvrant sur l'image de la Vierge Annunziata proposerait, par le biais d'un autre niveau de signification intégré mentalement à la cohérence du récit, une association, qui deviendra paradigmatique, de la princesse à l'Église, réalisée par le motif de la Vierge en prière, tel qu'on le trouve dans de nombreux tableaux (chez Uccello, Carpaccio, Raphaël, pour nommer les plus connus). Apparaît donc dans ce deuxième temps de l'*istoria*, qu'une dénégation des effets du dispositif ne permet absolument pas de saisir, le rachat du doute manifeste dans l'*istoria* première. Par cette dissociation de la signification théologique du message pictural et du potentiel dramatique et érotique du récit, le peintre peut se livrer à cette expressivité qui risque davantage d'émouvoir le fidèle tout en se donnant la possibilité de rivaliser avec cet art qui, à orgue ouvert, submerge l'espace de contemplation. Quant à l'image de la princesse, elle disparaîtra en laissant la place à celle de l'Ange annonciateur qu'il faut lire, cette fois, dans cette substitution qu'il incarne à son tour par rapport à l'image de saint Georges, comme le messager de Dieu qui annonce la venue du Christ et le Salut du monde. Cette virtualisation pointe la rencontre infigurée, et si importante d'un point de vue théologique, de saint Georges avec le peuple infidèle en vue de sa conversion. Aussi le corps de la vierge lybienne est-il médiateur de cette rencontre, comme celui de la Vierge Marie l'est de la rencontre des hommes avec Dieu dont elle porte la semence. Si le corps sauvé, mais non enfreint, de la vierge lybienne demeure intact lui aussi à travers cette opération sacrée, à la différence de Marie *il n'ouvre pas un espace pour recevoir le divin mais trace un chemin*, établit le contact par le passage rituel du territoire sauvage au territoire civilisé, circonscrit où le peuple recevra la baptême. Mais la conversion des infidèles se fait au prix d'une procédure retorse. Sacrifiée par la cité pour le monstre, la princesse, en revenant accompagnée du monstre vaincu mais toujours vivant, sacrifie la ville. Elle amène la menace à l'intérieur de l'espace menacé. Il s'agit là d'une infiltration du Mal voulue par Dieu qui expose ainsi le peuple du roi pour mieux se l'approprier. Ce renversement, qui marque le passage du sacrifice au sacrement, a des implications cruciales en termes de filiation charnelle et spirituelle et en termes de pouvoir que nous ne pouvons que signaler. La femme est la terre, le territoire du roi, et c'est cette terre non fécondée par le héros que le roi récupère encore comme sienne mais au prix d'une conversion, c'est-à-dire d'une conquête et d'une occupation de son territoire par la toute-puissance divine. Mais la fille du roi est, symboliquement parlant, celle par qui s'engendre le fils, soit le fils de l'Homme, c'est-à-dire le Christ. Comme Marie, elle est le corps par qui Dieu transite pour se manifester aux hommes. Elle est, en fait, une condensation de la figure du Christ et de Marie; agneau sacrifié et, épargné, vierge dont la vie *vaut*, en tant que représentation symbolique de la vie de tous, la conversion à la Foi chrétienne. Ainsi articulé à la figuration du Mystère de l'Incarnation et de l'annonce de son secret, le diptyque de saint Georges est à lire comme une représentation narrative du procès et du mystère de la conversion et du salut. Si Louis Marin a si justement évoqué les paroles de Bernardin de Sienne comme pôle possible pour appréhender la puissance théorique des *Annonciation*s de la Renaissance toscane:

L'éternité vient dans le temps, l'immensité dans la mesure, le créateur dans la créature . . . , l'infigurable dans la figure, l'ineffable dans la parole, l'incirconscriptible dans le lieu, l'invisible dans la vision, l'inaudible dans le son . . .[22]

comment entendre alors le rapport à un espace aussi sauvage à la construction rationnelle et à la mesure que ce *Saint Georges* sinon comme la revendication d'un territoire non encore conquis, en voie de l'être, et qui laisse au drame la possibilité d'avoir lieu.

Mais avant de revenir une dernière fois aux modalités d'expression du drame et à la figure névralgique du duel, il faut remarquer combien l'éclairage ou les accents lumineux sont producteurs d'effets. Dans l'*Annonciation*, les auréoles sont le signe de cette lumière indépendante, incorruptible, qui émane d'une zone circonscrite à la charnière de deux lieux qui ont aussi leur propre luminosité, celui intemporel de l'arrière-plan qui s'oppose à celui du premier plan, l'espace rationalisé où les objets sont révélés par une lumière réaliste venant de la droite et un peu de l'extérieur. Mais la lumière émanant des auréoles, qui est signe du divin, devient aussi le fond luminescent des panneaux encastrés, de la démonstration artistique du traitement de la figure, fond abstrait qui rappelle celui du panneau de *Saint Georges*. La singularité de Cosmè Tura consiste dans l'exaltation d'une co-présence de ces deux types de lumière, co-présence qui est contradictoire, ambivalente, et sert à l'élaboration savante d'un ensemble de relations articulées non pas naturellement mais intellectuellement en un discours qui traite ensemble les implications théoriques et théologiques de l'image.

Cette oeuvre montre aussi comment la translation du texte à l'image, ou de l'histoire à sa représentation, est un passage douloureux à la corporéité des figures dont l'artiste refuse de transcender le caractère fictif. S'il est trop facile de lire ces corps comme simples produits d'une tradition gothique, simplement pour les distinguer des formes plus organiques de l'école florentine, il convient davantage de dire qu'ils constituent une rupture avec la tradition plus ornementale, plus abstraite et stylisée du gothique tardif tout en refusant les formules plus organiques qui font la gloire des artistes italiens. Ici, le corps devient un moule et, contrairement à ce que l'étude anatomique représentera pour les peintres, c'est-à-dire une approche scientifique visant à atteindre un réalisme de la représentation de la figure humaine, pour Cosmè Tura elle devient le moyen d'une représentation cohérente des articulations, des ligaments, des veines, bref d'une architecture corporelle qui se montre dans son schématisme plutôt que dans l'enveloppe organique des chairs. Les figures de Cosmè Tura, impénétrables et osseuses, sont les produits d'un système noueux qui résiste à la séduction de l'incarnat et aux attraits de cette enveloppe malléable dans laquelle le peintre toscan modèle la figure idéale.

Il y aurait là une extroversion inhumaine de la crise. C'est dans l'apparence, le vêtement, le décor, que ça craque. Procédé qui a pour conséquence philosophique un renoncement à la représentation d'une individualité habitée, torturée, pleine. Tout est projeté à l'extérieur, mais non pas comme chez Rubens où il y a mélange des chairs et de la peinture, en un amalgame tourbillonnant. Ici, l'extroversion est maîtrisée par la ligne; extroversion apparente donc, qui ne remue pas un intérieur, qui ne menace pas l'image mais qui suppose une séparation absolue entre l'homme et sa représentation. On pense au *Printemps* de la National Gallery de Londres où la construction du trône est thématisée, comme le seront plus tard les portraits maniéristes d'Arcimboldi, et au fractionnement de la robe, dont le froissement raide participe de cette décomposition homogène du décor qui la présente, du décor dont elle émerge. On a ici un trône qui n'est pas la figure d'une démonstration perspective utilisée dans un contexte triomphal, mais un trône comme portrait allégorique du printemps en ce que ses éléments concourent à la définition de la figure féminine. Voilà donc un appareil d'éléments pétrifiés renvoyant à l'élément marin. L'image contredit par son traitement la nature de la référence qu'elle construit. Espèces de l'autre monde, de l'ailleurs, du fantastique, de ce qui n'est pas soumis aux règles de la mimésis, ces créatures stylisées affirment la fonction ornementale, imaginaire plutôt que la rationalité perspective et anatomique alors en vigueur. On a là quelque chose comme un délire linéaire mais organisé. Se côtoient ici dans la tension un sujet humaniste, une figure renaissante et ses conditions de présentation selon des codes déjà conventionnels, et un traitement anti-réaliste, anti-idéaliste qui se résout dans l'assemblage.

Ces observations à propos de la tension entre la rigidité de l'abstraction linéaire des figures et l'évocation de l'élément marin nous ramènent au duel. Entre les méandres fluviaux qui mènent vers la "Tour de Babel" et la fil distendu de la robe virginale, l'expression de la crise trouve son centre névralgique à la surface du corps cintré du cheval. L'effet de mouvement produit par l'animation du panneau de gauche trouve sa contrepartie dans cette figure, dans cette irradiation des lignes parcourant, telles des veines gonflées de sang, la robe de la bête immobilisée mais tendue. *Par cette innervation, l'emblème s'anime tout en conservant sa staticité*; la couleur vive se manifeste, dans ce trait incisif, comme puissance d'animation de la figure emblématisée du combat. Mais, simultanément, surgit au coeur de ce duel et à travers ce corps médiateur ainsi innervé, l'image étonnante d'une licorne dont la pique est dessinée par la lance du cavalier: corne dorée qui condense l'image d'un rayon divin, et celle de l'arme de combat. Cette métamorphose révèle une association qui appartient spécifiquement à l'imaginaire ferrarais. Elle emblématise très habilement la symbolique du bon gouvernement du duc Borso d'Este et vient enrichir le champ sémantique lié à l'image de saint Georges du mythe de la licorne. Puissance de purification, l'animal fabuleux qui, de sa corne, débarasse l'eau de toute souillure, comme le cavalier terrassant le monstre lacustre, symbolise l'action du Prince vainqueur des terres marécageuses de Ferrare. Par l'image de la licorne associée au portrait emblématique du duc et à la symbolique de la Vierge Marie, le rapport à la terre contamine le rapport au sacré, et l'image du Prince émerge par le pouvoir de condensation pictural dans l'espace de l'Église.

NOTES

* Ce travail s'est développé à partir du projet de recherche "La Figure d'Andromède, de la renaissance au Baroque", dirigé par Françoise Siguret et Alain Laframboise, professeurs à l'Université de Montréal, et a bénéficié d'une aide du Conseil de Recherches en Sciences Humaines du Canada.

[1] *Un santo guerriero. San Giorgio tra Ferrara e Praga, Dalle collezioni estensi a Konopiste*, catalogue d'exposition (Ferrare, *Castello Estense*, avril-juillet 1991), Ferrare, Gabriele Corbo Editore, 1991.

[2] "Consiglio ciascuno pittore molto si faccia famigliare ad i poeti, retorici e agli altri simili dotti di lettere, già che costoro doneranno nuove invenzioni, o certo aiuteranno a bello componere sua storia, per quali certo acquisteranno in sua pittura molte lode e nome"; Alberti, *Della pittura*, édité par Cecil Grayson, Rome-Bari, Gius, Laterza & Figli, "Biblioteca degli Scrittori d'Italia", 1975, p. 94, traduit par Alain Laframboise dans *Istoria et théorie de l'art. Italie, XVᵉ, XVIᵉ siècles*, Montréal, Presses de l'Université de Montréal, 1989, p. 53.

[3] "Dico composizione essere quella ragione di dipingere, per la quale le parti si compongono nella opera dipinta. Grandissima opera del pittore sarà l'istoria: parte della istoria sono i corpi: parte de'corpi sono i membri: parte de'membri sono le superficie. [. . .] Tutti i corpi per grandezza e suo officio s'aconfaranno a quello che ivi nella storia si facci"; Alberti, *Della pittura*, op. cit., pp. 56–58 et p. 68, traduit par Alain Laframboise, *Istoria et théorie de l'art*, op. cit., p. 48.

[4] *Ibid.*, p. 27.

[5] Imprese: "le imagini fatte per significare una diversa cosa da quella che si vede con l'occhio [. . .] nelle quali con pochi corpi, & poche parole un sol concetto s'accenna". Emblemi: "[imagini] ove maggior concetto con più quantità di parole, & di corpi si manifesta"; Proemio, ICONOLOGIA/OVERO/Descrittione di diverse Imagini/cavate dall'antichità, & di pro-/pria inventione;/Trovate, & dichiarate/DA CESARE RIPA/PERUGINO,/Cavaliere de Santi Mauritio, &/Lazaro./[. . .] OPERA/Non meno utile che necessaria a Poeti/Pittori, Scultori, & altri, per rappre-/sentare le Virtù, Vitij, Affetti,/& Passioni humane./IN ROMA,/[. . .] M. DC. III., PROEMIO; facsimile édité par Georg Olms Verlag, New York, Hildesheim, 1970.

[6] Le sens "littéral" et le sens "spirituel" se rapportent aux termes de Pierre Fontanier, qui range par ailleurs les allégories personnifiées dans la classe des fictions poétiques ou des figures de pensée, plus marquées, plus étendues que les figures d'expression "courtes, rapides, qui ne se font qu'en passant, sur lesquelles on ne s'appuie pas, et qui ne sont visiblement qu'une expression un peu plus recherchée, substituée à l'expression ordinaire"; Pierre Fontanier, *Les figures du discours* (1830), Paris, Flammarion, "Champ", 1977; des tropes en plusieurs mots, ou improprement dits: personnification et allégorie, pp. 113–114.

[7] *Ibid.*, p. 114.

[8]   Nicole Loraux, *Les expériences de Tirésias, Le féminin et l'homme grec*, Paris, Gallimard, 1989, p. 10.

[9]   "C'est lui surtout qui, en combinant les tendances du caractère national avec les principes du Squarcione et en mettant à profit la présence prolongée de Piero della Francesca dans sa propre patrie, vivifia l'étude de la nature par la puissance du modelé et par l'exactitude de la perspective. Souvent âpre et rigide dans son style, trop peu préoccupé de la souplesse des carnations, de la beauté des types et de la pureté des lignes, il prête à ses personnages des formes dures et anguleuses, donne à ses draperies des plis tourmentés et compliqués. En revanche, il possède à un haut degré le sentiment de la grandeur et de la noblesse; il a horreur du banal et du conventionnel, et il étudie avec soin la structure du corps humain; enfin son coloris, poli comme un émail, est à la fois clair et brillant"; G. Gruyer, *L'art ferrarais à l'époque des princes d'Este*, 1897: "La maggiore impressione di ferocia del Tura è nel silenzio astrale di codeste sofferenze. Il mondo del Tura, quel mondo contorto e laminato in acciaio, sfaccettato in diamante, è offerto traverso una parete di vetro: i rumori, le lagrime, sono rimasti al di là, sono avvenimenti di un momento prima. Parlare di Tura in termini di fragori, sia pure pietrificati, di stravolgimenti metallici, di mineralogia sontuosa e feroce, è parlare incentrando formalisticamente il discorso"; Claudio Savonuzzi, "I quattro pannelli del Tura a Ferrara", *Emporium*, 1949: pour ne citer, par ailleurs, que ces extraits tirés de l'excellente enquête historiographique de Jadranka Bentini parue dans *San Giorgio e la Principessa di Cosmè Tura. Dipinti restaurati per l'officina ferrarese*, sous la direction de Jadranka Bentini, Bologne, Nuova Alfa Editoriale, 1985, pp. 28 et 35. "Nelle mirabili pagine del Berenson e in parte in quelle del Venturi inizia quella lettura interpretativa di Cosmè, pittore sconcertante, irrazionale e fantastico, parossistico e allucinato, forgiatore di forme pietrificate e maniaco dell'espressione feroce, ascetico, magico, lucido e feroce che rimarrà sostanzialmente immutata fino a Roberto Longhi"; pp. 28–29.

[10] Cette oeuvre, remplie d'objets-signes insolites – en termes d'*istoria* – ayant fortement orienté le discours du côté des enquêtes symboliques, a fait l'objet, notamment, d'interprétations alchimiques poussées d'Enrico Guidoni et d'Angela Marino ("Cosmus Pictor. Il "nuovo organo" di Ferrara: armonia, storia, e alchimia della creazione". *Storia dell'Arte*, 1969, pp. 388–414) à Marco Bertozzi ("Il Signore della Serpe, Simbolismo ermetico e alchimia nel S. Giorgio e il drago di Cosmè Tura", *San Giorgio e la Principessa*, *op. cit.*, pp. 55–64.)

[11] Roland Barthes, "La lutte avec l'ange: analyse textuelle de *Genèse* 32.23–33", *L'aventure sémiologique*, Paris, Le Seuil, "Points-Essais", 1985, pp. 316 et 328 (*Analyse structurale et exégèse biblique*, Genève, Labor et Fides, 1972).

[12] Nous signalons notre analyse des rapports féminin/monstrueux dans quelques tableaux maniéristes représentant le combat de saint Georges: "Une iconographie parergonale du combat. Pour une problématique du corpus héroïque", *Trois (revue d'écriture et d'érudition)*, **8**/1, automne 1992.

[13] Enrico Guidoni et Angela Marino, "Cosmus Pictor . . .", cités par Jadranka Bentini dans *Antologia critica, op. cit.*, p. 39.

[14] Jacques de Voragine, *La légende dorée*, trad. J.-B. M. Roze, chronologie et introduction par le Révérend Père Hervé Savon, Paris, Garnier/Flammarion, 1967, tome I, p. 298.

[15] Ces notions, issues d'une codification théâtrale, opèrent une subdivision territoriale du champ figuratif qui rend compte de la dimension spatiale de la représentation. Dans

"La description de l'image: à propos d'un paysage de Poussin" (*Communications*, **15**, 1970, pp. 186–209), Louis Marin en fait les éléments d'une structure émergeant de l'analyse des lectures du *Paysage avec un homme tué par un serpent* de Poussin par Fénelon et Félibien. Il considère l'objet-texte qu'est le tableau en fonction du discours qui le constitue et le marque. Précisons ici que la "scène" chez Marin est directement liée à la spatialité alors qu'il en fait le moyen terme complexe entre le décor et les acteurs, là où se rencontrent la nature et l'action. C'est à ce titre qu'elle se distingue de la définition strictement narrative que lui assigne Jean Petitot-Cocorda dans son analyse sémiotique des représentations de *Saint Georges terrassant le dragon*: "[...] dans l'oeuvre figurative se répondent la scène et le lieu. Or, si la scène, signifiante parce qu'articulée topographiquement par la virtuosité combinatoire, relève d'une théorie générale de la narrativité, le lieu relève quant à lui d'une théorie générale de la spatialité"; *Sémiotique de l'espace, architecture, urbanisme. Sortir de l'impasse*, Paris, Denoël/Gonthier, p. 97.

[16] Roland Barthes, "Introduction à l'analyse structurale des récits", *L'analyse structurale du récit*, Paris, Le Seuil, "Points", 1981, p. 23 (*Communications*, **8**, 1966).

[17] Bernard Lamblin, *Peinture et temps*, Paris, Klincksieck, "Esthétiques", 1983. Mais l'auteur fait preuve d'une certaine prudence quant à la pertinence et à l'applicabilité de son modèle: "Est-il besoin de remarquer au passage que notre analyse n'a nullement l'intention de conclure à l'illégitimité des tentatives faites par [les] artistes pour s'écarter de la disposition traditionnelle? Il est évident que la qualité d'une oeuvre ne saurait être déduite de son acceptation ou de son refus d'une tradition ou des lois prétendument éternelles de la composition. C'est à l'artiste qu'il incombe d'imposer et de justifier la solution qu'il a choisie"; p. 96, note 94. L'auteur semble néanmoins privilégier les solutions plus évidentes ou "heureuses" (selon ses propres termes) facilitant l'exercice d'une interprétation en termes de vraisemblance, et se méfie des compositions artificielles qui menacent l'unité dramatique et que l'artiste devra toujours s'appliquer à *justifier* comme la laisse entendre cette remarque sur l'*Annonciation* de Lorenzo Lotto: "En nous faisant assister à la réaction de la Vierge avant de nous présenter l'action qui la commande, il renverse l'ordre temporel du dialogue et a besoin alors de tout son art pour nous dissimuler cette intervention"; p. 103. L'auteur soulève ainsi la portée signifiante des écarts ou des oppositions qui entravent le libre cheminement du regard et provoquent dans l'image des tensions dont le spectateur admirera les effets d'autant qu'ils soient légitimés.

[18] Cette étonnante montagne est un élément clé de l'interprétation symbolique hermétique qui fait de l'oeuvre de Cosmè Tura ce *magnum opus alchemico* dont parle Marco Bertozzi; le mythe de la *renovatio* philosophico-religieuse se fait ici oeuvre d'art. "È la via che conduce alla torre della sapienza che sovrasta la 'citadella simbolica', cinta da una triplice cerchia di mura. [...] Al di fuori della prima cerchia di mura, sempre nello scomparto della Principessa, scorgiamo la figura di un impiccato [...], alla cui forca è appoggiata una lunga scala. Questa immagine sintetizza ancora un episodio del faticoso cammino dell'ascesa verso la perfezione mistica e la rivelazione della verità divina. La morte per impiccagione, la sospensione nel vuoto, indica il distacco dalle influenze terrene: una sorta di prova rituale e iniziatica lungo il percorso che conduce all'apice della sapienza; una stazione intermedia della 'sofferenza' che si richiede a chi vuol portare a compimento la 'grande opera'"; "Il Signore della Serpe...", *op. cit.*, pp. 57–58.

[19] Louis Marin, "Annonciations toscanes", *Opacité de la peinture, Essais sur la représentation au Quattrocento*, Florence, Usher, 1989, p. 135.

[20] *Ibid.*, p. 127.

²¹ Louis Marin fait aussi de cette relation la base d'une réflexion sur l'affinité entre
la théorie de l'énonciation et l'économie du secret. "Énonciation – Annonciation: Le
rapprochement des deux termes n'est pas simple jeu de mots ou de lettres: le récit de
l'Annonciation – comme représentation narrative du secret du mystère (de l'Incarnation
rédemptrice) – peut être considéré comme l'*exemplum*, voire le paradigme (dans le domaine
du discours religieux mystique) de la *théorie* de l'énonciation; il exhibe narrativement
la structure théorique des modes de connaissance de l'énonciation de langue, tout comme,
à l'inverse, la théorie de l'énonciation constitue l'économie abstraite, générale, de la
logique en acte du secret dans l'espace de communication. [. . .] L'énonciation ne peut
être approchée qu'indirectement, à partir des marques, traces ou indices qu'elle laisse dans
les énoncés empiriques qu'elle fonde et qu'elle permet: pronoms personnels, démonstratifs,
adverbes de temps et de lieu, temps verbaux, modalités, tout le champ de la *deixis* discursive – orale ou écrite – s'ouvre à la connaissance théorique à partir d'une problématique
de la trace et de l'inscription. On comprend alors combien ces énonciations énoncées,
ces marques ou traces de l'énonciation ont une remarquable affinité avec la logique et
l'économie du secret dans le procès de communication, dans la mesure où elles 'signa-
lent' la structure énonciative 'virtuelle', en désignent obliquement la présence, en
'insinuant' le dispositif, et ce, même par leur absence, comme c'est le cas 'idéal-typique'
avec la modalité énonciative écrite de l'histoire;" *Ibid.*, p. 138.
²² Ibid., p. 136.

BRUCE ROSS

ISLAMIC HERMENEUTICS AND SHIHABUDDIN SUHRAWARDI'S *LANGUAGE OF THE ANTS*

In an allegorical animal tale by Shihabuddin Suhrawardi, the twelfth-century Sufi best known for his theosophy of light, a hoopoe is threatened with death by a group of fairies (20–22). Unlike the hoopoe, the fairies are nearly blind and have based their understanding of the world upon their blindness. The seeing hoopoe is thus considered a dangerous heretic because its version of the world differs from theirs. The hoopoe saves its life by deciding to "speak to the people according to their intelligence" and by consequently pretending to be blind (21). When the disheartened hoopoe finally leaves the fairies at the conclusion of the tale, he characterizes the fairies by quoting *sura* 27:25 of the Koran: ". . . they worship not Allah Who bringeth forth the hidden in the heavens and the earth" (22). This tale is a simple parable that contrasts those, like the hoopoe, who correctly perceive reality through the Islamic faith, to those, like the fairies, who are figuratively blind to that faith. The tale is also Suhrawardi's imaginative reconstruction of the narrative of Solomon in section two of *sura* 27, in which the hoopoe, Solomon's messenger, reports on the land of Saba whose inhabitants worship the sun rather than Allah, having been seduced by Satan into misperceiving reality. Suhrawardi's tale consequently depicts the fairies, like the people of Saba, as obvious heretics who are ruled by their senses rather than by faith.

A sub-text of Suhrawardi's tale concerns the narrative mechanisms through which revealed truth might be disclosed. The parable of the hoopoe in effect suggests that truth should be hidden from disbelievers. Suhrawardi comments on the idea of narrative concealment in discussing his *Book of Conversations:* ". . . if one were to study this present book carefully, one would find that it is not devoid of precious things and treasures hidden under a thin veil. If the half-wit is unable to discover them, the fault is not mine" (Corbin, *Spiritual Body*, 119). One reason for narrative concealment is that controversial, even heretical, ideas can be dangerous, as the hoopoe discovers. Suhrawardi himself, like other Sufis, was persecuted and in fact executed because of his heterodox beliefs. Another motive for narrative concealment, one voiced by the

179

A-T. Tymieniecka (ed.), Analecta Husserliana XLIII, 179–194.
© 1994 *Kluwer Academic Publishers. Printed in the Netherlands.*

hoopoe and evoked in world literature, is that the uninitiated, the un-
educated, Suhrawardi's "half-wit," is not able to comprehend canons
of moral law and abstract or difficult religious thought. Unconcealed
narrative, such as the philosophic essay, a social realist novel, or a
journalistic account, is more or less straightforward in its use of words
and images. In this case the linguistic sign occurs at the most literal of
semantic levels. Word or sign "x" conveys and is meant to convey a
conventional meaning in the most direct manner possible. Rather than
occurring as a predominant stylistic idiom, metaphoric expression and
figurative language are highlighted as examples in narratives that intend
to express a forthright presentation of ideas and "facts." Contrariwise,
concealed narrative uses symbols and allegory of varying degrees of
ambiguity to convey its message. Word or sign "x" becomes a symbol
for meaning "y." Common sense, a general understanding of a given
ideology or belief system, or the context of the narrative itself reveals
the hidden meaning of the symbols or allegory. The animal image, as
in Suhrawardi's tales, often serves as a symbol in popular traditional
narrative. It is a two-dimensional symbol of the prudential wisdom of
man in the fable traditions, a naturalistic emblem of the play of good
and evil according to medieval Christian theology in the bestiary traditions, and an ironical token of the failures and superfluities of human
nature and society in the satirical beast epic traditions. Like the
Suhrawardi tale that explicates its symbols through quotations from the
Koran, the fable elucidates its meaning through a concluding gloss of
its narrative, the bestiary interprets its animal subject through a concluding *significatio*, and the satirical beast epic clarifies its linked animal
tales through interspersed moral commentary.

The animal image also serves mythic narratives. Usually expressed
in a highly metaphoric idiom, these traditional narratives, which include
"delivered" scriptures like the Old Testament and the Koran, represent
a primordial sacred time or the convergence of sacred time or intention
with history. Myths are explanations of the origin and development of
the natural order, the social institutions, the religious rituals, and the
beliefs of a given culture. Offering narratives of supernatural beings
and forces, myths represent supernatural reality and are therefore sacred
texts, unlike the "made up" moral tales of the fable and satirical beast
epic traditions or the moralized natural histories of the bestiary traditions.
Mythic texts often include divinely prescribed rituals and moral codes
and passages that in their ambiguity or imagistic resonance elicit inter-

pretation. Likewise, with the advent of Greek philosophy, the embodiment of myth through rituals became differentiated from the thinking about myth. This in turn led to the allegorical interpretation of mythic narrative so that images became symbols of traditional moral wisdom. In such interpretation, myth, like the fable, the bestiary, and the satirical beast epic, provides symbols whose meaning is read into the narrative to convey its inner meaning. Allegorical interpretation thus "completes" the myth, just as moral commentary completes the fable, the bestiary, and the satirical beast epic. Allegorical interpretation is an intellectual method of reading that is predicated upon the connotative possibilities inherent in language. Here the interpretation of a symbol allows one to move from one system of meaning to another without taxing the plausible limits of intention and common knowledge. This method of interpretation has been commonly used in the hermeneutics applied to the sacred texts of the great world faiths. Ibn Arabi, the thirteenth-century theosophical Sufi, augments this mode of interpretation through his concept of *tatbiq* or the uncovering of parallels. Whereas allegorical interpretation "reads onto" the text through an established pattern of symbols, parallel interpretation considers sacred texts, history, and individual human acts to be symbols of the spiritual world. A principally intellectual exercise becomes here an examination of the ontology of spirit by "reading backwards" from an intuition of the spiritual world. As Helmut Gatje notes of *tatbiq*: "Underlying this is the idea that sensual forms stand dependant upon a more general spiritual world into which one may ' cross over'" (41). And "crossing over" is the central concept underlying Sufic hermeneutics.

The tradition of the Islamic hermeneutics of the Koran is clearly divided into two modes of interpretation, the exoteric and the esoteric.[1] Like the Judaic exegetical method *pardes*, and medieval Christian allegorical interpretation, Islamic hermeneutics designates hierarchical levels of significance, ranging from the literal to the anagogic. The orthodox Islamic spiritual authorities, the *ulama* or doctors of the Law who executed Suhrawardi, practice exoteric or literal interpretation. They may be contrasted with the Sufi Shaykhs or spiritual masters, and the Sufi theosophists, who practice esoteric or anagogic interpretation. The term for exoteric interpretation is *tafsir* or "external interpretation." To validate its methodology, *tafsir* relies solely upon the *shari'ah*, the revealed law of the Koran, and the *sunnah* or sayings of Muhammad that are found in the *hadith* collections. "Outer" interpretation of the Koran, like unconcealed narrative, emphasizes the denotative, literal, historically verifiable nature of language and meaning. *Tafsir* in fact shares the same linguistic root with the word for commentaries on philosophic and scientific works (Gatje, 267, n54). Thus the traditionalist exegete Tabari notes: "Man's duty (*fard*) is to believe in the external wording (*zahir*) of the revelation; he is not required to know anything which goes beyond this" (Gatje, 65). The term for esoteric interpretation is *ta'wil* or "internal interpretation." *Ta'wil* supplements the methodology of *tafsir* through an investigation of an intuited inner dimension of the *shari'ah*. "Inner" interpretation, like concealed narrative, emphasizes the connotative, figurative, symbolic, allegorical, and metaphoric nature of language and meaning. In Sufic terms, *ta'wil* reflects an uncovering of an esoteric dimension of the *shari'ah* that evokes an immanent spiritual realm. Even the great Muslim philosopher Ibn Rushd (Averroes) recommends the use of "internal interpretation," if only on purely rational grounds, when the "outer interpretation" of the Koran contradicts reason:

> If agreement [of *tafsir* and reason] is present, there is no need for discussion; however, if no agreement is present, then allegorical exegesis (*ta'wil*) is required. Allegorical exegesis thereby has the purpose of converting the meaning (*dalala*) of an expression from the literal meaning (*dalala haqiqiyya*) to a figurative meaning (*dalala majaziyya*), without thereby damaging the standard linguistic usage of the Arabs with regard to the foundation of metaphors. (Gatje, 232)

Ibn Rushd's definition of *ta'wil* is thus simply a linguistic one that would exclude the idea of intution that is the basis of the Sufic use of the term.

Al-Ghazzai, the eleventh-century Sufi theologian who tried to reconcile the two traditions of Islamic hermeneutics, would contest Ibn Rushd's reduction of all Koranic interpretation to the proceedings of rational thought. Al-Ghazzai also knows that a hermeneutics that contradicts the established exoteric mode of interpretation would be considered heretical. He accordingly notes: "The people who are acquainted with only the outer aspect of exegesis (*tafsir*) have . . . discredited the mystics in so far as they have been involved with exegesis, because they explain (*ta'wil*) the wording of the Qur'an other than according to the tradition of Ibn 'Abbas and the other interpreters. They have thus advocated the view that what is involved here is unbelief" (Gatje, 228). The doctors of the Law could justify their refutation of *ta'wil* and the Sufis by citing *sura* 3:7:

It is He who has revealed to you the Koran. Some of its verses are precise in meaning – they are the foundations of the Book – and others are ambiguous. Those whose hearts are infected with disbelief follow the ambiguous part, so as to create dissention by seeking to explain it. But no one knows its meaning except Allah. (*Koran*, 408)

Zamakhshari, the twelfth-century linguistic exegete, consequently glosses "Those (who) . . . follow the ambiguous part . . ." thus: "They confine themselves to the ambiguous verses, which (on the one hand) allow the point of view of the (heretical) innovations without harmonizing them with the (clearly) determined verses. However (on the other hand), (these verses) also allow an interpretation which agrees with the views of the orthodox" (Gatje, 57). Zamakhshari, like his fellow exegetes, has it both ways. For him, those who try to resolve obscure passages in the Koran are heretics unless they belong to the orthodoxy. That Suhrawardi and other Sufis were executed for transgressing such hegemonic reasoning makes a telling statement about the social the political under-pinnings inherent in the divergences between the two major hermeneutic traditions.

Al-Ghazzai attempts to liberate *ta'wil* and Sufic methodology from this reasoning by sketching a mode of interpretation that is not depen-dent upon the rational and linguistic elements of *tafsir* and yet is able to elucidate Koranic spiritual knowledge which would not be conceived through *tafsir*:

All in all, every kind of knowledge is included in the realm of actions and attributes of God, and the description of the nature of the actions and attributes of God is contained in the Qur'an. These kinds of knowledge are unending: yet, in the Qur'an is found (only) an indication of their general aspects. Thereby the (various) degrees (*magamat*) of the deeper penetration into the particulars of knowledge are traced back to the (actual) under-standing of the Qur'an. The mere outer aspect of interpretation yields no hint of this knowledge. Rather, the fact is that the Qur'an contains indications and hints, which certain select people with (correct) understanding can grasp, concerning all that remains obscure of the theoretical way of thinking and that about which the creatures (*al-khala'iq*) disagree regarding the theoretical sciences and rational ideas. (Gatje, 229)

In effect Al-Ghazzai develops a mystical, rather than conceptual or linguistic, approach to the interpretation of the Koran. An intuition ("deeper penetration") of divine reality as such is applied ("traced back") to the Koran. *Tafsir* or external interpretation, the "theoretical sciences and rational ideas," cannot explain the Koranic "indications and hints" about the ontology of divine reality. Only the Sufic *ta'wil* reaches the threshold of interpretation required to comprehend the "ambiguous" and "obscure" sections of the Koran. *Ta'wil* completes and goes beyond *tafsir*. The Sufis, rather than the doctors of the Law, are Al-Ghazzai's "select people" who can resolve the ambiguities and disclose the inner meaning (*batin*) of the Koran. Al-Ghazzai's idea of applying a direct knowledge of divine reality to the Koran in the act of *ta'wil* reaches a kind of culmination in Ibn Arabi's concept of linking the spiritual world to the Koran through *tatbiq* or parallel exegesis. In the century between these two figures, Shihabuddin Suhrawardi develops an elaborate theosophy in which the interplay between the spiritual dimension and man's existence is established. This interplay, which is predicated upon the idea of the Malakut or interworld between the divine world and the world of man, also provides, according to Henry Corbin, the mechanism for an "inner interpretation" of the Koran: ". . . it is through it [the Malakut] that the *ta'wil* is accomplished, that is, the exegesis which 'reconducts' the teachings of the Quranic Revelation back to their 'spiritual truth'" (quoted in Eliade, 143, n86). The superimposition of a dialectic between man's consciousness and spiritual reality upon the act of Koranic interpretation that is common to these three Sufis is characteristic of the emphasis that Sufism places on the centrality of direct spiritual experience.

Orthodox Muslim faith is predicated on the beliefs and duties derived from the *shari'ah*, the sacred Law of Islam, foremost of which is *tawhid*, the affirmation of divine unity. For the orthodox, this affirmation, "There is no divinity but God," is repeated daily, and for the majority of Muslims it is a purely verbal construct. The Sufis, however, attempt to experience the ontological ground of the spiritual reality inherent in this testimony. The Sufis do not reject the *shari'ah* of common faith; rather, they conceive of *haqigah* or divine reality as the center of a circle whose circumference is the Law. The Sufi path or *tariquah* leads from the Law at the outside of the circle to divine reality at the circle's midpoint.[2] This path, then, "has as its goal the spiritual realization of *tawhid* through gnosis . . ." (Danner, 242). The Sufis believe that each Muslim has a kind of divine essence that corresponds to the divine reality of God. The Sufic path has thus been defined as "perfecting one's *ihsan*, or one's spiritual life, through conformity to the indwelling spirit . . ." (Danner, 171). This mystical approach to the Muslim faith is also based on the idea of *dhikr* or the remembrance of God, often achieved through the actual repetition of God's name, which links the devotee to the divine presence, and on *bay'ah* or the transference of grace, the state necessary for spiritual enlightenment, from the Shaykh, the Sufi master, to his disciple.

Corbin has defined Suhrawardi's theosophy of light as a "hermeneutics of exile" (*Temple*, 277). It shares with all Sufism the Platonic idea that man has forgotten that he is ontologically part of a divine reality. Man's spiritual perception, as opposed to his sense perception or his normal mental operations, is centered in the transcendental *'ayn al-qalb* or eye of the heart. Beacuse of his primordial fall from grace and consequent immorality, man's inner eye became closed or veiled. By adhering to the Sufi path, one may cause this eye to open and reveal spiritual reality. The *'ayn al-qalb* presumably also implements the act of *ta'wil*, the interpretation of the inner meaning of the Koran.

Orthodox Muslims believe in a reality in which Allah, the supreme God, acts directly upon man and the natural universe as well as through the mediation of angels. The Muslim faith is established with Allah's presentation of the Koran to Muhammad and through the angel Gabriel's revelation of visions to Muhammad. Similarly, Suhrawardi develops his theosophy of light because of an encounter with a spiritual being: "Suddenly I was wrapped in gentleness; there was a blinding flash, then a very diaphanous light in the likeness of a human being. I watched attentively and there he was: Helper of souls, Imam of wisdom, *Primus Magister*, whose form filled me with wonder and whose shining beauty dazzled me" (Corbin, *Spiritual Body*, 118–19). This miraculous being's message is simple: "For the seeker, the way consists first of all in investigating his knowledge of himself, and then in raising himself to the knowledge of that which is above him" (Corbin, *Spirtual Body*, 119–20). Suhrawardi consequently constructs a metaphysical order, elaborated in his *Oriental Theosophy*, that includes a more complex angelology than that of orthodox Islam, and which may be derived from Zoroastrianism.[3] His metaphysics of light is similar to Platonic Idealism. It depicts levels of diminishing degrees of spiritual light which emanate from a godhead of primal light. An angel presides over each of these levels. The angel Gabriel directs the last level. Here mankind's souls and prophetic visions, like those of the Koran, issue from Gabriel. These souls, which Suhrawardi calls Beings of Light, are separated from their counterparts, the human souls of the natural world, by the intermediate world of the Malakut. Through the instrument of Surawardi's mystical psychology, a man's inner being ascends this metaphysical order so as to unite with his heavenly soul. Ultimately one may even experience God Himself, this being the supreme goal of Sufism. Accordingly, in Suhrawardi's visionary tales, a spiritual pilgrim unites with the *khangah* or divine temple at the heart of his own heavenly soul.[4] The pilgrim encounters Gabriel and is eventually surrounded by flashes of light which demarcate a union with the highest divine presence. When this state becomes permanent, the pilgrim attains *Sakinah*, the perpetual flooding of the soul with divine light.[5]

One of the impulses behind mysticism, the direct or intuitive experience of God or divine reality, is to justify faith in a way that rivals the powerful claims of ordinary sense perception. After all, aside from the devotees of mystic traditions, madmen, poets, saints and prophets are the only ones to claim that they have directly experienced divine reality. The long history of natural theology reflects the need to reconcile the perceived universe with a divine reality. The concept of origin or first creation serves, often through metaphor, analogy, and parable, as a means of explaining or proving the existence of a divine reality. Logic and natural law also provide mechanisms for establishing divine reality through reason, a direction that reaches a high point in western thought with the idea of a clockwork universe. The Deists thus conceived of a God completely removed from his perfectly ordered natural world. By extension, modern science conceives of a similarly ordered world but without any reference to a God at all. Natural law thus replaces faith in a divine will. The gradual displacement of the idea of divine will by natural law is mirrored in the reference in *sura* 27 to the people of Saba who worship the sun rather than Allah. The overwhelming domination of man by his sense perceptions leads to the pantheism of Saba through his religious urge, and to natural science through his faculty of reason. The difficult task of establishing proof for an abstract deity leads either to an act of faith in divine scriptures, the path of orthodoxy; to the development of arguements for God's existence, the goal of the theologians; or to the establishment of a gnosis of direct revelation, the direction of mysticism.

Suhrawardi's gnosticism of light attempts to establish the existence of divine reality as well as to reconcile the perceptual world with the spiritual one through a visionary psychology. This mode of gnosticism is illustrated by Corbin's outline of Suhrawardi's discussion of the various ways in which the visible sky could be perceived:

There are several ways of regarding the heavens. One of these is common to men and beasts. Another is that of the men of science, the astronomers and astrologers, who see the heavens with the eyes of heavens. Finally, there are those who see the heavens neither with the eyes of the flesh nor with the eyes of the heavens, but with the eyes of inner vision. In them the organ of the inner vision is an *Imago caeli* that does not originate in empirical perceptions, but that precedes and governs all such perceptions. (*Spiritual Body*, 271)

Thus, the *'ayn al-qalb*, the inner eye, shares in a Platonic-like spiritual world through which the natural world derives and maintains its existence. Ordinary sense perception is in effect filtered through this inner vision, but man must first purify his inner being, before he can correctly percieve reality. Suhrawardi's "hermeneutics of exile" represents the clouding of inner vision, a characteristic concept of all Sufism, and the consequent absence of spiritual light, an image used throughout Islamic thought but worked out in detail in Suhrawardi's theosophy of light. For Suhrawardi, light is not a metaphor but an essential reality, like the early Zoroastrian sun god Mithra or the light flowing out of the godhead in Plotinus's neo-Platonic metaphysics. Suhrawardi calls this divine source of illumination Bahman-Light, the origin of all spiritual forms which in turn generate the world of perceptual reality.[6]

Such ideas perhaps influenced the seventeenth-century Shiite theosopher Qummi's conception that spiritual light is the first thing to emerge from the godhead. Qummi represents this light as either a throne, an Intelligence such as Suhrawardi's angels, or Muhammadan Light, the manifestation of spiritual illumination in the visible universe through the presence of the prophet Muhammad.[7] The Koran itself justifies the use of light as an emblem of spiritual reality in *sura* 24:35:

Allah is the light of the heavens and the earth. His light may be compared to a niche that enshrines a lamp, the lamp within a crystal of star-like brilliance. It is lit from a blessed olive tree neither eastern or western. Its very oil would almost shine forth, though no fire touched it. Light upon light; Allah guides to His light whom He will. Allah coins metaphors for men.[8] (*Koran*, 217)

Through the imagery of light, this *sura* provides a model of how the parable could be used for religious instruction. The *sura* states that Allah actually offers or is this figurative illumination of the universe. The parable of the lamp serves as a metaphoric exposition of this concept. The figurative nature of the parable and the word "light" are underscored in the assertion that Allah uses metaphoric expressions to benefit or instruct man. The proponents of orthodox interpretation, *tafsir*, and the majority of Muslim believers would consider the *sura*'s equation of Allah with natural light to be merely a metaphor of Allah's omnipotence, if

they explicated this equation at all. In opposition, the proponents of
esoteric interpretation, *ta'wil*, and the Sufis would perceive this equation
not as a simple metaphor but as an expression of anagogic truth and,
for the Sufis, an ontological fact of existence: spiritual reality precedes
and determines natural reality. The Sufis would understand that they
possessed a spiritual light within themselves that was similiar to Allah's
illumination, and that this light linked them to spiritual reality and to
Allah. Suhrawardi and other Sufis, moreover, would adopt Koranic
metaphoric language to introduce unenlightened Muslims to the mystical
tenets of Sufism.

Suuhrawardi's collection of animal parables, *Language of the Ants*
(*Lughat-i-muran*), explains his theosophy of light through the veiled
narrative techniques of religious allegory. The preface to *Language of
the Ants* establishes the mystical psychology upon which the Sufic understanding of the relationship between the natural world and the spiritual
world is predicated: ". . . the existence of all existant things is due to witnessing the 'essence'" (13). The tales are intended as a way of "pointing
out the procedure" (13) through which this "essence" or spiritual perception might be acquired.

The first tale is Suhrawardi's imaginative response to *sura* 27:18:

Solomon marshalled his forces of jinn and men and birds, and set them in battle array.
When they came to the Valley of the Ants, an ant said to her sisters: "Go into your
dwellings, ants, lest Solomon and his warriors should unwittingly crush you." (*Koran*,
83)

This verse corresponds to the well-known proverb of Solomon:

Go to the ant, thou sluggard; consider her ways, and be wise; which having no guide,
overseer, or ruler, provideth her meat in the summer, and gathereth her food in the harvest.
How long wilt thou sleep, O sluggard? When wilt thou arise out of thy sleep . . . so
shall thy poverty come as one that travelleth, and thy want as an armed man. (*The Portable
World Bible*, 324)

Solomon's proverb, which is itself analogous to Aesop's fable of the
ant and the grasshopper, illustrates the virtue of industry. The industrious
ant that wisely arranges its life's activities for self-preservation is contrasted with a lazy man who, like Aesop's grasshopper that plays in the
summer and starves in the winter, will end up destitute. The industrious
wisdom of the proverbial ant carries over into the Koranic depiction of
the naive self-protective ant. An exoteric reading of the *sura* would interpret the ant as a symbol of common man's modest existence and practical

judgment.[9] Suhrawardi offers an esoteric reading of the *sura* by recon-
structing it in his parable of talking ants (13–14) and by connecting
this reworking to *sura* 24:35, which compares Allah to light.

The ants of Suhrawardi's tale are neither industrious nor humble;
instead they are introduced, in a blending of the ants and Solomon's army
of *sura* 27, as marauding soldiers in quest of food. Moreover, they are
portrayed as simpletons who argue about the origin of dew drops that
have formed like manna on blades of desert vegetation. Some of these
ants think that the dew comes from the earth. Others think that it comes
from the sea. A natural scientist among the ants invokes the law that
all things return to their origin and suggests that the ants observe what
element the dew is drawn to in order to determine its essential nature.
When the sun evaporates the dew, the ants realize that the dew comes
from the air. This tale is not a fable about simpletons and the obvious.
Rather, it is an allegory about the divine origin of man and the desired
union with God's light. Thus, the natural scientist ant, who promotes
Suhrawardi's theosophy, declares: "Whatever retreats to pure darkness
has also that [darkness] for its source. And on the other side of the
light of Divinity this fact is more evident with regard to a noble essence,
God forbid any supposition of a union. Whatever seeks light is also
from light" (14). The ants, except for the natural scientist among them,
are veiled souls who, like the uninitiated reader of this tale, must be
instructed in the spiritual truth of Sufism and in Suhrawardi's theosophy of light through the allegory of the dew. The tale therefore begins
with the ants emerging from the darkness of their symbolic spiritual blindness and concludes with a citation from *sura* 24:35 stating that Allah
will direct man to spiritual light. The ants need to clear their *'ayn al-
qalb*, the eye of the heart that senses spiritual reality, in order to perceive
spiritual light, the "noble essence" referred to in this tale and in the
preface to *Language of the Ants*. One expert on Sufism sums up this main
point of Suhrawardi: "The ontological status of a being depends on the
degree to which it is illuminated or veiled" (Schimmel, 261). The unenlightened Muslim, like the ants, must illuminate his soul with divine light
in order to exist as a spiritual being who may ultimately experience
God Himself.

The turtles in the following tale are also veiled souls, like the ants
(14–16). They discuss whether a speckled bird that occasionally dives
into the water inhabits the water element or the air element. A judge,
Suhrawardi's spokesman, attempts to resolve this question for the turtles

by interpreting the bird as a symbol of the soul's ascent from sense perception, the water, to spiritual reality, the air. Like this bird, the turtles should abandon their veiled perception, the world of their nest, and experience divine reality as a Sufi does. Accordingly, the judge even explicitly summarizes Suhrawardi's mystical psychology: "All are agreed that so long as the veils are not removed observation cannot be acquired. This essence which comes into observation is created and produced" (14–16). But the spiritually dense turtles are not able to comprehend a state of divine "essence," so they dismiss the judge and return to their nest. In another tale, like Suhrawardi's blind fairies who try to kill the Sufi-like hoopoe because of its divergent perception of the world, night-inhabiting bats are veiled souls who attempt to punish a chameleon by placing it in direct sunlight (19–20). Because the bats live in darkness, they cannot conceive of a worse punishment than sunlight, Suhrawardi's metaphor for spiritual truth. Thus the bats are unwittingly assisting the symbolic chameleon's spiritual progress.

The most dramatic depiction of the veiling of the soul in the tales is offered in the parable of the peacock and the king (22–25).[10] This king has one of his peacocks sewn up in leather and covered with a large basket so that the bird cannot observe its own beauty and has almost no contact with the world of the senses. Gradually the bird loses contact with the reality of the senses, here represented by the king's beautiful garden, which serves both as a traditional emblem of Islamic paradise and as a symbol of spiritual perception. The bird is released after a long imprisonment and gradually returns to its senses. The moral of the parable is expressed in a citation from the Koran (59:20): "They forgot Allah, therefore He caused them to forget their souls" (24). This parable illustrates the Islamic concept of *dhikr* or the remembrance of God's presence, and its opposite, *ghaflah*, the veiling of the *'ayn al-qalb*. The leather garment symbolizes the veiling of the soul and of spiritual perception. The peacock's yearning response to the few unfamiliar sense impressions that penetrate his leather garment and basket prison represents the inception of the movement from *ghaflah* to *dhikr* that occupies most of the tale.

Another Sufic concept that is illustrated in the tales is *fana* or the annihilation of the self by God's presence. Al-Hallaj, the ninth-century Sufi, offers a potent metaphor of this experience in his image of the moth being consumed by a candle's flame.[11] Thus in one tale a nightingale is the only bird not to respond to Solomon's request for a meeting (16).

The nightingale finally decides to leave its nest and meet Solomon outside because the nest, a symbol of ordinary sense identity, could not contain Solomon's meeting, which is a symbol of *fana* or union with Allah. The tale concludes with a poetic depiction of the ecstatic Sufic state of *fana* that highlights the selflessness of men saturated by God's presence: "He sang to me wholeheartedly, and I also sang as he did. And we were wherever they were, and they were wherever we were" (16). The process of achieving *fana*, the desired penultimate experience of mysticism, is depicted in another tale through the declarations of one of the kings of the jinns (17–19). This king outlines necessary acts of ritual purification that precede the experience of *fana* and quotes a ninth-century Persian Sufi, Kharraz, on the experience of *fana* itself:

"My qualities rose for the sovereign altogether,
My qualities disappeared when you disappeared from the prison,
And he disappeared on whose account was my absence,
So this was my annihilation, understand, O people of senses."

(18)

Ritual acts of purification, such as the establishment of the contemplative state of mind prescribed by the jinn king (18), lead to the elimination of sense perception and the annihilation of the self that are described by Kharraz. In line one, the speaker's attention is directed entirely towards Allah. Consequently, in the remaining lines ordinary sense perceptions, the "qualities," and the self based on such perceptions, are annihilated. Accordingly, the chameleon that was to be murdered by bats through exposure to the sun embodies the idea of *fana*. In contrast to the bats, veiled souls bound to sense perception, the chameleon actually views his death positively because it symbolizes the desired annihilation of the self through *fana* and unites it as an Islamic martyr with Allah. Thus Suhrawardi cites two lines of poetry whose oxymoronic figurative language evokes *fana*: "Kill me, O my confidents; killing me is my life, / My life is my death and my death is my life" (19). The tale concludes with the witty notion that the bats themselves would metaphorically die of rage if they became aware of the pleasure they were affording the chameleon (20).

Through spiritual allegory, the parables of *Language of the Ants* characterize the Sufic path with veiled illustrations of the *'ayn al-qalb*, *dhikr*, the process of purification, *fana*, and, finally, the ultimate experience of Sufism, the union with God. The Sufis have taken the general Islamic

concept of *tawhid*, a theological verbalization of divine unity, and transformed it into a declaration of the Sufic experience of spiritual ontology
in which God is seen in everything. The Sufic path that culminates in
spiritual union and spiritual perception is summed up in chapter eleven
of *Language of the Ants*:

Whatever is useful and good is bad; whatever is the veil of the way is the unbelief of
men. To be satisfied with self through what it acquires and to make up with that is a
weakness in the path of the [mystical] travelling and to be pleased with oneself is vanity,
although it is on account of truth. To turn the face towards God entirely is liberation.
(27)

One must exinguish the self of ordinary existence and replace it with
an awareness of God's presence in all things. This common thought of
Sufism is expressed in the imagery of light in Suhrawardi's theosophic
treatises and parables.

The imagery of light dominates Suhrawardi's parable of the candle
and the sun (27). A fool is upset because he cannot see the light of his
candle, the symbol of the ordinary self, when he holds it up to the sun,
the symbol of Allah and divine reality. From the perspective of the idea
of union, this parable of the annihilation of the self in God reflects a
desired experience, and therefore it closes with the rhetorical question,
"Is not everything except God in vain?" and a citation of *sura* 57:3 which
express the Sufic notion of *tawhid*: "He is the First and the Last, and
the Outward and the Inward; and He is the Knower of all things" (27).
A final parable uses the imagery of light to elaborate the relationship
between the self, here the moon, and divine reality, here the sun (25–26).
The other heavenly bodies wonder why the amount of light coming
from the moon varies. The moon explains that it does not have any
light of its own but reflects the light of the sun. The amount of light
reflected depends on the moon's relative closeness to the sun. The moon
symbolizes the purified soul that is able to annihilate the self in its
union with divine light. As the moon explains: ". . . all the smoothness
of my surface and the polish of my face is fixed for accepting his light.
So, every time when I look at myself I see his light" (26). Making use
of a tale-within-a-tale structure similar to that of the *Thousand and One
Nights*, Suhrawardi has the moon amplify the nature of the identification of the self with divine light through its own parable about a mirror
that was placed in front of the sun. The moon suggests that if the mirror
had eyes to look at itself, it would only see the sun and hence declare:

"I am the sun" (26). Again, as in the parable of the fool's candle and the sun, the desired union with divine light is made to seem foolish, and for a reason. When the moon, at the end of this parable, apologizes for the mirror's presumption in comparing itself to the sun: "If it says: 'I am the Truth' or 'Glory be to me! How great is my glory' its excuse must be accepted; even the blasphemy . . ." (26), it is reflecting Suhrawardi's concern for the survival of Sufism. "I am the Truth [= God]" is the statement that led to the execution of the Sufi mystic al-Hallaj, and it parallels the ideas that led to Suhrawardi's own execution.[12] Although the Sufic conception of the individual soul's identification with the godhead is meant to suggest an "essential – not material – identity" (Danner, 99),[13] the doctors of the Law would view such an idea as blasphemous and punishable by death. Suhrawardi's parable thus refects a central motive for veiled narrative – personal survival. Suhrawardi's spiritual allegories did not merely introduce sympathetic believers and the uninitiated to his mysticism of light; they were perhaps not so subtly presenting his case to the not so sympathetic orthodoxy. The mirror, the chameleon, and the hoopoe are the defamed Sufi theosopher Suhrawardi himself.

Empire State College

NOTES

[1] For a concise overview of Islamic hermeneutics see Danner, 69–71.

[2] See the definition of *haqiqah* in Danner, 234.

[3] For an extended discussion of Suhrawardi's theosophy of light in the context of the *Imago Templi*, see Corbin, *Spiritual Body*, 263–83.

[4] For a more detailed description of the soul's union with the divine temple see Corbin, *Spiritual Body*, 274.

[5] A comparison could be made between the *Sakinah* that is encountered at the tenth level of metaphysical light and the Judaic divine presence the *Shakinah*, that is associated with the tenth of the divine emanations or *sefirot* in Kabbalah.

[6] For the relation of Suhrawardi's Bahman-Light to earlier Iranian concepts see Corbin, *Spiritual Body*, 22.

[7] For a presentation of Qummi's theosophy of light see Corbin, *Spiritual Body*, 199–200.

[8] See the notes to *The Holy Koran*, 907–08 and also Appendix VII, 920–24 for a mystical interpretation of the parable of the lamp.

[9] See *The Holy Koran*, 982, n3258 and n3259 for an elaboration of this interpretation.

[10] An explanation of the king's actions is offered in the typical peacock entry of the western bestiary tradition. The peacock suffers for its undue pride in its beautiful feathers by suddenly observing its ugly feet. Suhrawardi's peacock may likewise be suffering from

pride. In one version of the bestiary a peacock cries out in the night because it is afraid that it has lost its beauty. The bestiary interprets this as the bird's fear that it has forfeited God's grace. Similarly, Suhrawardi's peacock, through *ghaflah*, has forgotten God's presence.

[11] This metaphor is elaborated in Schimmel, 142.
[12] See Eliade, 128, for a discussion of al-Hallaj's heretical statement.
[13] Compare this with Meister Eckhart's distinction between *Gott* and *Gottheit*.

REFERENCES

Corbin, Henry. *Spiritual Body and Celestial Earth, From Mazdean Iran to Shi'ite Iran.* Trans. Nancy Pearson. Princeton: Princeton University Press, 1977.

Corbin, Henry. *Temple and Contemplation.* Trans. Phillip Sheriard. London: Islamic Publications, 1986.

Danner, Victor. *The Islamic Tradition: An Introduction.* Amity: Amity House, 1988.

Eliade, Mircea. *A History of Religious Ideas, Vol. 3. From Muhammad to the Age of Reforms.* Trans. Alf Hiltebeitel and Diane Apostolos-Cappadona. Chicago: University of Chicago Press, 1985.

Gatje, Helmut. *The Qur'an and its Exegesis, Selected Texts with Classical and Modern Muslim Interpretations.* Trans. Alford T. Welch. London: Routledge, 1971.

The Holy Qur'an. Trans. A. Yusuf Ali. Riyadh: Khalil Al-Rawaf, 1978.

The Koran. Trans. N. J. Dawood. London: Penguin, 1988.

The Portable World Bible. Ed. Robert O. Ballou. New York: Viking, 1961.

Schimmel, Annemarie. *Mystical Dimensions of Islam.* Chapel Hill: University of North Carolina Press, 1975.

Suhrawardi Maqtul, Shihabuddin. "Language of the Ants" in *Three Treatises on Mysticism.* Trans. Otto Spies and S. K. Khatuk. Stuttgart: W. Kohlhammer, 1935. 13–17.

CYNTHIA OSOWIEC RUOFF

LE VÉRITABLE SAINT GENEST: CREATIVITY AND THE MOVEMENT FROM THE PROFANE TO THE SACRED

In Jean Rotrou's *Le Véritable Saint Genest* (1645), the illustrious pagan actor Genest emphatically states that he has become an actor in order to mock and deride Christianity. However, through the play-within-a-play structure incorporating the *mise-en-abyme* "Le Martyre d'Adrian," Genest, playing the martyr Adrian, demonstrates the operation of his creative imagination in his own surprising movement from the profane to the sacred. In *Logos and Life:* Book I: *Creative Experience and the Critique of Reason*, Anna-Teresa Tymieniecka describes the liberating force necessary to activate the creative process.

Imaginatio creatrix proposes to us "to leave it all" behind and to create for ourselves wings and devices to explore the extraordinary and the marvelous, the unprecedented and the infinite. The individual armed with these becomes *homo creator.*[1]

Genest freely and spontaneously responds to sense experience and the marvelous, leaves behind the established religious beliefs and gods of the Romans, assimilates the passion of Adrian the convert whom he plays, and joyfully creates his new being, a Christian martyr. The pagan actor Genest and the Christian martyr he plays form a new creation, a metamorphosis which astonishes the Roman spectators who thought they were witnessing and enjoying the creation of the illusion of reality.

While revealing the process of Genest's new creation and metamorphosis during the actor's rehearsal and performance on stage, *Le Véritable Saint Genest* emerges as an allegory of a soul in pursuit of salvation for himself and for the spectators. On the literal level, the Romans celebrate the forthcoming marriage of Valerie to the newly-appointed co-emperor Maximin by viewing the performance of "Le Martyre d'Adrian." They discuss drama and performance and intermittently critique the pagan troupe's performance. Moving beyond the initial literal signification, Genest's performance of Adrian's role functions as a springboard for the process of creative transfiguration of the pagan actor in an ascending movement leading to the sacred, ecstasy, and Absolute Truth. In *The Transformations of Allegory*, Gay Clifford emphasizes that allegory, unlike symbol, is concerned with the process or "the way in which the

195

A-T. Tymieniecka (ed.), Analecta Husserliana XLIII, 195–208.
© 1994 *Kluwer Academic Publishers. Printed in the Netherlands.*

characters go about achieving . . . objectives as much as with actual attainment, the conclusion of the narrative."[2] In Rotrou's orchestration of human existence, Genest's own process of conversion reinforces the representation of Adrian's conversion in the interior play and becomes the basis of the predominant message: a timeless call to spectators of any era to re-create their own life texts in a movement from the profane to the sacred.

Genest's own journey toward salvation is veiled by his fame as an illustrious pagan actor skilled in the creation of verisimilitude and celebrated for his previous realistic portrayals of other Christian martyrs. During the performance of "Le Martyre d'Adrian," the Roman court focuses on verisimilitude because the troupe is dramatizing the recent martyrdom of Adrian, a pagan turned Christian condemned to death by Maximin, a member of the Roman audience. Genest himself boasts to the newly elevated Roman emperor Maximin that his realistic portrayal of the recent martyrdom will prevent the Roman audience from distinguishing the illusion, the fictional representation, from the reality:

> Et la mort d'Adrian, l'un de ces obstinés
> Par vos derniers arrêts naguère condamnés,
> Vous sera figurée avec un art extrême,
> Et si peu différent de la vérité même
> Que vous nous avouerez de cette liberté
> Où César à César sera représenté
> Et que vous douterez si dans Nicomédie
> Vous verrez l'effet même ou bien la comédie.[3]

St. Augustine's explanation of hidden meaning in the Bible sheds light on Rotrou's technique of dissimulation. According to Augustine, the nature of God and the nature of His work lose some of their *prestige* if presented too clearly to humans; therefore, the Bible veils them, but does not hide them totally. Referring to St. Augustine's explanation, Jean Pépin in *La Tradition de l'Allégorie* states that allegory works in a similar fashion: "ce mélange de dissimulation et de dévoilement définit précisément l'expression allégorique."[4] As a result of Genest's exceptional ability to create verisimilitude, the pagan Romans do not suspect Genest's impending conversion. However, an alert seventeenth-century Christian audience, or an audience of any era, slowly discovers it by responding to the initial textual cues. This dual reaction to his transformation draws attention to spectator reaction and highlights Genest's own progressive movement from the profane to the sacred.

Although the pagan Romans believe in their own gods, throughout the dramatic text Rotrou identifies the profane with the pagan Romans and the sacred with the Christians.[5] In the interior play and in the principal play, the pagan gods are associated with images of blindness and obscurity; they are "des lumières sombres / Dont la faible clarté perce à peine les ombres" (IV, 7, 1379–80). In contrast, Christianity is a source of "la céleste lumière" (V, 1, 1465). Early in the play, during a pause in his rehearsal (a rehearsal which the Romans do not view), Genest reveals a momentary tendency to be seduced by his role, and convert. Addressing the pagan gods, he expresses his sudden rebellion against them. He then directly identifies the pagan Roman heritage as profane and the Christian heritage evolving from Christ's Incarnation, Crucifixion, and Death as sacred:

> J'ai pour suspects vos noms de Dieux et d'immortels,
> Je répugne aux respects qu'on rend à vos autels,
> Mon esprit, à vos lois secrètement rebelle,
> En conçoit un mépris qui fait mourir son zèle;
> Et, comme de profane enfin sanctifié,
> Semble se déclarer pour un crucifié. (II, 4, 411–16)

Immediately after his momentary lapse, he questions his change of position, reaffirms the powers of the pagan gods, and reminds himself that for an actor "Il s'agit d'imiter, et non de devenir" (II, 4, 420). However, Genest's conflict reveals that he is experiencing a "Creative stirring." Tymieniecka describes this state:

We are inwardly, all of a sudden, as if stung, shaken by the feeling of missing something crucial within ourselves, by an invading nostalgia prompting us to get out and to seek it . . ."to create it." (LL, 177)

His intuition, his "creative stirring," and his recognition of the difference between the profane and the sacred mark his initial step on the path to salvation.

Rotrou then undermines French seventeenth-century classical aesthetics promoting rules, reason, and verisimilitude and highlights an actor whose creativity is manifested in a spiritual quest sparked by his irrational passion and sense experience. In the interior play "Le Martyre d'Adrian," the Romans attribute Genest's conversion to a magic spell or a venom, in order to explain Adrian's revolt against his reason. Later, when Genest himself appears to be converting, Valerie, the emperor Diocletian's daughter, asks "Parle-t-il de bon sens?" (IV, 7, 1375) Following Adrian's path, this extraordinary pagan actor whom they admire is rejecting the Roman values of reason and judgement.

During the main play, while rehearsing the role of Adrian, Genest also shows his receptivity to sense experience and the supernatural in his reaction to the possible theophany or divine manifestation, the appearance of flames accompanied by a voice proclaiming:

> Poursuis, Genest, ton personnage;
> Tu n'imiteras point en vain;
> Ton salut ne dépend que d'un peu de courage,
> Et Dieu t'y prêtera la main. (II, 4, 421–24)

Whether feigned by another actor or miraculous, Genest's spontaneous response to this Voice, which tells him to follow his character's direction in life, identifies the Voice with the world of the sacred (sacré) and reveals his hidden but burning desire to follow the path to the heavens. Responding to the Voice, Genest comments:

> Souffle doux et sacré qui me viens enflammer,
> . . . .
> Guide mes pas douteux dans le chemin des cieux,
> . . . .
> Que du Ciel cette voix me doive être adressée!
> (II, 4, 427, 431, 434)

Mircea Eliade's description of the sacred in *The Sacred and the Profane* clarifies Genest's yearning: "Sacred power means reality and at the same time enduringness and efficacity . . . religious man desires to be, to participate in reality, to be saturated with power."[6] Although in the pagan's estimation Genest is emotional and irrational, his response to the flames and Voice is the reaction of a potential convert searching for eternal life.

For Genest, the flames and his receptivity to the intervention of the Voice during his rehearsal establish the elevated stage on which he performs as a sacred place, an avenue of spiritual progression. Flames signal purification and illumination, often of the Holy Spirit.

According to Eliade, it is in a sacred space that man is able to transcend the world:

the theophany that occurs in a place consecrates it by the very fact that it makes it open above – that is, in communication with heaven, the paradoxical point of passage from one mode of being to another.[7]

After the momentary spontaneous revelation of his inner yearning, Genest, in the interior play, recites Adrian's lines describing movement from one plane to another; as a result, Genest in performance intensifies the association of the stage with a sacred place. Genest/Adrian portrays Christ's martyrdom and death on the cross as a movement from the worldly plane to the celestial plane through the image of a ladder. Speaking of the crucifixion, Genest/Adrian observes that Christ died

> Sur un bois glorieux,
> Qui fut moins une croix qu'une échelle des Cieux.
>
> (11, 8, 593–94)

Later, Genest/Adrian, after having recounted the Redeemer's ascension to the heavens, intimates that he will follow Christ's example. In response to Flavie's comment that Caesar will strip him of his wealth if he converts, Genest as Adrian responds: "J'en serai plus léger pour monter dans les Cieux" (II, 8, 606). Genest in performance on the elevated stage, a plane closer to heaven than the surrounding profane space, is himself open to direct contact with Heaven. The communication and passage between earth and heaven is particularly evident in Act IV, when an angel descends from heaven to baptize Genest.

By demonstrating his spontaneity and receptivity to sense impressions and to Christianity, and by acknowledging the elevated stage as a potentially sacred space, Genest exhibits his freedom to change. Tymieniecka describes this type of individual who seeks to go beyond the restrictive boundaries imposed by his culture and by himself:

in forcing back the limits of the exterior world, the creative impulse responds to an interior drive toward the surpassing not only of the limits which the world fixes as a framework of our experience, but before all else of molds which we have forged for ourselves by our ways of feeling, seeing, evaluating, and which we passively perpetuate as the forms of our participation in the world, in others, in our own interiority. (LL, 33–34)

While speaking to the emperor Maximin in the interior play, Genest as Adrian pinpoints the exercise of liberty as the convert's crime:

Pour croire un Dieu, Seigneur, la liberté de croire
Est-elle en votre estime une action si noire,
Si digne de l'excès où vous vous emportez,
Et se peut-il souffrir de moindres libertés?

(III, 2, 727–30)

By accepting his own imminent suffering, torture, and death in addition
to the consequent financial disaster of his troupe, Genest challenges
the rational norms imposed by the Romans. Genest's creative call to
become a believer defies the value system of the pagan Roman world.
Eliade notes that "profane man is the result of a desacralization of human
existence – nonreligious man has been formed by attempting to 'empty'
himself of all religion"[8] – meaning Genest's conscious effort to reject
his family's religious system. Since he previously rejected his parents'
Christianity to openly ridicule and persecute the Christians through his
acting, Genest now also breaks the pagan "molds" he "forged" for himself
in order to reach beyond the limitations of his world and satisfy his
creative impulse.

Genest, following in Adrian's path, responds to his sense impressions, breaks with the established Roman codes, and creates himself.
While playing Adrian, Genest becomes aware of God's grace and
describes his freely-given response to God's invitation:

Il faut lever le masque et t'ouvrir ma pensée;
Le Dieu que j'ai haï m'inspire son amour;
Adrian a parlé, Genest parle à son tour!
Ce n'est plus Adrian, c'est Genest qui respire
La grâce du baptême et l'honneur du martyre.

(IV, 5. 1244–48)

Genest experiences what Tymieniecka identifies as a beginning point
of the creative process, "the illuminating notion of the work to be accomplished before we undertake it" (LL, 198). Now conscious of his task,
Genest, moved during his rehearsal and performance, decides to follow
Adrian's path and open the possibility of eternal life through baptism.

Intentionally dissociating himself from the dramatic text and profane
pagan values, Genest will not submit to the play-acting of Adrian's
baptism which the pagan actor Lentule's profane hands would have
administered. Genest insists:

Mais Christ n'a point commis à vos profanes mains
Ce sceau mystérieux dont il [Christ] marque ses Saints.

(IV, 5, 1249–50)

In contrast to the profane, the *merveilleux chrétien* intervenes, and flames and an angel appear with the "eau sacrée" for Genest's rite of baptism:

Un ministre céleste, avec une eau sacrée,
Pour laver mes forfaits fend la voûte azurée;
Sa clarté m'environne, et l'air de toutes parts
Résonne de concerts, et brille à mes regards,
Descends, céleste acteur; tu m'attends! tu m'appelles!
Attends, mon zèle ardent me fournira des ailes.

(IV, 5, 1251–57)

Genest responds spontaneously and enthusiastically to the apparition, encourages the angel to descend, and adds that his ardent zeal will provide him with wings to transport him to the celestial realm. Wings have a dual signification. First, they indicate his desire to transcend the human condition and join the angels. At the same time, the wings symbolize the liberation of his creative forces; for example, the poet or prophet has wings when he is inspired. In a similar way, Genest responds to inspiration and transforms himself through baptism. Stage directions indicate that Genest goes up two or three steps to be baptized by an angel. This symbolic ascent toward the "voûte azurée" recalls the imagery of Christ's ladder to the heavens and reinforces the imagery of the wings. Genest's rejection of the fictitious baptism by Lentule and his subsequent baptism by the angel reflect Eliade's statement that "*access to spiritual life always entails death to the profane condition, followed by a new birth*" (his emphasis).[9] In Christian theology, baptism is a sacrament symbolic of spiritual regeneration in which the recipient is considered cleansed of original sin and admitted into Christianity. Genest's freely-chosen baptism signals his progression from the profane to the sacred.

During his process of transformation, of creating his new being, Genest masterfully voices his newly-created lines and deludes the Roman spectators. After Genest's conversion and departure from the dramatic text, the actor Lentule, thinking that Genest suffers from a memory lapse, attests to Genest's spontaneity and improvisation skills: "Quoiqu'il manque au sujet, jamais il ne hésite" (IV, 7, 1315). Unaware of his metamorphosis, the Romans praise Genest's creation of the illusion of reality. Valerie remarks that "sa feinte passerait pour la vérité méme" (IV, 7, 1284). The Romans are blind to his spiritual journey, and they continue to critique and admire his acting. Genest's skillful improvisation stands in marked contrast to the other actors of his troupe who are unable to follow his lead and improvise their own lines.

Genest's facility in improvisation shows the real spectators of the whole play *Le Véritable Saint Genest* that he could successfully return to the dramatic text and conceal his conversion in order to save his life. However, Genest, like Adrian in the *mise-en-abyme*, feels compelled to reveal his conversion. After disclosing his experience of instantaneous intuition, Genest again insists:

> Et vous m'entendez mal, si dans cette action
> Mon rôle passe encor pour une fiction.
> . . . .
> Ce n'est plus Adrian, c'est Genest qui s'exprime.
>
> (IV, 7, 1318–19, 1324)

Tymieniecka's explanation of the function of a creative work illuminates Genest's need to reveal his conversion:

the work of art, a scientific theory, etc. essentially "communicate" something, and their very being may be identified with their function of communicating and the unique type of message to be conveyed. . . . By fixing its message and perduring, the creative result affirms itself and is received into the intersubjective life-world. (LL, 185–86)

Genest has to affirm his creative work; therefore, he directly confronts the Romans with his conversion:

> Je professe une loi que je dois déclarer,
> Ecoutez donc, Césars, et vous troupes romaines.
>
> (IV, 7, 1330–31)

By courageously attempting to disclose and describe his new life significance to the Roman spectators, and by extension to all spectators, Genest goes beyond conversion and directs his spiritual journey toward martyrdom.

Although witnessing Genest's declaration of Christian faith, the Romans, because of their cultural conditioning and values, ignore his statement of conversion. The pagans do not recognize that he is now performing in God's theatre because they cannot imagine that a revered pagan actor would rebel against their pagan beliefs. This conflict between pagan and Christian spiritual values reflects Angus Fletcher's comment in *Allegory: The Theory of a Symbolic Mode* that "in any allegory one idea is pitted against another" which results in "symbolic power struggles."[10] While the emperors Diocletian and Maximin believe they attain their glory through military conquest and the torture and murder of Christians, Genest believes his martyrdom will bring him "la gloire éternelle" in paradise, "un séjour de la gloire" (V, 2, 1600, 1610).

Genest himself recognizes that his metamorphosis into a Christian believer and then martyr exists as the pinnacle of his creative efforts. The Romans have seen Genest transform himself "cent fois," in a hundred different ways; the heroes he portrayed were "plutôt ressuscités / Qu'imités" (I, 5, 239–40). In addition, Valerie emphasizes that Genest excels in portraying Christian martyrs. His previous transformations into other Christian martyrs, however, were simply preparations for his final metamorphosis into a Christian believer and martyr. Tymieniecka's description of the evolution of a masterpiece explains Genest's need to reveal his movement to the realm of the sacred:

Each new created work of the same maker is a stepping stone to the next one . . . all these dispersed solutions find their synthesis in a master-piece. This masterpiece appears, then, as the aim toward which all the previous fragmentary efforts converge. (LL, 192–92)

Chained and on the way to prison, Genest realizes that this metamorphosis is his masterpiece; it leads to glorification and to eternal life. It is only by unveiling his masterpiece that Genest communicates his message of belief to the spectators.

Fletcher's description of an allegorical character conforms to Genest and his new thrust in life:

If we were to meet an allegorical character in real life, we would say of him that he was obsessed with only one idea, or that he had an absolutely one-track mind.[11]

Motivated by his fixed idea, Genest completes the final stages of his journey. Looking up from the sacred place, the stage, to address God in the heavens, Genest asks to work with Him in becoming the model of conversion and martyrdom:

Achève tes bontés, représente avec moi
Les saints progrès des coeurs convertis à ta Foi!
Faisons voir dans l'amour dont le feu nous consomme.
Toi le pouvoir d'un Dieu,
. . . .
Et moi, Seigneur, la force et l'ardeur d'un martyr.

                                        (IV, 7, 1277–81)

Flames, stretching toward the heavens and unifying the celestial and
terrestrial planes, introduce light, highlight Genest's comprehension of
his new spiritual goal, and point to the glorious rewards awaiting man
in the celestial realm. Although the Romans still continue to believe he
is acting, Genest intends to establish himself as the incarnation of man's
movement from the profane to the final glorification with God.

As a baroque creative artist now performing in God's theatre, Genest's
journey is not complete until he unveils Absolute Truth, models conversion, and attempts to persuade all spectators to believe. Allegories
are often used for this "didactic and moral suasion" and incite people
"to desire and action."[12] Early in the play, during his rehearsal of "The
Martyrdom of Adrian," visible only to the spectators of the entire play,
the pagan actor highlights his receptivity to change and conversion, but
also reveals his own doubt and uncertainty. Recognizing his interior
conflict and indecision, Genest asks the pagan gods and Christ to battle
each other, make him the prize, and give him peace. Clifford notes the
importance of relating an allegory to human experience, which, in this
case, is Genest's uncertainty:

It is only by retaining some element in the action that corresponds to human experience
and not solely to the abstract patterns of allegorical meaning, that the adventures of the
hero can be enlightening to the morally interested reader – or, of course, to the imaginatively interested reader.[13]

With Genest's disclosure, Rotrou prepares the doubting spectators first
to identify with Genest's uncertainty and then with his free and spontaneous emotional response to God's grace.

In advance of the famous quarrel between the Jesuits and the
Jansenists, Genest, after revealing his conversion, points out to the
actress Marcelle that everyone is sufficiently touched by God's grace
to attain salvation; however, not everyone responds to God's call. He
declares:

Ta grâce peut, Seigneur, détourner ce présage!
Mais, hélas! tous l'ayant, tous n'en ont pas l'usage;
De tant de conviés bien peu suivent tes pas,
Et pour être appelés, tous ne répondent pas.

(V, 2, 1575–78)

Explaining that martyrdom destroys death by granting eternal life, Genest exhorts Marcelle and the other Roman actors and spectators to respond to God's call by defying the Roman laws and converting to Christianity. Finally, since Genest believes all men have sufficient grace, he urges all spectators to assimilate his belief and follow in his footsteps to conversion.

The visionary imagery permeating *Le Véritable Saint Genest* draws the spectator's attention to eternal life in heaven and culminates in Genest's final expression of his creative freedom, his decision to become a martyr. During the interior play, Anthisme paints a joyful picture of the celestial glory and laurel crowns awaiting Adrian, and, by extension, all Christian martyrs:

Va donc, heureux ami, va présenter ta tête
Moins au coup qui t'attend qu'au laurier qu'on t'apprête;
Va de tes Saints propos éclore les effets,
De tous les choeurs des Cieux va remplir les souhaits;
Et vous, Hôtes du Ciel, saintes légions d'Anges,
Qui du nom trois fois saint célébrez les louanges,
Sans interruption de vos sacrés concerts,
A son aveuglement tenez les Cieux ouverts.

(IV, 5, 1223–30)

The actor's repetition of "Va," the opening to the Heavens, the sacred concerts of angels, and the laurel crown, a symbol of immortality and victory, together form a pictorial representation of eternal glory and prepare us for the play's transition to Genest's own passage to eternal life. Although Genest separates himself from the performance of his role and attempts to establish the reality of his own conversion, the celestial imagery surrounding his baptism continues, multiplies, and reinforces the imagery of transcendence introduced in the interior play "Le Martyre d'Adrian." As a result, it is difficult for the spectators to dissociate Genest from his performance of his role as Adrian and recognize his conversion. After Diocletian arrests Genest for his conversion, the actor refuses to recant his decision to convert and directly chooses martyrdom. While speaking to his guards, Genest reintroduces the visionary imagery of the Heavenly City:

> Les Anges, quelque jour, des fers que tu m'ordonnes
> Dans ce palais d'azur me feront des couronnes.
>
> (IV, 8, 1903–04)

The repetition of this visionary imagery, presented first in "Le Martyre d'Adrian" and then in Genest's own conversion, adds intricacy and depth to Rotrou's work. It helps the spectator understand the significance of the action and reinforces the meaning of events by association.

Approaching the final goal of his creative journey, Genest rejoices in a state of lyrical exaltation precipitated by his impending martyrdom. His final liberation from this world will make possible his ascension to eternal life in heaven. Reminiscent of Bernini's "The Ecstasy of Saint Teresa," Genest experiences a foretaste of heavenly glory, an "Essai de la gloire future" and an "Incroyable felicité." In this rapturous state, he explains that the suffering of martyrdom will fill him with a "douceur extrème" (V, 1). In her masterpiece *Interior Castle* (1577), the Spanish mystic St. Teresa of Avila describes this state of ecstasy which a soul may reach. Her explanation elucidates Genest's yearning for martyrdom:

what ardent desires it [the soul] has to be used for God in any and every way and in which He may be pleased to employ it! . . . It was not such a great matter for the martyrs to suffer all their tortures, for with the aid of our Lord such a thing becomes easy.[14]

Remaining in this ecstatic state, Genest continues the visionary imagery of the Heavenly City, in an emotional plea to the spectators to heed their senses and emotions and follow his spiritual path in order to attain salvation:

> Mourons donc, la cause y convie;
> Il doit être doux de mourir
> Quand se dépouiller de la vie
> Est travailler pour l'acquérir;
> Puisque la céleste lumière
> Ne se trouve qu'en la quittant
> Et qu'on ne vainc qu'en combattant;
> D'une vigueur mâle et guerrière
> Courons au bout de la carrière
> Où la couronne nous attend.
>
> (V, 1, 1461–70)

Genest enlarges and intensifies Anthisme's earlier directive to Adrian, "Va," in his call to the spectators, "Courons." This specific verb accelerates the movement and emphasizes the urgency of the action, while the use of the "nous" form of the imperative highlights the presence of the spectators Genest wishes to involve with him in attaining the goal of absolute reality. Consistent with the persuasive nature of moral and didactic allegory, Genest urges the spectators to contemplate and aspire to the joys of this celestial vision.

Genest's creative work, his metamorphosis into a Christian believer and martyr, his journey from the profane to the sacred, exists in this world through his performance as a pagan actor who chooses to enact his final transformation in God's theatre. His "creative stirring," baptism, state of ecstasy, and martyrdom transport him to eternal glory as a saint in heaven. Genest exhorts all spectators to focus on the goal of eternal life, and he becomes a model for all spectators to imitate, each one in his/her unique way. Like John Bunyan's allegory *Pilgrim's Progress* (1678), Rotrou's play demonstrates that "the present moment is always potentially the moment of salvation or damnation."[15] As a result, Genest exhorts all spectators to respond to their sense impressions now, to be inspired by his spiritual journey, and to re-create themselves to become Christian believers.

Western Michigan University

NOTES

[1] Anna-Teresa Tymieniecka, *Logos and Life*, Book I: *Creative Experience and the Critique of Reason* (Dordrecht: Kluwer Academic Publishers, 1988), 12. All further references to this edition will be indicated in parentheses in the text.

[2] Gay Clifford, *The Transformations of Allegory* (London: Routledge & Kegan Paul, 1974), 12.

[3] Jean Rotrou, *Le Véritable Saint Genest*, Théâtre du XVIIe siècle ed. Jacques Schérer (Paris: Gallimard, 1975), 953. All further references to this edition will be indicated in parentheses in the text.

[4] Jean Pépin, *La Tradition de l'allégorie* (Paris: Etudes augustiniennes, 1987), 94.

[5] J. Dubois and R. Lagane in *Dictionnaire de la langue francaise classique* (Paris: Librairie Classique Eugène Bélin, 1960) define profane as "sacrilège, impie. . . . Le XVIIe connaissait aussi le sens actuel: 'qui n'est pas sacré.'" 393. "sacré" means "consacré. . . . Au sens actuel de "Revêtu d'un caractère vénérable, religieux," il pouvait se placer aussi bien avant qu'après le nom dont il était épithète," 442.

[6] Mircea Eliade, *The Sacred and the Profane*, trans. Willard Trask (New York: Harcourt, Brace, & World, 1959). 12–13.

[7] Eliade, 26.

[8]   Eliade, 204.

[9]   Eliade, 201.

[10]   Angus Fletcher, *Allegory: The Theory of a Symbolic Mode* (New York: Cornell UP, 1964), 22–23.

[11]   Fletcher, 40.

[12]   Fletcher, 120–21.

[13]   Clifford, 20.

[14]   St. Teresa of Avila, *Interior Castle*, trans. E. Allison Peers (New York: Image Books Doubleday, 1989), 155.

[15]   Clifford, 98.

PART FOUR

SACRED SPACE AND POWER

DAVID CHIDESTER

THE POETICS AND POLITICS OF SACRED SPACE: TOWARDS A CRITICAL PHENOMENOLOGY OF RELIGION

What is the sacred? In the study of religion, two broad lines of definition have been advanced, one substantial, the other situational. The former claims to have penetrated and reported the essential experience of the sacred, while the latter analyzes the practical, relational, and often contested dynamics of its production and reproduction. In this essay, I have set myself the task of weaving together the substantial and the situational through a critical rereading, against the grain, perhaps, of the influential work of the Dutch phenomenologist of religion, Gerardus van der Leeuw. I hope to uncover, in the process, the situational, relational, and contested aspects that lie hidden at the heart of a classic substantial definition of the sacred.

Familiar substantial definitions – Otto's "holy," Van der Leeuw's "power," Eliade's "real" – might be regarded as attempts to replicate an insider's evocation of certain experiential qualities that could be associated with the sacred. From this perspective, the sacred has been identified as an awesome, powerful manifestation of reality, full of ultimate significance. By contrast, a situational analysis of the sacred, which can be traced back to Durkheim, has located the sacred at the nexus of human practices and social projects. Not full of meaning, the sacred, from this perspective, is an empty signifier. The sacred, as Lévi-Strauss proposed, is "a value of indeterminate signification, in itself empty of meaning and therefore susceptible to the reception of any meaning whatsoever."[1] In this respect, the term is better regarded as an adjectival or verbal form, a sign of difference that can be assigned to virtually anything through the human cultural labor of interpretation and ritualization. As a situational term, therefore, the sacred is nothing more nor less than a notional supplement to the ongoing cultural work of sacralizing space, time, persons, and social relations. The sacred is a byproduct of sacralization.

This divergence between a substantial and situational definition of the sacred is perhaps most evident in the analysis of sacred space. Mircea Eliade held that the sacred irrupted, manifested, or appeared in certain

211

A-T. Tymieniecka (ed.), Analecta Husserliana XLIII, 211–231.
© 1994 Kluwer Academic Publishers. Printed in the Netherlands.

places, causing them to become powerful centers of meaningful worlds. On the contrary, Jonathan Z. Smith has shown how place is sacralized as the result of the cultural labor of ritual, in specific historical situations, involving the hard work of attention, memory, design, construction, and control of place. Not merely an opposition between "insider" and "outsider" perspectives, this clash between substantial and situational approaches to definition and analysis represents a contrast between what might be called the poetics and the politics of sacred space.[2]

In his landmark text on the phenomenology of religion, *Religion in Essence and Manifestation*, Gerardus van der Leeuw imaginatively explored the implications of his substantial definition of the sacred, "power," in spatial terms.[3] In a chapter on sacred space, he outlined an inventory of typical sacred places that have appeared in the history of religions. That inventory, however, was also a series of homologies in which Van der Leeuw asserted the metaphoric equivalence of home, temple, settlement, pilgrimage site, and human body. A home was a temple, a temple a home. The city of Jerusalem, identified by Van der Leeuw as sacred space in its most "typical form," was a temple in the beginning and would be a temple in the end. The pilgrimage site, as a home, temple, or sacred settlement away from home, could ultimately be found at the center of the body in the human heart. Sacred places, therefore, formed a recursive series of metaphoric equivalences. In addition, and concurrently, Van der Leeuw tracked a second series of homologies, consisting of synecdoches for the items in the first series, that linked the hearth (of the home), the altar (of the temple), the sanctuary (of the settlement), the shrine (of the pilgrimage site), and the heart (of the human body). Although these homologies were not explicitly schematized or theorized by Van der Leeuw, the two series of equivalences established his basic vocabulary for an analysis of sacred places. As they recurred in his analysis, they provided evidence of a poetics of sacred space.

At the same time, even if unintended, Van der Leeuw laced his analysis with hints of a politics of sacred space. First, he provided hints of a politics of position. In some moments, like Eliade, he attributed sole, transcendent, and ultimate agency to sacred power, even holding that sacred power actually positioned itself in the world. However, this mystifying of power, a kind of "mystical intuitionism" of sacred space, was tempered by Van der Leeuw's recognition, however it might have been submerged in his text, that the positioning of a sacred place was a political act, whether that positioning involved, in his terms, selection, orientation, limitation, or conquest.

Second, Van der Leeuw hinted at another relational, situational aspect of sacred space by paying attention to the politics of exclusion. A sacred place, such as a home, was a space in which relations among persons could be negotiated and worked out. Some persons, however, were left out, kept out, or forced out. In fact, the sanctity of the inside was certified by maintaining and reinforcing boundaries that kept certain persons outside the sacred place. By recognizing this process of excluding persons, even if in passing, Van der Leeuw raised the possibility that a politics of exclusion might be an integral part of the making of sacred space.

Third, Van der Leeuw linked sacred space with a politics of property. A sacred place was not merely a meaningful place; it was a powerful place because it was appropriated, possessed, and owned. In several important passages of his text, Van der Leeuw referred to the sacred power of property, even suggesting, perhaps somewhat enigmatically, that property was the "realization of possibilities" (210). However, since "possibility" was a technical term in his analytical vocabulary, more attention will have to be paid to the connections between power, possibility, and property in Van der Leeuw's phenomenology of religion. To anticipate, we might find that the sacrality of place was directly related in his analysis to a politics of property.

Fourth, and finally, Van der Leeuw ultimately positioned sacred space, and his analysis of sacred space, in the context of a politics of exile. He insistently highlighted a "modern" loss of the sacred, or alienation from the sacred, or nostalgia for the sacred, in his use and interpretation of basic data of religion. Van der Leeuw repeatedly noted that "primitives" had the sacred; some common peasant folk have retained it; but "moderns" have entirely lost it. This historical and essentially political situation of exile from the sacred entailed two theoretical implications for Van der Leeuw's phenomenology of sacred space: the most sacred places were remote and the most authentic religious experience in relation to sacred space was homesickness. In the politics of exile, the sacred was positioned in relation to human beings who found themselves to be out of position.

1. POSITION

The sacred, Van der Leeuw held, "must possess a form: it must be 'local-izable,' spatially, temporally, visibly or audibly" (447).[4] In spatial terms, the sacred could only be localized by becoming a "position," a signifi-cant, valued, and even liberated *place* carved out of the vast extension of space. A sacred place was a position in which power and the effects of power were repeated. In some moments, Van der Leeuw announced a poetics of the sacred in which he attributed independent agency to sacred power, asserting that the sacred's "powerfulness creates for it a place of its own" (47). If that were the case, human beings could not select or make sacred places. Such places could not be founded; they could only be found. Once found, they could not really be lost, even if they were forgotten or neglected, because sacred power would continue to adhere to those positions, only waiting to be rediscovered. In these moments, Van der Leeuw celebrated a poetics of sacred space, a poetic imagination most evident in his enthusiasm for natural sacred sites, the forests and caverns, rocks and mountains, waterfalls and springs, in which the sacred has often been localized. However, Van der Leeuw's implicit distinction between natural and built environments was in tension with his recognition elsewhere that the very category of "Nature" was a nine-teenth-century invention, and, therefore, could not stand as a stable, independent term in his analysis of sacred space. In the poetics of the sacred, "natural" and "artificial" sacred sites were equivalent as positions in which power was localized (52–53).

Frequently, however, Van der Leeuw recognized the situational, rela-tional work of positioning through which human beings have carved sacred places out of the world. As a technical term, Van der Leeuw used the word "selection" for the practice of positioning sacred places. His understanding of the significance of this term was most evident in his treatment of temples and settlements. A temple was "selected" through a process of orientation, for example, by aligning its design and con-struction with the east/west trajectory of the sun. A settlement was "selected" through limitation, not only by drawing boundaries around it, but also by adjusting its pattern to conform to the right/left axis of the human body, a practice that Van der Leeuw regarded as the most prim-itive and important method of orientation. Positioning these sacred places, therefore, required the symbolic, cultural labor of orientation and limi-tation. At the same time, however, the establishment of position also required an essentially political conquest of space. A sacred place was not merely found; it was conquered. In his discussion of the human settlement as a sacred place, Van der Leeuw even made conquest a synonym for his technical term, selection. "For the settlement is always a conquest," he insisted, "a selection" (399). In the ancient world, the conquest of a city involved calling out, defeating, and capturing the city's gods. Selection, therefore, could also signify political and military relations of power, the conquest, domination, and control of space. In this respect, the positioning of a sacred city should be regarded as a political act.

Since Van der Leeuw's poetics of sacred space established a metaphoric equivalence between the settlement and the home, temple, pilgrimage site, and human heart, this politics of position could also be discerned in the "selection" of other sacred sites, even though Van der Leeuw's poetics often obscured the conquest and colonization of space necessary for the making of sacred places. Van der Leeuw advanced a poetics of the sacred consistent with what the geographer David Harvey has called the "aestheticization of politics," a mystification of political relations of power "in which appeal to the mythology of place and person has a strong role to play."[5] Van der Leeuw mystified the politics of sacred space through a poetics in which power was remythologized. In that mythology of sacred space, power was personalized, place positioned. However, as his discussion of the sacrality of settlements suggested, Van der Leeuw could also recognize a politics of position, a politics in which a city was sacred, not because power resided there, but because power was asserted through conquest and localized through domination. As Anthony Giddens has observed, cities have been "crucibles of power" in which interests are contested. In the city, power, always at stake in those political conflicts, has tended to carry a sacred aura. "Virtually everywhere," Giddens noted, "the generation of power in the city has been expressed in religious terms."[6] Van der Leeuw was not far from this line of analysis when he identified conquest as the process of selection that made a city sacred. Although he remythologized power from the vantage point of the conquerors, assuming that the sacralization of a city *required* its conquest, Van der Leeuw nevertheless introduced a political dynamic into his analysis of the human settlement as sacred space. In this politics of the sacred, the city could stand as a model of sacred space as contested space.

Like the city, the home was also a political arena, a site of a micropolitics, perhaps, but nevertheless a sacred place where power was contested. In its typical form, the home was a site in which relations among things, animals, and human beings were negotiated. Along similar lines, Pierre Bourdieu has analyzed the home as the center of a cultural *habitus*, a locale for the negotiation of social relations and practical knowledge of the world. "Through the intermediary of the divisions and hierarchies it sets up between things, persons, and practices," Bourdieu has observed, "this tangible classifying system continuously inculcates and reinforces the taxonomic principles underlying all the arbitrary provisions of this culture."[7] Van der Leeuw stressed the way in which the relations among persons, animals, and things were worked out in the home to form a unified whole. But he also hinted at the contested dynamics of the power relations that were localized in the sacred space of the home by suggesting that the home, like the city, was also a conquered place. In one of his most important illustrations of the sacrality of the home, and its sacred, central heart, the hearth, Van der Leeuw cited an account of a traditional Gelderland (or Guelders) home in Eastern Holland. At the hearth, "since ancient times, the hook has been the sacred position [*de heilige plaats*] in the house, around which the bride was led and which was seized to take possession of the house" (397).[8] Here the positioning of the home as a sacred place was also related to conquest, to the act of seizing the sacred hook above the hearth that signified the capture of the home. In this case, conquest signified not only possession, but also the relations of domination and subordination that were at stake in the sacred space of the house. The hearth focused the relations of power of a domestic micropolitics. A householder seized the hook as a sign of dominion, while a new bride was led around the hook, perhaps as a sign of submission, but definitely like a satellite revolving around the center of sacred power in the home. Not only property rights and gender roles, but also labor relations, were focused on that sacred center. A new laborer, Van der Leeuw recounted, was treated as a stranger to the household, apparently teased and tormented, until he went through a rite of passage by submitting to being doused with water, entering the house through a side door, and approaching the hearth to touch the sacred hook. Power relations among persons, therefore, were positioned in the sacred space of the home.

Sacred sites were centers in both a poetics and a politics of position. They were not only centers of sacred meaning and significance, but also "nodal points" in social and political networks of power.[9] As conquered places, sacred sites were inevitably entangled in power relations of domination and subordination. No conquest, however, goes uncontested. By mythologizing, and thereby apparently naturalizing, the conquered positions of person and place, an aestheticization of politics might deny the legitimacy of any resistance to the conquest that had established a sacred place. But power and resistance go together, defining, in practice, the contested process of positioning a sacred place. Along these lines, Michel Foucault described sacred sites as "heterotopias." As Foucault noted,

There are also, probably in every culture, in every civilization, real places – places that exist and that are formed in the very founding of society – which are something like counter-sites, a kind of effectively enacted utopia in which the real sites, all the other real sites that can be found within the culture, are simultaneously represented, contested and inverted. Places of this kind are outside of all places, even though it may be possible to indicate their location in reality.[10]

Unlike utopias, which have no real place in the world, heterotopias are anchored in specific sites. Van der Leeuw concentrated on how a sacred poetics could be represented and realized in selected places. He provided only hints to suggest that such a poetics of position, with its celebration of selection, orientation, limitation, and conquest, could be inherently, inevitably contested. Those hints can be found primarily in Van der Leeuw's recognition of the importance of two forces – exclusion and appropriation – in the making of sacred space. Both would be unnecessary if sacred space were not contested.

2. EXCLUSION

In developing a phenomenology of the sacred, Van der Leeuw paid considerable attention to the limits that have circumscribed power in the history of religions. "The sacred," he noted, "is what has been placed within boundaries" (47). Not only containing the sacred, boundaries have operated to keep out the profane. In this respect, a sacred place can be defined by what it excludes. Through practices of exclusion, a home achieves "prominence as against the surrounding entirety of space," a settlement "stands out from the surrounding extent of space" (397, 399). Space becomes place, isolated from the rest of the world, by means of exclusion. It becomes sacred place through a highly-charged, contested, and even violent politics of exclusion.

A sacred place excluded certain classes of persons. In Australian aboriginal shrines, sacred objects, the churinga (*tjurunga*), were hidden. The place could not be entered by the uninitiated, by women, or by children, as Van der Leeuw reported, "under pain of death" (395). Van der Leeuw interpreted this exclusion as a characteristic feature of any sanctuary: its separation from the ordinary world as a refuge from inter-personal strife. Clearly, however, this refuge was carved out of the social world through an exclusion that inserted the dynamics of inter-personal conflict directly into the heart of sacred space. It was precisely the relation between insiders and outsiders that was contested at the center and the boundaries of the sacred place. Although the exclusion of certain classes of persons already suggested an inherent violence in the estab-lishment of place, that exclusion was backed up by force or the threat of force. A sacred place was established and reinforced in the world under threat of death, signifying an ultimate, total exclusion.

While the exclusion of the uninitiated, women, and children elimi-nated from the sacred precincts persons who were nevertheless in-corporated in the local social world, the politics of sacred place also excluded foreigners. "The foreigner," Van der Leeuw remarked, "is one who is a stranger to the sacred" (251). Belonging outside the community, the foreigner or stranger was an "alien power," not only alien to the com-munity, but also to its sacred places. The boundaries that protected those places kept that alien power out; but doors and thresholds presented the threat that it might slip in. Accordingly, ritual gestures were neces-sary to block the dangerous alien power of the stranger.

> The stranger or foreigner must therefore be met with either the utmost courtesy (hospi-tality) or unconcealed enmity. Both are directed against his power, before which we bow or which we assail, since he is already severed from his own community; but in both cases it is feared. (248).

In Van der Leeuw's analysis, every sacred place had a door. But that point of entry was also a boundary, the dangerous point at which alien powers were confronted and excluded from the sacred place. Whether those aliens were foreigners, strangers, or demonic powers, they had to be excluded from access to sacred space.

Consistently, Van der Leeuw emphasized the importance of exclu-sion in his discussion of doors and thresholds in sacred space. In the sacred place of the home, the door and threshold were in place primarily "to separate the space inside the house from the power existing outside" (396). This exclusion was not only localized at the entrance, but pervaded the entire sacred space inside. Van der Leeuw related an Irish fairy tale to illustrate the way in which practices of exclusion maintained a sacred place. A woman enchanted every object in her household "to prevent the entrance of evil spirits." However, she had no power over the water in the bath, because it did not belong in the household, so she poured it outside before closing the door (396). In this parable, Van der Leeuw hinted at a politics of exclusion in which "alien powers" inside had to be thrown out and those outside had to be kept out. The closing of the door marked a finality of exclusion. Similarly, Van der Leeuw held, the gates of a city "play the part of the house door, separating the secure sphere of the human dwelling from the 'uncanny' realm of demonic powers" (399). Therefore, the door's most significant function in the construction and maintenance of sacred space only appeared when it was closed.

In the history of religions, a politics of exclusion has often been enforced in and through symbols of purity as well as of impurity, which has been defined in spatial terms by Mary Douglas as "matter out of place."[11] The maintenance of purity has often required the exclusion of defilement. At one point, Van der Leeuw noted the importance of purity regulations in the construction of the sacred space of the home by recalling that in the ancient Roman household no unclean person could enter or touch the larder (397). For the most part, however, the importance of purity as a symbol of sacred order, an internal order protected by arranging the inside and excluding the outside, was submerged under Van der Leeuw's preoccupation with the dynamics of power. Instead of defilement, therefore, the primary danger of desecration that had to be blocked was dispossession. A sacred place achieved prominence against the surrounding entirety of space because it was always at risk of dispossession. It was always threatened by the prospect that an "alien power" might cross its boundaries and steal the symbols of power residing inside. Therefore, the threat of dispossession had to be met by the force of exclusion. Returning to the Dutch Gelderland home of rural Eastern Holland, Van der Leeuw recounted a traditional practice of exclusion: On Christmas Eve, every object inside the house was carefully arranged, while every tool or farming implement outside was brought into the barn. All doors and gates were locked shut. "Everything must be locked up under cover in its right place," Van der Leeuw explained, otherwise, it was feared, " 'Derk met den beer' (the wild huntsmen) would take it with them" (46).[12] Like the foreigner, the wildman was a stranger to the sacred.

The danger posed by this "alien power" was not defilement but dispossession. The home could be protected by a ritual arrangement of space, with everything locked into its "right place." In this case, however, placement was not a matter of purity, of assuring that there was no "matter out of place" in the home. Instead, placement, guarded by rituals of exclusion that kept out the stranger, served the interests of property.

3. PROPERTY

In the sacred politics of Dutch Gelderland, the possession of the home was certified by seizing the hook above the sacred hearth; it was reinforced by the ritual exclusion of any competing claims. By symbolic acts of appropriation and exclusion, therefore, the home was registered as sacred property. In Van der Leeuw's phenomenology, property in general held a sacred aura, establishing relations between persons and objects, as well as relations among persons, that displayed an essentially religious character. Property, in fact, was a synonym for sacred power. As Van der Leeuw declared, "property is not just the object which the owner possesses. It is a power, and indeed a common power" (249). In references to property which are scattered throughout his text, Van der Leeuw referred to the sacred mystery of the ownership of property. In its "primitive" sense, Van der Leeuw observed, property "is a 'mystical' relation between owner and owned; the possessor is . . . the depository of a power that is superior to himself" (50–51). Property, therefore, was a sacred bond between object and owner, a bond that was most evident in ritual sacrifice, where the roles of giver and gift, according to Van der Leeuw, were interchangeable. "He who makes a sacrifice," he explained, "sacrifices his property, that is, himself" (355). In this respect, property was not really a relation between a person and an object. Property, as a mystical union between owner and owned, was thoroughly personal and interpersonal. It personified objects, while it objectified persons as depositories of sacred power.

Accordingly, property signified not only the owner's identification with an object, but, more importantly, with a superior power, a power that Van der Leeuw identified more specifically as "the realization of possibilities." In Van der Leeuw's scheme, a basic distinction obtained between the "given" and the "possible." By this dichotomy, Van der Leeuw specified two modes of the sacred. "The sacredness of life," he held, "is a matter of either *What is given*, or *Possibility*" (206). In "primitive" life, the "given" could be found in the sacrality of blood, family, and the totemic ties that held a community together. The "possible," however, appeared in property. Beyond the "given," the sacred, "powerful life," manifested "as *property*, which exhibits life's 'possibility'" (244). In property, as the realization of possibilities, a transcendent power could be achieved. Therefore, Van der Leeuw concluded, power could be enshrined in "the sacredness and inalienability of possessions" (210). Ownership, in these terms, was a way of actualizing the possibility of holding and wielding sacred power in the world.

The power of property, however, was clearly relational and contested. According to Van der Leeuw, the Polynesian term *tabu*, for example, represented a sacred prohibition that combined the forces of exclusion and appropriation to reinforce contested claims on the ownership of property. As Van der Leeuw explained, "the *tabu* is a means of asserting unquestionable right of possession to a piece of ground; some sign indicates the prohibition of stealing it or trespassing on it" (50). The *tabu*, in this sense, was a sacred sign of ownership. Property, as real estate, became sacred simply by virtue of being owned. Claims on ownership, however, were inevitably or perhaps inherently contested, thus requiring the interdictions against stealing and trespassing. Therefore, the sacred power of property had to be reinforced by prohibitions against alternative, competing acts of appropriation.

If property was sacred, then the sacred, in its tangible localized forms, was property. A ritual object, for example, was a power object in Van der Leeuw's terms, partly because it could be owned. The "possession of the power object," Van der Leeuw observed, "means *salvation*" (101). Recently cultural analysts have shown a growing interest in the importance of symbolic objects as sacred property. In particular, analysts have documented the ways in which exclusive claims on the ownership of sacred objects can serve political interests. As Norbert Peabody has recently noted, "For many years now it has been a commonplace observation in history and anthropology that the monopolistic possession of sacred objects, heirlooms, talismans, or regalia helps perpetuate political rule."[13] Likewise, the ownership of the "intellectual property" of religious symbols, myths, or rituals can be shown to operate in economic contexts and to serve specific social or political interests.[14] As I have suggested elsewhere, religion might even be regarded as a process of "stealing back and forth sacred symbols."[15] Sacred symbols are not merely made meaningful through interpretation; they are made powerful through competing, contested acts of appropriation.

Like property, therefore, the sacred could be lost or stolen. Certainly, sacred sites could be neglected or forgotten, as were the ancient pre-Christian shrines in the Netherlands, but they could also be dispossessed. In "primitive" practice, the sacrality of property surrounded sacred places with defenses against the loss of privileged, exclusive ownership of the sacred. In the "modern" world, however, the sacred has been stolen, and people do not even know what they have lost. In basic tone, as well as in specific terms, Van der Leeuw lamented a modern loss of the sacred, a loss most evident in a modern alienation from sacred space. Although he ostensibly focused on identifying the essential, timeless forms of sacred space, Van der Leeuw also showed a recurring preoccupation with the historical condition of dislocation in the modern world. Modernization has deprived human beings of the sacred; it has dispossessed them of their sacred places. Alienated from the sacred, modern human beings have to engage sacred space from a position of exile, participating in a politics of exile in which sacred power resides either in distant places or in irredeemably lost places.

4. EXILE

To return one last time to the sacred space of the old Dutch Gelderland home, Van der Leeuw noted that the significance of the hearth-hook had been forgotten, yet somehow was also oddly remembered, by local peasants. Citing an account of one Dutch informant, a farmer's son employed as a bailiff, Van der Leeuw reported that Gelderland children had been told that they must not set the hook swinging when they took the pot off the fire because "our dear Lord will get a headache" (397). In forgetting the original ancient significance of the sacred hook, peasants in the Gelderland nevertheless continued to associate it with a potent sacrality, however distorted that recollection might have been in its popular redaction. According to Van der Leeuw, that distorted recollection proved that there was a surplus of the sacred that could not be contained in the world. Although it was "localizable" in space and time, experienced as visible and audible, the sacred transcended location. It was a power both in and outside of this world. Even when its precise, local significance had been forgotten, "this cosmic significance of the sacred places," Van der Leeuw concluded, "was still haunting the mind of the bailiff in Eastern Holland when he feared that the swinging of the hook would give the dear Lord a headache" (398). In Van der Leeuw's reading of this evidence, therefore, the sacred was forgotten but not gone, because its cosmic traces lingered around the hearth in the rural peasant home of Dutch Gelderland.

In modern urban society, however, sacred space is both forgotten and gone, with even its cosmic traces erased in the modern world. In particular, Van der Leeuw complained that the sacrality of the home, its special position in traditional religious life as a self-contained, unified world, had been irrecoverably lost in modern society. "The house is an organic unity," Van der Leeuw recalled, "whose essence is some definite power, just as much as is the temple or church." Modern houses, however, are not sacred. Their unity has been dispersed, their boundaries dissolved, their sovereign ownership alienated. As a result of modernization, Van der Leeuw observed, "it is difficult for us, semi-americanized as we already are, living in flats and having what we need brought into the house, to form any idea of its unitary power . . . which not very long ago was an unquestioned reality" (395–96). In the modern world, therefore, the home no longer represents a sacred position, a sacred unity confirmed by rituals of appropriation and reinforced by rituals of exclusion. It is just a house, not a sacred home. Therefore, modern human beings are profoundly homeless, deprived of a sacred, domestic center. All modern people are "strangers to the sacred," exiles from sacred space.

In this modern context of dislocation, Van der Leeuw's analysis of sacred space was pervaded with a nostalgia for lost places and a longing for distant places. Like the home, the temple had become a lost sacred place in the modern world. Deprived of its "cosmic-sacred character" that had been achieved by orienting its architecture to the heavens, modern Protestant churches, Van der Leeuw observed, had become "merely places to stay in and talk." No one believed, he complained, that "anything really happens there." As the home had been drained of its sacrality to become "a mere place of residence," the temple, in modern Protestant practice, had been reduced to "an oratory or meeting place," losing, in the process, its once powerful position as a sacred place (398). Under the impact of modernization, therefore, local sacred places had become dislocated, as the modern world had dispossessed the home, temple, and city of their sacred possibility.

In this context of exile from the sacred, however, Van der Leeuw pointed to the pilgrimage site, that most remote sacred place, as the most sacred place in the world, the place of "superior sacredness." The pilgrim's destination was a sacred home away from home, the "home of the second power." The pilgrim, like modern people, lived in a condition similar to exile, occupying a peripheral position, far from the sacred center of power. Pilgrimage, Van der Leeuw noted, required an emigration from, and abandonment of, "one's own place." That place of departure, however, was not really one's own, because it was not really sacred property, being unsecured, as in the modern world, by powerful rituals of appropriation and exclusion. The ultimate realization of the possibility of ownership could only be found at the distant pilgrimage site. By leaving one's own place, one could journey to a distant place that could be claimed as truly one's own. "The world, which can actually be one's own," Van der Leeuw concluded, "is then found in remote regions." Geographically separated from what anthropologist Victor Turner called the sacred "center out there," people could still claim ownership of a distant place for themselves.[16] Jews could claim Jerusalem, Muslims could claim Mecca, Christians could claim Rome, and, as a result, Van der Leeuw concluded, "whole peoples and religious communities can have their home" (401–402).

In its basic structure, therefore, pilgrimage represents a symbolic antidote to homelessness. Although an ancient practice, pilgrimage nevertheless fits the modern condition of dislocation from the sacred. Van der Leeuw found echoes of this modern condition in ancient and "primitive" sacred places. For example, Van der Leeuw referred to another home, not in Dutch Gelderland, but on an Indonesian island, to illustrate a metaphoric equivalence between home and pilgrimage site. On the Celebes Island, a Minahassa village sanctuary that was built of stones, and supported by wooden planks representing birds' notes heard at the foundation of the village (along with some captured heads), was apparently called "the salvation and strength of the village" (393). For those at home in the village, therefore, the shrine signified its legitimate ownership, which, in Van der Leeuw's terms, represented the realization of its "possibility" as sacred property, as well as the exclusion of any foreign, competing claims. However, villagers who found themselves away from home knew the shrine was also referred to as "the callers," calling villagers from foreign regions by its power to "arouse home-sickness in their breasts." This "longing for house and home," Van der Leeuw concluded, "is ultimately therefore the yearning for salvation, for the consciousness of powerfulness bestowed by one's own selected place" (401). Accordingly, salvation, as the most authentic experience of the sacred, was anticipated in such feelings of homesickness. In order to find one's sacred home, Van der Leeuw seemed to be suggesting, one must first lose it. Therefore, although modern people have lost sacred space, they are well positioned to find it, precisely by virtue of their historical condition of dislocation.

Van der Leeuw's phenomenology of religion, therefore, was itself positioned in exile, deprived, under modern conditions, of any stable anchorage in sacred locations. Indeed, Van der Leeuw cited the remoteness or withdrawal of sacred space as a defining characteristic of religion, quoting the first-century Roman jurist Masurius Sabinus to the effect that "*religiosum* is that which because of some sacred quality is removed and withdrawn [*remotum ac sepositum*] from us."[17] This separation, Van der Leeuw declared, "is, precisely, the sacred" (49). Significantly, perhaps, Van der Leeuw drew this definition from an author writing in the context of the massive social disruptions of the first century, in which imperial boundaries were threatened and the older, supposedly stable sacred centers of the ancient world no longer held their power. In analyzing this religious change in the ancient Near Eastern and Mediterranean worlds, Jonathan Z. Smith has drawn a useful distinction between two basic orientations toward sacred space, the locative and the utopian. Anchored in specific sacred sites, particularly in the sacred city-temple complexes that localized divine kingship in the ancient world, the locative orientation identified sacred space with fixed, stable centers of power. Revolving around a sacred axis, the locative orientation required the maintenance of place and position in an ordered cosmos. By contrast, however, a utopian orientation toward sacred space was in principle unanchored in any specific site in the world. Whether resulting from the destruction of a locative center, or from resistance to the imposition of a dominant, oppressive locative order, this utopian orientation could find sacred space either in no place or in every place in the world.[18]

This distinction between locative and utopian orientations can illuminate the dynamics of sacred space in situations as apparently diverse, for example, as the development of Rabbinic Judaism, following the destruction of the locative center represented by the temple in Jerusalem, or the development of Ch'an Buddhism in China. In both cases, in response to local situational circumstances, a utopian orientation towards sacred space emerged in which sacred space could be found, in principle, everywhere, precisely because it was not anchored in a specific locative center.[19] No longer localized in the temple, God could be present anywhere. Not tied to specific, local sites, the Buddha-essence could be perceived to be everywhere. In such utopian orientations sacred place was essentially portable, whether it was carried in a text, a ritual, a mediation practice, a sacred calendar, gestures of recognition, or in the intimacy of the human heart.

The utopian orientation, with its portable sacred place, was particularly suited to a politics of exile. In the modern exile from the sacred, Van der Leeuw found that the most profound orientation toward sacred space revolved around the portable center of the human heart. In the end, he declared, "the holiest of holies is the heart." To illustrate, he cited the example of the Sufi mystic al-Hallaj, who asserted that the pilgrimage, that sacred journey to the remote "home of the second power," might be undertaken simply by staying at home, because "the true sanctuary lay within the heart." As the culmination of his analysis of sacred space, therefore, Van der Leeuw concluded that all sacred places, the home, temple, city, and pilgrimage site, coalesced in the heart, because "the real sanctuary is man" (402). However, as Van der Leeuw also realized, al-Hallaj had been executed for declaring that the genuine sanctuary was the heart. Even the heart, therefore, was a situational, relational, and contested sacred place. Like every other sacred place, the heart provided no purely poetic, mystical refuge from the politics of the sacred.

5. TOWARDS A CRITICAL PHENOMENOLOGY OF RELIGION

As we have seen, Van der Leeuw's analysis of sacred space recycled the domestic metaphors of home, homelessness, and homesickness in fashioning a poetics of the sacred. At the center of every sacred place, from hearth to heart, Van der Leeuw domesticated the sacred, asserting, in the end, that a sacred place was ultimately a place in which a person could truly be at home. However, as a cross-cultural, comparative category in a phenomenology of religion, the home may not actually travel very well. It is entangled in at least two theoretical problems. First, as a term for domestic space that is imbued with a range of specific feelings, cultural expectations, and symbolic associations, the English word "home" or the German word "Heim" may not be precisely translated across linguistic boundaries. They may not even translate each other. Indeed, literary theorist George Steiner has pointed directly to the cross-cultural translation problems posed by "mutually untranslatable cognates such as English *home* and German *Heim*."[20] As the central term in Van der Leeuw's poetics of sacred space, home might have been where his heart was, but it was a metaphor that did not necessarily transfer easily among different cultural contexts as if it were the single, recurring essence of sacred space. Therefore, whether as the *Heim* of the German original or the *home* of the authorized English translation, Van der Leeuw's domestic metaphor provided an inherently unstable, mutable "essence" at the heart of sacred space.

In any case, it was not the English or the German, but the Dutch home, and, more precisely, the lost *huiselijkheid* and *haardvuur*, the homeliness and the hearthfire of Dutch Gelderland, that seem to have preoccupied Van der Leeuw. Accordingly, a second problem arises in his domestic poetics of the sacred: the pervasive nostalgia for a lost home that informed his entire analysis of sacred space. In Van der Leeuw's method, the restraint of *epochē*, the intentional act of clearing a cognitive space in which religious phenomena could appear, was combined with the corresponding but opposite motion of empathy, interpolating religious phenomena into one's own experience, taking them, so to speak, to heart. Van der Leeuw interpolated sacred space into his own experience in 1933 when, living in urban Groningen, if not in a rented flat but at least in a "semi-americanized" manner, as he put it, he found that every sacred place was a lost or distant home. Located, or dislocated, in this context, Van der Leeuw's poetics of sacred space seems to have configured a modern sense of alienation or anomie in the midst of what has widely been regarded as the existential homelessness of the modern world. Accordingly, Van der Leeuw's phenomenology of sacred space was formulated from a peculiarly modern position of placelessness that the humanistic geographer E. C. Relph has called "existential outsideness."[21] Although he tried to give an "insider's" account, Van der Leeuw, an exile from the sacred like all moderns, could only develop a poetics of the sacred from a position outside the secure precincts of any sacred place.

As I have tried to show, Van der Leeuw's poetics contained hints of a politics of the sacred. Irrespective of the feelings that might be aroused by the poetic metaphors of home, *Heim*, or *heilig haardvuur*, situational assertions of power, as well as resistance to it, define the inherently contested politics of sacred space. Following hints provided but undeveloped by Van der Leeuw, it might be possible to advance a critical

phenomenology of religion that merges in a single field of analysis both
the poetics and politics of sacred space. While a poetics of the sacred has
enabled a recognition that home, temple, city, pilgrimage site, and human
heart are comparable in some respects, an analysis of the politics of sacred
space reveals the differential dynamics of power that go into the construction, as well as the contestation, of any sacred place. Significant
research has recently been advanced along these lines, taking, but also
taking apart, Van der Leeuw's basic ideal types of sacred space. Recent
studies of the sacred space of homes, temples and other sacred built
environments, cities, and pilgrimage sites, including, incidentally, tourist
attractions and battlefields, have repositioned sacred places within the
contested politics of power relations.[22] Even the human heart has been
placed within a politics of the sacred by research that has directed attention to the disciplines of the body, those ritualized "gestures of approach"
that provide the only outward indication that the inner heart is conformed
to the sacred.[23]

    In conclusion, and in keeping with these recent advances, I would
like to formulate, perhaps more schematically than necessary, four basic
principles of the politics of sacred space. Although submerged under Van
der Leeuw's poetics, these principles, as I have tried to show, were
interwoven in his phenomenological project. I record them here not
only to itemize a political subtext in a classic phenomenological text,
but also to suggest a direction that might be taken in developing a critical
phenomenology of religion, a phenomenology that is attentive not only
to the poetics, but also to the situational, relational, and contested politics
of the sacred. Accordingly, I offer these four axioms for a critical situational analysis of sacred space:

1.) In the politics of position, a place is sacred because the conquest
and colonization of space that established its location is contested.

2.) In the politics of exclusion, a place is sacred because it is at risk of
desecration or defilement by the very "alien" forces that are excluded.

3.) In the politics of property, a place is sacred because it is at risk of
being dispossessed by competing claims on its ownership.

4.) In the politics of exile, a place is most sacred when it is remote, or
lost, or experienced as sacred under conditions of extreme dislocation
or disorientation.

These, I submit, are the basic situational aspects of the politics of sacred space. These principles recall the struggles over conquest, exclusion, and appropriation that are intrinsic to sacred space. They stand for all the inherently contested power relations that are always at stake in the making and unmaking of sacred places. However, as we have seen, even if all the situational forces that make a place sacred have been canceled – that is, if its conquest has been successfully overturned, its exclusions violated, and its ownership alienated – a sacred place might still remain sacred, but it will only register as sacred to its formerly dominant, centered inhabitants from a decentered position of exile.

If we follow Van der Leeuw's reading of the modern world, then we must conclude that a modern poetics of sacred space can only be formulated within a politics of exile. As Van der Leeuw suggested, the phenomenology of religion itself, as a modern intellectual discipline, is unavoidably positioned in exile, a modern stranger to the sacred. In this respect, therefore, Van der Leeuw's phenomenology of sacred space can be regarded as a gesture of recentering, an attempt to recover the hauntingly familiar but nevertheless estranged feelings that might be attached to home in the midst of the decentered, homeless world of the modern. At the same time, however, by providing hints of a politics of the sacred, Van der Leeuw exposed the situational, relational, and contested power relations at stake in any attempt to recover a sense of sacred place. A spatial "disalienation," particularly in the midst of the endlessly signifying but essentially meaningless "hyperreality" of a post-modern world, as the critic Frederic Jameson has observed, requires more than merely a new recognition of the significance of place. It depends upon more than merely developing new techniques for "cognitive mapping." A recovery of place, in Jameson's terms, requires a cultural politics dedicated to "a practical reconquest of a sense of place."[24] It is not the home, but the battlefield, that provides the governing metaphor in such a poetics and politics of space. It might also inform the emergence of a critical phenomenology of religion that is not only dedicated to uncovering substantial meaning, but also to exposing the situational and contested power relations that permeate the space of the sacred.

University of Stellenbosh, S.A.

230   DAVID CHIDESTER

NOTES

[1] Claude Lévi-Strauss, "Introduction à l'oeuvre de Marcel Mauss," in Marcel Mauss, *Sociologie et anthropologie* (Paris: P. U. F., 1950): xlix; cited in Jonathan Z. Smith, *To Take Place: Toward Theory in Ritual* (Chicago: University of Chicago Press, 1987): 107. See also Jacques Derrida, "Structure, Sign, and Play in the Discourse of the Human Sciences," in *Writing and Difference*, trans. Alan Bass (Chicago: University of Chicago Press, 1978): 289–91.

[2] Mircea Eliade, *Patterns in Comparative Religion*, trans. Rosemary Sheed (New York: Harper and Row, 1958): 367–85; Eliade, *Sacred and Profane*, trans. Willard R. Trask (New York: Harcourt, Brace, 1961): 20–65; Jonathan Z. Smith, "The Wobbling Pivot," in *Map is Not Territory: Studies in the History of Religions* (Leiden: E. J. Brill, 1978): 88–103; and Smith, *To Take Place, passim.* On the subject of spatial poetics and politics, see Peter Stallybrass and Allon White, *The Politics and Poetics of Transgression* (London: Methuen, 1986).

[3] Gerardus van der Leeuw, *Religion in Essence and Manifestation*, trans. J. E. Turner, Foreword by Ninian Smart (Princeton: Princeton University Press, 1986; orig. German ed. 1933; orig. English trans. 1938). References to *Religion in Essence and Manifestation*, cited by page number from the 1986 edition, will appear in the body of the text. The best overview of Van der Leeuw's life and work remains Jacques Waardenburg, "Gerardus van der Leeuw as a Theologian and Phenomenologist," in *Reflections on the Study of Religion* (The Hague: Mouton, 1978): 187–247.

[4] On the topic of the visible and the audible, see David Chidester, *Word and Light: Seeing, Hearing, and Religious Discourse* (Urbana and Chicago: University of Illinois Press, 1992).

[5] David Harvey, *The Condition of Postmodernity: An Enquiry into the Origins of Cultural Change* (Oxford: Basil Blackwell, 1989): 209.

[6] Anthony Giddens, *A Contemporary Critique of Historical Materialism.* Volume 1: *Power, Property, and the State* (London: Macmillan, 1981): 145.

[7] Pierre Bourdieu, *Outline of a Theory of Practice*, trans. Richard Nice (Cambridge: Cambridge University Press, 1977): 89.

[8] H. W. Heuvel, *Oud-Achterhoeksch Boerenleven: Het Geheele Jaar Rond*, 2nd ed. (Deventer: AE. E. Kluwer, 1928; orig. ed. 1927): 17.

[9] Edward W. Soja, *Postmodern Geographies: The Reassertion of Space in Critical Social Theory* (London: Verso, 1989): 149, 151.

[10] Michel Foucault, "Of Other Spaces," *Diacritics* **16** (Spring 1986): 24.

[11] Mary Douglas, *Purity and Danger* (London: Routledge and Kegan Paul, 1966).

[12] Heuvel, *Oud-Achterhoeksch Boerenleven*, 483–84.

[13] Norbert Peabody, "In Whose Turban Does the Lord Reside? The Objectification of Charisma and the Fetishism of Objects in the Hindu Kingdom of Kota," *Comparative Studies in Society and History* **33** (1991): 727.

[14] Simon Harrison, "Ritual as Intellectual Property," *Man* (N. S.) **27** (1992): 225–44.

[15] David Chidester, "Stealing the Sacred Symbols: Biblical Interpretation in the Peoples Temple and the Unification Church," *Religion* **18** (1988): 137–62.

[16] Victor Turner, "The Center Out There: Pilgrim's Goal," *History of Religions* **12** (1973): 191–230.

[17] Aulus Gellius, *Noctes Atticae*, ed. P. K. Marshall (Oxford: Oxford University Press, 1968): IV, ix, 8.

[18]   Smith, *Map is Not Territory*, 101. See also Jonathan Z. Smith, *Drudgery Divine: On the Comparison of Early Christianities and the Religions of Late Antiquity* (Chicago: University of Chicago Press, 1990): 121–42.

[19]   Baruch M. Bokser, "Approaching Sacred Space," *Harvard Theological Review* **78** (1985): 279–99; Bernard Faure, "Space and Place in Chinese Religious Traditions," *History of Religions* **26** (1987): 337–56.

[20]   George Steiner, *After Babel: Aspects of Language and Translation* (London: Oxford University Press, 1975): 28. See Smith, *To Take Place*, 30; and David E. Sopher, "The Landscape of Home: Myth, Experience, Social Meaning," in D. W. Meinig (ed.) *The Interpretation of Ordinary Landscapes: Geographical Essays* (Oxford: Oxford University Press, 1979).

[21]   E. C. Relph, *Place and Placelessness* (London: Pion, 1976): 55.

[22]   On the topic of the sacred home, see not only Bourdieu, *Outline of a Theory of Practice*, but also Juan E. Campo, "Shrines and Talismans: Domestic Islam in the Pilgrimage Paintings of Egypt," *Journal of the American Academy of Religion* **55** (1987): 285–305. One of the subject of politics of sacred built environments, see Smith, *To Take Place*, 47–73, David L. Carrasco, "Templo Mayor: The Aztec Vision of Place," *Religion* **11** (1981): 275–97, and Pamela C. Graves, "Social Space in the English Medieval Parish Church," *Economy and Society* **18** (1989): 297–322. On the city, see the now classic works of Paul Wheatley, *The Pivot of the Four Quarters* (Chicago: Aldine, 1971), and Stanley J. Tambiah, "The Galactic Polity in Southeast Asia," in *Culture, Thought, and Social Action* (Cambridge: Harvard University Press, 1985): 252–86, but also David L. Carrasco, "City as Symbol in Aztec Thought: The Clues from the *Codex Mendoza*," *History of Religions* **20** (1981): 199–223, Bardwell Smith and Holly Baker Reynolds (eds.), *The City as a Sacred Center: Essays on Six Asian Contexts* (Leiden: E. J. Brill, 1987), and the remarkable analysis of Protestant and Catholic conflicts over sacred space in the city in Natalie Z. Davis, "The Sacred and the Body Social in Sixteenth-Century Lyon," *Past and Present* **90** (1981): 40–70. On the subject of pilgrimages to tourist sites and battlefields, see John Sears, *Sacred Places: American Tourist Attractions in the Nineteenth Century* (New York and Oxford: Oxford University Press, 1989), and Edward Tabor Linenthal, *Sacred Ground: Americans and Their Battlefields* (Urbana and Chicago: University of Illinois Press, 1991). An excellent analysis of sacred space in Japan, with particular attention to pilgrimage in its historical context, can be found in Allan G. Grapard, "Flying Mountains and Walkers of Emptiness: Toward a Definition of Sacred Space in Japanese Religions," *History of Religions* **20** (1982): 195–221. For a discussion of aimless, utopian pilgrimage, see Stephen Prothero, "On the Holy Road: The Beat Movement as Spiritual Protest," *Harvard Theological Review* **84** (1991): 205–22.

[23]   Resources for analyzing the body as sacred space can be drawn from Marcel Mauss, "Techniques of the Body," trans. Ben Brewster, *Economic Sociology* **2** (1973): 70–88; Mary Douglas, *Natural Symbols* (New York: Random House, 1973); and Michel Foucault, *Discipline and Punish: The Birth of the Prison*, trans. Alan Sheridan (New York: Vintage Books, 1975). See Chidester, *Word and Light*, 27–30; *Salvation and Suicide: An Interpretation of Jim Jones, the Peoples Temple, and Jonestown* (Bloomington: Indiana University Press, 1988): 97–104; and *Patterns of Action: Religion and Ethics in a Comparative Perspective* (Belmont: Wadsworth, 1987): 135–41.

[24]   Frederic Jameson, "Postmodernism, or the Cultural Logic of Late Capitalism," *New Left Review* **146** (July/August 1984): 89.

GIORGIO PENZO

THE NEW DIMENSION OF THE SACRED
AS NON-POWER

1. MAN AS FREEDOM AND AUTONOMY

To define man as a rational animal, according to the classical conception, signifies overlooking the authentic existential dimension of man.
The classical definition is limited to a determined sphere, and particularly underlines the negative aspect of man, emphasizing that which
man is not with respect to animals. Thus, this definition points out the
aspect of specific difference, reason, which enables the human species
to distinguish itself from the animal species. But man, in the most deeply
philosophical sense, cannot be reduced to a human species. This is a
typically scientific procedure. In a positive perspective, considered in his
unrepeatable individuality, man does not find his deepest essence in the
knowing intellect. Man is above all freedom. And the authentic horizon
of freedom cannot be grasped through pure knowledge, which is the
typical category of the sciences.

If we travel the path of knowledge to its end, we always find ourselves
facing the relationship between the knowing subject and the known
object. But in this sphere, rather than speak of freedom, we must speak
strictly of autonomy. This means that, step by step, as we travel the
path of knowledge, we acquire ever greater awareness of our own
autonomy, which we gain by means of our power over the objects before
us. This power can be measured in the contention that, if the object is
not yet known, it can nevertheless be known in the course of time.
Obviously, this concerns a horizon of possibilities on a logical level,
which, precisely, can be actualized in the course of time. In the sphere
of freedom, however, man becomes conscious, not of his power over
the things that surround him, but of his non-power. Thus, if autonomy
is linked to power, freedom is linked to non-power. The relationship
between power and non-power is a polar-dialectic one, given that the
latter is intrinsically united with the former. Non-power arises precisely
out of the consciousness of the limits of the former. Thus, the relationship between autonomy and freedom is also a polar-dialectic one, given
that it expresses the same intrinsic affinity that exists between power

233

A-T. Tymieniecka (ed.), Analecta Husserliana XLIII, 233–250.
© 1994 Kluwer Academic Publishers. Printed in the Netherlands.

and non-power. Hence, any possible venture into mysticism is eliminated, precisely because the moment of non-power remains firmly linked to that of power.

2. POWER AND NON-POWER AND THE RELATIONSHIP BETWEEN REASON AND TRUTH

Both of these moments constantly remain on the plane of rationality, even if they express two different ways of being of rationality. The plane of power, and thus of autonomy, is linked to the knowing intellect that unfolds in the relationship between knowing subject and known object. The plane of non-power, which emerges when man acquires consciousness of the limits of knowledge, itself remains linked to the plane of knowledge, even if in an indirect manner. Thus, the plane of knowledge is not eliminated, but an awareness of its limits is acquired. But, if power and non-power both remain on the field of rationality, only on the plane of non-power may we speak of the fullness of rationality. This fullness is given by the fact that in the logical sphere of knowledge, awareness of the new ontological implication of the rational dimension is acquired. This context no longer exactly concerns the limits of knowledge in regard to the object before us, because we are aware that, in time, these limits can, in some way, be overcome. But it does concern awareness of the limits of one's own cognitive faculty. In other words, the limit is displaced from the object that is or can be known, in order to reach the final root of the very possibility of knowledge. And it is in this acquisition of consciousness that the logical plane of knowledge reveals itself to be an ontological plane.

In this new context, the dimension of the "I" as a knowing being reveals itself in its deepest essence as being-itself. These two faces of consciousness are intrinsically united and their relationship is itself polar-dialectical, as is clear from their relationship with the dimension of freedom. As the I as a knowing-subject, man stays within the restricted sphere of autonomy, since the entire expression of freedom is limited to the relationship with the object which is or can be known. On the other hand, as being-itself, there occurs in man the passage from autonomy to freedom in the full sense, which coincides with the passage from the plane of power to that of non-power. Clearly these reflections on power and non-power, and thus on autonomy and freedom, lead us to confront two different ways of considering truth.

The dimension of power opens for us a truth which is measured in the very categories of scientific procedure. The dimension of non-power opens for us a horizon of truth which stands outside these categories. On the level of non-power, truth concerns the foundation of man as being-himself; thus, it involves not only the plane of knowledge, but also the plane of being. In this context, we cannot speak of a conception of being as a category, but of a conception of being that infuses the existence of man, as understood in its unrepeatable singularity. This occurs when the subject-object relationship is superseded by the relationship between subject and non-object. The truth on the level of being is revealed with the emergence of the "feeling" of facing the non-object, that is to say, of facing the nothingness of the object, thus facing nothingness. Herein lies the intrinsic link between truth and nihilism. Consequently, this dimension of truth as being-nothingness always appears as a mystery. This arises from the feeling of facing the non-object, and more precisely from the feeling of being dependent-on insofar as one is not master-of.

3. POWER AND NON-POWER AND THE SACRED

There is a reality of mystery, or of the sacred, which is quite different from that which arises on the plane of mere knowledge, which is resolved in the fact that the object in front of the knowing "I" is still not within the reach of knowledge. It is obvious that in this sphere, the term "mystery" is understood in a mistaken sense, given the awareness that, in the course of time, that object will be known. Thus, this dimension of mystery in the mistaken sense is intrinsically linked to the dimension of time.

The question strictly concerned with the mystery or the sacred is different. In contrast to that which arises on the plane of knowledge, mystery in the narrow sense is not linked to time. This is because this horizon of mystery, in its essence, withdraws from knowledge. Thus, we can say that this ontological reality of mystery only unfolds on the horizon of eternity. This is not considered on the metaphysical level, as a reality outside of time and thus in an objective sense, but it is considered on an existential level. On this level, it unfolds in each moment. The act of decision, even though it occurs in time, does not exhaust its existential reality in time. In fact, the moment encloses the act of decision which man accomplishes facing his foundation, and not in relation to the things that surround him and that are all in time. In this way, in this horizon of existential eternity, the dimensions of non-power, freedom, truth, and mystery are rediscovered in their existential-ontological implications.

Clearly, the reality of the mystery or of the sacred is ambiguous in its demonstration of two different faces of reality, one on a logical level, and one on an ontological level. Though these two faces are intrinsically united, they are at the same time profoundly different. Both are linked to the dimension of rationality, given that the mystery concerning being arises along the consciousness of the limits of knowledge. But, if both fall in the dimension of rationality, they distinguish themselves on the basis of two different ways of considering the dimension of rationality. The mystery concerning knowledge belongs to an illuministic rationalism which depends on the presupposition that all reality is resolved in its being-known, either in action, or in power.

On the other hand, the mystery concerning being is typical of a rationalism that could be called "non-illuministic", or "a-illuministic", though these terms do not imply "anti-illuministic". This kind of rationalism, which pervades the very horizon of being, depends on the fact that, if everything which is part of the experience of the things surrounding us can, and indeed must, become an object of knowledge, this still does not necessarily lead us to conclude that the whole sphere of reality can be traced back to this act of being-known. If then the mystery which pervades the plane of being expresses the horizon of non-power, understood as a feeling of dependence-on, consequently, this feeling announces that horizon of reality that, in its essence, cannot be represented, and thus, cannot be known. All this occurs outside of time, even outside of future time. The feeling of dependence-on reveals the very foundation of man, who, as I have said, is not in essence only a rational animal, but is, above all, freedom.

Rather than speak of two different modes of mystery, we can speak of two different ways of being of the sacred or the divine. We can thus open a discourse on the sacred as linked to a conception of illuministic rationalism, and a discourse on the sacred as linked to a dimension of a-illuministic rationalism. The former is inauthentic, the latter is authentic. The former presents us with the myth of the serpent that alludes to man's dream to be like God, precisely because man is aware of his ability to know all the things that surround him. The latter presents us with the awareness of the finitude of man, given that the sacred or divine is announced in that feeling of non-power, or of dependence-on, of which we have already spoken.

4. POWER AND NON-POWER AND SECULARIZATION

If we remember these two aspects of the sacred or divine, we can then make sense of the phenomenon known on a historical-cultural plane as secularization.[1] Even this dimension presents itself in two perspectives, one authentic and one inauthentic. Unfortunately, in modern and contemporary culture, inauthentic secularization has prevailed, and thus it is now rare to even consider the possibility of speaking of secularization in an authentic sense. Indeed, "secularization" is most often understood as the progressive elimination of the sacred in the cultural world. In reality, however, this description of secularization encompasses only its negative face, thus hiding its positive face, which is immeasurably more profound. In this new angle, secularization is not so much the progressive elimination of the sacred, but rather the progressive purification of the sacred. Thus, the planes of that same demythicizing phenomenon are overturned.

We may attempt to clarify this distinction, which I believe to be of fundamental importance in the elucidation of the most profound sense of culture, keeping in mind the two different modes of considering rationalism: the illuministic and the a-illuministic. In this light inauthentic or negative secularization can be explained in terms of an illuministic rationalism, while authentic or positive secularizaton can be explained in terms of an a-illuministic rationalism. Negative secularization thus shows itself to be connected to the plane of power, and positive secularization to the plane of non-power. In this manner we can see how, in the sphere of negative secularization, man acquires always greater consciousness of his power-to, at the same time as he succeeds in eliminating all so-called "mysteries" linked to the plane of knowledge. More precisely, man acquires consciousness when things reveal their proper nature because of the action of the knowing intellect and thus because of the action of science which, in a way, takes the place of religion, when understood in the inauthentic sense.[2]

Positive secularization linked to non-power properly belongs to the domain of a-illuministic rationalism in which mystery reveals itself to be on the level of being. Mystery manifests itself, as I have said, wherever consciousness of the limits of knowledge arises. From this perspective, secularization signifies the purification of the sacred, given that the sacred cannot exhaust itself in its inauthentic aspect of mystery, understood as that which is not yet known by the intellect. As purification of the sacred, authentic secularization implies that act of "making the world worldly". In other words, the world must be known according to its laws, which are the object of the knowing intellect and thus of scientific procedure. It is obvious that we cannot speak, in the proper sense, of mystery or the sacred within the domain of the world's laws, since in the course of time, these are fated to all fall within the domain of the knowing intellect.

On the other hand, the two expressions of secularization, negative and positive, even though of different natures, find themselves together on the same field, if only to a certain extent. And in this proceeding together, we can see how the task of negative secularization fundamentally serves to prepare the way for positive secularization, in which, in this context, even negative secularization finds its justification. In fact, once intellect removes the veils of mystery or the sacred that surround things, we cannot say that, with this act of knowledge, the authentic mystery or sacredness disappears. All that is eliminated is that inauthentic aspect of the sacred that consists in the mere fact that things hide their nature only because they are not yet known. The reality of this so-called sacred is thus resolved entirely on the logical plane. The deepest nature of this act of negative secularization is thus revealed in the act of "making the world worldly". And it is precisely in this sphere that negative secularization shows its positive face. Indeed, in this context, there is no distinction between the two modes of being of secularization. In its deepest nature, however, secularization is not confined only to the act of "making the world worldly", where justly the reality of the so-called sacred is found. It goes much deeper.

The act of a continual "making the world worldly" reveals itself in turn as a necessary act for the purification of that most profound dimension of the sacred whose nature is not only resolved on the logical plane. The most profound sacrality of the sacred is, at heart, that which withdraws in essence from the violence of the cognitive act. Thus, if negative secularization is entirely resolved on the plane of power, positive secularization occurs within the horizon of non-power. Nevertheless, positive secularization coincides above all with the act of elucidating the limits of knowledge and thus the limits of culture, without abandoning the plane of culture, however. Thus there is an intrinsic, polar-dialectic relationship between negative and positive secularization, just as there is between knowledge and non-knowledge, or between culture and meta-culture. Positive secularization presents us with the dimension of meta-culture, as that particular horizon of reality in which culture is continually thrown into crisis. Considered from this angle, it is clear how the dimension of secularization acquires an extremely particular sense, given that it is not only exhausted culturally but reveals itself above all as a category on the ontological level.

5. SECULARIZATION AND THE RELATIONSHIP BETWEEN REASON AND CHRISTIAN REASON

If we keep in mind secularization in its positive aspect as a category on the ontological level, I believe we can more fully clarify the same dimension of faith. In regard to faith, we can make the fundamental distinction between its authentic and inauthentic moments. In its inauthentic moment, faith presents itself as incredulity. It is linked to the object, and thus to knowledge. This is the dimension of faith which belongs to the sphere of power. In its authentic moment, faith is not linked to the object or to knowledge. Its extreme expression is that of being as nothingness. This dimension of faith, then, belongs to the sphere of non-power.

The context of faith as power not only encompasses the phenomenon of religion, but also that of science and of other cultural expressions whenever they are considered in a totalizing perspective. In this sphere, their entire reality is resolved in being-represented, and consequently it all falls under the power of the knowing intellect. On this level, faith presents itself as incredulity. Obviously, if we speak of the religion encompassed in the sphere of power, we intend to refer to the inauthentic moment of religion. The authentic moment of religion is not resolved in its being connected-to, but transcends any possible closure in any objective dimension. In this act of transcending, religion shows its face of authenticity and itself falls into the horizon of non-power. Herein lie the two faces of religion: as authentic faith, linked to non-power, and as incredulity, linked to power.

This distinction between incredulity (i.e., the negative moment of faith) and faith in the deepest sense of the terms, helps us to clarify the problematic contained in the relationship between reason and Christian reason.

This is not only a problematic on the historical-cultural level, but also on the existential-ontological level, given that it concerns culture as meta-culture and thus reaches the ultimate foundation of man.

With this consideration, we have taken a further step towards eluci-dating the problematic of the divine. After having clarified, in the philosophical sphere, the difference between the inauthentic mystery or sacred, linked to knowledge, and the authentic mystery or sacred, linked to understanding and thus to being, we can focus on another relation-ship – that between the authentic sacred on a simply philosophical level, and the authentic sacred on the level of theological or Christian thought, given that both these dimensions of the sacred are connected to under-standing. "Christian thought" may describe either the conception of Christian culture or that of the God of Christianity, which is the ultimate foundation of that conception considered in its historical and cultural aspects. We can thus see how the relationship between the sacred on the philosophical level and the sacred on the level of the Christian con-ception is ambiguous, given that it can present itself either in its intrinsic aspect or in its extrinsic aspect.

The ambiguity is clarified if we remember the distinction just made between the historical-cultural dimension of Christianity, linked to the plane of knowledge, and the same dimension of the God of Christianity, linked to the plane of understanding. The relationship between these two aspects of the same existential and historical-cultural phenomenon recalls the relationship between, respectively, culture and meta-culture. The reality of the divinity of the God of Christianity, even while present in the historical-cultural phenomenon of Christianity, is always, by definition, that reality which goes beyond any historical-cultural expres-sion. This reality of the divinity of the God of Christianity reveals itself finally within the sphere of the foundation of man as that extremely particular reality that, even though it is present, never lets itself be com-pletely grasped in its being present. It is thus present and absent at the same time, precisely because it is of a transcendent nature. The "meta" dimension of meta-culture as regards the existential-historical phenom-enon of Christianity is given by that reality of the divine which can never be grasped in the fullness of its being as nothingness, precisely because it eludes understanding and thus, power.

6. SECULARIZATION AND THE LANGUAGE OF FAITH

In this context, the problem of the reality of the God of Christianity can be proposed anew in the sphere of the existential reality of faith. We can thus elucidate a new relationship between faith on the authentic philosophical level, and faith on the authentic theological level. The faith linked to the authentic dimension of philosophy is, as we have seen, that of the sacred linked to the dimension of understanding. The faith linked to the ontological dimension of theological thought is that of the sacred linked to the God of Christianity, which is itself elucidated in the sphere of understanding. Therefore, in the horizon of the onto-logical difference or of the "between" or of the crisis, where the dimension of understanding is revealed either in its philosophical aspect or in its theological aspect, it is possible to identify an intrinsic relationship between the two moments of faith.

Nevertheless, even the intrinsic relationship between reason and Christian reason can be clarified in this problematic context, where faith is identified in its double nature, philosophical and theological. We have said that the dimension of the sacred in the philosophical sphere can be double-sided, on the inauthentic level of knowledge, when "sacred" signifies that which is not yet known but which may be known in the course of time – and on the authentic level of understanding, or of being – when "sacred" signifies the very limit of knowledge which does not so much concern the object as the cognitive faculty itself. Because of this limit or constraint, or because of this crisis which occurs in the sphere of reason as understanding, reason itself becomes aware of its limits. Thus man perceives himself to be a limited being. In the context of reason as pure knowledge, on the other hand, man may be exposed to the temptation of believing himself to be a being without limits and thus, in a way, similar to God, given that he can always know. The sensation of being limited implies the consciousness of no being master-of. Now, within this horizon of philosophy, where philo-sophical faith is liberated on the level of understanding that unfolds in the foundation of man, it is possible to proceed further. The mystery or the sacred on the philosophical level can thus reveal itself on the theological level as well. This is possible, clearly, if the historical-cultural phenomenon of Christianity also reveals itself in its meta-cultural aspect.

In this philosophical-theological context on the level of understanding, we can still observe the dimension of constraint, of crisis which occurs because of secularization, understood in its positive aspect. In other words, this secularization brings Christianity as a historical-cultural phenomenon back to its deeper dimension of meta-culture as crisis. Only if they are placed on this hermeneutic field can philosophical and theological faith be rediscovered on an intrinsic level. In this way, even the relationship between reason and Christian reason will reveal itself. That is to say, the relationship between reason in its dimension of understanding on one hand, and Christian reason on the other, will reveal itself when the "Christian" dimension of reason is considered as the "meta" of meta-culture, or as transparence. All this fundamentally concerns the problem of the language of faith, which is elucidated within the horizon of constraints and crises, considered on the level of philosophical reason as well as on that of philosophical-theological reason. Only thus, in the problematic of the relationship between reason and Christian reason, is the language of faith intrinsic in relation to the language of theological faith. Both languages, in fact, belong to the same terrain of understanding.

This implies the fundamental principle that Christian thought cannot be reduced to a simple conception of the world, given that this is entirely resolved in its cultural aspect. This is true even if, in its historical expression, Christian thought might seem to be a conception of the world. Thus the problem is not whether or not to consider Christianity as a model of culture that can be compared with other models of culture, in order to see which of these is the most authentic humanistic expression. The desire to clarify within the domain of culture whether one humanism is more "human" than another, and thus whether the Christian conception of the world is more profoundly human than other conceptions of the world, entails enclosing a discourse within its cultural context, and thus within the context of time. This we can particularly see when this discourse is inserted into future time, considered as the horizon of a possible utopian conception.

In my opinion it is not particularly important to open the discourse to a utopian vision of Christianity, one which could be more profoundly human than another, precisely because this vision unfolds in time, and thus only on the cultural plane. In the perspective of a philosophical-theological hermeneutic, the Christian conception denotes more exactly the continual openness of the individual man to his own foundation. Only in this horizon can the light of God considered according to the announcement of Christ be disclosed. Thus, if we speak of Christian reason, we mean above all to underline the place in which the existential-ontological phenomenon of the transparence of the sacred announced by Jesus Christ can be unfolded. This act can be elucidated on the theological plane as the very act of putting into crisis any cultural expression in which the Christian conception of the world is present. If there is no doubt that the announcement of Jesus is also a phenomenon on the historical-cultural level, nevertheless, when considered in its essence, it continually withdraws from any possible cultural language, given that language is by nature linked to the knowledge of man. Nonetheless, this message, considered in its non-cultural or meta-cultural aspect, is destined to put into crisis every possible cultural language that pretends to exhaust the fullness of this message in its being said.

7. SECULARIZATION AND THE LANGUAGE OF FAITH AS SILENCE

Clearly this problem concerns the dimension of language that in its hermeneutic nature is, at the same time, "saying" and "not-saying". If saying expresses the cultural moment on the ontic level and thus on the level of power, then not-saying expresses the meta-cultural moment on the ontological level, and thus on the level of non-power. The dimension of crisis marks precisely the limit between saying as "having said" and saying as "not having said", or rather as "not being able to say". The dimension of constraint or the crisis coincides with that of the "not" of not-saying as not-being-able-to-say. If we bring this problematic into the sphere of the relationship between reason and Christian reason, we can see how this relationship holds at an intrinsic level when reason is considered in the context of understanding as not being able to say. The same can be affirmed with regard to the Christian aspect in the context of Christian reason, and precisely, when the aspect of "Christian" is considered in its hermeneutic nature as the sacred that reveals itself on the level of the foundation of man as not-being-able-to-say. In other words, the relationship is intrinsic when the two aspects, that of reason and that of Christian reason, meet within the horizon of not being able to say, or within the horizon of silence, horizons which are identical.

This silence, which is opened in the same dimension of crisis, continually presents us with the horizon of being as nothingness. The dimension of crisis expresses the continual questioning of saying as having said, in order to bring saying back to not being able to say, that is, to silence. In this sense, the dimension of silence is clearly on an onto-logical level. But, on an ontic level, silence is clarified within the sphere of knowledge as that which has not yet been said, but which even-tually, will be said. On the level of being as nothingness, silence as crisis falls outside of the dimension of time, given that this silence is linked to the decision occurring on the level of the same foundation of man, and thus outside of time. Thus, saying is in time, as is the dimen-sion of power, while not being able to say is outside of time, as is the dimension of non-power. And given that power and non-power are expressions of a polar dialectic, the same can be affirmed for the moments of saying and not being able to say.

We have seen that the eternity in which non-power unfolds always remains within time, even if it is transversal to it, since that eternity can never exhaust itself in time. The same is true for saying as for not being able to say, or for silence. Thus even this silence is a matter of transcendence, because not being able to say always remains beyond all attempts to say. In other words, the ontological possibility of not being able to say always remains as that ontological possibility. But we must never forget the polar dialectic between power and non-power which is represented precisely in the relationship between saying and not being able to say. In fact, because of this polar dialectic, the transcendence of non-power in the expression of not being able to say can never take the shape of metaphysical transcendence, given that it always remains fundamentally linked to the phenomonological plane of power as saying. In this manner, I intend to emphasize that there can be no qualitative leap between saying and not being able to say. For the same reason, there is no qualitative leap between reason and Christian reason.

The historical-cultural phenomenon of Christianity does not signify in its profound hermeneutic nature a doctrine that emerged in a deter-mined place and time, but rather expresses the announcement that involves man, every single man, in its foundation. The eternal dimen-sion of the announcement as a dimension outside of time withdraws from every possible saying as having said in order to continually establish itself as unsaid in the sense of not being able to say. The announcement reveals itself fully in silence. In silence, truth must strip itself of all its cultural expressions in order to manifest itself only in the problematic form of crisis and risk. It must strip itself of all dogmatic expressions. Thus, the relationship between saying and not being able to say is expressed as the relationship, respectively, between dogmatism and truth.

The term "dogmatism" does not concern only the dogmatic expression typical of the old metaphysical theology, but every expression of truth that wants to be seen as law. We can thus distinguish truth as law or dogmatism from truth as a contesting of every well-established dimension of law. In this context, we can even speak of truth as crisis or truth as being-in-revolt. In its hermeneutic nature on the theological level, this truth as being-in-revolt closely recalls the typical truth of the Gospels. Thus we can see that the opposition between law and the Gospel is also resolved in the polar-dialectic field between power and non-power. Clearly, the relationship between reason and Christian reason in its internal polar-dialectic dynamic coincides with the fundamental relationship between power and non-power, between saying and not being able to say, and between truth in its dogmatic aspect as law and truth in its aspect of being-in-revolt which recalls the evangelical truth.

In this sense, we can speak of theological philosophy, given that one attributes to the term "theological" a new sense that finds its final explanation in the polar-dialectic relationship between power and non-power. The relationship between philosophical thought and theological thought is not a relationship of dependence of the former on the latter, nor of the latter on the former, as if between two different conceptions of the world or two opposing forces. In fact, it is a relationship that is disclosed in the sphere of the foundation of man and thus on an intrinsic level. Both of these moments, that of philosophy on an authentic level and that of theological philosophy, also on an authentic level, are disclosed in the hermeneutic field that falls outside of time and thus in eternity. In other words, eternity in its philosophical aspect can be further deepened in the context of eternity in its theological aspect. This deepening always occurs in the same field of the foundation of man and thus in the field of transcendence and not in that of immanence, since it still concerns the horizon of non-power. In this way, silence on the philosophical level as not being able to say meets with silence on the philosophical-theological level.

By my insistence, I intend to underline this affinity in order to show how the passage between the moment of faith on the philosophical level is not extrinsic, but intrinsic to the moment of faith on the theological level. It is not by accident that these two moments are disclosed on the rational horizon of understanding which, even while remaining in the context of human reason, overcomes in its essence the rational context of explanation. Fundamentally, these two planes of faith reveal themselves to be intrinsic because both are disclosed on the horizon of a transcendence which, even though it is not unfolded outside of man, still can never exhaust itself within man.

8. SECULARIZATION, SUPERSTITION, AND FIDEISM

Nevertheless, if we consider the fundamental question of the relationship between reason and Christian reason in this perspective, we can see how there is no longer any sense in posing the dilemma of the rationality or irrationality of faith. This entails that all disourses on the validity of fideism be exposed as unphilosophic, however fideism might be understood. This dilemma has sense only if we remain attached to a rational conception of the illuministic kind, to reason understood as pure knowledge. In other words, this dilemma retains sense only in a philosophical context that has not yet understood the power of ontological difference. In the sphere of metaphysical difference, the moment of faith is constantly exposed to the grave danger of falling onto an extrinsic level with respect to reason, with the consequence that faith is revealed to be fideism. Fundamentally, faith as fideism finds its final justification in the illuministic assumption that all reality is resolved in its being known and thus in the sphere of saying as having said. In turn, the illuministic assumption has its reason only in the fact that human reason unfolds in its most profound reality only in the cognitive act, in explaining.

I have underlined how reason is revealed in its most profound essence also as understanding, which aims to elucidate the intrinsic limit of all knowledge, thus becoming manifest in crisis. The dimension of crisis prevents the authentic reality of faith on the philosophical or theological level from expressing itself in the non-rational reality of fideism. This is because crisis is always revealed in a rational field, whether it be more typically on a philosophical or a theological level. In the theological context, crisis becomes the final justification for why theological faith in general, and thus also Christian faith, does not present itself as a well-defined conception in the conceptual sense, according to the typical categories of the scientific sphere. This does not imply that the dimension of faith as content, as it is guarded by the Church, must be eliminated. It is instead necessary to operate on this content a continual demythicization or secularization, whose task is only to make transparent that which is expressed in the cultural context. Fundamentally, this act of demythicization or secularization becomes confused with the very horizon of crisis.

In the most strictly philosophical sphere, this dimension of crisis or this becoming transparent signifies, as we have seen, the continual passage from a dimension of reason understood as pure knowledge to a dimension of reason understood as understanding. Only in the latter is the further passage between the authentic sacred on the philosophical level to the authentic sacred on the theological level possible. Both of these dimensions unfold precisely within the horizon of understanding. In the theological context, there is thus a further deepening of understanding, without the danger that the intimate nature of this understanding will be covered with a theological dimension of the sacred that could contain a dogmatic aspect.

Clearly, in this problematic context, faith withdraws from the danger of revealing itself as superstition or fideism. In the first case, faith presents itself as "being linked-to," that is, to a determined object or a determined culture. In the second case, faith reveals itself as a non-rational leap into a more or less mystical horizon, given that obviously one thinks that reason cannot explain the principles of Christian faith. Actually, the inauthentic moments of faith as superstition or fideism can find their legitimate justification only in the presupposition that reason is limited only to the dimension of knowledge. Consequently, these moments are linked to a conception of authority understood in its inauthentic nature as authoritarianism. In this way, in the sphere of faith as superstition, authoritarianism is revealed in the act of recognizing a well-determined conception of the world as the final necessity. In the sphere of faith as fideism, authoritarianism reveals itself to be linked to a conception of the world delineated in the sphere of the time of religion, understood only in its dogmatic or negative aspect.

Nevertheless, superstition and fideism fail if the inauthentic dimension of authority as authoritarianism is made problematic by the authentic dimension which is founded on a rational horizon of faith, which finds its terrain precisely in the sphere of understanding. Fundamentally, these inauthentic moments of faith find their justification in the fact that their philosophical-theological roots lie in the context of ontological difference. It is known that this implies the difference between entity and being. But, in contrast to the typical metaphysical difference of traditional philosophical and theological thought which plays on the rational field of only one dimension, that of knowing, ontological difference plays on the rational field of two dimensions, that of knowledge as explanation and that of knowledge as understanding. This latter dimension, in the act of continually making the former problematic because of the dimension of crisis, ensures that the authority implicit in the existential act of faith does not fall into authoritarianism, in which context that sense of dependence-on, which I have already spoken about, becomes dependence within a well-determined dimension.

But in this case, the oppression of a law of any nature takes the place of the expression on the ontological level of the being-in-revolt, and thus on an external, not internal, level. And then, in the sphere of faith, the internal moment of adhesion is replaced by an external moment of obedience, which becomes decisive. This entails that faith be presented precisely in its inauthentic nature as superstition. This can be defined as being linked-to, which can present itself as a being linked-to a determined object or conception of the world, where the dimension of crisis as being-in-revolt is not presented. Fundamentally, this is precisely the danger that confronts every religion. In this case, religion turns from the authentic to the inauthentic, because an internal authority is replaced by an external authority. The external sign in its objective expression takes the place of the internal one. Fundamentally, this concerns the dominance of the law over the Gospel.

Analogous observations can be made about the inauthentic dimension of faith as fideism. I believe that there are two presuppositions at the root of the phenomenon of fideism: the first is justified and the second is not. According to the first presupposition, faith cannot be explained by reason when, obviously, it is considered in one dimension, on the level of knowing only. In fact, faith cannot be the object of those rational categories that are typical of the scientific process. The second presupposition on which fideism is founded is fundamentally common to Illuminism, Positivism, or Neo-Positivism. According to this presupposition, the whole reality of our experience must exhaust itself in the sphere of knowledge. Obviously, this affirmation presupposes that the dimension of knowledge resolves the reality of the rational dimension. And it is precisely this principle that I have continually put into question in these reflections.

If we consider fideism in this sense, we can see how this entails the very alienation of man. This in fact implies the act of looking for the foundation of man outside of man, and not in the same rational dimension of man that is understanding, which is manifested in the sphere of the foundation. Fideism overlooks the I as being-itself and thus remains closed within the extremely limited relationship between the knowing I and the known object. On the other hand, in the horizon of being-itself, the object that is or that can be known is replaced by the non-object, the dimension of nothingness. This cannot be known on the level of essences and thus cannot be expressed. In this context, non-saying as not being able to say is decisive, and thus so is silence. Only in this horizon can faith overcome the danger of falling into its inauthentic moments of superstition or fideism. In the horizon of silence is revealed the very horizon of God in its most profound aspect as that dimension of the divine that emerges in man through the feeling of dependence-on, thus in the sphere of man's unrepeatable singularity. In this way, the passage between reason and Christian reason occurs intrinsically, given that the horizon of silence offers the common field of understanding on the philosophical and theological levels.

Thus the concept of atheism is reshaped. I believe that we cannot call one who challenges Christianity as a conception of the world an atheist given that this falls into the sphere of scientific knowledge and thus can always be challenged. Instead, one who does not recognize the limits of reason and who thus places himself outside of the field of ontological difference can be called atheist. In this context, in fact, the distinction between that which is finite (the creature) and that which is infinite (the creator) is surpassed. This is the Faustian attitude of the man who places himself in the center of the universe so that he can know and thus explain every object. In religious terms, the creature takes the place of the creator.

University of Padua

NOTES

[1] Concerning the problem of secularization, the philosophic-theological thought of Friedrich Gogarten is a fundamental reference. Among his works, we can cite: F. Gogarten, *Destino e speranza dell'epoca moderna*, F. Coppellotti, ed. (Brescia: Morelliana, 1972); *L'annuncio di Gesù Cristo*, Giorgio Penzo, ed. (Brescia: Queriniana, 1978); *L'uomo tra Dio e il mondo*, A. Molinari, ed. (Bologna: Dehoniane, 1971). On the thought of F. Gogarten, see Giorgio Penzo, *F. Gogarten. Il problema di Dio tra storicismo ed esisten- zialismo* (Rome: Città Nuova, 1981); E. Arrigoni, *Alle radici della secolarizzazione. La teologia di F. Gogarten* (Turin: Marietti, 1981).

[2] Regarding the thematics of the philosophy of existence and of nihilism which lie at the root of secularization in the philosophical sense, see: Max Stirner, *L'unico e la sua proprietà* (Milan: Mursia, 1990); on Stirner, see: Giorgio Penzo, *Max Stirner. La rivolta esistenziale* (Turin: Marietti, 1971; 3rd ed., 1992); F. Nietzsche, *L'Anticristo* (Milan: Mursia, 1982); on Nietzsche, see: Giorgio Penzo, *Invito al pensiero di Nietzsche* (Milan: Mursia, 1990); G. Vattimo, *Ipotesi su Nietzsche* (Milan: Giappichelli, 1967); K. Jaspers, *La filosofia dell'esistenza* (Milan: Bompiani; 4th ed., 1967); K. Jaspers, *Cifre della trascendenza* (Genoa: Marietti, 1990); on Jaspers, see: Girogio Penzo, *Il comprendere in K. Jaspers e il problema dell'ermeneutica* (Rome: Armando, 1985); U. Galimberti, "Jaspers" in *Questioni di storiografia filosofica*, A. Bausola, ed., Vol. IV (Brescia: La Scuola, 1978).

PART FIVE

THE SACRED, THE DIVINE, RELIGION

J. N. Mohanty and George H. Williams at our session devoted to the phenomenology of the Sacred at the American Philosophical Association, Eastern Division Meeting in Boston, December 1990.

WHAT IS SPECIAL ABOUT
PHENOMENOLOGY OF RELIGION?
(Remarks on Works on Phenomenology of Religion by
Steven Laycock and Anna-Teresa Tymieniecka)

The question "What is special about phenomenology of religion?" may mean, depending upon where one places the emphasis, either "What is special about *phenomenology* of religion, compared to other ways of philosophically dealing with religion (such as rational theology)?", or "What is special about the phenomenology of *religion* qua phenomenology, that is to say, as compared to, e.g., phenomenology of perception?"

I intend to touch upon both senses of the question—the former insofar as I am interested in religion, which I believe is an important and central concern of philosophy, and the latter insofar as I am interested in phenomenology, in its strength and weakness as a method.

In dealing with both of these questions, I will be commenting on two books on phenomenology of religion: Steven Laycock's *Foundations for a Phenomenological Theology* and Anna-Teresa Tymieniecka's *The Three Movements of the Soul*. The two books are as different from each other in their central project, styles of execution, and methods as is conceivable within an overall framework of phenomenology. Whether this last term entails a significant commonality needs to be asked; and if it does, then it is worthwhile to make an effort to precisely bring out that commonality.

Let me begin with a few remarks on the two questions. One way of bringing out the difference of phenomenology from the standard

A-T. Tymieniecka (ed.), Analecta Husserliana XLIII, 253–264.
© 1994 Kluwer Academic Publishers. Printed in the Netherlands.

philosophies of religion is to ask: what sorts of questions that figure in the central core of standard philosophy of religion do not figure in phenomenology of religion? Or, if there are important questions that translate from the one to the other, how do they—their sense and import—get transformed thereby? I think it may be fair to say that two kinds of questions are ruled out of a phenomenology: questions that ask for a rational argument for a thesis (such as proof that God, answering the Judeo-Christian description, exists), and questions that have a hypothetical "If-Then" form (such as, If God is omniscient, omnipotent, and good, how can there be evil?). Much standard philosophy of religion is concerned with questions such as these, and phenomenology, with its appeal to the evidence of originary experience, has no need even of taking these concerns seriously. However, phenomenology's abjuring of such issues belonging to rational theology need not be construed as entailing that phenomenology is indifferent to the particular religions in their particularities. It would seek for each, not an argument, but an experience as the original source of meaning and validity.

But this last remark leads me to the second of the two questions asked at the beginning: how is phenomenology of *religion* distinguished from phenomenology of, say, perception, or of mathematics, or of logical thinking? It does appear, at the very outset, that there is a problem which seriously affects the fortunes of phenomenology of religion but which leaves phenomenology as applied to the other areas of experience untouched. This is the problem of radical alternation—of either-or—and not of conjunction, summation, or equalization. One is either a Hindu or a Buddhist or a Christian. The perceived world is not so divided: one perceives the same world under descriptions which are commensurable.˜ That is why a phenomenology of perception, of perceptual experience (not of the perceived world, to be sure) can come up with eidetic descriptive features (such as perspectivity, temporality, historicity, and the like) which are indifferent as to *what* one perceives and as *what*. Can we say the same of phenomenology of religious experience? Faced with the radical alternation that divides religious life, should it immediately ascend to an eidetic level and focus on religious experience as such (with a capital 'R' possibly)? And what guarantee is there that eidetic reduction has not too hastily persuaded us to take what is a dispensable feature of Religion for an essential feature (even though it be essential for one religion in particular)?

But are not the fields of logic and mathematics (or also of art) split by similar radical alternations? You are either a classical mathematician or an intuitionist. Much of what makes sense for the former (such as Cantor's transfinite sets) does not make sense for the latter. You either accept a logic of two truth-values, or a logic of many such. Consider also the deep divide between classical physics and quantum physics. If you are doing phenomenology of these disciplines, how do you proceed? Skipping over differences, and proceeding by a hasty eidetic reduction to the logical as such, the mathematical as such, to art as such? No. Here eidetic reduction must give way to a transcendental-constitutive phenomenology which lays bare the many different processes of meaning-giving underlying the many different object domains before capping the enquiry with an eidetic reduction. So do I think at present, and the case is not very different in the case of religion, although in the case of religion the plurality is bewildering, for you cannot consider the world-religions only, you need also to take into account the so-called pre-literate religions.

My concern with phenomenology of religion is partly due to this: here is a good testing ground for phenomenology as a method, with its twin methodological stances, eidetic reduction and transcendental-phenomenological constitution analysis. A good phenomenology should be able to keep them in a proper balance. But more of this later.

However, we encounter questioning from another direction—in effect, a calling into question the very possibility of extending the transcendental-phenomenological constitution analysis to the domain of religious experience. Tymieniecka joins a host of thinkers, more notably Levinas, in this fundamental questioning. I will focus on this questioning in a little while. For the present, let me look at the two books which provide the occasion for these remarks.

The word 'phenomenology' is often used in a broad, liberal, open-ended sense in which the only constraint on its application is laid down by the imperative of validating one's theoretical-cognitive claims, and of clarifying one's meanings, by the evidence of originary experience. In a narrower, historically grounded sense, one means by 'phenomenology' Husserl's work, and whatever carries that work forward in conformity with its guiding intention. Tymieniecka's work, if I understand her aright, is closer to, even if it does not coincide with, the first sense of 'phenomenology,' and Laycock's is closer to the second sense. I hope Dr. Laycock will understand that having been concerned with understanding and interpreting Husserl's works for exactly four decades, his conceptualization of the basic demands of religious experience comes closer to my way of looking at things, and that criticism of his project, then, will serve to highlight the significance of Dr. Tymieniecka's project. But then again, I will return from her work to his in order to bring out just where my questioning of her work precisely lies. In thus contrasting two such different projects, each carried out with exemplary care as to details, we may begin to see where the path to a satisfactory phenomenology shall take us.

Strangely enough, Laycock's basic question is: What would it be like to see the world as God sees it? (Recall Nagel's question, what is it like to be a bat?) Is this very questioning not phenomenologically illegitimate? Is this not the sort of hypothetical "If-then" question I ruled out at the outset? "If there is God, how does he see the world?" In addition, does not the question bypass the *access* through human intentionality and seek to go directly over to the divine intentionality intending the world—when all that we are legitimately permitted to ask is, how is the sense 'divine intentionality intending the world' constituted in the appropriate sort of human intentionality?

As a matter of fact, Laycock's move is not as phenomenologically illegitimate as I have just made it out to be. What he is doing is starting with an eidetic reduction to the eidos 'mind.' Finite minds are characterised by intentionality, teleological directedness, perspectival character, and intersubjectivity. Such features must apply to divine mind, if there is a divine being. Consequently, for Laycock, divine consciousness is teleologically directed towards *its* object pole—and what should be its object save the world as a whole? Ruled out is divine omniscience—on purely eidetic grounds, as being incompatible with the necessarily egological character of God, for the eidetic structure of intentionality requires as much an ego-pole as an object-pole. Again, not unlike finite human intentionality, divine intentionality also requires a hyletic datum, this being provided by the universal intersubjective community. Consequently, God perceives the world through, and only through, our eyes. Laycock gives us the idea of a finite, developing God whom absolute presence of the world eludes, but who, he nevertheless tells us, us is "implicit" within each act of finite consciousness in the form of a *de jure we* (insofar as asserting a proposition is claiming that *any one* with assent). Through a synthesis of perspectives, this *de jure*, implicit we moves towards being actualized: which is nothing other than the constitution of an ever higher humanity, of what Husserl calls *Gottes-Welt*. In this sense, God's empty intending of the world-pole is concretised through our "compassionate" practice of mutual understanding. God's future is thus in our hands. How nicely does Laycock succeed in fitting together elements from Husserlian thought to give shape to a concept of God?

But can he avoid the question of access? Is such a God given to us in religious experience? He may bracket the question of the real existence of such a (or any other) God, but he cannot bypass the question, is God so described also presented to human intentionality? To this question, Laycock has an answer. Phenomenology, he tells us, can only be concerned with the God-phenomenon. Thus far, he is right, but then he goes on to add: the God-phenomenon is God *as experienced by me in my reflective act*. Since nothing is revealed to me through reflection which is not itself either a consciousness or a moment or structure of consciousness, the God-phenomenon is possible only if it is a divine consciousness partially congruent with mine. We can reflectively imagine what it would be like to see as God sees. If divine mind is in no way revealed through reflection upon my lived experience, there will be for me no God-phenomenon.

I think Laycock's one move here is both crucial and highly questionable. If God is to be a phenomenon, one may wish to argue, it can be so only to the pre-reflective consciousness. If numbers are phenomena, they are so to the intentionality of the mathematician, not to our—the philosopher's—reflection. We as phenomenologists need to be able to catch hold of that pre-reflective intentionality in order to focus upon what was to it its intended object. If this is the case, Laycock still has on his hands the problem of access. He cannot bypass the question of religious experience and simply base all on the eidetic congruence between finite consciousness and divine consciousness. What prevents one from saying that the eidos he depends upon is not the eidos 'mind in general' but, rather, the eidos 'finite mind in general'?

Whereas Laycock gives us a picture without providing an access (note that he provides a conceptual access, not an experiential access), Tymieniecka provides us with that access, a genetic phenomenology of religious experience, but with no picture of that to which it is an access. She knows her phenomenology well, and so rejects the role of intentionality altogether in such matters. Let me therefore focus on this last issue, so crucial for the very conception of a phenomenology of religion.

I can only begin by formulating the issue in my own way. One of the questions I have been asking myself for some time is: Is there any specifically religious intentionality? I mean an intentional act of a type such that its object is only a religious object. One speaks of love, faith, worship, prayer, for example, as religious acts. So they are. But they are not presumably specifically religious acts, for they take on objects which are not religious. Otto, Scheler, and Stavenhagen, amongst others, tried to identify some. This is not the place to go into the question of why I am not satisfied with their answers.

Failing to identify such specifically religious acts, one may choose either of two alternatives. Either deny that religious experience is at all a mode of intentionality and assert that true religiosity requires transcending the intentional (Levinas takes this route), or hold that religious experience, not an intentional experience *sui generis*, is rather an interpretation of the totality of all our intentional experiences (cognitive, affective, and volitional)—in which the totality of relationships to the world and others is given in some deep and profound sort of sense. Tymieniecka has something in common with both of these views, but she forges her own unique path. Is the path phenomenological?

She starts with the idea that man is involved in an ongoing process of self-interpretation in existence and traces out a route from the "pre-experiential evidences" of this process up to the "ultimate fulfillment" of the soul. The secret intention which guides this process is to transcend and be free from all objectifying sense.

Note that if the specific hallmark of religiosity is sacredness, for Tymieniecka nothing that is "outside" the human soul (nature, soil, vegetation) is sacred. Only the human soul is capable of acquiring sacredness, and of thereby investing the world with that significance. She asks a sort of transcendental question: How is the human being—a natural being of the world—capable of sacredness and also of conceiving the sacred as emerging from an other-worldly sphere? The emphasis is on "other-worldly"—if I understand her aright.

In dealing with this question, Tymieniecka claims to have reversed the direction of classical phenomenology. Classical phenomenology focused on consciousness, she focuses on life. Consciousness is only a moment in the process of life's self-individualisation. Classical phenomenology privileges intellect, cognition—in fine, objectivating intentionalities; she privileges the creative, emotional life. Classical phenomenology, we are told, starts with transcendental consciousness, she starts with life at its pre-empirical "stirrings, strivings, pulsations," with "brute vital forces." While doing this, Tymieniecka also wants to remain a phenomenologist, and that—as far as I can see—on two scores. First, she resolves to be faithful to the primacy of the *intuition* of religious experience over all other approaches to the religious phenomenon. By "religious experience" she means—what one cannot just set aside—mystical experience. Secondly, not unlike Heidegger in his course on phenomenology of religion, Tymieniecka insists that religious experience has to be examined in the context of man's situation in the lifeworld, his inward development, and his quest for the destiny of his soul. However, in doing the last-mentioned, she undertakes what looks like her version of Husserl's genetic phenomenology: spiritual experience is traced back to its genesis in that life-process from which all else originates.

There are two distinctive features of all this which bear examination. First, there is the concept of *life* which Tymieniecka expounds with a great deal of vigor, and secondly, the account of the spiritual act that she gives. The first, to my mind, moves towards a metaphysics of life; the second shows genuine phenomenological restraints.

Looking back briefly to classical phenomenology, it is interesting to note here how in the course of time (and partly under the influence of Dilthey) Husserl's expressions "intentional act," "consciousness," and their derivatives slowly gave way—beginning in the twenties—to the language of "life" ("intentional life," "life of consciousness"). This was not a mere change of locution. The change of locution reflects Husserl's perception of the interconnectedness of acts, of their horizonal structure, and of their teleological directedness. But when Tymieniecka speaks of "stirrings of life," of brute vital powers, she is talking about a domain that lies at the borderline of biology and psychology. To come to terms with the issue of the phenomenological accessibility of the stratum of life in what I take to be Tymieniecka's sense, we can best begin by asking to what extent the Freudian discourse is amenable to appropriation and then extend that query to Tymieniecka's seemingly expansive claim. Note that there is nothing as such wrong in this expansive claim about a subterranean life. The question is whether such a concept can be phenomenologically validated—a question that also arose in connection with some similar ideas of Max Scheler.

Let us now take up Tymieniecka's conception of 'spiritual act.' Her description of the specific traits of spiritual acts largely, but not entirely, coincides with that of Scheler. She lists the following: immanent perception of such an act is accompanied by the conviction of a presence; a spiritual act penetrates the entire depth of consciousness; a spiritual act wants or demands to be continued and makes claim to a validity superior to that of objectifying acts; it has an affective quality of peace and serenity; it does not "aim at an object," it has no noetic-noematic structure; it eventually aims at transcending all objectivity; it is not a cognitive act, it has no distinctive contours and structures; it always appears to be unpredictable, sporadic, and ephemeral; it appears devoid of a horizon of possible acts—"out of context," so to speak; it involves a tonality, a harmonic and polyphonic unity lived at many different conscious levels. The spiritual act contains a message about which Tymieniecka has many important things to say. The message itself has several levels of meaning. In this act all human faculties participate. As and when a spiritual act emerges, it shows the limits of objectification, of intentionality, of the transcendental-constitutive system. The constitutive act aims at rest and stability (of the constituted objectivity), the spiritual act is characterised by a restless dynamism to transcend the objective world. The spiritual act is not a positional act, it is rather proclamatory. It proclaims a truth, makes an appeal, and it also seeks to communicate.

Two general features stand out in Tymieniecka's account of the spiritual act (besides its non-objectifying and non-intentional character): its telos towards world-transcendence, and its demand for communication with the other. We are given marvelous accounts of the stages by which the spiritual soul passes beyond the natural finitude of man, and yet the "message" of the spiritual experience, though personal and situational, requires communication with others. In her inimitable language: "The Unknowable One is...our Star in the attempt to surpass finiteness," while "other human beings are the soul's only and last hope."(p. 86) Added to these two features, is the continuing theme of the genesis of the spiritual life in elementary nature, in pre-predicative life. As a matter of fact, we are told the story of how the human condition arises out of this vital substratum and how it struggles to transcend its mundaneity, a story of which only the broad landmarks can be given, in terms of the traces left behind by the emerging spirituality.

Commenting upon Laycock's work, I have said that he gives us a picture of divine life but does not tell us how we can have an access to it. Tymieniecka gives an account of the genesis and the path of the spiritual life, but no clear conception of the goal emerges. This may well be a merit of her work: her concern is with the nature of spiritual experience and how it is related to the totality of human life; it does not seek to validate any specific theory of religious reality (God, or anything else). In this respect, it is a phenomenological work. My concerns, after all of its undoubted merits are recognised, are the following.

How precisely to understand the non-intentionality of the spiritual act? One reason why the spiritual act is taken to be non-intentional is the anxiety that if it were intentional, then its telos, i.e., God, would be an *object*, and so would be open to 'constitution' by the transcendental ego. In other words, the ontological primacy of God as the creator of all things and as Being which is *causa sui* would have to be given up. God would become constituted, rather than being the ultimate ground of all constitution. Thus, from the religious point of view, transcendental phenomenology would seem to be an inversion of the true order of things. To protect, then, the primacy of God, one must either limit transcendental phenomenology to the domain of objects, or do away with the transcendental project altogether in favor of an ontological thesis such as Heidegger's which leaves human existence open to transcendence but does not constitute it.

Religious thinking moves along either of three different paths: either it posits its 'object' (which is a non-object) as the first cause and *causa sui*; or it posits it as a person, a transcendent subjectivity; or it thinks of its goal as an impersonal spirit which is the ground of all things. Transcendental phenomenology puts within brackets that imperious validity which religious life claims for its 'object,' reduces that validity to a validity-claim, the putative object to a noematic structure; and it is to this noema, to this sense, that it assigns a constituting subjectivity. To a certain extent, neither the external world (which claims to cause the states of consciousness within an ego) nor the other person (who is encountered as an irreducible other) gives in to this constituting analysis without protest. They too have their claims to transcendence. But it is precisely their sense of transcendence—not those things out there—that transcendental phenomenology seeks to capture in its genesis. If this be so, then the resistance that religious belief and religious experience offer to transcendental phenomenology should be nothing new in principle. It is only that the transcendence-claim of this new 'object' is far more imperious, its putative transcendence far in excess of that which the external world and the other person carry with them. It would not cut deep, then, if one conceded to transcendental subjectivity in all domains save and except the religious. One thus understands Levinas' refusal even to concede that the other person, in his otherness, can be a proper 'object' for transcendental phenomenology. Let us, for the present, leave it undecided whether Husserl's attempt to exhibit the constitution of the ego of the other succeeds or not. But quite apart from the fate of constitutive phenomenology, should one even deny that the other person, in his otherness, becomes the object of a whole class of intentional acts—acts such as love, sympathy, and moral judgment? One still needs to ask whether these acts could be specifically religious in the sense articulated earlier in this commentary.

It is in this connection that we begin to see the relevance of a much larger question which, for phenomenology, seems to have been decided in advance: namely, whether there is a dimension of consciousness that is non-intentional, and if there is such a dimension, what is its relevance for religion, on the one hand, and for transcendental phenomenology, on the other?

To be fair to Husserl, it should be noted that the domain of consciousness, even for him, is far wider than the narrow region of intentional acts. First, there is the horizonal intentionality which is a sort of pointing without being an object-directed act. Inner time consciousness is characterised by such horizonal intentionalities (retention and protention amongst others). The account of the constitution of temporality leads Husserl to what he characterises as the streaming flux which yet remains the standing living present. This dimension of consciousness, again, is not an act. I need not recall here how Husserl extended the account of transcendental constitution beyond the static theory of *Ideas* I. It is in the light of this enriched theory, then, that the question of the role of intentionality within religious experience needs to be re-examined.

A brief remark about 'experience': sometimes it is held that what must constitute the core of religion must be some non-conceptual, non-intentional experience beyond the subject-object distinction. This sort of view is pressed in many different forms by different thinkers. I do not want on this occasion to go into a detailed treatment of these in their specificities. The remark I want to make should be relevant to all such views in general. No experience, however overwhelming, strong and impressive, tells its own story. The story that emerges is the result of either an intepretation of that experience, or of the role that experience may play in fulfilling a prior empty intention. Without such a conceptual intention coming into relation with the experience, not much can be said about the experience. This is not to say that there is no such religious experience, or no mystic experience. But the cognitive value that we ascribe to any such experience involves an interpretation in terms of some already available conceptual scheme (either Christian or Judaic or Hindu or Buddhist). The pure uninterpreted experience that sweeps you away off your feet, flows into your empty vessel (so the Yogasutras describe it), and simply dazzles you does not *tell* you anything.

Temple University

FILIPPO LIVERZIANI

TOWARD A PHENOMENOLOGY OF
THE ABSOLUTE

A Copernican revolution is taking place in phenomenology, one which will, I believe, enable it to inquire in a more effective and appropriate way into certain aspects of reality which, though they are among the most fundamental, have been left in something like a shadow zone by Husserlian orthodoxy. The work of Anna-Teresa Tymieniecka strikes me as very important in this connection. I obtained particular stimulus from reading her latest book *The Three Movements of the Soul.*

I want to put forward a series of considerations which should prove to be well in line with the essential content of this book, and which could even represent an integration thereof, albeit a very modest one. Each one of us, of course, owes his personal valuations to a maturation process that is inevitably different from that of all others and can neither be given nor received as a loan: therefore, even though themes may be shared in very close intersubjective harmony, they are inevitably lived by each person in his own particular way. I must, therefore, begin by saying something about my own *iter*, the process that has led me to what I believe are conclusions analogous to those of the Author.

Following Descartes, Husserl renewed the discovery of the *cogito*, not only reliving it, though once again in his own way, but delving deeper into it: he thematized and illustrated it, and gave an account of it. At a certain point, however, it seems that even Husserl ends up by enclosing the cogito within itself: indeed, he seems to put the cogito into the cage of a concept that is far too rigid, far too intellectually defined and circumscribed.

Even Husserl at a certain point seems to be saying: the cogito is this and this; and therefore everything that is not in line with this precise definition is outside the cogito, is related to the cogito as the famous "Non A" of traditional logic is related to "A". And, since one

A-T. Tymieniecka (ed.), Analecta Husserliana XLIII, 265–273.

can only have a phenomenology of the lived experiences of the cogito, it follows that whatever does not fall within the ultrarigorous definition of the cogito and its *Erlebnisse* is phenomenologically irrelevant.

A phenomenology that considers nothing but the lived experiences of the cogito conceptualized in this particular manner, experiences that in their turn can be conceptualized in a similar manner, ends up by excluding everything else; it, thus, comes to lack the possibility of phenomenologically considering the subtler aspects of life that cannot very readily be marshaled into the schemes and patterns of the intellect. Ultimately, it confronts the lack of possibility of a phenomenological consideration of the sacred.

All this, of course, has to be said in less absolute and more differentiated terms. Indeed, one needs to take into account the many oscillations that Husserl's thought underwent in the course of time; and, again, one has to remember that he sought, above all, to develop a methodology, something that could always be revised in order to be applied to new sectors of inquiry, especially to the very sectors that he—in actual fact—neglected in his life. Let us, therefore, declare that such a phenomenology excludes life, excludes the sacred, *to the extent to which* the sacred cannot be reduced to the particular schemes that Husserl de facto employed in his analyses. Historically, it is well known that Husserl's analysis set out to be rigorously scientific: and it is by virtue of this second choice—which is by no means either essential or inevitable—that Husserl's phenomenology assumed an intellectualisitic imprint right from the beginning, with the consequences we have just noted.

Descartes enclosed consciousness in the concept of it. Everything that does not in fact form part of consciousness in the clearest and most distinct manner is excluded from direct, authentic, and certain experience, from what could be defined as originary experience. Everything that is not in fact part of consciousness by full right can only be inferred. Thus, God Himself is inferred from the cogito, and in His turn He ensures that our sensations will not be deceived.

It is only human that a reality of which we no longer have any experience, a reality that we limit ourselves to inferring, should increasingly lose sense and meaning for us. Thus, in the course of the development of modern philosophy, the Cartesian approach becomes converted into a more and more markedly idealistic approach: if everything that is outside the cogito becomes less and less thinkable for me, it is clear that ultimately only the cogito will exist for me.

The more the Cartesian cogito excludes an interchange with outside reality, with objective reality, the more it becomes liable to becoming enclosed within itself. The concept—by its very nature—is static and immobile. Whoever reduces consciousness to its concept will therefore tend to consider it as a reality that, notwithstanding all its becoming, always remains absolutely distinct and different from any and all reality which is external to it or which in some way transcends it. Conceptualizing consciousness, seeing it as being enclosed in its concept and as being in some way identified with this concept, will deprive us of other possibilities: anybody who conceptualizes consciousness will not find it very easy then to see it as a living reality, one in continuous transformation, in continuous interchange with the external world.

Only a vision free of intellectualism would enable us to grasp consciousness in the process of its continuous acquisition of realities that, but a moment earlier, were transcendent or extraneous to it.

In temporal becoming there is gradually established a continuous copresence of what we might call "the last instant of the past" and "the first instant of the future." Here we have the copresence of two instants of time that, even though they are successive, enables the subject to live its becoming—something that would no longer be possible if the second instant were to be experienced as an absolute "after" with respect to the first.

In the last instant of the past a given reality is not yet seen, not yet heard, not yet learned, not yet ingested (in the case of food or drink), or not yet breathed in, and so on. This selfsame reality, which at the last instant of the past is still extraneous to the subject, becomes an intimate part of him at the first instant of the future. And it is the copresence of the two moments that enables the subject to have a simultaneous vision of the first instant, when the reality to be acquired is still external, and of the second instant, when that selfsame reality enters to form part of the subject.

Descartes' static consciousness tends to become absolute at the

moment at which it becomes enclosed within itself: in fact, everything that is in consciousness is direct knowledge and perfectly
adequate, articulated in clear and distinct ideas, at least as ideas;
everything else, everything, that is, that cannot be reduced to one's
own cogito in the same terms, remains extraneous to the subject, is
doubtful, evanescent, shadowy, and tends to lose all relevance and
meaning.

For Descartes, the consciousness of the cogito (which he always
understands as a human and created *res cogitans*) depends on God,
that is to say, on a reality that transcends consciousness itself. But
in the wake of Cartesianism, there germinated the idealism that
reduces everything to consciousness, so that even the God Who
transcends consciousness came to be effaced. And thus the Cartesian consciousness itself became the absolute.

The same may be said of Husserl's consciousness, albeit in a
different—but equally significant—sense. Husserl, in the well-
known Paragraph 55 of *Ideen I*, affirms the absolute being of
consciousness. Consciousness is absolute in its intentional aspect,
because it confers sense upon things. Inasmuch as it confers sense
upon all realities, consciousness does not refer to any other, nor does
it depend on any other. In Husserlian terms, then, consciousness is
absolute because it gives sense to everything, to the world itself: it
is therefore placed above the mundane.

But at this point one must surely ask oneself: How is it possible
for consciousness to be above the world if, one the one hand, it is
incarnate in it and forms part of it? Here we come face to face with
the famous "paradox of human subjectivity, which is subject for the
world and also object in the world" (as it is put in the title of
Paragraph 53 of the *Krisis*). If consciousness forms part of the world,
this means that there is a part of the world that is not accessible to
consciousness or, at least, to my consciousness as it is at this
moment.

Certainly, the impact of the world limits consciousness: the act
of thought that gives sense to all things can be the consciousness of
me, John Smith, who at this particular moment is afflicted by a
terrible toothache. I may try to make it pass by not thinking of it; but
the toothache is what it is, it obliges me to think of it, to confer upon

it the sense of being.

This experience of my toothache is thus undoubtedly brought into being by my consciousness, but only by it: a contribution to bringing it into being is also made by a reality that, at least at this moment, appears as something external to this consciousness. There can be no doubt that my consciousness, such as it is here and now, depends on something extraneous and to some extent refers to it.

If it is true that consciousness can confer a sense of being upon every reality, what is it that can confer a sense of being upon this *quid* that is outside my ongoing consciousness if not an absolute Consciousness, a Consciousness very different from the one that is incarnated in me in my present situation? One must therefore postulate an absolute Consciousness, a Consciousness that is absolute in a true and full sense that goes far beyond the sense of Husserl's definition just noted: one has to postulate a divine Consciousness. It is only from a divine Consciousness that all things receive their true sense of being, while in human consciousness they receive only a relative sense of being that depends on the way individuals are conditioned and on their limited and imperfect vision.

Only the divine Consciousness confers sense of being upon all those things that I do not know and to the sum total of the facts and events that occur on the most distant planets and stars, where— leaving aside the possibility of other sentient beings—no human consciousness can confer any sense of being, or that occurred on our own planet before the advent of man or before any possible development of his consciousness.

Now, is a divine Consciousness really outside my actual consciousness? Perhaps this is not so if one postulates that this actual consciousness of mine is temporal by its very nature and, what is more, is destined to run its course in such a way as to in the end flow into and coalesce with the divine Consciousness together with the consciousness of all other men. This illation of a metaphysical nature undoubtedly has a touch of temerity, perhaps even to the point of seeming a little fanciful, but as a hypothesis it can help to give sense to the idea that consciousness, this very consciousness of mine, can confer significance upon all things: it does, indeed, confer this significance, even in the most total and absolute manner, but does so from a particular perspective, that is to say, inasmuch as my consciousness is dynamic, open to the future, and tendering protentions toward a real absoluteness that it may some day attain.

What I have said so far, albeit only very succinctly, explains for what reasons I was already prepared to accept and receive the Copernican revolution of which I spoke at the beginning. I had prepared myself for it, as I said, in my own particular way.

Here we have a revolution in phenomenology wherein the central place of the cogito is taken by the Absolute itself, the true Absolute. A phenomenology conceived in these terms will still move from a consideration of phenomena as lived experiences of my incarnate human consciousness but will thereafter set itself the problem of what the phenomena of an absolute Consciousness could be. The phenomena of an absolute Consciousness, as it were, are "things" as they "are in themselves." They are things not as I see them, but in their absolute truth.

If, then, the Absolute manifests itself in the relative through a continuous creative action, there arises the problem of yet another way of conceiving phenomena: one can conceive all the realities and events of this world as the manifestations, more or less direct and genuine, of that creative activity that is the presence of the living God in ourselves, in space and in time, through cosmic evolution and the history of man.

In "gathering the phenomena" (*leghein ta phainomena*, phenomenology), we also look for their sense and, at the limit, their ultimate sense. We shall certainly end up by finding this ultimate sense of all things, of all events, and, indeed, of everything that in some way manifests itself, in what Tymieniecka calls "the genesis of life itself, in its constructive workings." What is there at the basis, at the erstwhile spring of this continuous creative action that expresses itself in the universe and of this selfsame creativity of us men? And what is the sense of our existence?

More than from an intellectualistic analysis of consciousness, Anna-Teresa Tymieniecka moves from a concrete analysis of our creative action. She sees it as an act of life which all men have in common. We are here concerned with a "human nature" no longer conceived in accordance with the traditional and static—and, therefore, very rightly obsolete—scheme, but rather in more concrete and dynamic terms. Given this perspective, the inquiry into the fundamental sense—the first and ultimate sense inherent in the creative act of man—becomes man's own questioning, his wondering about the meaning of his own life. And human life in this context has to be conceived in the widest, most intense, and richest sense. What, then, is the sense of this gigantic game of human creation?

A phenomenology understood in the new terms we have just enounced does in fact show itself capable of grasping the sense of human creativity in the creativity of God Himself. At the ultimate origin of the True, the Just, and Beautiful that man pursues, there is the Sacred, there is the active and creative presence of the living God.

And man himself is called upon to cooperate with God so that the creation may be carried forward to its ultimate end, to what Teilhard de Chardin calls its "omega point." Here we have man's most authentic vocation, the innermost destiny of the human being.

Here we have a divine presence that has its privileged place in man's interiority, whence it expresses itself through the unconscious and, little by little, emerges into consciousness through a language that often appears mysterious and ciphered. It is up to us to interpret these messages; and this interpretation becomes possible, little by little, as the interior experience deepens within us and, with it, our sensitivity to it. In this sense, therefore, one may speak of a "phenomenology of 'inward sacredness' in the human condition," to use Tymieniecka's own words. A phenomenology thus enacted in the first person becomes hermeneutical. It sets out to discover within ourselves "the subliminal realm of the soul." And it is from thence that phenomenological analysis must move rather than from the lived experiences of a consciousness that has attained its clearest and most translucent evidence. The limpid clarity of rationality will come at a later stage, whereas the really important thing is to grasp the manifestations of the self-revelation of the Absolute when it first emerges and is born in the interiority, the inwardness of man.

If the essence of phenomenology can be expressed, above all, by Husserl's famous motto "to the things themselves," it seems to me that Tymieniecka makes a particularly appropriate observation when she says that the field that lends itself most readily to the application of this principle is undoubtedly the field of spiritual experience.

Spiritual-religious experience is at the bottom of all human experience. No human experience can do without this fundamental experience of God, which is the only experience that can give sense to any human experience, act, or initiative. Every creative act of man has true and full sense and value if and when it is grafted onto divine creativity and it continues it; going to the other extreme, any human enterprise not founded on God's creativity is vain.

There is a precise dialectic in what Tymieniecka expresses by means of the formula of "the three movements of the soul." By virtue of the first of these three movements, "radical examination," man emerges from the humdrum everydayness of an anonymous existence and enters into the next movement, "exalted existence." Here, in keeping with each individual vocation, man pursues the various forms of science, art, economic-political activity, etc. and seeks to give the greatest possible expression to his ideals, among which one might mention love, friendship, and happiness. Man turns each of these ideals into an absolute, almost as if they could be self-subsistent. But in the end, he realizes that—in purely human terms—absolute love cannot exist, just as—within the limits of our actual condition—there can be neither absolute beauty, nor pure and stable happiness or perfect good. Man thus ends up by experiencing his own finiteness in the most vivid manner, as the vanity of all purely human aspiration that is not sustained by the creative and transforming action of the Absolute.

It is at this point that the third movement of the soul, the movement "toward transcendence," can set man on the way to the discovery of his own interiority and, in the very depth thereof, of the absolute Spring that brings all things into being and confers true and eternal significance upon them.

Any humanism without God is empty and vain. Only in God can humanism find its true sense. Only in God can human creativity rediscover its authentic significance and, what is more, its true efficacy: an efficacy that is no longer ephemeral, but a real contribution to the construction of the eternal kingdom of God. The search for God and the building of His kingdom is a collective task, a work to be pursued in common, in a continuous dialogue wherein each gives whatever he is capable of giving.

We are now approaching the end of the modern epoch—the epoch characterized by a humanism that sought to rely solely on the powers of man to know and dominate and transform a reality conceived in exclusively wordly terms. And there thus comes the moment of rediscovering the further reality and, with it, God, Who is its only absolute foundation and beginning. There thus comes the moment for us to realize that only God is the true protagonist, and that we men are called upon to collaborate with Him in the creation of the universe until such time as this work will attain its fullness, its ultimate goal of perfection. At the threshold of the third millennium, this awareness indeed becomes more essential than ever before, and phenomenology can and must do more, its best, to bring all to attain this awareness.

Italian Centre of Phenomenological Research

YNHUI PARK

THE DESTINY OF THE SOUL
AND THE PATH OF THE TAO:
TWO PHILOSOPHICAL ANTHROPOLOGIES

At the very beginning of his book *The Myth of Sisyphus,* Camus claims that the most fundamental philosophical question is to know whether a life is worth living, and that all the other philosophical questions are secondary. If Camus is right, the primary question in philosophy is that of how a human being is to be defined, what the worth of life consists of, and finally how one should then live in order to make life worthwhile. These questions belong to philosophical anthropology. Both existentialism and Taoism are exemplary philosophical anthropologies. Whatever else they may address, existentialism and Taoism are primarily concerned with the questions of what it is to exist as a human being, where the worth of life can be found, and accordingly how one should live. 'Existentialism' I would here understand broadly. It refers not only to the philosophies of Sartre, Heidegger, Kierkegaard, Nietzsche, and Pascal, but also to the similar philosophical thinking of many others, among whom I would include Tymieniecka. And by Taoism I mean the philosophical thought of Lao Tzu and Chuang Tzu .

These two philosophical anthropologies are very similar inasmuch as they are not totalitarian but individualistic, and not rationalistic but romantic visions of human life. Their most striking common features are a strong emphasis on creative freedom, and an aspiration for transcendence toward something that can only be called 'sacred.' Accordingly the fundamental impulse of both anthropologies is to give us the right directions we should take and the right signs we should follow.

However, existentialism and Taoism are quite distant from each other in their respective conception of human nature, and they propose two conflicting itineraries for a human life. I would characterize the existentialist itinerary as that of 'the destiny of the soul' and the itinerary of the Taoist as 'the path of the Tao.'

A-T. Tymieniecka (ed.), Analecta Husserliana XLIII, 275–291.
© 1994 *Kluwer Academic Publishers. Printed in the Netherlands.*

Which conception, i.e., ontology of the human being is true? Which itinerary, i.e., ethics, will correctly guide us to Damascus or to Enlightenment? The present paper intends to examine the different answers to these questions to be found in existentialism and Taoism respectively. I shall do so by contrasting, in succession, two epistemological perspectives on man, two ontologies of man, two ethics, two types of human beings, and finally two dimensions of man.

I. Two Perspectives: Anthropocentric and Cosmocentric

As philosophical anthropologies, existentialism and taoism equally attempt to describe and understand human beings as distinct from other creatures within the universe. What are their respective perspectives?

Existentialism is unmistakably anthropocentric while Taoism is clearly cosmocentric. The former sees the universe, to paraphrase Nietzsche, through the lens of the human, whereas the latter observes through the lens of the universe.

For the existentialist, as Sartre says with reference to the Cartesian philosophical method, the starting-point is subjectivity. In Descartes, after methodical doubt, it is only the thinking "I" that survives. It is only this thinking substance that can guarantee the existence of the world, God, and each being. Whatever his radical differences with Descartes, Pascal is a Cartesian in that he also affirms the subjective starting point when he states that a man, as the thinking reed, *comprehends*, i.e., encompasses the infinitely immense universe insofar as he understands it. In Nietzsche, the shape of reality, and all values are seen and determined through the lens of the individual's will-to-power. The Cartesian thinking 'I' or ego, the Pascalian 'thinking reed,' and the Nietzschean 'will-to-power' in Heidegger acquire the name 'Dasein' (human existence), referring to a living individual in the world. To quote Kierkegaard, "truth is subjectivity." With Tymieniecka, the essence of subjectivity is the soul.

For an existentialist, then, subjectivity constitutes the epistemological center of the universe. This is the essence of the anthropocentric view of reality. On this view man is, at least cognitively, at once the center, the shaper, and thus the master of the universe. In this respect existentialism extends the deep and long Western anthropocentric philosophical tradition running from Protagoras to Kant. At the center of this human center we find something variably called 'self,' 'ego,' 'consciousness,' and the 'soul.' Thus, we can characterize this conception of reality as being ego-centric as much as anthropocentric. For the universe and all things themselves are seen and understood only through the human, more precisely, ego-centric grid, and thus surreptitiously identified with the human or, more specifically, with the ego-centric representation of them.

Taoism, however, holds what I would call the cosmocentric or alter-centric view of reality. Standing on the cosmic perspective, the Taoist is well aware of the fact that far from being the center of the universe, man is infinitely peripheral to the universe. It is in light of, and with reference to, the universe that the true aspect of man is to be for the first time seen. Chuang Tzu's amusing parable about the frog in a well makes this point clear. Because it lives in a small deep well, its perspective is unbelievably limited, and thus it cannot understand the broad perspective of a tortoise living in an immense ocean. From the tortoise's point of view the frog is, far from being the center of the universe, infinitely peripheral. Instead of standing apart from, against, and in isolation from, all else in the universe at large, man is a marginal and yet integral part of the universe. Reality taken as a whole is indivisibly one.

The first line of the ultimate Taoist text, Tao Teh Ching, begins with a statement that says: "The Tao that can be told is not the eternal Tao." Here Lao Tzu To warns of the inevitable blindness of all conceptualization of reality and suggests that all conceptual representations are necessarily distortive and superficial, if not fictive. One of the central points of Chuang Tzu's philosophy is the demonstration of the fact that all of our views on reality are doomed to be relative to our limited different perspectives. Reality as a whole is ultimately an indivisible and undifferentiated totality, where, as another of Chuang Tzu's famous parables, that of the dream of butterfly, illustrates, even the distinction between reality and dream is ultimately impossible to make. Seen from this cosmic and metaphysically totalizing perspective, a human being apart from the rest of beings, in isolation from the totality of the universe, does not exist. The self, the ego, and the soul, which is supposed to constitute the ultimate, ontologically nonphysical essence of a human being does not exist either.

For a Taoist, a particular individual or a self is to be defined not in terms of the particularity of an alleged essence, referred to often as ego or soul, but only in terms of his *Tao*, understood in terms the modality of a dimension or aspect of reality in general and not as the metaphysically identifiable unchanging essence of that individual. The *Tao* is impersonal, while the self, or the ego, or the soul refers to some kind of personalized agent. As we all know, the Taoist critique of the conceptualizing of ego-centrism is also found in the Buddhist theory of *anatta* or nonself and *anicca* or nonreality. According this theory, insofar as it is not conceptualizable, reality or Being is said to be 'void' or 'nothingness,' and what is referred to as 'ego,' or 'I,' or 'the soul' are only convenient fictions.

The contrast between the anthropocentric perspective of existentialism with the cosmocentric perspective of Taoism seems to reflect a problem, if not an aporia, arising from the conflict which I have elsewhere called the conflict between the semantical perspective and the ontological perspective, which in turn is reflected in the perennial Western philosophical questions of the nature of the relationship between reality and its representation, between the cognitive object and the cognitive subject, between the known and the knower.

The question is: Is the way in which the universe is dependent on a man's cognitive ability to somehow survey it from above or from without? Or is not only our knowledge of the universe but also our cognitive ability itself the mere reflection of the universe? Is the universe our construction? Or is our construction itself merely an aspect of the universe? The problem is to resolve the dilemma that if, as the Berkeleyian idealist says, it is unintelligible to talk about any unperceived or unknown truth of reality, then, as any realist would point out, it is equally absurd to think that reality is what we humans have happened to make it out to be. Epistemologically speaking, the semantic perspective that corresponds to the anthropocentric perspective is right, while ontologically speaking, the ontological perspective that corresponds to the cosmocentric perspective is right. Whatever perspective is taken, there is always a logical tension.

However, I believe the cosmocentric perspective, i.e., the Taoist standpoint is right, even though I can not provide any scientifically adequate argument for it. But my most primordial intuitive conviction is that, contrary to Goodman, the stars are not fabricated by men, and the eye is not a human creation. Reality as reality is independent of our description of it. Ontologically a man with his consciousness and soul is not outside, but within, the universe. He is an integral part, a dimension, of it.

II. Two Ontologies: Monism and Dualism

The above two epistemological perspectives generate two different ontologies. The anthropo-ego-centric perspective of existentialism engenders ontological dualism, whereas the cosmo-alter-centric perspective of Taoism leads to ontological monism.

Seen from the existentialist perspective, as the knower, as the shaper of the world, and as a conscious agent, man is radically apart from the known, from the shaped world, and from object-things. It is his reflective consciousness that constitutes him as knower, or as cognitive subject, and that defines and sets him radically apart from the rest of beings. According to Descartes, there is nothing that is more certain than the thinking 'I,' i.e., consciousness. The existence of my consciousness is alone self-evident. The same is true in Husserl and Sartre. Consciousness is transcendental through and through, thus irreducible to its object. Mind and body are distinct substances even though they are somehow conjoined in a living human being. For Sartre, consciousness and its objects are named respectively being *pour-soi*, or being-for-itself, and being *en-soi*, or being-in-itself. The perfect being, i.e., God must be at the same time both being-in-itself and being-for-itself. Man, insofar as he is a being-for-itself, ultimately dreams of overcoming the dichotomy between itself and its object in order to synthesize them into a single whole. Therefore man's ultimate passion is to be God. Yet this attempt is doomed to failure. It is for this reason that Sartre says, "Man is a useless passion" for a great gulf separates him from his dream. It is in this way that reality is radically divided into two kinds of being.

Ontological dualism is not unique to Descartes, Husserl, Sartre, and all the existentialists. It is very much a characteristic feature of Western thought in general. The Platonic distinction between the intelligible and the visible realms, and the Kantian distinction between noumena and phenomena manifest how deeply rooted the assumption of ontological dualism is in the West. Judaeo-Christian religion is another example of the underlying fundamentally dualistic vision of the Western mind, for the fundamental assumption of this tradition is the distinction between the sacred and the profane, between the spiritual and the temporal world.

Confronted with this radical dualism, Heidegger's philosophical project was meant to in part overcome this dualism in defining human being in terms of *Dasein* or being-in-the-world. And yet, *Dasein* is conceived of as a being through which the meaning of Being manifests itself, or as the "shepherd of Being," namely, as a subject, as a practical agent as much as a cognitive one. In this way reality is once again surreptitiously divided into two kinds of being: human being and objects. Tymieniecka, in line with Bergson and Whitehead, subscribes to an evolutionary view of the origin of the human being and his soul. According to her, the soul is an emergent being, and thus she speaks of "the truly primogenital zone of the primal life in which the soul has its root."[1] Thus, ontological dualism has presumably been overcome. And yet, the soul is conceived of as "the source of the ultimate significant principle of principles,"[2] and as something which "rises above the common."[3] In this fashion the soul is yet again ontologically distinguished from other kinds of being. Hence Tymieniecka too remains still an ontological dualist.

In place of ontological dualism, Taoism offers ontological monism. It denies any ontological difference between any kinds of things, between mind and body, between man and the rest of creatures, between animals and inanimate things. In the context of contemporary Western philosophy, it is with Merleau-Ponty that a successful attempt to overcome ontological dualism was undertaken. On his account mind and body are not two separate things. A concrete living human being is not composed of two different beings called mind and body, but is, rather, an indivisible single integral entity in which mind and body are holistically intertwined and interwoven. Insofar as its ontology is monist, Merleau-Ponty's philosophy is Taoist.

Ontological monism is not a feature unique to Taoism. The underlying fundamental characteristic of the Oriental metaphysical vision is its monism. The identification of *nirvana* and *samsara* in Buddhism as well as the identification of Brahman and Atman in Hinduism illustrates the ontological monism underlying all typically Oriental philosophy.

In accord with this Oriental vision of reality, Taoism stresses the indivisible unity of all things including human beings and their consciousness, selves, or souls. Thus, Chuang Tzu writes:

> The universe is the unity of all things. If one once recognizes his identity with this unity, then the part of his body means no more to him than so much dirt, and death and life, end and beginning, disturb his tranquility no more than the succession of day and night.[4]

However different they may be from each other, all the phenomena that can be differentiated are in reality continuous. It is in this perspective that the Buddhist idea that the world as we see it is nothing but *Maya*, understood as cosmic illusion, can be grasped. The idea consists in belief in an ultimately undifferentiated unity, an unbroken continuous oneness of all things in the universe. The *Tao* in Taoism, literally the "Way," in fact refers to the Way everything is, or, to be more precise, to the way in which everything is articulated in continuity with the way in which other things are articulated—as "ontological waves," as it were, of the one indivisible ocean of the universe, or reality, or Being. Between mind and body, between man and the world, between the soul and matter, between subject and object, and between being-for-itself and being-in-itself, there is no metaphysical difference. The differences among things are only different articulations of the ultimately same thing.

Dualism or monism, which ontology is true? No views and no theories can claim absolute authority. The scientific vision of reality as it is is not compatible with the religious vision of reality. Yet there is no ultimate way of adjudicating between the two. The debate is still going on, even though religion has been in decline for more than two centuries. This fact, however, does not mean that some views and theories are not more reasonable than others. If consistency, predicability, positivity, universality, simplicity, and practicality are important measures for evaluating theories, the scientific vision seems to be more reasonable than the religious vision.

Religion in general and Western religion, in particular rests on ontological dualism, while the scientific vision implies, and is founded upon, ontological monism, even though it may apply to a limited domain. This makes it plausible that Taoist ontological monism is probably right, and that existentialist ontological dualism is probably mistaken.

III. Two Ethics: The Destiny of the Soul and the Path of the Tao

The existentialist anthropocentric perspective has led us to ontological dualism, and the Taoist cosmocentric perspective, to ontological monism. These two different ontologies in turn lead to two different ethics. On the one hand, ontological dualism involves such notions as consciousness, ego, and self with reference to a human being, all of which are variously understood as a kind of active agent which is, ontologically speaking, radically different from the remainder of things in the universe. And the soul is understood as a kind of agent within this agent, as it were, as the essence of the agent. On the other hand, ontological monism leaves no room for the existence of things ontologically distinct from the rest of things. From the Taoist point of view such notions as consciousness, ego, self, and the soul are ontologically empty words because there are no real things corresponding to these words. If these words are meaningful, this is so only insofar as they refer not to the ontologically separate and separable essence of the human species, but simply to the different modalities or articulations of the human existence ontologically continuous with the universe. Thus the existence of each human individual is seen as the 'the Tao' rather than as the 'soul.'

The soul refers to an autonomous free agent, whereas the Tao signifies a certain mode of being. If it be an autonomous agent, the soul is condemned to have certain desires and projects and must make choices among many alternatives. But, with the Tao, there not being an agent or a metaphysical subject, the very notion of project and that of choice do not arise. Defined in terms of the soul, a man is inherently teleological; when understood, not as an agent, but as the Tao, man is merely contingent. If man has a telos, then to live as a human being is to constantly set certain objectives in accord with one's desires and projects, to *act* in view of the satisfaction of these desires, and to achieve these goals or fail to do so. If man's being is contingent, then to live as a human being is to *be* in tune with nature. Thus, whereas the existentialist has a destiny to dare, the Taoist has a path to follow.

The teleological life of an existentialist is then quite different from the natural life of a Taoist. If to live is to follow a certain itinerary, then to follow the existentialist itinerary is to follow the soul in its struggle with its destiny, and to follow the Taoist itinerary is to harmoniously follow the path of the tao. To put it differently, ontological dualism personalizes, that is, anthropomorphizes human nature, and ontological monism depersonalizes, that is, naturalizes it.

For Kierkegaard, life is meaningful only insofar one seeks God with a knightly faith in eternity. Although Nietzsche finds himself in a world where God is dead, nevertheless, for him the true meaning of life consists in the fulfillment of the Will-to-Power defining us. For Heidegger, *Dasein* must listen to the call of Being and remain a Shepherd of Being. This constitutes his metaphysical vocation as an authentic human being. The Sartrean authentic man owns an absolute freedom to choose his own values without believing that they have any other foundation, in the absence, then, of any transcendental and divine goal to be attained. Whatever the differences there are among these philosophers, for all of them as existentialists there

are at least purposes in life, if not a purpose of life. For them it is
obvious that human life is permeated by or pregnant with purposes.
All human actions are goal-orientated, i.e., teleological.

But the teleological view is not restricted in application to the
nature of human actions. Insofar as it stands on the anthropocentric
perspective, and adopts ontological dualism, any given philosophical view will tend to presuppose a teleological metaphysics. Not only
the actions taken by a man in his life but also his life taken as an
event as much as his story, and, likewise, the universe as much as
its history will be assumed to have a metaphysical, transcendental
purpose.

We wonder whether there is a meaning of life besides the
various meanings in life. Western religion and Hegelian philosophy
answer affirmatively. Teilhard de Chardin represents, the best
example of recent teleological-scientific metaphysics. Here, not
only do all human lives have a meaning in the sense of a purpose for
living entire lives but also cosmic history as much as human
history has a meaning in the sense that it has a definitive purpose
transcending all the purposes we humans have in our lives. It is in
this manner that the entire universe is surreptitiously personified, as it were, anthropomorphized. This way of thinking that may
be called 'teleological metaphysics,' constitutes the culmination of
anthropomorphism.

Anthropomorphic teleological metaphysics is evident as well
even in such anti-traditional, anti-theological thinkers as Nietzsche,
Heidegger, and even Sartre. And although she claims that she has
overcome, indeed, transcended the limit of classical philosophic
thinking, this deep-rooted "teleologism" is also evident in
Tymieniecka, for she states:

> Though sometimes the passion to be true to oneself degenerates
> into a soul-searching quest for one's "dignity," or "authenticity,"
> that goes in futile directions, and though it is sometimes misled by
> willfulness, and lack of discernment, Occidental man's quest for
> "being true" to himself is more alive than ever.[5]

She speaks as if there were a cosmic non-human norm to which
we ought to conform our conduct, and cosmic values we ought to

adopt. And yet, we may wonder whether it is necessary to see a human life, the history of the human species, and the universe teleologically? Can these things be seen in a quite different light, i.e., non-teleologically?

The Taoist emphatically says "Yes." From the Taoist point of view the notion of purpose applies to an intentional animal, more specifically, to human beings. Values and norms as much as the notion of 'ought' are intelligible only with reference to human desires and man's rational faculty. Thus it is absurd to apply these concepts not only to the universe but also to the history of humanity and to the life of an individual. The universe, the history of humanity, and the life of an individual are neither meaningful or meaningless, neither devoid of purpose nor pregnant with purpose. They are simply as they are.

In sharp contrast to existentialism, Taoism naturalizes an individual's consciousness, decentralizes the self/subject, and tries to depersonalize it in order to see it as an integral part of impersonal nature or the universe. In the Taoist perspective, just as it is absurd to talk about the purpose of a stone or a mountain or the universe, it is equally nonsensical to talk about the project or goal of an individual person because, for a Taoist, a person is not an actor, or agent, or a soul residing within the individual and independent of the universe, but a state, or a way, or the Tao as a spatio-temporal aspect of the indivisible whole of reality. Human beings are blended into one great featureless and indistinguishable mass: nature and humanity constitute an unbroken unity.

Given the teleological conception of human life, man is condemned to be free, to make choices, to take responsibility for his freely chosen action and thus to be constantly in a state of anguish. Since life is then the setting of endless goals to be achieved, the complete fulfillment or meaning of life is logically impossible to find at any moment, but is merely to be hoped for in the never present future. In Sartre's words life is a useless passion in the sense of both drive and suffering. In contrast to the existentialist, for a Taoist the point of life is neither physico-intellectual competition, nor spiritual strife, nor the seeking of any specific goal, but a wandering through the Tao along one's path, which constitutes the natural order of the universe. As Lao Tzu says: "Gentle and yielding is the disciple of life."[6]

It is at this juncture that the concept of nonaction or *wu-wei*—along with *tao*, one of the key concepts in Taoism—can be understood. Having no goals to aim at, the Taoist does not need to act insofar as to act means to perform contrived actions. If to live means in part to perform certain actions, the actions should not be contrived. *Wu-wei* or nonaction does not mean not to act, but to act spontaneously, naturally, without strife and struggle. As Eastman puts it, "No salvation is sought by the Taoist, no liberation from this world. We are children of cosmic nature, and we follow and trust its ways." As Smullyan, a Taoist mathematician puts it in a simple but wonderful metaphor, in a nutshell, to be a Taoist simply means to be able to fall asleep without taking nap, just as one's dog does.[7]

An existentialist finds within himself his soul, while a Taoist sees no soul, but only his tao. Whereas the existentialist's soul seriously faces the challenge of its destiny, the Taoist tao is only a path to be spontaneously followed. While the existentialist's soul has its goal to achieve, the Taoist's path is without any purpose other than itself. What is it to live as a human being? How should a man live? Or what is the meaning of life? The meaning for the existentialist's soul can only found in daring its destiny. Since the existentialist's soul is fated to dare its destiny, the meaning of his life can be found only outside of, and transcendent to, itself. Since the Taoist's tao is to be on his path, the meaning of his life lies only inside, and immanent in, itself. The meaning of the existentialist's life is external to his life, and thus transcendent, while the meaning, of the Taoist's existence is internal to itself, and thus immanent.

The existentialist and the Taoist, who is right? Do each human life, other creatures, and the universe have a purpose or purposes, as the former thinks? In the absence of either a vision or the voice of God, it is rather impossible to give an answer definitively. However, I am very much inclined to take side with the Taoist anthropology. Whatever there is simply exists, or could exist without purpose, without reason. All is simply there. Whatever there is, all things are integral parts of the one indivisible universe, both the physical and the metaphysical, and existing from eternity. If there is any purpose for each life at all, the purpose could only be to simply *live*. In the cosmocentric monistic metaphysics the concept of a purpose of any thing standing outside that thing is unintelligible. The teleological conception of reality is only a by-product of our unfortunate anthropomorpho-centric dualistic vision of reality.

IV. Two Types of Persons: Adolescent and Adult

Anthropocentric, dualistic, and teleological existentialism projects one ideal type of man, while cosmocentric, monistic, and naturalistic Taoism projects another ideal type of man. An existentialist whose soul struggles with its destiny reveals himself as one type of person, while a Taoist on his path manifests himself as another kind of human being.

If the existentialist can be described as contriving, intense, passionate, heroic, and emotional, the Taoist can be characterized as natural, relaxed, contemplative, moderate, and rational. Because of his strong sense of ego, self, or the soul, the existentialist tends to be self-assertive, uncompromising, and militant, while because of his denial of an isolated self or ego, the Taoist tends to be self-yielding, compromising, and peaceful. If the former looks more like an adolescent full of energy and expansive vitality, the Taoist can seem more like an adult full of serenity and sophisticated wisdom. The existentialist is too serious and always combative, whereas the Taoist is by nature light-hearted and always yielding. To the existentialist the Taoist may appear unbearably dull, if not a useless *passe*. But to the Taoist the existentialist appears pointlessly agitated. The existentialist may think that the relaxed and contemplative Taoist is too old and too boring to be with, while the Taoist may feel that the serious and intense existentialist is too childish and too tiresome to be taken very seriously. While the existentialist is a struggling person never content with the present, the Taoist is a joyful person who never worries about the future. In sum, if an existentialist is a man of tragedy and turmoil, a Taoist is a person of peace and harmony. Which kind of man would you like to be? Which life would you like to live? In *Tao Teh Ching*, the Taoist answers are as follows:

> He who stands on tiptoe is not steady.
> He who strides cannot maintain the pace.
> He who makes a show is not enlightened.
> He who is self-righteous is not respected.
> He who boasts achieves nothing.
> He who brags will not endure.
> According to followers of the Tao,
> These are extra food and unnecessary luggage.
> They do not bring happiness.
> The followers of the Tao avoid them.

This verse resonates deep down in my heart. I prefer the Taoist to the Existentialist because the former is emotionally more attractive than the latter. I choose the Taoist life because that life is aesthetically more appealing. More importantly, however, my preference and choice stem from the fact that the Taoist conception of man and the universe rings true, while the alternative conception does not. It seems simply true that a man is an integral part of the universe, never completely discontinuous with it, and that whatever there is is part of the nature, that is, simply there without reason simply because it is.

V. The Paradox of Man: Transcendence and Immanence

Nevertheless, we are not entirely comfortable with Taoism, or more specifically, with the Taoist anthropology. The central point of Taoism is that man is ultimately part of nature, which is immanent in him, and this implies that man is incapable of transcending nature. And yet, the other point of Taoism is living according to the principle of *wu-wei*, or nonaction, even though it consists in acting in accordance with the natural order. Taoism is not a simple description of how things are. It also prescribes how we *should* live, which is, I suppose, its primary intent. It is designed to provide us with a norm of conduct and values. This Taoist intent, however, presupposes that man can transcend nature, i.e., what

Kant calls the realm of phenomena, to some extent and thus belong, in part, to the realm of noumena. This entails that man is more than nature. And that in turn implies not only the intelligibility but also the necessity of the notion of a soul residing at the heart of a human being. Taoism itself is a manifestation of transcendence then.

These two different implications of Taoism are contradictory. The transcendence of a human being cannot be made intelligible unless the reality of the soul as an ultimate agent within him is presupposed. Since the soul refers to something nonphysical, then a human being cannot be explained solely in the terms of naturalism as natural science attempts to do. The problem of the soul is still alive. In spite of astounding advances in neuropsychology, the metaphysical question of the nature of the mind or reflective consciousness remains as puzzling as ever, and the nature of the somewhat murky thing called the 'soul' perplexes us more deeply than ever before.

In a recent article "Neurology and the Soul,"[8] Sacks attempts to overcome mind-body dualism and to make the concept of brain and the concept of mind consistent—"so that finally neurology and the soul do come together completely in a way which dignifies neurology, and which is no indignity to the soul." However, insofar as mind or consciousness is explained in terms of a metastructure built upon the real world in the brain, Sacks is a physicalist in the sense that in the last analysis he sees the soul in terms of the functioning of the brain. Here we are back to our original question.

However the ultimate nature of the soul is to be defined, it refers to an undeniable spontaneous urge and felt inner necessity impelling toward transcendence which is inherent to all human beings. This is, I believe, one of the most immediate phenomenological facts. It is this notion of soul that makes it intelligible for us to endure things that, as Saint-Exupery puts it in his novel *Wind, Sand and Stars*, "no animal would have gone through."[9] The Soul is essentially a moral, indeed, spiritual power, manifested, at least potentially, only in the human species, in each member of the human species. All great literature is about moral power, about the transcendence of the soul, as exemplified in such literary characters as Antigone in *Antigone*, Ishmael in *Moby Dick*, and Jim in *Lord*

Jim, to cite only characters explored by Tymieniecka in her *The Passions of the Soul and the Elements in the Onto-Poiesis of Culture, the Life Significance of Literature.*

If a man cannot be rendered entirely intelligible in the terms of naturalism, he cannot be entirely governed by deterministic causal laws, and thus must be free. It seems then to follow that he is in some sense, as it were, outside nature in transcending it. However, in the face of recent neurophysiology, neuropsychology, genetics, and cosmology, it is equally difficult to think that man, his mind, and his soul are ontologically different from physical reality—that they are not at all somehow causally connected to physical elements. It may be the case that what we refer to as consciousness, spirit, the soul, freedom, and transcendence may be different from the physical not in kind, but only in degree. All these things may turn out to be merely different descriptions of the ultimately same stuff as the stuff we call matter.

According to a Chinese Buddhist story, which is designed to show the infinite greatness of Buddha, the greatest knight, one Son Oh Kong, has supernatural power to run as fast as a horse and to jump as high as the Himalayas, but no matter how hard he tries to show his great power, has always in the end finds himself in the palm of Buddha. The existentialist is committed to the idea of the transcendence of man. To that extent, as Sartre states, man is condemned to freedom, indeed, absolutely free, in other words, irreducible to nature, and thus can soar over it. Upon some reflection, however, consciousness, spirit, the soul, and freedom always end up falling flatly on the ground, for they are only different parts of the single ultimate stuff called 'nature.'

Given the above considerations, it is difficult to understand man in terms of transcendence as existentialism does, because as the Taoist tries to show, man is immanent in nature. But it seems equally difficult to comprehend man in terms of immanence alone as Taoism does because, as the existentialist tries to show, man is transcendence. Seeing man in terms of transcendence generates a paradox, and so does seeing him in terms of immanence. What then is man? Is this question itself an expression of his transcendence or a symptom of his immanence? Is he in some sense spiritual? Or is he entirely part of nature as science understands it? This question seems to be an echo of the paradox involved in the relationship between the ontological perspective and the semantic perspective, between reality and its representation, which I have alluded to earlier. The ultimate philosophical puzzle remains, and philosophical debates drag on. At this point, as Wittgenstein asks us to do, we should keep silence on unsayable things. The trouble, however, is that we, as human beings, cannot keep our mouths shut, not even before such matters.

Pohang Institute of Science

NOTES

1. Anna-Teresa Tymieniecka, *The Passions of the Soul and the Elements in the Onto-Poiesis of Culture* (Dordrecht: Kluwer Academic Publishers, 1990), p. 24.
2. *Ibid.*, p. 31.
3. *Ibid.*, p. 31.
4. Chuang Tzu, in *Chuang Tzu.*
5. Tymieniecka, *op. cit.*, p. 140.
6. Lao Tzu, in *Tao Teh Ching.*
7. Raymond M. Smullyan, *The Tao is Silent* (Harper & Row, 1977), p. 3.
8. Oliver Sacks, *The New York Review of Books*, Nov. 22, 1990.
9. Antoine de Saint-Exupery, *Wind, Sand and Stars*, trans. Lewis Glantiere (New York: Harcourt, Brace and World, 1967).

STEVEN W. LAYCOCK

THE PHENOMENOLOGIST'S ANSELM

Anselm's *Proslogion* opens with the statement of a distinctively phenomenological program seldom taken seriously as such. Most contemporary discussions of the ontological argument concern the strictly logical and ontological dimensions of Anselm's reasoning. I believe, however, that much remains to be seen of this argument which will be concealed in any other but a pheonomenological luminescence. I shall attempt, then, to make explicit the implicit phenomenology of the *Proslogion*'s first chapter, emphasizing the striking parallelism between Anselm and Husserl. It will still be necessary at that point to reinterpret the ontological argument in the light of fundamental phenomenological insights, thus providing us with a distinctively phenomenological *demonstration* – a "showing" – of the existence of God, as opposed to an *a priori* proof (*proba*) rendering the divine existence merely "probable."

I

Anselm withdrew from the ongoing life of perceptual consciousness, attempting to "escape for a little while from the tumult of [his] thought,"[1] and thereby to rouse his mind to the contemplation of God. He admonishes us, in accordance with his own practice, to:

[e]nter into the inner chamber of [our] soul, shut out everything save God and what can be of help in [our] quest for Him and having locked the door seek Him out. . . .[2]

Anselm recognized that the "weighty cares" and "wearisome toils"[3] of quotidian existence were a distraction to the contemplative life. One cannot simultaneously collect oneself in meditation and be dispersed in the hectic round of daily affairs. Everyday existence levies upon us demands for attention which are not our own, tearing our attentive consciousness away like so many wild stallions. We may attend to this or that object temporarily, but, inasmuch as what calls for our attention poorly accords with our own wishes, the overall posture of daily mindfulness can scarcely be called that of deliberate concentration. We may,

A-T. Tymieniecka (ed.), Analecta Husserliana XLIII, 293–305.
© 1994 *Kluwer Academic Publishers. Printed in the Netherlands.*

that is, succeed in centering the mind upon given objects of attention until called away by other concerns, but our consciousness of the systematic totality of such objects – the World – remains dispersed, inattentive, centrifugal.

Anselm thus admonishes us to "shut out" the distractions of daily life. We must disconnect ourselves from the mad torrent of quotidian affairs in such a way that we are no longer drawn in by them. Only then will we be prepared to deliberately center our attention, not upon this or that fleeting object, but upon their systematic totality. It is only in the decisive attitude of meditation that we are liberated from servitude to this or that particular object and freed from the specific patterns of ignorance which particularity induces. Searching for my keys, I view each object in the room simply as *not being my keys*. In the frantic search for my keys, no object except my keys is what I desire to see. No other object is an object of interest. I greet non-keys only to reject them. Their presence, to my perceptual consciousness, is an accident which I had no part in bringing about, an obstacle in my path, an obstruction to my search, an *ob-ject*: that which obturates, stops the gaze, hinders. I assuredly do not attend to such objects, except fleetingly; I do not deliberately attend to them at all. It is thus with all the specific pursuits of daily existence. Each pursuit, each finite seeking involves a specific pattern of rejection, inattention perhaps blindness. And the attainment of any finite end is invariably the inception of some further pursuit. Small wonder then, that for the most part daily activity does not involve authentically attending to the systematic totality of objects as such. Lost among the trees of particular pursuits, we lose sight of the forest itself.

Only by "entering into the inner chamber of our soul" are we enabled to lend concerted attention to the world. And it is only in this posture of world-attentiveness that Anselm can achieve the reflective self-distance required to address himself: "Speak now, my whole heart, speak now to God: 'I seek Your countenance, O Lord, Your countenance I seek.' . . .".[4] Anselm's act of disconnection, of "shutting out" and "locking the door," is inescapably an act of reflection. He stands now *at a distance* from his "whole heart," from that most profound of desires presupposed by every specific desire. Only now does his heart "speak." Only now is it made explicit and articulate that the "whole heart" is a perfervid desire for the Divine Countenance.

The whole heart is not a mere aggregation or bundle. It does not correspond to the manifold of specific pedestrian desires as a button collection does to collected buttons, but is itself quite clearly a desire. The whole heart is the fundamental desire for that End with respect to which the objects of the specific desires are the "means." Only the Divine Countenance is desired, for its own sake alone. Everything else is desired as a *means* to this Supreme End. An object of a specific desire is thus a *medium, that-through-which* the Divine Countenance is revealed.

A countenance – a "look" – is, of course, the overall expression manifested by a face. There could be no countenance without a face which reveals the hidden subjectivity "behind" it. The face "bodies forth" the mind. And this "bodying forth" is the countenance. The countenance is the manifestation of subjectivity through the bodily mediation of the face. In seeking the Divine Countenance, the whole heart is seeking God-as-manifested, God-as-revealed. And the "Face" of God – the medium of deific manifestation – can be no less than the systematic totality of "facets" confronting consciousness in its clarifying, concentrated attitude of world-attentiveness in which the specific, dispersive claims to attention of mundane concerns have been silenced. The World is the divine "Face," and the whole heart is the centering attentiveness of consciousness to *God as revealed through the World.*

II

In the foregoing extrapolation I have attempted to "tease out" and emphasize what in Anselm might be regarded as inchoate phenomenological insights. The *Proslogion* contains in its opening paragraph an implicit phenomenology of God of which every detail can be reclaimed by contemporary phenomenology in its own Husserlian vocabulary. Anselm's "shutting out" can be interpreted in terms of the phenomenological reduction; the "whole heart" can be interpreted in terms of the General Thesis and Husserl's disclosure of "empty" intentionality; the Divine Countenance can be interpreted in terms of the Husserlian understanding of phenomena; and God can be understood in terms of phenomenological transcendence.

Rotating a coin between my fingers, I see it now as circular, now as eliptical, now as rectangular. But in each case, I see the coin itself. Each view is a view *of the coin.* The coin, that is, is an *identity* within a *manifold* of appearances. The coin itself "transcends" any given appearance, thus presenting itself in the manner of a transcendent object. It is worth noting that the appearance of a transcendent object may itself function "opaquely." Thus, a still-life painter may return repeatedly to the arrangement of objects, reidentifying not merely the objects, but also the particular *view* of those objects as a guide to artistic representation. In this sense at least, appearances may themselves appear. Yet, since an appearance is necessarily the appearance *of something*, no such series of appearances of appearances of . . . can continue without end. We err, however, in taking the termini of such series to be the "ordinary" objects of everyday experience (tables, chairs, etc.). Each such object is only relatively transcendent. Each is seen within an external "horizon" of possible contextual situations, possible background arrangements of objects in the world. Thus, each functions as a "mirror" reflecting within it every other object which might possibly be seen in its background, and reflecting within it, moreover, the ultimate background of all backgrounds: what Husserl calls the "World-horizon" (*Welt-horizont*). Thus is established a clear sense in which ordinary objects are themselves *appearances of the world*. The world is the object of all objects, the "World-ground" (*Welt-boden*), precisely because it is the World-horizon "reflected" in each worldly object.

Husserl's understanding of phenomena can be characterized in terms of transcendent objects. A transcendent object, X, is an identity appearing through a manifold of appearances: $A1$, $A2$, etc. X-as-appearing-through-A-1, X-as-appearing-through-$A2$, etc., are, then, the phenomena of X. A phenomenon is an object precisely as and only as it appears. Anselm's proto-phenomenology becomes evident at this point. The object of the whole heart is, as we have seen, the Divine Countenance: *God-as-revealed-through-the-world*. In the Husserlian accent, the Divine countenance is the *God-phenomenon*. God is that which appears through every possible world-appearance.

Husserl speaks of a divine Being "beyond the world" which "would be *transcendent in a totally different sense* from the transcendent in the sense of the world."[5] For Husserl, every possible object of experience (except, of course, the world itself) functions as an appearance of the world. We can therefore speak of a "world-pole" which centers and unites the manifold of objectual "world-appearances." We may even extend the notion of "world-appearance" to encompass not merely given transcendent objects but also the actual configurations of the objects of our experience (themselves possible contextual situations going to comprise the horizons of given transcendent objects). Such a configuration could no doubt have been different. Hence, any such configuration is simply one possibility among others. Husserl's remark is perhaps best understood by taking "world" to refer to the *actual* configuration of transcendent objects. The God "beyond the world" is therefore that identical world-pole which is revealed through *every possible* object-configuration.

At the same time, God, for Husserl, is "an *'Absolute' is a totally different sense from the Absolute of Consciousness.*"[6] God is not merely the highest genus of *esse apparens*, but also the highest-order appearance, the appearance of all appearances, and hence, that within which God-as-transcendent appears. The World-ground appears within the World-horizon, and this appearing is the act of divine self-revelation.

The omniscient simultaneous display of all possible aspects of an object to a given consciousness would, in Husserl's view, destroy the distinction between transcendence and its contrasting presentational character, immanence.[7] For such a consciousness, the object would be given *in its entirety* through a single comprehensive appearance, thus losing its transcendence altogether. The object, it might be said, would *be* its omniscient display in the sense that a putatively omniscient mind, viewing the object under every possible aspect simultaneously, would see everything there is to see of it. In this sense, then, we may interpret the divine "Face" as the omniscient display of all possible object-configurations. The "Face" of God is fully revelatory. Who sees the "Face" sees God in God's entirety.

However, Anselm as well as Husserl recognized that to be conscious of the divine "Face" is phenomenologically impossible.

Lord, if You are not present here, where, since You are absent, shall I look for You? On the other hand, if You are everywhere why then, since You are present, do I not see You? . . . Again, by what signs, under what aspect, shall I seek You? Never have I seen You, Lord my God, I do not know Your face . . . [Your servant] yearns to see You and Your countenance is too far away from him.[8]

God is never wholly presented under any aspect, but remains "transcendent" in the strictly phenomenological sense. God's being is never wholly captured through any manifestation. God remains indefinitely revealable; God's *absence* remains strictly proportional to the not yet realized possibility for divine *presence*. The Divine "Face" must ever remain "too far away." We know no more of God than is revealed through experienced world-appearances. The "Face" of God is necessarily hidden, and could be revealed only at the cost of divine transcendence. Deprived of the "Face," how shall we come to know the Divine Countenance?

Anselm's response is contained *in semine* in his explicit avowal that "I do not seek to understand so that I may believe; but I believe so that I may understand."[9] Understanding presupposes belief, but not conversely, since genuine understanding is precisely understanding *of belief*. What God *is* is understood only through reflection upon our doxastic positing of God's existence. What we understand God to be is what we posit God to be. We shall see that at least in this respect Anselmian reflection is strikingly comparable to the phenomenological reduction.

In the straightforward "natural" attitude of consciousness, we are, so to speak, "taken in" by appearances. The cartoon commonplace of the life-sized picture of a tunnel placed against a solid mountainside (with its slapstick consequences) is a superb illustration. The fate of the villainous pursuer could be averted were he only to see the tunnel-picture *as a picture*. The ill-fated villain is "taken in" by the appearance, convinced that that-which-appears (the apparent) really exists. The appearing of an apparent, however, is no guarantee of its existence, and to suspend our belief in the existence of an apparent is not only to divest ourselves of the fateful naivete of such a belief, but is furthermore to place ourselves in a position to see the appearances of the apparent *as appearances*. The apparent is not lost in the act of suspension, but the appearance is gained. In the view of Husserlian phenomenology, every specific commitment to the reality of an apparent object presupposes the fundamental belief in the reality of the world (the systematic totality of apparents). And the phenomenological attitude is assumed when this "General Thesis" is itself suspended.

For Anselm, the "shutting out" of mundane distractions involves the silencing of all specific claims to attention. But our attention is claimed only in virtue of the existential beliefs we maintain with respect to the apparents of daily experience. Watching a film of ghastly ghoulish deeds, we may very well feel our heart pound, our palms sweat and our hair stand on end. But the apparents of the film do not in and of themselves have the power to engender such reactions. We may "step back," disengage, refuse to be "taken in" by the appearances, and thereby be free from their claims. We are affected, drawn in, only by yielding credence to the apparents.

Our impression that Anselm's "shutting out" coincides in significant respects with Husserl's phenomenological reduction is reinforced by

Anselm's account of what is disclosed through "shutting out." The act of "shutting out" displays to his reflecting consciousness his "whole heart" – that fundamental yearning whose "Object" is the End of all finite ends, the End with respect to which the objects of the pedestrian desires serve only as means. The whole heart remains to be fulfilled, and thus represents a root-form of consciousness which, essentially, is "empty." In perfect alignment is Husserl's exposition of "empty" intentionality. We emptily intend an object *in its absence*. For example, one might think of a package waiting to be picked up at the post office, and in this way consciousness is directed toward an object which is not perceptually present. This empty intention is later, at least relatively, "filled." Perceiving the package before us, we intend *in presence* what was previously intended *in absence*. An indefinite array of sensuous profiles is given to our intending consciousness, thus saturating to some degree the sensuous vacuity of empty intentionality.

The "whole heart" involves an empty intending of the divine "Face," the vacuity of this intentional act being understood as the "space" within which the End of ends is progressively brought to presence. The "whole heart" yearns for the plenary saturation of this emptiness, for the coincidence of the divine "Face" and the fulfilling presence of the world. But to emptily intend the world is necessarily to posit it as existing. Hence, reflection upon the "whole heart" involves reflection upon the General Thesis, and reflection upon the General Thesis is the defining characteristic of the phenomenological reduction.

III

It is therefore through the discovery of this ineluctable commitment to the existence of the divine "Face" – that medium of revelation through which God appears, the world-horizon – that Anselm came to understand God (the divine apparent) as "that-than-which-no-greater-can-be-thought." Commitment to the existence of the divine "Face" is the fundamental necessary condition for the meaningfulness of any thought. Hence, even the thought "God exists" must presuppose the thought "the world-horizon exists." Yet according to Anselm's definition, no thought presupposing that "the world-horizon exists" concerns anything greater than God. The thought "God exists" is unique among thoughts in that it concerns that-than-which-no-greater-can-be-thought. Commitment to the general Thesis maintains the meaningfulness of the

Theistic Thesis. And Anselm was convinced that the meaningfulness of the Theistic Thesis guaranteed its truth.

God, as the apparent appearing through every possible world-appearance, is indefinitely revealable, an identity within an inexhaustible manifold of appearances. An identity is always that which motivates recurrence, reidentification, that in which interest is invested. We return to an object, continually reidentifying it through its profiles, because that object is of value to us. Identities are loci of value. The End of ends for which the "whole heart" yearns, the Transcendent of transcendents, is thus the locus of absolute value, that-than-which-no-greater-can-be-thought. God is "the Good." Being ultimate in respect of transcendence, a greater locus of value is simply inconceivable.

A final point awaits consideration before we can do full justice to a phenomenological reinterpretation of the ontological argument. We must come to understand the notion of "existence" pheonomenologically. The existence of an object no doubt involves more than its transcendence. A given object of the imagination may, presumably, be imaginatively presented in a variety of ways. We may imagine the same object from this or that angle without in any way supposing it to exist. While insufficient, transcendence is nonetheless at least a necessary condition for existence. Nothing exists which is not variously presentable.

A viable phenomenological conception of existence must, however, supplement transcendence with the notion of *will-independence*. What distinguishes the imaginary object imagined from various angles from the extra-imaginary object actually perceived from various angles is not richness of detail, for there are no *a priori* limits to the power of the imagination. Theoretically, for every detail of the real object, one could imagine a corresponding detail of the imaginary object. And in this respect Kant was certainly correct. The existent cannot be distinguished from the imaginary by appealing to the sensory qualities which the one possesses and the other lacks. Rather, the pheonomenologist appeals to the presentational character of *givenness*. The object presents itself as *there for the taking* – whether we wish to take it or not. An object is a "gift," as it were. We may welcome the object, or recoil from it. But its being *given* is not directly a function of our will. Again, the object obtrudes upon us, "bursting in" upon our consciousness with a peculiarly emphatic implosive force of its own. We are, as we say, "struck" by the object, in its "grip."

Of course we may, by exercising the will, move the object or

manoeuvre ourselves with respect to the object, thus acquiring alternative views of it. But the object's being there, given in *just this way*
under *just these conditions* or from *just this angle*, is not the realization of an act of willing. And the extra-imaginary object remains
will-independent in precisely this sense. For the phenomenologist, then,
existence entails and is entailed by at least the presentational characters of *transcendence* and *will-independence*. In Husserl's formulation,
an object "actually 'exists' if one succeeds in fulfilling the judicative
intentions with an intuition which is given at first hand."[10]

Kant argued that "exists" is not a "real predicate" on the grounds
that, for every property of an actually existing object, that very property
may be imagined to characterize a corresponding imaginary object; hence,
since the imaginary object may at least theoretically be imagined to
possess all and only the properties actually possessed by the existent
object without thereby forfeiting its imaginary status, existing cannot
be a property which accounts for the existence of the one and the non-
existence of the other. The phenomenologist agrees with Kant that
existence is not the property of any *object*. But, as we have begun to
see, existence may be anlayzed in terms of *presentational characters*
(e.g., transcendence and will-independnece). That is, while existence
is not a property attributable to *objects*, it is nonetheless a property
attributable to *the way objects appear*. What instantiates the property
of existence is not the *content*, but the *mode*, of presentation. As Husserl
maintains, we predicate "being," not of the "true identical self" of the
object judged to exist, but of its sense.[11] Objects appear "existingly" or
not, depending upon the presentational character instantiated by their
mode of presentation.

IV

Given this understanding of existence as a presentational character, we
are now prepared to turn directly to Anselm's ontological argument, while
offering a phenomenological reinterpretation of it in light of the insights
thus far achieved.

Surely that-than-which-a-greater-cannot-be-thought cannot exist in the mind alone. For
if it exists solely in the mind even, it can be thought to exist in reality also, which is
greater. If then that-than-which-a-greater-cannot-be-thought exists in the mind alone,
this same that-than-which-a-greater-*cannot*-be-thought is that-than-which-a-greater-*can*-

be-thought. But this is obviously impossible. Therefore there is absolutely no doubt that something-than-which-a-greater-cannot-be-thought exists both in the mind and in reality.[12]

A transcendent object, as we have seen, is a locus of value. And God, being transcendent in the most profound sense, is the locus of absolute value. A transcendent object is a *telos*, both in the sense of centering interest and motivating recurrence and in the sense of being indefinitely approximable, though unattainable. Each appearance acquired of a given transcendent object is a step toward the *telos* of enjoying its *absolute presence*, the simultaneous plenary display of all its appearances. God is thus the *telos* of enjoying the absolute presence of the world.

Suppose now that God, as the absolute *telos*, does not exist. This entails either that the God-phenomenon lacks the presentational character of transcendence, that God does not appear transcendently, or that God is not *given* in experience. But no apparent can appear non-transcendently and be taken *as God*, since God is understood precisely as the ultimately transcendent. If God appears at all, then God appears as transcendent.

"*If* God appears at all . . ." – This is precisely the issue. The modal counterpart of this statement runs: "If a necessarily existent being exists, then it exists." And it is justifiably argued that existence might even be thought to comprise part of the essence of God, much as three-sidedness comprises part of the essence of the triangle; yet, just as triangles may well fail to exist, so too might an essentially existing being fail to exist. The essence must actually be instantiated *before* the object can be said to actually possess the properties comprising its essence. The phenomenologist, however, remains untouched. Existence cannot comprise the essence of any object – even God – since existence is not an object-property, but a presentational character. Existence is not derivable from the concept of God, but from the way God appears, the way God is "taken" or conceptualized, the *mode of conceptualization.*

What is there, then, about the *way* God is taken which guarantees that God appears transcendently? First, it must be seen that phenomenology is not about the business of applying concepts to things-in-themselves. Phenomenology delivers pronouncements concerning *the way things are* only on the basis of *the way things appear.* A phenomenological ontology flows strictly from the discipline of describing objects *as they appear.* Existence is attributed only if required by the structure of appearances. Hence, a phenomenological demonstration of the existence of God must rely strictly upon a description of God *as God appears*, of the *God-pheonomenon* or Divine Countenance.

Existence, we have insisted, is not a property of God, conceived as a noumenal "thing-in-itself," but rather a presentational character attributable to the mode of divine appearing, God *as* God appears, the God-phenomenon, God *for us*. Existence is a phenomenal, not a noumenal, property. But we already know that nothing which is not transcendent in the most profound sense can count as the God-phenomenon. God appears transcendently, or not at all.

V

Perhaps, then, God does not appear at all. And if not, then our claim that *were* God to appear, He *would* appear transcendently, is of no avail. We must now turn to the strictly phenomenological task of *demonstrating – showing –* the existence of the God-phenomenon.

The (external) "horizon" of a given intentional object is the whole range of possible contexts within which it may appear. Husserl says of this "intuitively clear or dark, distinct or indistinct *co-present* margin, which forms a continuous ring around the actual field of perception," that

> it reaches . . . in a fixed order of being the limitless beyond. What is actually perceived, and what is more or less clearly co-present and determinate (to some extent at least), is partly pervaded, partly girt about with a *dimly apprehended depth or fringe of indeterminate reality* . . . An empty mist of dim indeterminacy gets studded over with intuitive possibilities or presumptions, and only the "form" of the world as "world" is foretokened. Moreover, the zone of indeterminacy is infinite. The misty horizon that can never be completely outlined remains necessarily there.[13]

The "world-form," the range of "intuitive possibilities" for intentional activity, the horizon of all horizons, or *World-horizon*, is "foretokened" in every intentional act. Every intentional act occurs within this framework, or "space," of intentional possibilities. And every act involves a pre-thematic awareness of its horizon which can be brought to thematic givenness through the discipline of phenomenological reflection. What then confronts the reflective gaze is a transcendent object; the world-horizon, originally accessible to "natural" consciousness only as prethematic immanence, is "gathered" into transcendence. *World-horizon* has become *world-pole*. Equivalently, we may say that the World-horizon is the world as presented to "natural" consciousness; and the world-pole is the world as encountered – will-independently *discovered*, not *created* – within the pheonomenological reduction. But the World-pole, that which is transcendent in the most profound sense, the ultimate *telos*, that-than-which-no-greater-can-be-thought, is precisely the God-phenomenon. Phenomenology has thus performed its task of exhibiting God-as-revealed-through-the-world, the Divine Countenance.

VI

By "shutting out" the distractions of everyday life, Anselm ascended to that reflective stance whereby his "whole heart" was revealed as yearning for the "Divine Countenance," God as revealed through the divine "Face." So long as quotidian distraction remained, he was unable to "shut out everything save God." Only by "locking the door" could he achieve the requisite concentration. Yet once enabled to focus not merely upon the "trees" of particular concerns but upon the entire "forest," which remained invisible so long as he was lost among the "trees," the Divine Countenance became manifest to him. His meditation enabled him to see the "sense" of the Divine Countenance, to describe the God-phenomenon, to understand, instead of merely believing.

I give thanks to You, since what I believed before through Your free gift I now so understand through Your illumination, that if I did not want to *believe* that You existed, I should nevertheless be unable not to *understand* it.[14]

Anselm is explicit in saying that what he understands of God, including God's existence, is given *through God's illumination*, through the manifestation of the God-phenomenon. the ontological argument must then be set in this context. God, as that-than-which-no-greater-can-be-thought, is the object of phenomenological description. The ontological argument receives its understanding of God through phenomenological reflection upon the manifest God-phenomenon. Indeed, we may see the ontological "proof" as a descriptive elaboration of the phenomenological "demonstration."

University of Toledo
Toledo, Ohio

NOTES

[1]   M. J. Charlesworth, trans., *St. Anselm's Proslogion with a Reply on Behalf of the Fool by Gaunilo and the Author's Reply to Gaunilo* (Notre Dame: University of Notre Dame Press, 1979), p. 111.

[2]   *Ibid.*, p. 111.

[3]   *Ibid.*, p. 111.

[4]   *Ibid.*, p. 111.

[5]   Edmund Husserl, *Ideas: General Introduction to Pure Phenomenology*, translated by W. R. Boyce Gibson (London: Collier-Macmillan, 1969), p. 158.

[6]   *Ibid.*, p. 158.

[7]   Husserl criticizes as a "fundamental error" the notion of God as: "the Subject of absolutely perfect knowledge, and therefore also of every possible adequate perception, [who] naturally possesses what to us finite beings is denied, the perception of things in themselves." Such a view, in Husserl's straightforward characterization, is "nonsensical." "It implies that there is no essential difference between transcendent and immanent, that in the postulated divine intuition a spatial thing is a real (*reell*) constituent, and indeed an experience itself, a constituent of the stream of the divine consciousness and the divine experience." (*Ibid.*, p. 123.)

[8]   Charlesworth, *op. cit.*, p. 111.

[9]   *Ibid.*, p. 115.

[10]   Edmund Husserl, *Experience and Judgment: Investigations in a Genealogy of Logic*, Ludwig Landgrebe, ed., James S. Churchill & Karl Ameriks, trans. (Evanston: Northwestern University Press, 1973), p. 294.

[11]   *Ibid.*, p. 295.

[12]   Charlesworth, *op. cit.*, p. 117.

[13]   Husserl, *op. cit.*, p. 92.

[14]   Charlesworth, *op. cit.*, p. 121.

THOMAS RYBA

THE *MAGISTER INTERNUS:* AN AUGUSTINIAN PROTO-PHENOMENOLOGY OF FAITH AS DESIRE AND TEACHER

INTRODUCTION

In his book *The Idea of the Holy*, in the second footnote to the chapter entitled "The Holy as an *A Priori* Category, Part II," Rudolf Otto makes the following suggestive comparison:

The most interesting features in Luther . . . are the passages upon 'Faith', in which Faith is described as a unique cognitive faculty for the apprehension of divine truth, and as such is contrasted with 'natural' capacities of the Understanding, as elsewhere the 'Spirit' is contrasted. 'Faith' is here like the 'Synteresis' in the theory of knowledge of the mystics, the 'inward teacher' (*magister internus*) of Augustine, and the 'inward light' light of the Quakers, which are all of them of course 'above reason', but yet an *a priori* element in ourselves.[1]

In this paper, it is *not* my purpose to evaluate the essential rectitude of the comparison which Otto makes, though – as a historian of religions (somewhat) given to the nominalization of religious phenomena – my first inclination is to be skeptical of Otto's facile comparison of these four very complex (but not historically unrelated) notions. It *is* my purpose, however, to examine one of the supposed religious *a prioris* which Otto mentions in the above passage, because of its interesting potential to illuminate the Christian experience of faith. What I should like to do in this paper is to describe the Augustinian notion of the *magister internus*, not only as a pivotal notion for the Augustinian epistemology and understanding of faith, but also as an idea which has significant potential to carry the Husserlian phenomenology to the point of *rapprochement* with the Christian notion of supernatural revelation.

The question which immediately arises is: "What has Augustine's theology to do with Husserlian phenomenology?" Why choose a concept from the Augustinian theology to serve as an interpretive bridge between Husserlian phenomenology and Christian religious experience? The serviceability of the notion of the *magister internus* itself derives from the philosophical and historical affinities between the phenomenological project as Husserl conceived it and the end of Christian philos-

307

A-T. Tymieniecka (ed.), Analecta Husserliana XLIII, 307–329.
© 1994 Kluwer Academic Publishers. Printed in the Netherlands.

ophy as Augustine understood it. These were affinities which were not
missed by some of Husserl's students – to Husserl's eventual conster-
nation – nor, paradoxically, were they missed by even the master himself.
Let us examine the superficial evidences, first, and then move to the more
significant structural similarities.

THE SUPERFICIAL EVIDENCE FOR THE AFFINITY BETWEEN AUGUSTINIAN AND HUSSERLIAN PHILOSOPHY

Among (what I call) the superficial evidence for the affinities between
the Husserlian and the Augustinian philosophical projects are the following facts: (1) that many of the students of Husserl were led to varieties
of Augustinian Neoplatonism by Husserl's thought and (2) that Husserl
himself was responsible for encouraging a judgment of continuity
between Augustinian philosophy and his own thought by explicitly
quoting – with approval – those insights of Augustine expressive of those
features of Western philosophy which his own phenomenology was
designed to sustain.

About the first variety of superficial evidence I have little to say except
what others have already said in greater detail, namely, that Husserl's
early development – particularly that leading up to and issuing in the
Logical Investigations – produced in many of the Göttingen circle, and
even in some of his later students, a tendency to interpret Husserlian
philosophy as – at the very least – an *entrée* into the realist philosophical program. In the main, this annexation was accomplished under one
of two forms: a neo-Augustinian interpretation of Husserl or a neo-
Thomist interpretation of Husserl. Among the students who adhered either
to one or the other, or even to a combination of these formal appropri-
ations of Husserlian phenomenology, were Adolf Reinach, Dietrich von
Hildebrand, Max Scheler, Edith Stein and Ludwig Langrebe.[2] Among
contemporary thinkers, the neo-Augustinian reformulation of phenomenology is sustained by thinkers such as Josef Seifert and Ludger Holscher,
and the neo-Thomist reformulation is sustained by thinkers such as Robert
Sokolowski and Thomas Prufer.[3] In the case of the Göttingen circle and
Husserl's students, the annexation of Husserlian philosophy to neo-
Augustinianism or neo-Thomism was based upon the predisposition
toward realism held by many students before they came to study with
Husserl at Göttingen and, hence, their predisposition to interpret his
thought as being in line with one or another variety of classical realism.

But this annexation was also based upon the disappointment caused by Husserl's abrupt left turn toward transcendental idealism and the (supposed) inability of this new movement to deal with ontological *aporiai* nested in idealism's bosom. In contemporary approaches to phenomenological realism, only the neo-Augustinians continue to press strongly for an ontological critique of Husserlian idealism and relativism, while the neo-Thomists, in the main, have accepted an uneasy reconciliation between their realism and Husserlian idealism, accepting the party line of the latter as a response to the Augustinians, namely, that the distinction between realism and idealism has indeed been transcended in the Husserlian project.

Alone, the simple fact that many of the students of Husserl found his philosophy to be a bridge to what they considered the more adequate formulations of a ramified Augustinianism proves nothing, until one examines their reasons for doing so. Since it is not my purpose to involve myself in a dispute about these reasons, I simply offer the observation that if some individuals (discontented with the adequacy of Husserlian phenomenology) found rest in Augustinianism, then this constitutes, at least, a superficial affinity between the two positions. To put it another way: the Husserlian phenomenology posed certain questions which – at least in the perceptions of some – could be better answered by Augustinianism. My own discussion will not be aimed at reviving old disputes about the adequacy or inadequacy of either position. My major concern later in this paper will be to describe the structural features of the Augustinian philosophy and theology – and particularly the notion of faith – to suggest how they might be serviceable within a Husserlian phenomenology.

With respect to the second class of superficial evidences, it is clear that Husserl, himself, in print, encouraged the perception of continuity between his own thought and Augustinian philosophy. He did this by referencing some of his works to the quotations or treatises of Augustine. In *The Phenomenology of Internal Time Consciousness*, for example, Husserl calls our attention to the *locus classicus* for the investigation of consciously experienced time as none other than Book Eleven of Augustine's *Confessions*.[4] Here, the implicit suggestion is that Augustine has accomplished something in the way of a proto-phenomenological analysis of lived time which remains foundational even today.

In both the *Paris Lectures* (1929) and their expansion, the *Cartesian Meditations* (1929), Husserl – in virtually identical language – calls

philosophy back to its proper foundation. For philosophy to be justified in its "highest sense" it must become nothing less than *"universal
self-knowledge*, first in a monadic and then in an intermonadic sense.
. . . One must first lose the world through *epochê* so as to regain it in
universal self-examination."[5] Here, there are two touchstones which summarize the project of the Western scientific endeavor as it is expressed
in Husserlian phenomenology. They are the Delphic oracle's γνῶθι
σεαυτόν! and Augustine's sentence from *Of the True Religion*: "Do
not wish to go out; go back into yourself; truth dwells in the inner man."[6]
Superficial though it well may seem, Husserl's referencing of all the
above passages is symptomatic of a deep appreciation of their significance. In his affirmation of Augustine's analysis of time-consciousness,
Husserl is approving a concrete example of proto-phenomenological
analysis; in other words, he finds merit and even truth in those
Augustinian analyses which proceed according to a descriptive methodology which is anticipatory of his own more rigorous phenomenology.
In contrast, in his affirmation of Augustine's sentence from *Of the True
Religion*, Husserl is not approving an individual phenomenological
analysis but a fundamental principle of scientific knowledge: it is only
by instrumentally employing self-knowledge that we arrive at apodictic
knowledge of the things themselves.

One might well argue that neither set of superficial evidences makes
the case that the philosophies of Husserl and Augustine have any real
affinities. After all, students often get the meaning of their professors
wrong and attribute to them all manner of wild esoteric and exoteric
teachings. Moreover, what a teacher teaches positively is often reacted
to negatively by his/her students. Under this interpretation, one might
construe Husserl's students' drift into Augustinianism a result of the
profound disquiet induced by instruction in the difficult and – from the
point of view of realism – highly skeptical phenomenological approach.
Under this interpretation, Husserl's Augustinian students became so only
because they were after cheap truth, and were not willing to do the
phenomenological work required to purchase real truth at its requisitely
higher price. Similarly, one might dismiss Husserl's references to the
Augustinian canon as mere rhetorical flourishes, as either paying homage
to one of the late greats or as playing to an audience (as in the case of
the *Paris Lectures* delivered at the Sorbonne), or as a demonstration of
literacy. It strikes me that none of *these* alternatives is adequate. In enter-
taining them, we gainsay both the intelligence and diligence of a large

set of Husserl's students – and it is important to realize that the size of the group casts doubt upon the accusations posed. Moreover, we impugn the integrity of Husserl himself by reading the works of an otherwise unswervingly cautious philosopher as though he was capricious in precisely these instances. The remaining alternative is to take a brief look at the Augustinian philosophy to determine whether it indeed anticipates, and yet also supplements, Husserlian phenomenology.

CONCEPTUAL AFFINITIES BETWEEN AUGUSTINIAN AND HUSSERLIAN PHENOMENOLOGY

a. *Skepticism and the Augustinian Proto-Phenomenology*

In his work *The Phenomenological Movement: A Historical Introduction*, Herbert Spiegelberg locates one of the fonts of the Husserlian notion of the *epoché* in the positive second moment of the philosophy of skeptical Academicians such as Arcesilaus and Carneades.[7] The difficulty with this assertion is that there is no single, universally agreed upon interpretation of how the *epoché* functioned in the philosophy of these Academicians. Sextus Empiricus provides the most skeptical reading of their intentions, while Cicero (in what counts as little more than a throwaway line) suggests that the Academicians' use of the *epoché* was to be followed by a philosophy founded upon apodictic verities in a fashion which anticipated the Husserlian phenomenology. In an earlier work, I suggested that the safest course was to come down on the side of Sextus Empiricus' interpretation of these Academicians and view their notion of the *epoché* as essentially negative.[8] Although I still think that this interpretation is the safest to follow in light of the evidence we have (at this historical moment, at least), both Augustine and Cicero (before him) thought differently.[9] It is in the context of the Ciceronian interpretation of these Academicians that Augustine formulated his proto-phenomenology as a response to the minimalist understanding of the methodological principle of the *epoché*.

The skepticism which Augustine set himself against involved the prescription of a suspension (*epoché*) of judgment when two equiprobable conclusions were reached, particularly with respect to the reality or unreality of some object.[10] The sceptics maintained that it was impossible to provide any infallible criterion by which true appearances might be distinguished from false appearances. Accepting the general accuracy of this principle (with respect to perceptual data), Augustine followed the Platonic and Neoplatonic response. And it was in following this response that Augustine anticipated Husserlian phenomenology in its quest for apodictic evidences.

Augustine's position can be described as follows: The notion of the suspension of judgment (*epochê*) cannot be applied to everything, because then it must be applied to itself, and this very application is tantamount to an act by which the world is uncritically restored. But the uncritical restoration of the world is something which neither the Sceptics nor Augustine desire. What must be sought is a principle or foundation upon which some notion of the suspension of judgment can be based. Without an epistemological or ontological foundation, radical doubt or suspension of judgment are self-referentially refuting. The Sceptics see this problem, however, and take as their basis for the application of the *epochê* the proposition of Zeno, to whit, "A sense datum can be known and understood if it reveals itself with such marks as a false thing could not have."[11] They read this as meaning negatively that nothing given to human experience is given without the mark of the false in it. But Augustine, again, responds to this attempt to ground the *epochê* by pointing out that at least the statement of Zeno makes the claim to that which the Academics universally deny. However, if they allow that Zeno's statement is a truth, then they must employ a criterion as its guarantor.

What precisely is this measure of the true and the false to be? Augustine, without initially providing this criterion, begins with a set of examples designed to establish that there are truths. First, there are disjunctive assertions which are true, such as: "Either there are many worlds or there is one world," or "There is an infinite number of worlds or there is a finite number of worlds," or "Either the world had no beginning and will have no end or it had a beginning in time but will have no end or it had no beginning but it will have no end or it had a beginning and will have an end." By exhausting all alternative possibilities, these propositions must be true.[12] Second, there are the truths of mathematics which – as he puts it – are true whether we sleep or wake.[13] Third, there is the appearance of bent oars in water. In this case, Augustine asks the very astute phenomenological question whether the appearance of the oars is necessitated by the sight of the eyes, which is to say, whether the eyes truly see the way the oars appear. He answers this again in the affirmative, making an oblique reference to the necessity of the laws of refraction of light and their relation to the structure of the eye.[14] Finally, in a passage which approaches the insight of the Husserlian charge ("Back to the things themselves!"), Augustine describes the foundation for his proto-phenomenology as follows:

Restrict your assent to the mere fact of your being convinced that it appears thus to you. Then there is no deception, for I do not see how even an Academic can refute a man who says: "I know that this appears white to me. I know that I am delighted by what I am hearing. I know that this smells pleasant to me. I know that this tastes sweet to me. I know that this feels cold to me." . . . This is what I say: that when a man tastes something, he can in good faith swear that it is sweet to his palate or that it is not, and that by no Greek sophistry can he be beguiled out of this knowledge. If I am relishing the taste of something, who would be so brazen to say to me: "Perhaps you are not tasting it: it may only be a dream?" Would I discontinue? Why, that would afford me pleasure even in a dream. Wherefore, no resemblance to falsity can confuse what I have said that I know. . . . There are some philosophers who profess an opinion can be engendered by what the mind receives through a bodily sense, but maintain no certain knowledge [*scientia*] can be thus engendered. They hold that such knowledge is contained in the intelligence, far remote from the senses. Perhaps it is among those philosophers that we shall find the wise man we are looking for.[15]

This passage is ramified later in the *City of God* and in *On the Trinity* where Augustine employs a methodological doubt very much like that of the Sceptics and in clear anticipation of the Cartesian variety. He concludes that any fabric of doubt woven with skeptical questions has substance only because the very possibility of posing those questions is guaranteed by deeper certainties. If I doubt, I live; if I doubt, I remember the origin of my doubt; if I doubt, I understand that I doubt; if I doubt, I know I wish to be certain; if I doubt, I think; if I doubt, I know that I do not know; if I doubt, I know that I must seek certainty and avoid rash judgments.[16] Doubt calls up the proofs for the certainty of existence, the certainty of memory, the certainty of the doubting itself, the certainty that there is a desire to resolve doubt in truth, the certainty of thought in the process of doubting, the certainty that I do not know that which I doubt and with it the implication that I would know certainly – what I now doubt – were I only to find the answer. Every doubt leads to a certainty and suggests the means for establishing an internal, infallible criterion of truth.

It is within his own Christianization of the Neoplatonic philosophy that Augustine, indeed, discovers: (1) the wise man, (2) a criteriology, (3) the impersonal criteria of truth and (4) the personal criterion – or *internal master* – of truth. The conclusion that Augustine comes to is that what unites all certainties is that they are true by necessity and intuition. Like Husserl, Augustine does not settle for a psychologistic determination of intuition. The Augustinian notion of intuition, rather, implies a certainty which is incorrigible, *a priori* and logically necessary. In the realm of the intelligibles – which is convertible with both the personal and impersonal dimensions of the Λόγoζ – Augustine discovers a variety of guarantors of truthful judgements. Among the *res intelligibiles* are truth, unity, eternity, similarity, the good, wisdom, charity, justice, beauty and the mathematicals, among others.[17]

Despite his arriving at a Neoplatonic essentialism, Augustine preserves the philosophical usefulness of the suspension of judgment. Its legitimate use is as a form of methodological doubt driving the thinker to a truthful conclusion. In this sense, the *epochê* is employed by Augustine as a useful tool throughout his writings, but particularly in his early dialogues.

b. *The Augustinian Erotetics and the* Magister Internus

In his dialogue, *Concerning the Teacher*, Augustine takes his insights concerning methodological doubt and turns them into a positive theory of questioning (or *erotetics*). Augustine realizes that the process of questioning is nothing more than making the object and intentionality of a doubt conceptually explicit to one's self or others. Like Husserl, he recognizes, that every doubt seeks resolution in the apodicticity of evidence, so that questioning becomes the chief instrumentality by which one comes to positive knowledge about the world.

The peculiarity of the results of Augustine's erotetics is that they derive from premises introduced from the Neoplatonic program which Augustine accepted in large portions. They are not the products of pure inquiry. Specifically, Augustine had to contend with the Platonic premise of *anamnêsis* – the theory that all scientific knowledge was a remembering of the eternals from a time when the individual souls were in a deeper ontological union with the One. Because Augustine rejects both the Manichean/Platonic/Pythagorean doctrine of the transmigration of souls and the Plotinian emanational henology, he must explain certain knowledge on other bases than these. With these conceptions as a foil, he develops an alternative theory to account for the possibility of certain knowledge, an alternative theory which gives the savant immediate access to an internal teacher through the mediating relation of divine illumination.

Augustine formulates the process of scientific inquiry as follows: All things known are known on the basis of either a bodily sense or on the basis of the mind. The former are called sensibles (and are carnal in both the theological and anthropological sense), the latter are called intelligibles (and are spiritual in both the theological and anthropological sense). (One can see that Augustine already operates with a dualism which is far from value neutral.) When we query about the former we seek a scientific resolution in the sensibles on hand, or we seek it in sensible traces stored as images impressed upon the mind. When we query about the latter, however, we seek scientific resolution in another realm and on the basis of an intuition which has no sensory component and which is a single unbroken contemplative act. There is a mixed form of knowledge as well, which – being in a sense the most challenging – consists of the application of the eternals to the sensory realm.[18] Both the sensory experiences and the experiences of the eternals are limited in scope, the former by the intensity and extensivity of the individual's life, the latter by the individual's *spiritual* capacity, conditioned by his innate capacity and intellectual/spiritual development. Knowledge comes from no other sources.

When we inquire, therefore, we attempt to bring to resolution acts of judgment about which we are uncertain, and this inquiry may take place monadically (for example, when I question myself) or dyadically (for example, when I question another). In either erotetic situation I am attempting to resolve a judgment on the basis of experiences which either are my own possessions or are not possessed by me. Now to resolve the doubt of inquiry it may be possible to have new experiences and thus acquire new possessions by which my questions are resolved, or it may be possible to reason on the basis of analogies drawn from others' experiences. In the latter case, however, the questions raised can never be brought to perfect apodictic resolution, but, to some extent, must rely upon the *authority* of the other. Augustine recognizes that much of what goes by the name of knowledge is unavoidably based upon authority, but teaching by authority never resolves doubt perfectly. The perfect resolution of doubt must be based upon the self-presencing of the evidence within the monadic ego, whether one is assisted by another or not. The preferred variety of knowledge is that which is based upon direct experience of the sensibles or the intelligibles.

It is this analysis of knowledge which allows Augustine to arrive at the conclusion that no dyadic teaching relationship – save the relationship between the internal teacher and the individual ego – can ever result in the impartation of new scientific knowledge. Scientific knowledge demands intimate acquaintance and conformity with the objects of knowledge, whether these be objects in the world or in the realm of the intelligibles. An external teacher queries the student so that the evidences already in the possession of the student are employed to resolve doubt. When the student queries the teacher, the student is merely bringing the teacher to the resolution of doubt about what the student doubts, and this is accomplished on the basis of the inter-subjective dialectic of question and answer in the teaching session, as well as on the basis of the intelligibles which the teacher already knows and to which the student, internally, has potential access. Those occasions in which either teacher or student has a false start, and must later deny something originally affirmed, represent those situations in which the queries had not achieved apodictic resolution in one or the other's mind.

In the teaching situation in which the individual queries him or herself, Augustine views the origin of certainty a bit differently. He thinks that the ability to resolve questions regarding the intelligibility of objects is dependent upon an internal presence which stands guard at the flood-gate of insight. And he thinks that the ability to know with intelligible certainty is, in some sense, at the discretion of this internal regulator. We intuit intelligible truth only because the Internal Teacher allows access to it. What seems to be the subject's possession is actually on loan from another source. We have knowledge of the eternals only because we are able to *reflect* those eternals; they do not have actual residence within us. For the eternals *to be* reflected, they must have a locus other than in the mirror which reflects them.

The *magister internus* is called into service in Augustine's erotetic analysis because he finds it impossible to believe that all individuals can be brought to the same degree of certainty about all things. We all know according to the varying lights given us. Thus, it is conceivable that with respect both to external discrimination and to internal discrimination it may be impossible to teach a student scientifically because of a limited capacity. But there is a difference between those who are organically limited and those who are merely ignorant. The sensorially or intellectually exceptional are organically limited in what they may know; they do not have the normal instrumentalities by which to mediate the external or internal realities around them. For the ignorant, the liberal arts (the *trivium* and *quadrivium* suffice to bring the inherent potentialities of individuals to actualization.

It is, thus, in his erotetics that Augustine attempts to work out the *philosophical import* of the notion of the *magister internus* (or internal master). But this philosophical treatment hardly exhausts the Augustinian understanding of the importance of the Internal Teacher. The *magister internus* has relevance to theology as well, because Augustine views theology both as the highest science and as the fulfillment of philosophy. His tendency to conflate the impersonal characteristics of his Neoplatonic predecessors' notion of the *logos* (or *Noûs*) with the Christian notion of Jesus Christ as incarnate *Logos* (or second person of the Trinity) must, therefore, be understood in this context. This conflation means that Augustine places at the ground of consciousness a metaphysical reality which possess both personal and impersonal aspects but which transcends those aspects of the human subject. This metaphysical reality must be distinguishable – according to some criteria – from the consciousness within which it is lodged. For Augustine, there is no question of confusing this *fundus animae* or *Seelengrund* with the human person in its most interior reality. For that most interior human stratum Augustine reserves the description: "the image and likeness of God."

c. *The Stratification of Consciousness in the Augustinian Proto-Phenomenology*

Augustine's view of consciousness presupposes the stratification of the human person into a number of different levels which have as their major division an "outside" and an "inside." The human person exists as a functional unity straddling this division, half-existing in the outer world and half-existing in the inner world, and Augustine names these relatively differentiable components the "outer man" and the "inner man" (which I, in order to stave off offense, will term the "outer" and "inner human"). Both the outer and the inner humans represent trinitarian analogies, the scalar trinities approaching greater similitude as one moves up the higher cognitive functions toward what Augustine calls the "image and likeness of God." Augustine describes the movement from the lower to the higher cognitive functions according to a preferred spatial metaphor as a movement inwards, just as the movement from the higher to the lower cognitive functions is described as a movement outwards.

The meanest of these scalar trinities in humans occurs at the level of visual sensation, and consists of three components: (1) the object seen or visually sensed (which may or may not be preexistent to the activity of sensation), (2) the act of sight or visual sensation (which does not preexist the presence of some object) and (3) the attention of the mind which keeps the act of sight or visual sensation focused upon the object.[19] The object is in a sense primordial to the experience, since there cannot be an act of visual sensation without it. Visual sensation comes to be in the activation of the sense of sight, but the sense of sight itself, preexists *in potentia* prior to its activation by an object. Likewise, there would be no sensation were it not for the act of attention, though attention as a desire [*appetitus*] to see exists even when the sense of sight is destroyed.[20] The desire to see is one of the primordial components of consciousness and, as such, cannot be explained by something more fundamental. It represents one of the grounds of knowledge below which nothing more fundamental may be sought. Of the three components to this scalar trinity, attention is the only one which belongs to the mind (the inner human), as the sense and sensation belong to the body (the outer human) and the object belongs either to the world or the body (the outer human).

Since visual sensation is the product of the cooperation of attention, the sense of sight and the object, the object cannot alone be said to be constitutive of it, nor can it be said to produce it.[21] Yet the object contributes its form to the sensation, which is a likeness of itself present in the sensation. According to Augustine, it is impossible from within sensation itself to distinguish the body (as it is outside the act of sensation) from the sensation which is the product of attention, the object and the sense. The will, operating through the appetite of conscious attention, is responsible for fusing the constituted sensation with the pure contributions of the object so that the two become apparently indistinguishable, or better, so that the object cannot be known except through the constituted sensation. It is possible that through an act of rational inference the object may be distinguished from the sensation of the object. Here Augustine comes close to a distinction between the noema and the noesis of a sensorial act, for he is forced to admit that the examination of the constituted sensation can reveal the willful distortions of that sensation, but the means of this revelation are not cognitive acts at the level of the formation of sensations but at the higher level of rational inference. Rational inference is a higher operation of consciousness

belonging to the sphere of the "inner human." Moreover, in those individuals who are particularly willful or lustful, the object becomes so fixed
that rational inference is completely subordinated to the distortions of the
appetitus, so that no clear sight is even possible. Augustine goes even
further to suggest – as a kind of sensorial Lamarckianism – that this will-
fulness or superabundance of appetite is genetically transmittable to
subsequent generations! "For the more tender, and . . . the more formable,
are the primary seeds, the more effectually and capably they follow the
bent of the soul of their mother, and the phantasy that is wrought in it
through that body, which it has greedily beheld."[22] It is by analogy with
this understanding of sensation that Augustine constructs his teaching
of the spiritual transmissibility of the concupiscence of original sin
from the first generation of humans to the humans of his own time. For
Augustine, to live on this level – that is, to pursue the attractions of
appetite and a sensual existence – is degenerate.

The next scalar trinity which functionally contributes to the constitution of experience is the triad of memory, will and internal vision.
This triad is a structure of the higher consciousness which may be termed
"conceptualization" or "cogitation" [*cogitatio*] and thus is operative
within the inner human.[23] It begins to function simultaneously with the
sensory stimulus but persists even after the sensory stimulus is withdrawn.
Augustine suggests that the persistence of the sensation in memory is
a persistence of a mental sign of a higher order because it consists of
an icon (a perception) of the original contribution of the sensed object
which is shrouded in the willful and attentive alterations of the act of
sensation; all of which are shrouded in the contributions of the will and
the "eye of the mind" (or the internal vision) and mnemonically crystalized. The combination [*coactus*] of these three sets of contributions
form the conception of cogitation [*cogitatio*] stored as a memory.
Recourse to Augustine's own words helps to clarify what he has in
mind.

[I]n place of that bodily species which was perceived from without, there comes the
memory retaining that species which the soul has imbibed through the bodily sense; and
in place of that vision which was outward . . ., there comes a similar vision within,
while the eye of the mind is informed from that which the memory retains . . . ; and
the will itself . . . now converts the vision of the recollecting mind to memory, in order
that the mental sight may be informed by that which the memory has retained, and so there
may be in the conception a like vision. And as it was reason that distinguished the
visible appearance . . . from the similitude of it . . . ; so . . . that phantasy . . . which
arises from the mind thinking of the appearance of a body that it has seen, consists of

the similitude of the body which the memory retains, together with that which is . . . formed
in the eye of the mind that recollects; yet it so seems to be one and single, that it can
only be discovered to be two by the judgment of reason . . .[24]

Augustine, here, seems to anticipate the Husserlian notion that
anything which consciousness grasps can be reactivated according to any
of the numerous conscious acts by which it was originally thematized.
As in Husserlian phenomenology, perception has a peculiar primacy
inasmuch as it represents the lowest level of the constitution of experience which can be consciously examined. Augustine, like Husserl, also
recognizes the possibility that intentional distortions can render the examination of the sensorial contributions of the object to the perception
impossible in some circumstances. For Husserl, the solution is the association of different forms of conscious intentionality with different
perceptions of the object. Some of these will fail to do justice to the
object's transcendence, while others in their richness will respect that
transcendence. Husserl has a much more dynamic view of the intentional
contributions to consciousness than does Augustine. He must therefore
try to preserve the continuity of the object by understanding the precise
effect of various intentionalities on the subject's constitution of the object.
In the case of Augustine, however, the grasp of the object involves
many fewer conscious contributions. Through its species, the object
comes into the consciousness of the subject wholesale, as it were, the
experience of an object being much more passive than for Husserl.
Nevertheless, both Augustine and Husserl recognize that the experience of the object is the result of conscious acts and that through an
analysis of these acts the fullness of the object may be attained.

In the perception and conceptualization of an object, Augustine detects
a grand lattice of analogies, the most important constant being the contribution of will to human consciousness.

What . . . a body in place is to the bodily sense, that, the similitude of a body in memory
is to the eye of the mind; and what the vision of one who looks at a thing is to the
appearance of the body from which the sense is informed, that, the vision of the concipient
is to the image of the body established in memory, from which the eye of the mind is
informed; and what the intention of the will is towards a body seen and combined with
it, . . . that, the same intention of the will is towards combining the image of the body
which is in memory, and the vision of the concipient, that is, the form which the eye of
the mind has taken in returning to the memory. . . .[25]

Four species of the sensed object issue in tandem: the first, which is
the contribution of the object; the second, which is the result of the

will and attention; the third, which is the result of will and the "eye of the mind"; and the fourth, which is the result of the will and intuition (*contuitu*).[26] Because he emphasizes the primacy of the will in the constitution of perception and conceptualization, the will becomes the focal point of Augustine's understanding of how knowledge is frustrated or distorted. Even given the relative passivity of consciousness, the will possesses a mighty power over the mind's experience. At the level of conceptualization, the will may become so powerful and unruly, so effective at turning the mind's eye away from the bodily species from the object's contribution to sensation, that "so exact a likeness of the bodily species from memory is presented, that not even the reason itself is permitted to discern whether the body itself is seen without, or only something of the kind thought within."[27] In extreme alterations of consciousness – that is, in the states of madness, ecstasy, prophecy, illness, fearfulness, daydreaming, etc. – one mistakes these vain imaginings for reality, but most generally the distortions of the will are of a much milder variety than those involving such intense eidetic imagery. Nevertheless, the will is responsible for the distortion of reality – without exception – in all unredeemed humans.

Sustained clear understanding, both of the world and of the supernatural realm, is made impossible by the distortions of the will. Augustine's point, here, is aretalogical. He believes that defective (read sinful) wills are responsible for the mischief wrought on our intersubjective experience of reality. Here there is no question that an *epochê* alone, driven by the will to truth, can rescue distortions of perception or understanding and bring the true nature of reality into clear resolution or to apodictic certainty. The problem is the very will itself. No will to truth, goodness or beauty will have any effect, because, in Augustine's understanding, all wills are defective. All wills distort reality to greater or lesser extents. The closest thing in Augustine's proto-phenomenology is a *sine qua non* for either phenomenological or eidetic reduction may be found in his notion of the purification of the will, and this notion of purification can only be achieved supernaturally.

Now, in saying that Augustine believes all wills to be defective, we must not understand him to argue for a theological position that means complete *thelemic* depravity and thus, complete *noetic* depravity. Neither the will nor cognition are so depraved as to make all knowledge impossible. Rather, Augustine believes the will to be defective to the point that it is no longer possible not to sin. The nature of its defect is a matter of sustainability, not complete corruption. The same is true with respect to the notion of inner illumination. We are all illuminated to a degree, but nowhere near as much as we would have been had we not sinned, and nowhere near as much as we would be were we to have faith.

Conceptualization, however, does not exhaust the conscious structures which, Augustine believes, comprise the inner human. Beyond the stratum of conceptualization is the stratum which Augustine calls "the image and likeness of God." This stratum – the human mind – is responsible for the direct intuition of the truth of lower conscious constructions as well as of the truth of its own operations and of the truth of supernatural wisdom. Here in the image and likeness of God we find the ultimate trinitarian analogy, that of the mind's remembering, understanding and living. In the mind's reflection on itself, there is no question of this knowledge introducing the impression of a phantasm or sensorially filled concept into memory. When the mind reflects on its own operations it does so on the basis of memory, because as soon as those operations stop they must be preserved in some medium to be reactivated and examined later. The memories thus resulting are of an immaterial and higher intellectual order than those of perceptions or conceptions requiring some sensorial filling. This follows from Augustine's notion that the species through which the mind knows must always be like the thing known and must cause the mind to conform to the thing known. When it knows lower things, the mind, as the seat of knowledge, knows them according to a meaner and more turgid knowledge. Put another way, the sensorial filling attendant upon the conceptualization and perception of external things stands as a material component over and against their intelligible species; it stands as matter to the intelligible form of the object. However, when the mind knows itself, its knowledge is of the same order, and there is a perfect parity between the subject and object. The object – the mind as known – becomes perfectly transparent to the subject – the mind as knowing. When the mind knows itself it is on a par with its object, the resultant knowledge being neither of a higher nor of a lower variety. When the mind knows itself, its knowing results in a perfect likeness in which the image and the word (or intuition) are one.[28]

Peculiarly, the mind is also conceived by Augustine – in almost monopsychistic fashion – as being tantamount to the Aristotelian species form or the Marxist notion of species being. When the mind dwells in its individuality – an individuality which is the result of its own peculiar accidents and desires – it lowers itself in its dignity. The diversification of instantiated minds (which results in equal parts from their being joined to matter and from their willful pursuit of what makes them trivially unique) is set against the transcendental unity of the image and likeness of God. When the mind throws off its individuality and selfish desires and searches for its common and eternal nature, then it moves closer to wisdom and the restoration of the *imago Dei*. This understanding of the mind has important practical implications. Since there can be no question of wisdom or *scientia* (in the highest sense) being subverted to mean ends, only that form of knowledge which has an empirical component and practical use can be thus subverted. If this variety of knowledge is to be employed licitly, then it must be employed "to the end of the chief [or unchangeable] good" which is "public and common."[29] If it is employed for the attainment of "some private good of its own" then the mind "neglects the love of wisdom, which remains always after the same fashion, and lusts after knowledge by experiment upon things temporal and mutable, [and] that knowledge puffs up, it does not edify: so the mind is overweighed and thrust out . . . from blessedness . . ."[30]

Coversely, when the mind turns to the contemplation of God – since it already possess a species which is analogous to the object of its knowledge (and by virtue of which it is the image and likeness of God), and even though God is of a non-material and purely intelligible order – God's own nature can be only dimly intuited. Just as the mind finds it impossible to bring the sensorial content of worldly conceptions to perfect intelligibility because of its subintelligible materiality, so it also finds it impossible to comprehend the form of God because of its hyper-intelligible compass and simplicity. What is known by God, in God, as a simple simultaneous act, can only be known to humans by division or composition, two intentionalities which fracture the divine simplicity.

Augustine follows his Neoplatonic predecessors by lodging the *logos prophorikos intra mentem* (the *logos* manifest in the mind) in the center of this stratum of human consciousness. Although the image and likeness of God is like the trinity in the simplicity of its knowledge, love and memory, its ability to know and love are capacities with horizons open to divinity and divinization (or *theosis*). Put another way, though knowledge and love are natural capacities of all humans, they are natural capacities because they were created to mirror God's own nature.

Moreover, they are natural capacities susceptible to supernatural expansion. When we intuit the intelligibility of some geometrical object, we do so only because we are illuminated by the *magister internus* (the Internal Teacher) which is none other that the Word of God who dwells in us; but as *logos prophorikos intra mentem*, the Internal Teacher has a presence within all humans because all humans bear – in however distorted a form – the image and likeness of God. The more a human mind turns contemplatively toward objects of knowledge which are beyond the material world (and hence beyond images and signs), the more it becomes conformed to the species of those objects and the more it develops the theoretical capacity for wisdom. Still, even in the world the human mind finds signs and vestiges of God which are manifest through its order and harmony. This is the *logos prophorikos extra mentem* (the *logos* manifest outside the mind) which can only be read, however, by using the intelligibles in the *logos prophorikos intra mentem*. Without the virtue of faith (*fides*) and its perfection in the virtue of love (*caritas*) there is a limit to the wisdom which can be attained naturally. The greater the faith, the more the mind opens itself as a channel of supernatural illumination. The capacity for intuition or direct insights into the necessity of intellectual objects represents for Augustine that dimension of human consciousness which best mirrors God's own understanding.

d. *Faith's Role in Bringing Us to Scientific Certainty*

The purpose of the preceding discussion was to provide an outline of the Augustinian philosophy, and to draw parallels with the Husserlian phenomenological project where these parallels obviously suggest themselves. However, this is the appropriate place to draw these related discussions together on the thread running through them all. Having presented Augustine's proto-phenomenology in some detail, we are now in a better position to understand the meaning of faith for the Augustinian notion of scientific certainty.

Every sophomore philosophy major has been taught that Augustine's approach to knowledge can be summarized in his command: "*Crede ut intelligas*": "Believe in order that you may understand!"[31] Unfortunately, to encapsulate the thought of a philosopher in a single principle – as is the case in most one-sentence summaries – tends to flatten the topography of his or her thought to the point of trivializing it. It would be easy to distort Augustine's thought according to this principle and to see it as a matter of empty-minded fideism, to see the notion of the *Magister Internus*, for example, only as a theologically loaded conception whose fundamental purpose in Augustinian thought was to put Christians in the know – because they have faith – and to exclude non-Christians from knowledge – because they don't have faith. However, to do this would be a gross distortion of Augustine's intent as a philosopher. A more accurate reading of Augustine would be to understand this command as the imperative form of a conclusion drawn from careful phenomenological analysis of how humans come to certainty about the world.

For Augustine, 'faith' denotes an analogical concept. It has descriptive capacities far beyond its theological referents, although its theological referents are certainly central to Augustine's purpose. In fact, faith operates at every level of the human intentionality. Most generally – and bracketing momentarily the dimension of personal trust the Christian tradition introduces into its theological meaning – faith is the desire to bring an anticipation to certain resolution at some future point. It results in actions necessary to make this resolution possible, even when the time of the resolution's accomplishment is not immediately apparent. To put this in Neoplatonic terms which Augustine would probably accept, faith is the unwavering desire to seek union with the desired. If the object desired in sensory, the result will be a sensation. If the object is knowledge, then the result will be conformity between the knower and the known. According to this meaning, we can see how faith is analogically operative at every level of Augustine's model of consciousness and, if his model is correct, in the lives of all humans.

At the lowest level of human experience, there is that variety of faith associated with sensory fulfillment. We desire – and this variety of faith is little more than desire – the resolution of the yearning which our senses naturally possess for stimulation. The will which drives this desire is irrational and below the level of explication. Yet it is this will which makes the subsequent tiers of experience possible. In a sense, faith-as-raw-desire-for-stimulation is the blindest faith of all because it is sustained by the irrational determination of will and is completely subordinate to its strength.[32]

At the level of simple cognition, faith is little more that the desire to achieve a crude conceptual familiarity with things, to have experiences, to store up memories, to see the world. The ends of faith, here, are proximate. They are not based upon any distant ends or proficiencies, the development of great art or science. Rather, this variety of faith is directed to a resolution which occurs when the sought after state-of-affairs is finally experienced. It is fundamentally passive. It is experience as understood by the American tourist. The kind of knowledge which results from simple cognition is nothing more than that of the collector, raconteur or master of trivia, and this variety of faith is satisfied when this kind of knowledge is obtained.[33]

At the level of the acquisition of knowledge in the outer or inner worlds, there is a decided shift in the nature of faith. With respect to the other world, faith becomes an essentially practical virtue, but one from which, nevertheless, high technical skill results. Faith is useful until the achievement of some desired effect is made possible. The tendency here is to equate the end of faith with practical success so that all the skills learned in faithfulness to the promise that practice might eventually result, reach their completion and fulfillment in the awarding of a diploma, or license, or in the discovery of a new means of propulsion, or in the winning of a gold medal, or in making "a killing" on Wall Street, etc. Faith – as it is discovered among the practitioners of the world – has its utility in sustaining people for long durations until a certain homogeneity of production is achieved. The utility of this variety of faith is measured in results and these results are equated with knowledge. In America, this variety of faith is most prized – it being associated with the professionalism of the Protestant work ethic – because it results in the things Americans most value.[34]

In contrast, faith which produces knowledge of the inner world refers to the suspension of the cognitive satisfaction, a suspension associated with the theoretical disciplines. In Augustine's terms, it is a prerequisite for knowledge of the intelligibles. Here, faith is applied as long as the process of inquiry is sustained, and in the theoretical disciplines there is no end to inquiry, just as there is no end to faith. To be sure, interim results are achieved; were it not for such results, even the most ardent theoreticians might become discouraged. But among theoreticians, faith has a decidedly different aspect because it is essentially contemplative; it is directed to the appreciation of the objects of knowledge for themselves, and to no other purpose. Because Augustine believes that neither the world nor the realm of the intelligibles offers anything like a depletable source of knowledge, the desire for knowledge for its own sake is never-ending. As a Christian believer, however, Augustine thinks that the desire to circumscribe the whole meaning of existence can be satisfied neither in the fragmentary evidences which the natural external world presents, nor from the fragmentary natural knowledge of the intelligibles which are reflected within the consciousness of all humans. The faith invested in the attempt to achieve complete insight into the impersonal side of the *logos prophorikos extra mentem* and the impersonal side of the *logos prophorikos intra mentem*, though it may result in numerous successes, can never achieve its object. This is because it requires an added illumination which is possible only through initiation into the Christian mysteries. For Augustine, Christian faith in the Logos incarnate is the means to the transformation of the will, and the will must be transformed for reality to be seen as it is. Until the philosopher understands that the Internal Teacher is none other that the Physician of Grace, a phenomenology which results in a full and complete wisdom will be impossible.[35]

CONCLUSION

I began this paper by posing the question of the relationship between Augustinian philosophy and the Husserlian phenomenology. It seems to me that the answer to that questions lies in the very issue of faith itself. Husserl felt comfortable referencing Augustine's philosophy as expressing the deepest insight into phenomenology, but not because he could accept the theological loadings of the Augustinian philosophy, nor because he was prescient and could see that the eventual outcome of his phenomenological program would be identical to that of Augustine's. As he well knew, the horizon of phenomenology is infinite in its scope both extensively and intensively. No, Husserl quoted Augustine because Husserl had *faith* – and not a little proof – that the project begun by Plato and sustained by Augustine could be adapted, refined and continued in a new age. And if, in Husserl's case, this faith did not extend to Augustine's theological views, nevertheless these theological views did appeal to some of Husserl's own students, who found Husserl's *faith* in what phenomenology *could be* too narrow to reflect the religious experience of Augustine.

St. Thomas Aquinas Center
Purdue University

NOTES

[1] Rudolf Otto, *The Idea of the Holy*, Trans. John Harvey (New York: Oxford University Press, 1958), p. 138.

[2] See: Herbert Spiegelberg, *The Phenomenological Movement: A Historical Introduction* (The Hague: Martinus Nijhoff, 1982). The relevant portions are as follows: Adolf Reinach, pp. 191–200; Dietrich von Hildebrand, 235–237; Max Scheler, 268–305; Edith Stein, 238–239; and Ludwig Landgrebe, 242–244.

[3] See, for example: Josef Seifert, *Back to the Things Themselves: A Phenomenological Foundation for Classical Realism* (New York: Routledge & Kegan Paul, 1987); Ludger Holscher, *The Reality of the Mind: St. Augustine's Philosophical Arguments for the Human Soul as Spiritual Substance* (New York: Routledge & Kegan Paul, 1986); Robert Sokolowski, *The God of Faith and Reason* (South Bend: University of Notre Dame Press, 1982).

[4] Edmund Husserl, *The Phenomenology of Internal Time Consciousness*, Martin Heidegger, ed., James Churchill, trans. (Bloomington: Indiana University Press, 1964), Part I: Introduction, p. 21. Husserl's exact words are: "The analysis of time consciousness is an age-old crux of descriptive psychology and theory of knowledge. The first thinker to be deeply sensitive to the immense difficulties to be found there was Augustine, who larbored almost to despair over this problem. Chapters 13–18 of Book XI of the *Confessions* must even today be thoroughly studied by everyone concerned with the problem of time. For no one in this knowledge-proud modern generation has made more masterful of significant progress in these matters than this great thinker who struggled so earnestly with the problem. One may still say with Augustine: *si nemo a me quaerat, scio, si quaerenti explicare velim, nescio.*"

[5] See: Edmund Husserl, *The Cartesian Meditations* (The Hague: Nijhoff, 1970), pp. 156–157 (182–183) and Edmund Husserl, *The Paris Lectures* (The Hague: Nijhoff, 1973), p. 39 (39).

[6] Augustine of Hippo, *Of True Religion* in J. H. S. Burleigh, ed., *Augustine: Earlier Writings* (Philadelphia: Westminster Press, 1953), 39:72, p. 262. All subsequent quotations are from this English translation.

[7] Herbert Spiegelberg, *The Phenomenological Movement: A Historical Introduction* (The Hague: Martinus Nijhoff), pp. 119 & 159–160, Note 103.

[8] Thomas Ryba, *The Essence of Phenomenology and Its Meaning for the Scientific Study of Religion*, Toronto Studies in Religion, Vol. 7 (New York: Peter Lang Press, 1991), pp. 208–209, n. 106.

[9] Augustine of Hippo, *Contra academicos*, II:13:29, III:7:14; III:17:38. this and all subsequent quotations are from the following English translation: *Answer to Skeptics*, Denis Kavanagh, trans., in *The Writings of St. Augustine* Vol. I (New York: CIMA Publishing, 1948). See also: Cicero, *Academica*, I:9:10, II:18:60.

[10] Sextus Empiricus, *Outlines of Pyrrhonism*, I:232–235.

[11] Augustine of Hippo, *op. cit.*, III:9:18; Cicero, *Academica* 2:24:77.

[12] *Ibid.*, III:10:23.

[13] *Ibid.*, III:10:25.

[14] *Ibid.*, III:11:26.

[15] *Ibid.*, III:11:26.

¹⁶   *Civitas dei*, XI:26; *De trinitate*, XV:12:20. See also the illuminating discussion in: George Howie. *Educational Theory and Practice in St. Augustine*. New York: Teachers College Press, 1969. pp. 130–137.

¹⁷   *Soliloquia* I:15:27; *De vera religione*. 66; *De diversis questionibus*, 83: q. 23; *De libero arbitrio*, II:19:52.

¹⁸   *De magistro*, XII.

¹⁹   *De trinitate*, XI:2:2. This and all subsequent quotations are from the following English translation: Augustine of Hippo. *On the Trinity*. A. W. Hadden, Trans. *Nicene and Post-Nicene Fathers*. Vol. 3. Grand Rapids: Eerdmans, 1956.

²⁰   *Ibid.*, XI:2:3.

²¹   *Ibid.*, XI:2.3.

²²   *Ibid.*, XI:2:5.

²³   *Ibid.*, XI:3:6.

²⁴   *Ibid.*, XI:3:6.

²⁵   *Ibid.*, XI:4:7.

²⁶   *Ibid.*, XI:9:16.

²⁷   *Ibid.*, XI:4:7.

²⁸   *Ibid.*, IX:11:16.

²⁹   *Ibid.*, XII:12:17.

³⁰   *Ibid.*, XII:11:16 & 12:17.

³¹   *Tract. Johan.*, XXIX:6; *Sermones*, 43:7; *De libero arbitrio*, II:5; *Contra academicos*, II:9.

³²   *Op. cit.*, X:2:2.

³³   *Ibid.*, XI:3:6.

³⁴   *Ibid.*, XII:12:17.

³⁵   *Ibid.*, XII:11:16; XII:12:23.

EVANGHELOS A. MOUTSOPOULOS

TEMPORAL AND "KAIRIC" CATEGORIES APPLIED TO PROVIDENTIAL HISTORY

I. THE NOTION OF KAIRICITY

The three-fold system of fundamental temporal categories: "past", "present", "future", helps in defining and concretizing the scheme that contains becoming. According to the basic Bergsonian distinction, the flow of duration being indivisible, time is introduced into the process of becoming by human understanding in order to make possible its divisibility, which is, of course, a "factice" conception, but which results from a typical application of a certain aspect of the Cartesian method (the more complicated the problems faced by the understanding are the more they are susceptible to being solved by analysis. Hence the "revolutionary" conception of Bergson, that time is an invention aiming towards practical activity, whereas duration, which corresponds to the reality of becoming, helps in grasping its meaning theoretically.

Now, another distinction is possible within the framework determined by the preceding considerations, and its meaning will be clarified through some examples. The system of temporal categories described previously seems to be strictly static. Indeed, it implies that propositions formulated according to it correspond to mere statements which are entirely independent of any kind of commitment of consciousness to the process of becoming, the latter remaining definitely external to this system. The following propositions: "it rained yesterday", "it is raining today", "it will (probably) rain tomorrow", imply no immediate consequence for the consciousness itself, which remains that of an indifferent observer.

Consider, however, the following propositions: "it has not rained yet", "it will (probably) not rain any more (this autumn)". In these propositions the commitment of consciousness to the facts described is obvious and direct. Now, suppose these statements are made by a ploughman. They immediately acquire a very precise meaning: they respectively express on one hand the ploughman's anxiety and hope, and on the other hand his frustration, for his own existential activities are tied to the facts that he states.

331

A-T. Tymieniecka (ed.), Analecta Husserliana XLIII, 331–334.
© 1994 *Kluwer Academic Publishers. Printed in the Netherlands.*

Furthermore, these propositions express the ploughman's deep interest in specifying an advantageous moment, which they help locate between the two distinct periods they respectively indicate, and during which this activity will be exerted in the best way and with the best possible results under the best objective conditions as more than mere statements, they are equivalent to some extent to axiological propositions, for they indicate the ploughman's interest in, and intention of recognizing this advantageous moment as a "kairos", i.e. both as a minimal and as an optimal one, and as a minimality and an optimality in itself.

II. THE DIVISIBILITY AND DISCONTINUITY OF BECOMING

"Not . . . yet" and "not . . . any more" (or even: "never more") represent the two elements of a two-fold or dual categorical system which one may call "kairic", and which is generally disguised and screened by the former static system of temporal categories. The "kairos" is defined and determined by the minimal difference between the period covered by the application of the category of "not yet" and the period covered by the category of "never more". This implies the confirmation of the validity of certain notions, such as: the objective uniqueness of the "kairos", which is due to the objective impossibility of it being repeated within the limits of the process it engenders; the actualization of the future (and of the past as well, depending on the orientation of the procedure), which consists in reducing it to the present; and the intentionality of consciousness, understood not in a static Husserlian sense as a reference to its contents, but in a dynamic Bergsonian sense as an orientation towards a goal to reach.

Combined with the "kairic" categories, these notions allow us to understand the vectoral attitude of consciousness when it is introduced and integrated into reality. Such an attitude of the consciousness entails the possibility of real restructuring, not by statically proceeding to some kind of theoretical and phenomenal division of the indivisible duration, but by dynamically imposing on it a discontinuity which makes possible a radical distinction between its two subsequent yet henceforth irreducible portions.

The "kairic" moment definitively inserts into and imposes upon the process of becoming a restructuring, as well as a catalytic distinction between what precedes and what follows. Divisibility does not disrupt the continuity of becoming. "Kairification", on the contrary, implies a fundamental discontinuity according to which there is no way to reconcile "before" and "after". The whole life of consciousness is thus reducible to a chain of "kairifications", its main activity consisting in theoretically, yet intentionally, conceiving the aim of its immediate or subsequent action.

III. KAIRICITY IN PROVIDENTIAL HISTORY

Since history is the field *par excellence* of human exertion, it is evident that it concentrates the major part of man's intentional activity. The history of mankind is mainly a succession of "kairifying" actions. From this level, the notion of intentionality may easily be raised by means of an "economic" transfer (in the theological acceptation of the term) to the level of divine action. At this level, God is considered mainly as an "acting person" who plans, decides and executes his acts by actualizing, through "kairification", the moments at which his activity will prove most efficient.

Thus the "history" of God's deeds since the creation of time (in the sense attributed to it by St. Augustine, *Confessions*, XI, 13), is a series of actions that one might improperly call "timing" but which are in fact "kairifications", according to the nature of God's own intentionality; the most prominent of these are creation and redemption, completed by the prevision of the last judgement. An infinity of major or minor acts, scheduled and executed according to the same model of divine activity and interpolated between these basic actions, then incorporated and integrated into their fundamental system, constitute the comprehensive form of divine providence.

Considered from this viewpoint, divine providence proves to be a continuity of discontinuous acts which is an elaboration of the basic model of "kairification", i.e. the actualization of remote instants within the range of divine intentionality. Thus, time turns out to be a typical illusion, and its creation in fact only a static form of the dynamic reality of God's activity. Such an 'activity actualizes eternity itself through a series of successive disruption which entail the existence of gaps that God's activity fills up simultaneously, and finally surpasses by means of a series of "stridings" and "overlappings".

Providential history thus comes to mean a highly dynamic field in which divine intentionality is exerted in a creative form that is inconceivable through the static system of temporal categories, but is fully realizable through the dynamic system of "kairic" categories. Such a system acquires the importance of an instrument that helps us understand divine activity as a creative historical process comparable to usual human creativity, a comparison which would otherwise be unacceptable, namely in the form of traditional insights based on mere temporality. Moreover, God's activity itself thus acquires a meaning which, even if not fully understandable, is necessarily the very reason for providential history.

University of Athens

ALAN M. OLSON

PHENOMENOLOGY, RELIGIOUS
STUDIES, AND THEOLOGY

The possibility and prospect of a phenomenological theology is a difficult but recurrent question. Recent works by Anna-Teresa Tymieniecka and Steven Laycock, however, provide considerable help with respect to clarifying the parameters of the problem—especially with respect to the questions of God and creativity.*

Now the prospect of *phenomenological theology*, it seems to me, is not the same as considering the place of phenomenology in religious studies generally. There is much in religious studies which characterizes itself as *phenomenological*. Some of this work is critical philosophically, but much characterizes itself phenomenological simply because it is concerned with *description*. But since descriptive utilizations of phenomenology remain "uncritical" of their starting point, as James Hart points out (*PT*, 99), they cannot be called phenomenological in the rigorous sense. To be rigorous, phenomenology must be *critical* in the transcendental, epistemic, methodological sense. Our task, then, is to adduce how a critically rigorous phenomenology, such as represented by Laycock and Tymieniecka, might be deployed not only in *religious* but also in *theological* studies.

One's notion of a phenomenological theology, of course, depends heavily upon what one thinks phenomenology is—and there are, as the literature indicates, a wide variety of positions on the matter. And in contrast to deciding what a *phenomenological* philosophy might be, the task of defining phenomenological theology is doubly problematical for, owing to the peculiar nature of theology's object, there is almost as much disagreement regarding what the discipline of theology is or should be as there is in the case of phenomenology. Needless to say, what the two terms signify when brought together in terms of a *phenomenological theology* presents us with a highly perplexing set of problems. One might argue, on the one hand, that a *phenomenological theology* is an oxymoron if one happens to be of

A-T. Tymieniecka (ed.), Analecta Husserliana XLIII, 335–347.
© 1994 *Kluwer Academic Publishers. Printed in the Netherlands.*

the view that only one or the other of these disciplines has scientific validity (whether as a correlation or as a modification); one may be of the view, on the other hand, that they constitute an absurdity if one thinks that neither phenomenology nor theology have scientific validity. Therefore, while the attempt to arrive at a *phenomenological theology* seems to arise from the motive to sharpen the question with respect to phenomenology's place in religious studies, one must also be willing to ask whether extending phenomenology also to theological studies does not make an already confused situation worse.

For purposes of general argument we will begin by assuming that both phenomenology and theology have legitimacy as disciplines, each in its own right, our task being one of determining whether they maintain this legitimacy and coherence when connected one to the other and what such a linkage might suggest or imply when the connecting link is *religion*. Such a question also includes asking whether the prospect of a *theological phenomenology* might not ultimately be more coherent than a *phenomenological theology*. Indeed, I will be suggesting, in the remarks which follow, that the project of Tymieniecka in *The Three Movements of the Soul* might very well be viewed in terms of the latter, namely, a *theological phenomenology*, with Laycock very strictly viewed in terms of the former or what he terms a *phenomenological theology*.

My reasons for this typological characterization will, I hope, become more evident as I proceed—especially given the fact that Tymieniecka's work can only be viewed as a *theological phenomenology* under special conditions. Suffice it here to say that a theological phenomenology would not be unlike an existential phenomenology—the project of a pure, transcendental phenomenology being modified, as in Heidegger and Jaspers, by the purpose of elucidating specific meanings about possible *Existenz* or, in the case of a theological phenomenology, modified by the attempt to elucidate, as does Tymieniecka, those ciphers of Divine Transcendence psychologically discernible in the spiritual life of the soul which, she contends, are the enigmatic and paradoxical origins of what we call *creativity* while not being identical with their source. Tymieniecka's project in *The Three Movements of the Soul*, therefore and as I understand it, presupposes *faith* with respect to the fundamental validity of basic symbols and values of Western tradition and uses phenomenology to make this faith more lucid and coherent. In contrast to the more hermeneutical nature of *theological phenomenology*, then, I view *phenomenological theology* as the speculative attempt to establish and/or determine the validity of theology itself by phenomenological method and, having once done so, to arrive thereby at the possibility of knowledge and faith.

As background, it seems to me that there are basically three positions with respect to the place of phenomenology in religious studies, two of which are represented in the works of Steven Laycock and Anna-Teresa Tymieniecka. Laycock's position represents a strictly Husserlian, transcendental or immanentist *consciousness* model of phenomenological inquiry—a phenomenology intent upon establishing what he terms the epistemic "foundations" for a phenomenological theology. Tymieniecka's approach, on the other hand, has more in common with a late-Husserlian or *Lebenswelt-Existenz* phenomenological approach. As a project in philosophical anthropology, her approach recalls, prior to Heidegger and Jaspers, the *Freiheits-philosophie* of creative *potenz* in Schelling. For this creative potency consists of pre-reflective, pre-predicative, intuitive experiences of Spirit or the "dianoiac thread," as Tymieniecka calls it, to be elucidated phenomenologically. Yet a third model, here unrepresented, might be broadly identified as the *Chicago Model* of phenomenology in the study of religions developed by the students of Joachim Wach and Mircea Eliade and under the continuing influence of Rudolf Otto, Brede Kristensen, and Gerardus van der Leeuw.[1]

This three-fold categorization roughly approximates Laycock's formal description of philosophical orientations, namely, (1) "...philosophy which takes phenomena as its subject matter and is reflectively achieved," as in the case of his own and, to an extent, Tymieniecka's; and a combination of (2) and (3), namely, "...philosophy which [partially] takes phenomena as its subject matter and is only [partially] achieved reflectively"—the key being how consistently *phenomena* and *reflection* are understood in terms of the Husserlian project of phenomenology (*PT*, 4). The Chicago model of phenomenology of religion, as I understand it, generally falls under this latter *mixed* heading since it is used in combination with other methods of analysis and interpretation as insisted upon, for example, by Ninian Smart. Because this poly-methodological approach is so well-established in religious studies, however, we will use it as our point of reference—even though there are many scholars who question its empirical validity and/or reliability in religious studies. As such, the prevailing utilizations of phenomenology in religious studies tend to satisfy neither the rigorous empiricist nor the rigorous phenomenologist—the obvious question being whether it is possible to develop a phenomenology which is capable of doing both.

The approaches of Tymieniecka and especially Laycock can be viewed as alternative pioneering attempts in this regard. The basic difference between these more rigorous utilizations of phenomenology is that only Laycock states explicitly that it is his task to develop a phenomenological theology or, more precisely, to establish *foundations* for a phenomenological theology, thus making it capable of displacing other approaches. Tymieniecka makes no such claim. Her intent, as I see it, is rather to develop a phenomenology which, while it might serve as a propaedeutic to traditional theology, stands entirely on its own. For through her phenomenological elucidation of the psychological structures of spirituality and creativity, Tymieniecka provides a cogent basis for the amplification, appreciation, and adjudication of truth claims in the history of theology, religious philosophy, and aesthetics. Her work may also be identified, therefore, with sapiential philosophy, that is, with the philosophy of moral wisdom and value, which presupposes and does not explicitly challenge the validity of traditional dogmatic or systematic theology and its normative or quasi-normative claims, but rather attempts to show how and under what conditions of experience such claims may be viewed as being true.

As I understand the position of Laycock, however, the validity of traditional dogmatic or systematic theology is challenged both explicitly and implicitly, in the attempt to displace it by what he terms *phenomenological theology*. Laycock's approach, therefore, stands in some sharp contrast to conventional phenomenology of religion which simply brackets the normative claims of theology in its proper and/or established sense (viz. *Church* Theology, as in Karl Barth, or dogmatic, apologetical, evangelical theology) and limits itself to the history, morphology, and comparative philosophy of religions. For to be consistently phenomenological, one must (consistent with the Neo-Kantian roots of the phenomenology of religion) rely upon the presence of "phenomena" in order to carry out one's project—that is, there must be identifiable religious phenomena present to the experience of the individual attempting to construct a phenomenology of and/or about religion and religions.

In most instances, such so-called *religious* phenomena present themselves to the phenomenologist through the experiences of others and/or the living expressions and artifacts of such experiences accessible to the experience of the scholar. Moreover, if one's concern is to describe manifestations of the sacred or the experiences of such manifestations, one must refrain, as previously stated, from making judgments regarding their metaphysical or ontological status beyond or outside of this description. One may say something about their value or meaning or how they bear witness to what one might term the authority of the *sacred*, but one cannot make truth-claims regarding the ontological reality of what they signify beyond the realm of meaning. As Erazim Kohak maintains, "phenomenology is the systematic study of the meaning-patterns which structure the life-world, including humans and their lives and actions"—a position entirely consistent with Kristensen's famous observation that "the only object in the study of religions is the faith of the religious." One may, of course, combine phenomenology with hermeneutic philosophy, as does Ricoeur, with respect to interpretations of the moral and social implications of such descriptions—including what they imply or commend personally and apologetically from the standpoint of the personal appropriation and/or conversion of the phenomenologist and his or her students and readers. But if one does this, one must also attempt to make clear, as does Ricoeur (at least most of the time), when it is the case that one's operation is phenomenological and when it is hermeneutical—especially when questions of meaning encroach on questions of Being.

Finally, one may arrive at a phenomenology of religion by way of a speculative phenomenology of religious consciousness-as-such, as, for example, Hegel attempted to do in his *Phänomenologie* and his *Vorlesungen über die Philosophie der Religion*. While Hegel's pioneering attempt was, for him, a regional but utterly critical attempt to chart out the larger operations and implications of consciousness with respect to the reality of Spirit, it is to Hegel's analysis that all subsequent phenomenologists of religion must ultimately defer as the originating source. Laycock's project has much in common with Hegel's speculative philosophy—even though he is troubled by what he refers to as the *theological* aspects of Hegel and is intent upon correcting him by way of what he terms a phenomenological *via eminentiae* through a reduction of the Divine very strictly to a datum of consciousness—the reality of which is deemed to be identical with consciousness. The *speculative* side of Hegel is, therefore, rejected by Laycock on the view that the Hegelian Absolute is, in some sense, "finished" and, as such, a violation of the processual, open-ended, and unfinished nature of consciousness.

A phenomenological thematization of the noetic/noematic structures of experience will not itself suffice unless one has decided, a priori, that the reality of God, the Divine, or the Sacred, is *intra nos* and *intra nos* or subjective only as distinct from being also *extra* and *supra nos*. Indeed, it is just such notions which are bracketed in order to distinguish a phenomenological from a strictly psychological approach to the meaning of religion. Hegel understood this well on two levels. First, he understood that transcendental attempts bent upon clarifying the ontological status of theology's primary object or referent have negative implications for theology's larger speculative claims regarding the nature of Being. For example, Hegel's concept of Spirit, as in the case of Jaspers' Comprehensive-Encompassing (*das Umgriefende*), like Hegel's Absolute, obviously tends to commend some kind of monism—even though both Spirit and the Encompassing are vague enough to resist this as a strict identification. But monistic metaphysical commendations also have serious negative consequences for those complexes of meaning arising from the quasi-dualistic narratological framework of Western theology, especially in the areas of ethics and soteriology. Hegel, I would argue, does not ultimately solve this problem, viz., the "dialectic of belief and pure insight," but views it, as does Tillich, in terms of the "dynamics of faith" or "life in the Spirit." The question is whether Laycock's speculative phenomenological theology which, in contrast to Tymnieniecka's position, dissolves the dialectical tension between *Glauben* and *Wissen*, can avoid these consequences, assuming that he wishes to do so.[2]

Indeed, if a phenomenological theology has to do with a systematic thematization of the meaning patterns that structure those experiences we call "religious," we have to ascertain what kind of an experience a *religious* experience is. To do so requires that we arrive at some kind of working consensus regarding the nature of *religion*— and this is not an easy thing to do. If we take as normative the prevailing sociological definitions, then a *religious* experience (*religio* qua *re-ligare*) is any experience mediated within and through the ritual, mythical, and dogmatical structures of a given cultus—for example, the experience of blessedness and serenity which comes as the result of participation in the Mass or some other form of worship and meditation. If one has such experiences *sui generis* and allegedly independent of a cultically specific mediating context, for example, if one had an experience of the *sacred* in a dream or when walking by the sea, there is still the mediating context of language with which one has to deal, as Heidegger and Gadamer have shown. This means that one is still forced to "make sense" out of the meaning of one's experience (viz., to decide whether this experience is or is not *religious* in the proper sense) by way of culturally specific language, even though it be asserted that the origins of such experiences are pre-reflective, pre-linguistic, and in some sense immediate.

This being the case, it might be possible, on some version of the Chicago model, to develop what might be termed a *phenomenology of theologies*—in other words, to engage in the phenomenological analysis and description of the theological positions, assertions, claims, and symbolizations of individuals, groups, traditions, etc. Such positions are, after all, also part of the lifeworld prior to my reflections about them. This is the notion which seems to inform Gordon Kaufmann's Neo-Kantian approach to theology as an "imaginative reconstruction." But one would not, thereby, arrive at a *phenomenological theology* as Laycock defines it. One remains rather with a phenomenology of theology or theologies, and the fundamental question as to whether one's religious experience (or experience of theology) is also an experience of God remains, it seems to me, unanswered apart from the faith of the experient.

What is unique about experiences of the sacred, however, is that they not only refer to themselves in terms of meaning, but beyond themselves with respect to Being—the shift from the former to the latter requiring a kind of Kierkegaardian *leap*. The only exception to such experiences of double-reference and the logic of double-meaning necessary to elucidate them might be the quasi-empirical investigations of the so-called *numinous* as in paranormal psychology or in the social sciences generally where investigators attempt to isolate the objects and/or states-of-affairs allegedly underlying or generating such experiences, including one's own experiences—if it is the case that the investigator is given to psychic-states and visitations by paranormal phenomena (which is not infrequently the case amongst uncritical empiricists still intent upon locating the lost divine object).

But in Laycock's approach, the question of meaning and Being are collapsed—the reason being that the "God phenomenon," as Laycock himself points out, "is no ordinary phenomenon" (*FPT*, 234) and that subjectivity and objectivity cannot be differentiated as easily as in the case of other phenomena. This being the case, it would seem that a phenomenological theology is impossible if by this we mean a phenomenology of *Theos*. In short, it would seem that there can only be a phenomenology of the various *logia* about *Theos* as such. And if we take Ricoeur's famous statement about bracketing the false *logos* of *mythos* as a normative statement regarding what is necessary in the project of *demythologizing* in the history of religions (viz., "to release myth as *muthos*"), then it is even more true, it seems to me, with respect to what is required of a phenomenological theology. In this case, phenomenological theology, as the endless comparative play of theologies, really turns out to be some kind of hermeneutic phenomenology, as Eide calls it with respect to Ricoeur's philosophical anthropology, or simply philosophical theology. Indeed, this obtains in the case of most philosophical theologians for whom the pioneering work of Schleiermacher is an important model and who also like to call themselves phenomenologists. In this context, commitments to phenomenology are limited by a certain Neo-Kantianism, as in the work of Paul Ricoeur and, indeed, of John Findlay, who insists that philosophical theology (i.e., metaphysics) has to be carried out "between Kant and Hegel"—that is, "between" a strictly phenomenological "discipline of the Cave" and a speculative metaphysical "transcendence of the Cave."

Such a position, it seems to me, is considerably at odds with what Laycock sets out to do, for it is just the above dichotomy which he sets out to dismantle. At first glance, in fact, Laycock's comment on Husserl's *itinerarium ad mentis deum* in the latter's conversation with Sr. Adelgundis Jaegerschmidt, viz., "to arrive at God without God" (*FPT*, 1) is somewhat reminiscent of the rather dubious project of Hazel Motes in Flannery O'Connor's *Wise Blood*, namely, to establish "the Church of Christ Without Christ." Nevertheless, by this radical strategy Laycock poses fascinating methodological questions with respect to the prospect of a phenomenological theology—not least, the question of *normativity* which has always been central to any theology, especially *fundamental* and/or *foundational* theology.

In order to expand on this a bit, let us look rather carefully at Laycock's definition of a phenomenological theology: "A distinctively *phenomenological theology*," he says, must be viewed in sharp "contradistinction to either a *positive* theology, with its assumption of textual or traditional authoritarianism, or a speculative-natural theology, with its procedures of deductive and inductive derivation." Such a phenomenological theology, he says, "...seeks to discover its subject matter, the Divine (*theos*), in that web of intuitively articulate necessities in which phenomena are caught and seeks to do so by means of the reductive-eidetic-reconstructive techniques characteristic of phenomenology" (*FPT*, 5). Such a project, then, attempts to collapse the distinctions mentioned above and is, therefore, *transcendental* in the strict Husserlian sense by way of thematizing the ways in which so-called Divine phenomena are not only present to *my* individual experience and the structures present thereto, but also present to *all* consciousnesses in a similar manner.

The properties of such a phenomenological theology are explicitly and lucidly set forth by Laycock under the leading axiomatic proposition that "...if phenomenological theology is possible at all, the divine mind qua mind must be [understood as being] isomorphic with the human [mind]" (*FPT*, 22). By granting this isomorphism, we not only discover that the human self-consciousness of God is identical with God's self-consciousness, but we also discover, according to Laycock, that the divine consciousness is "intentional," "cognitively finite," "teleological," and "intersubjectively mediated" (*FPT*, 25).

Now it seems to me that this proposition not only contains the primary intention of discovering the God *entheos* in consciousness-as-such, but also the secondary intention of demonstrating that this is the only God which *can* exist. If this is the case, then it scarcely needs mentioning that one is unlikely, by this strategy, to encounter the God of Abraham, Isaac, and Jacob, that the mainstream of Western tradition owns. I do not draw this opposition in order to affirm Pascal's exclamation or to argue for some kind of revelational positivism (of the type Laycock rightly rejects). I do so rather out of the conviction that distinctions regarding divine and human consciousness and self-consciousness are not merely distinctions having to do with properties of mind but have to do with properties of *Spirit*. Hegel saw this better than anyone, perhaps, and that is why he draws such a radical distinction between *Verstand* and *Vernunft*—Reason qua *Geist*, in his view (and also Derrida's), being different with respect to the meaning of Transcendence than what one finds in a transcendental philosophy of reflection limited to an immanent content.

But Hegel's speculative category of Spirit, as Robert Williams rightly indicates (*PT*, 80ff.), encompasses both the prereflective, prethematic, primordial experience of the Divine (Being) and the post-reflective, thematized understanding of the Divine, and it has this dialectical power because Spirit is ultimately a "social-ontological" category. What Spirit means ontologically apart from the *normativity* of this social-cultural context, then, is impossible to determine. This is why, it seems to me, all late and postmodern talk about *presence* and *absence* remains and must necessarily remain vague, for it is a discourse detached from all social contexts save the context (if indeed it be a *context*) of pluralistic individualism.[3]

Laycock, however, wants to achieve some kind of trans-social and trans-cultural normativity for his *speculative cosmology*—a "phenomenological speculation [that] is a genuine *seeing into*" (*PFT*, 154) the ultimate nature of things through his thematization of the Divine/human consciousness. It remains unclear to me, however, why one would call this consciousness *Divine*. For it seems to me that his project provides valuable insights when it is strictly limited to human consciousness and does not need to be further complicated by the God question. Indeed, little knowledge of the Divine Mind is obtained by this strategy unless one accepts, a priori, his contention that mind and Spirit are the same.

If the Divine is to be invoked, then it makes better sense to inquire, as does Tymieniecka, into the meaning of those ciphers of creative Transcendence present to the life of the soul which cannot be objectified by conventional science, and into why there ultimately seems to be a disjunction between *Logos* and *Life*.

To illustrate from the history of religions, it makes sense to ask whether or not Jesus was in the natural attitude just as much as it makes sense to ask whether any allegedly inspired intra-cosmic divine being was or is in the natural attitude. But it does not make sense to ask whether an Absolute Mind—the Mind of an extra-cosmic or wholly transcendent absolute—is in the natural attitude except, as Augustine saw for moral/soteriological reasons, as an act of self-limitation. For the natural attitude is precisely what an extra-cosmic divine mind qua Spirit formally excludes—and this, of course, was what Job eventually discovered in the "silence" of dust and ashes. Another way of putting it is by drawing a distinction between what Laycock refers to as the "roundness of Being" (*PT*, 4), following Cusanus and the medieval notion that "the reality of God can be likened to an infinite circle whose center is everywhere and whose circumference is nowhere" (or Vedantic and Buddhist notions of *samsara*), and the "circularity" of consciousness. One's failure to recognize the immanent circularity of consciousness (as Hegel indicates in Chapter One of his *Logik*) is precisely what leads one to pseudo-ontological conclusions regarding the nature of Being.

Therefore, it makes much better sense to ask regional phenomenological questions in theology such as "Was Jesus in the Natural Attitude?" Lest this question sound preposterous, I pose it in the view that phenomenological christology seems to me entirely possible and highly desirable (just as it is possible to develop any number of varieties of phenomenologies in the history of religions). On the other hand, a phenomenological theology in the strict sense, that is, a phenomenology of the consciousness of God, seems to me a rather questionable prospect. For we do not, it seems to me, have access to the consciousness of God as such, that is, to the divine self-consciousness. Hegel's great insight regarding the nature of the *revealed* Western religious traditions (and here especially Christianity) had to do with *how* they were revealed, that is, with how religion came to conceptual self-consciousness, and not with *what* was revealed. But if we accept Laycock's assertion that the Divine Consciousness is "isomorphic" with the human and that it is, thereby, "intentional, cognitively finite, teleological and intersubjectively mediated," we are still stuck with Feuerbach's struggles with the *what* of revelation. In short, we may have described certain properties of human self-consciousness, but we have said nothing about God other than a claim, a posteriori, that God's consciousness and human consciousness are the same because such a God is the only God accessible to consciousness. Such a notion is oblivious to the God who, in the phrase of Pseudo-Dionysius, "...has made the dark His hiding place." What the *logos* of *Theos* is when he, she, or it is *not* phenomenologically incognito remains and must remain a complete and total mystery for the phenomenologist—perhaps for the phenomenologist *most of all*, in Tymieniecka's view.

Boston University

NOTES

*Abbreviations: *PT* = *Essays in Phenomenological Theology*, ed. Steven W. Laycock and James G. Hart (Albany: SUNY Press, 1986); *FPT* = Steven W. Laycock, *Foundations for a Phenomenological Theology* (Lewiston, NY: Mellon, 1988); *TM* = Anna-Teresa Tymieniecka, *Logos and Life*, Book 2: *The Three Movements of the Soul* [*Analecta Husserliana*, Vol. XXV] (Dordrecht: Kluwer, 1989).
1. For a cogent overview of the Chicago School, see Charles H. Long's article, "A Look at the Chicago Tradition in the History of Religions: Retrospect and Future" in *The History of Religions: Retrospect and Prospect*, ed. Joseph Kitagawa (Chicago: 1985), pp. 87-104. William Paden's recent book, *Religious Worlds* (Boston: Beacon Press, 1989) is an excellent example of the blending together of the sociological, historical,

and phenomenological approaches to the study of religions with which Wach, Eliade, Van der Leeuw, and Otto are variously identified.

2. Laycock's concluding "Epilogue," viz., "The God-Phenomenon and Compassionate Praxis," seems to be a preliminary attempt to deal with these problems (*FPT*, 231-234).

3. Alisdair MacIntyre's views on the "tradition constituted, tradition constituting" community as the only possible context for a constructive philosophy of value are instructive in this regard. See *Whose Justice? Which Rationality?* (Notre Dame, IN: Univ. of Notre Dame Press, 1988) and, more recently, his Gifford Lectures, *Three Rival Versions of Moral Enquiry: Encyclopedia, Genealogy, and Tradition* (Notre Dame, IN: Univ. of Notre Dame Press, 1990).

INDEX OF NAMES

Analecta Husserliana

The Yearbook of Phenomenological Research

Editor-in-Chief

Anna-Teresa Tymieniecka

The World Institute for Advanced Phenomenological Research and Learning,
Belmont, Massachusetts, U.S.A.

Analecta Husserliana

the Territory for Interdisciplinary Communication. 1983
Part II see below under Volume 21.   ISBN 90-277-1447-9

15. Tymieniecka, A-T. and Calvin O. Schrag (eds.), *Foundations of Morality, Human Rights, and the Human Sciences.* Phenomenology in a Foundational Dialogue with Human Sciences. 1983   ISBN 90-277-1453-3

16. Tymieniecka, A-T. (ed.), *Soul and Body in Husserlian Phenomenology.* Man and Nature. 1983   ISBN 90-277-1518-1

17. Tymieniecka, A-T. (ed.), *Phenomenology of Life in a Dialogue Between Chinese and Occidental Philosophy.* 1984   ISBN 90-277-1620-X

18. Tymieniecka, A-T. (ed.), *The Existential Coordinates of the Human Condition: Poetic – Epic – Tragic.* The Literary Genre. 1984   ISBN 90-277-1702-8

19. Tymieniecka, A-T. (ed.), *Poetics of the Elements in the Human Condition.* (Part 1:) The Sea. From Elemental Stirrings to Symbolic Inspiration, Language, and Life-Significance in Literary Interpretation and Theory. 1985
For Part 2 and 3 *see below* under Volumes 23 and 28.   ISBN 90-277-1906-3

20. Tymieniecka, A-T. (ed.), *The Moral Sense in the Communal Significance of Life.* Investigations in Phenomenological Praxeology: Psychiatric Therapeutics, Medical Ethics and Social Praxis within the Life- and Communal World. 1986
                    ISBN 90-277-2085-1

21. Tymieniecka, A-T. (ed.), *The Phenomenology of Man and of the Human Condition.* Part II: The Meeting Point Between Occidental and Oriental Philosophies. 1986   ISBN 90-277-2185-8

22. Tymieniecka, A-T. (ed.), *Morality within the Life- and Social World.* Interdisciplinary Phenomenology of the Authentic Life in the 'Moral Sense'. 1987
Sequel to Volumes 15 and 20.   ISBN 90-277-2411-3

23. Tymieniecka, A-T. (ed.), *Poetics of the Elements in the Human Condition.* Part 2: The Airy Elements in Poetic Imagination. Breath, Breeze, Wind, Tempest, Thunder, Snow, Flame, Fire, Volcano... 1988   ISBN 90-277-2569-1

24. Tymieniecka, A-T., *Logos and Life.* Book I: Creative Experience and the Critique of Reason. 1988   ISBN Hb 90-277-2539-X; Pb 90-277-2540-3

25. Tymieniecka, A-T., *Logos and Life.* Book II: The Three Movements of the Soul. 1988   ISBN Hb 90-277-2556-X; Pb 90-277-2557-8

26. Kaelin, E. F. and Calvin O. Schrag (eds.), *American Phenomenology.* Origins and Developments. 1989   ISBN 90-277-2690-6

27. Tymieniecka, A-T. (ed.), *Man within his Life-World.* Contributions to Phenomenology by Scholars from East-Central Europe. 1989
                    ISBN 90-277-2767-8

28. Tymieniecka, A-T. (ed.), *The Elemental Passions of the Soul.* Poetics of the Elements in the Human Condition, Part 3. 1990   ISBN 0-7923-0180-3

Analecta Husserliana

29. Tymieniecka, A-T. (ed.), *Man's Self-Interpretation-in-Existence*. Phenomenology and Philosophy of Life. – Introducing the Spanish Perspective. 1990
ISBN 0-7923-0324-5

30. Rudnick, H. H. (ed.), *Ingardeniana II*. New Studies in the Philosophy of Roman Ingarden. With a New International Ingarden Bibliography. 1990
ISBN 0-7923-0627-9

31. Tymieniecka, A-T. (ed.), *The Moral Sense and Its Foundational Significance: Self, Person, Historicity, Community*. Phenomenological Praxeology and Psychiatry. 1990
ISBN 0-7923-0678-3

32. Kronegger, M. (ed.), *Phenomenology and Aesthetics*. Approaches to Comparative Literature and Other Arts. Homages to A-T. Tymieniecka. 1991
ISBN 0-7923-0738-0

33. Tymieniecka, A-T. (ed.), *Ingardeniana III*. Roman Ingarden's Aesthetics in a New Key and the Independent Approaches of Others: The Performing Arts, the Fine Arts, and Literature. 1991
Sequel to Volumes 4 and 30
ISBN 0-7923-1014-4

34. Tymieniecka, A-T. (ed.), *The Turning Points of the New Phenomenological Era*. Husserl Research – Drawing upon the Full Extent of His Development. 1991
ISBN 0-7923-1134-5

35. Tymieniecka, A-T. (ed.), *Husserlian Phenomenology in a New Key*. Intersubjectivity, Ethos, the Societal Sphere, Human Encounter, Pathos. 1991
ISBN 0-7923-1146-9

36. Tymieniecka, A-T. (ed.), *Husserl's Legacy in Phenomenological Philosophies*. New Approaches to Reason, Language, Hermeneutics, the Human Condition. 1991
ISBN 0-7923-1178-7

37. Tymieniecka, A-T. (ed.), *New Queries in Aesthetics and Metaphysics*. Time, Historicity, Art, Culture, Metaphysics, the Transnatural. 1991
ISBN 0-7923-1195-7

38. Tymieniecka, A-T. (ed.), *The Elemental Dialectic of Light and Darkness*. The Passions of the Soul in the Onto-Poiesis of Life. 1992   ISBN 0-7923-1601-0

39. Tymieniecka, A-T. (ed.), *Reason, Life, Culture, Part I*. Phenomenology in the Baltics. 1993
ISBN 0-7923-1902-8

40. Tymieniecka, A-T. (ed.), *Manifestations of Reason: Life, Historicity, Culture*. Reason, Life, Culture, Part II. Phenomenology in the Adriatic Countries. 1993
ISBN 0-7923-2215-0

41. Tymieniecka, A-T. (ed.), *Allegory Revisited*. Ideals of Mankind. 1994
ISBN 0-7923-2312-2

Analecta Husserliana

42. Kronegger, M. and Tymieniecka, A-T. (eds.), *Allegory Old and New*. In Literature, the Fine Arts, Music and Theatre, and Its Continuity in Culture. 1994   ISBN 0-7923-2348-3

43. Tymieniecka, A-T. (ed.): *From the Sacred to the Divine*. A New Phenomenological Approach. 1994   ISBN 0-7923-2690-3

Kluwer Academic Publishers – Dordrecht / Boston / London